EARLY CHRISTIANITY IN CONTEXT

Editor
John M.G. Barclay

Editorial Board
Loveday Alexander, Troels Engberg-Pedersen,
Bart Ehrman, Joel Marcus, John Riches

Published under

JOURNAL FOR THE STUDY OF THE NEW TESTAMENT
SUPPLEMENT SERIES
263

Editor
Mark Goodacre

Editorial Board
Craig Blomberg, Elizabeth A. Castelli, David Catchpole,
Kathleen E. Corley, R. Alan Culpepper, James D.G. Dunn,
Craig A. Evans, Stephen Fowl, Robert Fowler, George H.
Guthrie, Robert Jewett, Robert W. Wall

Early Jewish and
Christian Monotheism

edited by

Loren T. Stuckenbruck
and Wendy E.S. North

T & T CLARK INTERNATIONAL
A Continuum imprint
LONDON • NEW YORK

Copyright © 2004 T&T Clark International
A Continuum imprint

Published by T&T Clark International
The Tower Building, 11 York Road, London SE1 7NX
15 East 26th Street, Suite 1703, New York, NY 10010

www.tandtclark.com

British Library Cataloguing-in-Publication Data
A catalogue record for this book is available from the British Library

Library of Congress Cataloging-in-Publication Data
A catalogue record for this book is available from the Library of Congress

Typeset by CA Typesetting, Sheffield
Printed on acid-free paper in Great Britain by The Bath Press, Bath

ISBN   0–567–08363–2 (hardback)
           0–567–08293–8 (paperback)

CONTENTS

ABBREVIATIONS

AB	Anchor Bible
ABD	David Noel Freedman (ed.), *The Anchor Bible Dictionary* (New York: Doubleday, 1992)
AGJU	Arbeiten zur Geschichte des antiken Judentums und des Urchristentums
ASSR	*Archives des Sciences Sociales des Religions*
ASTI	*Annual of the Swedish Theological Institute*
ATSAT	Arbeiten zu Text und Sprache im Alten Testament
BASOR	*Bulletin of the American Schools of Oriental Research*
BDB	Francis Brown, S.R. Driver and Charles A. Briggs, *A Hebrew and English Lexicon of the Old Testament* (Oxford: Clarendon Press, 1907)
BETL	Bibliotheca ephemeridum theologicarum lovaniensium
Bib	*Biblica*
BibInt	*Biblical Interpretation: A Journal of Contemporary Approaches*
BIOSCS	*Bulletin of the International Organization for Septuagint and Cognate Studies*
BNTC	Black's New Testament Commentaries
BR	Biblical Research
BWANT	Beiträge zur Wissenschaft vom Alten und Neuen Testament
CBET	Contributions to Biblical Exegesis and Theology
CBQ	*Catholic Biblical Quarterly*
CIS	*Corpus inscriptionum semiticarum*
CSC	James D.G. Dunn, *The Christ and the Spirit: Christology* (Edinburgh: T. & T. Clark, 1998), I
DJD	Discoveries in the Judaean Desert
DSD	*Dead Sea Discoveries*
EKKNT	Evangelisch-Katholischer Kommentar zum Neuen Testament
EPRO	Études préliminaires aux religions orientales dans l'Empire romain
ExpTim	*Expository Times*
FAT	Forschungen zum Alten Testament
FRLANT	Forschungen zur Religion und Literatur des Alten und Neuen Testaments
HTR	*Harvard Theological Review*
HUCA	*Hebrew Union College Annual*
ICC	International Critical Commentary
IEJ	*Israel Exploration Journal*
JBL	*Journal of Biblical Literature*
JJS	*Journal of Jewish Studies*
JRCM	C.C. Newman, J.R. Davila and G.S. Lewis (eds.), *The Jewish Roots of Christological Monotheism: Papers from the St. Andrews Conference on the Historical Origins of the Worship of Jesus* (JSJSup, 63; Leiden: E.J. Brill, 1999)

JRS	*Journal of Roman Studies*
JSJ	*Journal for the Study of Judaism in the Persian, Hellenistic and Roman Period*
JSJSup	*Journal for the Study of Judaism in the Persian, Hellenistic and Roman Period*, Supplement Series
JSNT	*Journal for the Study of the New Testament*
JSNTSup	*Journal for the Study of the New Testament*, Supplement Series
JSOT	*Journal for the Study of the Old Testament*
JSOTSup	*Journal for the Study of the Old Testament*, Supplement Series
JSPSup	*Journal for the Study of the Pseudepigrapha*, Supplement Series
JSS	*Journal of Semitic Studies*
JTS	*Journal of Theological Studies*
LD	Lectio divina
NCB	New Century Bible
JTS	*Journal of Theological Studies*
NovTSup	*Novum Testamentum*, Supplements
NTOA	Novum Testamentum et orbis antiquus
NTS	*New Testament Studies*
OBO	Orbis biblicus et orientalis
OED	Oxford English Dictionary
PEQ	*Palestine Exploration Quarterly*
PGM	Papyri Graecae Magicae
PSB	*Princeton Seminary Bulletin*
PTS	Patristische Texte und Studien
RB	*Revue biblique*
SBL	Society of Biblical Literature
SBLDS	SBL Dissertation Series
SBLSP	SBL Seminar Papers
SCI	*Scripta Classica Israelica*
SEÅ	*Svensk exegetisk årsbok*
SHR	Studies in the History of Religions
SJLA	Studies in Judaism in Late Antiquity
SJ	Studia judaica
SJT	*Scottish Journal of Theology*
SNTSM	Studiorum Novi Testamenti Societas
SNTSMS	Society for New Testament Studies Monograph Series
SP	*Studia Patristica*
SPB	Studia postbiblica
STDJ	Studies on the Text of the Desert of Judah
TB	Tyndale Bulletin
TDNT	Gerhard Kittel and Gerhard Friedrich (eds.), *Theological Dictionary of the New Testament* (trans. Geoffrey W. Bromiley; 10 vols.; Grand Rapids: Eerdmans, 1964–)
TDOT	G.J. Botterweck and H. Ringgren (eds.), *Theological Dictionary of the Old Testament*
TED	Translations of Early Documents
TJT	*Toronto Journal of Theology*
TSAJ	Texte und Studien zum antiken Judentum
TynBul	*Tyndale Bulletin*
WBC	Word Biblical Commentary
WMANT	Wissenschaftliche Monographien zum Alten und Neuen Testament
WUNT	Wissenschaftliche Untersuchungen zum Neuen Testament
ZNW	*Zeitschrift für die neutestamentliche Wissenschaft*

INTRODUCTION

Wendy North and Loren T. Stuckenbruck,
University of Durham

The present volume is a collection of essays that investigate the contours of early Christian beliefs about Jesus in relation to the one God of Israel. These essays address a number of topics that may be grouped under three areas relating to the question of 'monotheism': (1) the religious world of the New Testament; (2) selected New Testament documents; and (3) problems inherent in terminology.

In this introduction, we would like to summarize the arguments and identify the contributions made by the collection. Before focusing on the essays themselves, it is appropriate at the outset, without providing a comprehensive history of research, to sketch how they relate to several major areas of scholarly and religious activity: (1) New Testament theology (i.e. the place of Christology in relation to an understanding of God); (2) interfaith (especially Jewish-Christian) dialogue; and (3) the study of Christian origins (i.e. religious- and tradition-historical explanations for the rise of faith in Jesus). By considering these, we hope that, despite the diversity of perspectives reflected in the essays, the reader will recognize among them a large current of common understanding.

First, the essays in this book are informed by biblical theological concerns. In particular, it is in New Testament theology where the problem addressed in this book emerges. To the extent that the task of New Testament theology is conceptually and systematically conceived, it is confronted by a logical, indeed 'modernist', tension that has attracted considerable attention. How can the claim to an exclusive belief in 'one God' be reconciled with claims about Jesus? Although some recent interpreters of the New Testament have doubted that its documents as a whole contain unambiguous evidence for a belief in Jesus as an exalted being alongside God,[1] many others have been convinced that the position ascribed to Jesus was both distinct and, in essence, unprecedented. Whatever the view, however, few have been willing to dispense with the notion that 'monotheism' in some sense characterized the faith of the earliest Christians. Insofar as it refers to instruction about an exclusive religious devotion to the one God of Israel, 'monotheism' has thus been regarded in many circles as one of the fundamental presuppositions of New Testament theology.[2]

---

1. See, e.g., the publications of J.D.G. Dunn and P.M. Casey referred to in n. 8 below.
2. See, e.g., M. Burrows, *An Outline of Biblical Theology* (Philadelphia: Westminster Press, 1946), pp. 59–60, who one-sidedly declared that 'The New Testament throughout takes monothe-

The authors of the New Testament documents were, undeniably, primarily and most immediately concerned with explaining the significance of the 'Christ-event' (i.e. the life, death and resurrection of Jesus). While this event is conceived not simply as Christ's activity but, more fundamentally, as the activity of the God of Israel, the latter has often – until more recently – not been sufficiently perceived. The New Testament understanding of God is, as in the contemporary Jewish documents of its time, dynamic and relational. One would therefore be mistaken to suppose that any of the New Testament authors began with an *a priori* or static notion of God and then overlaid it with more novel and creative Christologies. Even if engagement with Christology motivated the composition of the New Testament documents, it is inappropriate to argue that reflections about 'God' are not, in the end, the proper domain of New Testament theologies.[3] Indeed, it is perhaps precisely here where the dynamic of New Testament thought may be fruitfully explored. Early Christology was shaped by ideas about God and humanity from a Jewish-Hellenistic environment; and, in terms of Christ's soteriological significance, Christology was necessarily perceived as an outgrowth or extension of God's covenantal relationship with people embodied and exemplified in Israel. So also Christology, in turn, gave shape to what early Christian communities came to think about God. The earliest Christians – and then the authors and compilers of their writings – were revisionists; for many, if not most of them, Christology became a foundation for theological reflection about a God whose activity among humanity was not being primarily or even ultimately defined in relation to Jews alone.[4] The 'God of Jesus Christ', creator of the cosmos, was at the same time the God who calls, challenges, and embraces Jews and non-Jews alike. This expansion of the understanding of Israel's God to include, on equal terms, non-Jews within a covenantal framework, made the reconceptualization of God, at the very least, a sociological necessity. But the 'Christian' reconfiguration, though not regarded by insiders as anything but a singular devotion to God, came with time – to some

ism for granted'; R. Bultmann, *Theology of the New Testament* (trans. K. Grobel; New York: Charles Scribner's Sons, 1951–1955), who regarded 'the message of Jesus' (about God and God's rule) as 'a presupposition for', rather than the content of, 'the theology of the New Testament theology' (p. 3). This understanding is likewise reflected by the more balanced discussions of J. Bassler, 'God in the NT', in *ABD*, II, pp. 1049–55 (esp. 1049: 'always and everywhere the New Testament's most fundamental presupposition') and J.D.G. Dunn, *The Theology of Paul the Apostle* (Grand Rapids: Eerdmans, 1998), pp. 28–31 ('God as Axiom', though this does not seem ultimately to reflect Dunn's position; see n. 6 on pp. 29–30).

3.   An indispensable role in theological reflection about 'God' is, of course, played by those who study the biblical documents concerned more directly with the God of Israel, namely, the Hebrew Bible or Jewish scriptures; it is here where the significance of worship devoted to one God is developed in a way that, in turn, lays the foundations for Christology. However, this does not mean that the task of New Testament interpretation does not include, even directly, an attempt to understand Israel's God.

4.   To be sure, this function of Christology was not entirely novel; concern with humanity as a whole, that is, beyond Israel, came well within the purview of Jewish apocalyptic and sapiential traditions. However, the early Christian communities, including Gentile adherents, rapidly subsumed such traditions under their respective Christologies, so that the universalizing impact of the gospel could no longer be entertained without reference to Christ.

extent already attested in the New Testament itself – to be apprehended variously by non-Christian Jews as a violation of conceptual and practical boundaries.[5]

Thus, as has been generally (though not always sufficiently) recognized, theologians of the New Testament cannot dispense with the question of 'God' without, at the same time, sacrificing or playing down the Jewish matrix within which the life of Jesus and the religious devotion of his followers began to take shape. In other words, Christology cannot stand on its own. On this most contemporary scholars of the New Testament are agreed; despite real definitional problems (see Moberly and MacDonald's essays in this volume), the 'monotheistic' question asserts itself time and again. This is certainly true if the New Testament writings are being read and interpreted in relation to their historical context. But the importance of reflection on God by New Testament specialists and scholars in contemporary Judaism reaches well beyond its impact on historical study to the basic socio-theological question of religious identity itself. Here, various scholars and confessions will find themselves parting company. For example, how much may Christology be allowed to shape reflection and doctrine about God? Does the 'Christ-event' and its significance mark the beginnings – even in the New Testament – of a trajectory that leads inevitably to a reconceptualization of God as a 'Trinity' of Father, Son, and Holy Spirit;[6] does it already express seeds of a 'binitarianism' which centres on the exalted status of Christ as one worthy of worship alongside God;[7] or does it, in the earliest stages, function as an additive essentially subordinate to and in service of a religious devotion to the God who called Israel to be God's people?[8] These are not

---

5.   Note the absence of any evidence that the Jewish opposition to Paul had anything to do with the exalted nature of Jesus even though this was clearly part of Paul's own thinking. On the other hand, the Johannine literature witnesses to the problem that a 'high' Christology posed for the exclusive devotion to God amongst opposing non-Christian Jews.

6.   So, e.g., Ethelbert Stauffer, *New Testament Theology* (New York: MacMillan, 1955), pp. 233–57. Going a step further and less plausibly, John O'Neill has argued that the notion of Trinity is not essentially new to early Christianity, i.e. it is already present in some expressions of Hellenistic Judaism; cf. 'The Trinity and Incarnation as Jewish Doctrines', in *idem, Who Did Jesus Think He Was?* (Leiden: E.J. Brill, 1996), pp. 94–114.

7.   Despite the differences between Larry Hurtado and P.M. Casey, the question of accommodating Jesus alongside God lies at the centre of their published studies; for instance, cf. Hurtado, *One God, One Lord: Early Christian Devotion and Ancient Jewish Monotheism* (Philadelphia: Fortress Press; London: SCM Press, 1988) and Casey, *From Jewish Prophet to Gentile God: The Origins and Development of New Testament Christology* (Cambridge: James Clarke; Louisville, KY: Westminster/John Knox Press, 1991). While not applying the language of 'binitarianism', N.T. Wright nevertheless argues that in 1 Cor. 8.4–6 Paul was already formulating a 'christological monotheism', i.e. a 'specifically and uniquely Christian' theology that appropriated, but redefined, the Jewish Shema'; cf. 'Monotheism, Christology and Ethics: 1 Corinthians 8', in *The Climax of the Covenant: Christ and the Law in Pauline Theology* (Edinburgh: T. & T. Clark, 1991), pp. 120–36. Further literature devoted to various aspects of this problem will be considered below.

8.   This perspective is reflected by those who argue that 'high' Christology did not flower until the latter part of the first century; see James D.G. Dunn, e.g. in *Christology in the Making: A New Testament Inquiry into the Origins of the Doctrine of the Incarnation* (Philadelphia: Westminster Press, 1980) and *The Partings of the Ways between Christianity and Judaism and their Significance for the Character of Christianity* (London: SCM Press, 1991), esp. pp. 182–206; and Casey, *From Jewish Prophet to Gentile God.*

the only alternatives. And yet, as such, they show how contemporary interpreters have chosen to express the 'oneness' or 'uniqueness' of God in the New Testament in different ways. While none of the essays in this volume is addressed directly to antecedents to later trinitarian formulations within the New Testament, the interpretation of New Testament traditions regarding the identity of the exalted Jesus, both within particular documents and in relation to later Christian formulations, is taken up in the essays of Bauckham, Dunn, Hayward, W. North, and L. North. To this extent, the volume contains discussions that impinge on New Testament theology.

Second, the present volume reflects an awareness of, indeed interest in, Jewish-Christian dialogue, a concern that intersects with the questions already outlined above. Although none of the essays is explicitly formulated as a contribution to this area of religious activity, the growing discussions among Christians and Jews about religious identity have added poignancy, or even a sense of urgency, to 'monotheistic' understandings of Jesus in the New Testament. Aware of this context, numerous scholarly publications have, in the wake of the Holocaust and especially during the last thirty years, considered the theme of 'God' in the New Testament.

Broadly speaking, these publications have explored the New Testament in order, variously, to assess readings that have led (and continue to lead) to anti-Judaism and even anti-Semitism, on the one hand, and to explore readings that open up common ground for Jews and Christians, on the other.[9] Others have sought to recover a 'neglected' dynamic in order to place 'God' nearer to the centre of early Christian concerns.[10] To the extent that Christians, as Jews, thought of themselves

---

9. The secondary literature is voluminous; we note here a few of the more significant, though varied, contributions: R. Ruether, *Faith and Fratricide: The Theological Roots of Anti-Semitism* (New York: Seabury, 1979); F.-W. Marquardt, *Die Gegenwart des Auferstandenen bei seinem Volk Israel: Ein dogmatisches Experiment* (München: Kaiser, 1983) and already in *Die Juden im Römerbrief* (Theologische Studien, 107; Zürich: Theologischer Verlag, 1971); E.P. Sanders, *Paul and Palestinian Judaism: A Comparison of Patterns of Religion* (London: SCM Press, 1977); P. van Buren, *Theology of Jewish-Christian Reality* (3 vols.; San Francisco: Harper & Row, 1987–1988); M. Barth, e.g. in *The People of God* (JSNTSup, 5; Sheffield: JSOT Press, 1983) and *Das Mahl des Herrn: Gemeinschaft mit Israel, mit Christus und unter den Gästen* (Neukirchen–Vluyn: Neukirchener Verlag, 1987); A.F. Segal, *Rebecca's Children: Judaism and Christianity in the Roman World* (Cambridge, MA; London: Harvard University Press, 1986); Dunn, *The Partings of the Ways*; J.H. Charlesworth (ed.), *Jesus' Jewishness: Exploring the Place of Jesus within Early Judaism* (New York: Crossroad, 1991); J.J. Gager, in *The Origins of Anti-Semitism: Attitudes towards Judaism in Pagan and Christian Antiquity* (New York and Oxford: Oxford University Press, 1985) and *Reinventing Paul* (Oxford: Oxford University Press, 2000); L. Gaston, *Paul and the Torah* (Vancouver: University of British Columbia Press, 1987); and R. Bieringer, D. Pollefeyt and F. Vandecasteele-Vanneuville (eds.), *Anti-Judaism and the Fourth Gospel* (Assen: Van Gorcum, 2001).

10. In this respect, see e.g. the following, again widely diverging, publications: N.A. Dahl, 'The One God of Jews and Gentiles (Romans 3.29–30)', in *idem, Studies in Paul: Theology for the Early Christian Mission* (Minneapolis: Fortress Press, 1977), pp. 178–91; T. Holtz, 'Gott in der Apokalypse', in J. Lambrecht (ed.), *L'Apocalypse johannique et l'Apocalyptique dans le Nouveau Testament* (BETL, 53; Leuven: Leuven University Press, 1980), pp. 247–65; J.C. Beker, *Paul the Apostle: The Triumph of God in Life and Thought* (Philadelphia: Fortress Press, 1980); E. Boring,

as believers and worshippers of 'one God', how did they, in view of their affir-mation of Jesus' exalted status, go about formulating this conviction? The fol-lowing rhetorical, and theological, questions lurk underneath the surface: Would the attempt by Christians to retain language about 'one God' have been a matter of salvaging something that was no longer really there, or were Christians expressing something that non-Christian Judaism already contained within its bounds? Finally, aware of the theological repercussions of their work, a number of scholars have devoted research to determine what kind of matrix in Judaism, if any, provided the groundwork that explains or renders plausible why and how unprecedented claims about the Jesus could have been made by his followers.[11] This last-mentioned enterprise anticipates the third area outlined below.

Third, the essays of this volume participate in and relate to a discussion about the religious- and tradition-historical context within which the exalted status of Jesus arose. However, they assume, rather than review, the more remote history of discussion that has determined the sorts of questions recent research has brought to the ancient documents. Since numerous publications over the last fifteen years in this area regard themselves as revisions of the old *religionsgeschichtliche Schule* (that wielded so much influence on perceptions of Early Judaism and Christianity from the late 19th to the mid-20th centuries), it is useful here to provide a brief outline of just what it is that is now being called into question.[12]

Much of the recent scholarship on the rise of early Christology has taken shape out of an awareness of the theses of Wilhelm Bousset. Bousset's work on early Christianity and contemporary Judaism (which with his contemporaries he called '*Spätjudentum*') marked the culmination of the history-of-religions school that had its beginnings in Göttingen under the tutelage of Albrecht Ritschl.[13] As is well known, in determining the background to convictions about Christ articulated in the New Testament, Bousset distinguished between Palestinian Judaism, on the one side, and Hellenistic Judaism, on the other. Hellenistic ideas and practices, whether directly or through their influence on Judaism of the diaspora, played a decisive

---

'The Theology of Revelation: "The Lord our God the Almighty Reigns"', *Interpretation* 40 (1986), pp. 257–69; U.W. Mauser, 'One God Alone: A Pillar of Biblical Theology', *PSB* 12 (1991), pp. 255–65; J.T. Squires, *The Plan of God in Luke–Acts* (SNTSMS, 79; Cambridge: Cambridge University Press, 1993); M.M. Thompson, *The God of the Gospel of John* (Grand Rapids: Eerdmans, 2001).

11. See the literature cited below.

12. Hence the title of J. Fossum's article, 'The New *religionsgeschichtliche Schule*: The Quest for Jewish Christology', in E.H. Lovering (ed.), *SBL 1991 Seminar Papers* (Atlanta: Scholars Press, 1991), pp. 638–46.

13. See W. Bousset, in *Die Religion des Judentums im späthellenistischen Zeitalter*, revised by H. Gressmann (Tübingen: J.C.B. Mohr [Paul Siebeck], 3rd edn, 1926), pp. 302–57 ('Der Mono-theismus und die den Monotheismus Beschränkenden Unterströmungen') and, in relation to the development of Christology, *Kyrios Christos: Geschichte des Christusglaubens von den Anfängen des Christentums bis Irenaeus* (Göttingen: Vandenhoeck & Ruprecht, 1913). A similar, more broadly focused perspective was of course espoused by the influential treatment of A. von Harnack in his *History of Dogma* (7 vols.; London: Williams & Norgate, 3rd edn, 1894–1899), esp. vol. 1 (trans. N. Buchanan).

role in the deification of Jesus. The worship of Jesus in early Christianity, therefore, was for Bousset best explained by a religious environment in which the strict
monotheism of the Old Testament prophets (and Jesus himself) had been significantly weakened. He argued that this compromise of religious devotion to the
one God of Israel may be discerned in several features that were contaminating
the essential purity of post-exilic Jewish thought: (a) a growing interest in angels
(he refers to an 'Engelkultus'); (b) the rise of dualism, marked by increasing
concern with demonology; and (c) a belief in divine 'hypostases' such as 'Logos'
and 'Sophia'.

While Bousset admitted that Christianity may have inherited these developments
from Judaism, he nevertheless maintained that the ultimate source of this was
'paganising elements' and, to the extent that Judaism was involved, it was in a
theologically aberrant form. Post-exilic Judaism held generally a weakened sense
of God's presence in the world; in distinguishing Palestinian from Hellenistic
Judaism, Bousset held that while in Palestine the distance of God manifested itself
through an intensified legalism among pious Jews, in the diaspora this was
reflected in widespread belief in the existence of divine beings independent of God.
Though in Jesus' day Judaism remained concerned with the worship of God, many
Jews, especially those in apocalyptic circles, were attempting to compensate for
God's remoteness by offering 'cultic' worship to intermediary beings. And so
Bousset derived the rise of the 'Christ-cult', which he maintained occurred as the
church gained an increasingly Gentile profile, from 'foreign', Hellenistic elements
in Judaism (esp. Hellenistic and Persian) that threatened to undermine Jewish mono-
theistic convictions.

Bousset was, even then, not without his critics. One of these was George Foot
Moore,[14] who took issue with aspects of Bousset's programme in two main areas:
first, he questioned whether it is appropriate to ascribe a belief in 'hypostatic
beings' independent of God to Jews of the Second Temple period. On the contrary,
he concluded that references, for example, to 'Logos' and 'Sophia' (in Philo and
the Targumic literature) were not absolute or literal, but rather metaphorical. Moore
wanted to protect the notion of divine transcendence in Second Temple Judaism
and, along with it, a monotheistic understanding of God. Second, he questioned
whether the Jewish apocalyptic literature on which Bousset so much relied for data
ought to be a starting point for characterizing the Judaism of Jesus' day. He proposed instead that the more 'classic' literature (namely, the rabbinic writings) be
allowed to represent 'normative' Judaism near the turn of the Common Era. While
the criticism by Moore of Bousset's caricatures of Second Temple Judaism provided an important corrective, his own location of Jewish apocalyptic thought on
the sidelines of mainstream Judaism has not been found convincing. Not only have
the studies of scholars like Jacob Neusner called attention to the problem of dating
rabbinic traditions to the pre-70 CE period, but also marginalization of apocalyptic

---

14. See esp. his 'Intermediaries in Jewish Theology: Memra, Shekinah, Metatron', *HTR* 15
(1992), pp. 41–85. For a similar critique of Bousset's work, from the side of modern Judaism, see
F. Perles, *Bousset's Religion des Judentums im neutestamentlichen Zeitalter kritisch untersucht*
(Berlin: Wolf Peiser, 1903).

thought runs counter to the growth of early apocalyptic teaching alongside strong emphasis on Torah instruction in Jewish circles during the 3rd and 2nd centuries BCE. The corollary of this for the question of 'monotheism' and Judaism is that apocalyptic cosmologies, which involved a belief in the existence and activities of heavenly beings other than God, are not – indeed, were not – necessarily perceived as antithetical to 'monotheistic' convictions. By the same token, one is not to infer inaccessibility to God from stratified conceptions of the universe; transcendence – yes, remoteness – no.

Revision of the Boussetian approach has become possible on two main counts: (1) the distinction between Palestinian and Hellenistic Judaism, for purposes of discerning the background to early Christian ideas, has been found wanting; and (2) the considerable material gains in and increasing study of early Jewish sources since the mid-20th century. First, several comprehensive studies of Judaism during the Graeco-Roman era – especially those of Elias Bickerman, Victor Tcherikower, and Martin Hengel – have demonstrated the extent to which Palestinian versus diaspora (i.e. especially Hellenistic) Judaism is misleading.[15] In particular, Hengel's work has stressed that the Palestine-Mediterranean Diaspora divide among Jews of antiquity cannot be understood in terms of an ideological difference between a 'Semitic' Judaism, on the one hand, and a 'Hellenised' Judaism, on the other. The implications of this perspective for Christology were obvious enough. Developments in 'high Christology', attributed by many scholars during the first part of the 20th century to the growing influence of Hellenistic culture on an increasingly Gentile church, could now be thought to have taken root on 'Palestinian' soil where, since the conquests of Alexander the Great and their immediate aftermath, virtually all sectors of Judaism either absorbed or reacted to Greek-speaking culture. Hengel found in his religious-historical framework sufficient reason to assign a belief in Christ's exaltation to 'God's right hand' (cf. Ps. 110.1) to the earliest post-Easter followers of Jesus.[16]

Second, during the last fifty years the discoveries of many new documents from the Dead Sea, archaeological excavations in Israel, and the publication of editions and translations of Second Temple Jewish literature have led scholars to recognize the multi-cultural, apocalyptic, and yet monotheistic, character of Palestinian Judaism at the turn of the Common Era. This has resulted in a greater willingness on the part of scholars to seek antecedents for 'high' Christology within the contemporary Jewish thought world of earliest Christianity. Scholarly activity in both professional meetings and publications since the early 1990s shows how this approach, in particular the study of intermediary figures in Early Judaism, has gained momentum.

15. So E. Bickerman, e.g., *The Jews in the Greek Age* (Cambridge, MA; London: Harvard University Press, 1988), a collection of previously published essays; V. Tcherikower, *Hellenistic Civilization and the Jews* (trans. S. Applebaum; Philadelphia: Jewish Publication Society of America and Jerusalem: Magnes Press, 1959); and M. Hengel, *Judaism and Hellenism* (trans. J. Bowden [German, 1973]; 2 vols.; Philadelphia: Fortress Press, 1974).

16. Hengel's work on Christology has emphasized the extent of developments within the first post-Easter generation of the Christian community; see his *The Son of God: The Origin of Christology and the History of Jewish-Hellenistic Religion* (London: SCM Press, 1976) and *Studies in Early Christology* (Edinburgh: T. & T. Clark, 1995).

In particular the recent secondary literature has referred time and again to several publications that are thought to have posed the sorts of questions being asked. Especially influential have been Alan Segal's *Two Powers in Heaven* (1977), Richard Bauckham's study on 'The Worship of Jesus in Early Christianity' (1981–1982), and Larry Hurtado's *One God, One Lord* (1988).[17] Already several articles and discussions have documented and characterized the recent history of research in this area;[18] thus, without repeating what has been said, we may, for purposes of the present volume, at least identify the issues that have been raised.

If Jewish institutions and ideas are, in contrast to Bousset, to be taken seriously as having played a formative role for the rise of earliest Christology, including a belief in the exaltation of Jesus, then the question of where Christian faith began and non-Christian Judaism left off, becomes acute. With respect to the history of thought, the issue arising from Segal's earlier work consists in the degree to which, beyond early Christianity and gnostic circles, the rabbinic polemics against the notion of 'two powers' reflected a concern to curb possible implications of ideas espoused amongst some Jewish writers at the turn of the Common Era (e.g. Philo). With respect to religious 'cultic' practice, as especially emphasized by Hurtado, the overriding question may be formulated as follows: How could the followers of Jesus think of themselves as worshippers of 'one God' when, at the same time, they came to worship Jesus alongside God as well? Did the status and role of Christ among first-century Christian communities represent a new and unprecedented development in the history of religions, or can these be explained by already existing beliefs (i.e. concerning mediator figures or personified ideas), practices in worship, and interpretations of scripture? The studies in the first two sections of this book either directly address or respond to these questions. Related problems raised here may also be noted: What is 'worship' (as opposed to, for example, 'veneration' or '*proskunesis*'; see Horbury, Stuckenbruck, Crispin-Fletcher Louis, and North)? Was the exalted status of Jesus as 'deity' a feature of early Christian belief from the beginning; what is 'deity'; and what does it mean to ascribe to Jesus a 'divine identity' (see Dunn, Capes, Bauckham)?

However, a further line of inquiry is opening up as recent studies which, under the shadow cast by scholarship from the 19th through early 20th centuries, have

---

17. For the details of these publications, see the bibliography at the end of this volume.

18. See, e.g., Fossum (article cited in n. 12); Hurtado, *One God, One Lord* (2nd edn), pp. i–xv; L.T. Stuckenbruck, *Angel Veneration and Christology* (WUNT, II/70; Tübingen: J.C.B. Mohr [Paul Siebeck], 1995), pp. 3–21; J. Knight, *Disciples of the Beloved One: The Christology, Social Setting and Theological Context of the Ascension of Isaiah* (JSPSup, 19; Sheffield: Sheffield Academic Press, 1997), pp. 71–185 (in relation to the background to Christology in *Asc. Isa.*); C.H.T. Fletcher-Louis, *Luke–Acts: Angels, Christology and Soteriology* (WUNT, II/94; Tübingen: J.C.B. Mohr [Paul Siebeck], 1997), pp. 1–17; C. Gieschen, *Angelomorphic Christology: Antecedents and Early Evidence* (AGJU, 42; Leiden: E.J. Brill, 1998), pp. 7–25; R. Bauckham, *God Crucified: Monotheism and Christology in the New Testament* (Didsbury Lectures, 1996; Carlisle: Paternoster Press, 1998), pp. 1–22; S. Vollenweider, 'Zwischen Monotheismus und Engelchristologie: Überlegungen zur Frühgeschichte des Christusglaubens', *ZTK* 99 (2002), pp. 21–44; T. Eskola, *Merkabah Mysticism and Early Christian Exaltation Discourse* (WUNT, II/142; Tübingen: J.C.B. Mohr [Paul Siebeck], 2002), pp. 1–11.

tended to adopt terminology that reflects potentially unexamined ideological categories. While to speak of 'one God' draws directly on Jewish and Christian tradition, how satisfactory are the expressions 'monotheism', 'henotheism', and 'polytheism' (including their cognates) if we wish to *describe* the theological perspectives of the ancient texts? The last essays in the third section of this volume by MacDonald and Moberly raise this concern in a bid to draw more sympathetic attention to the ancient sources being subjected to theological and historical analysis.

There now follows a brief description of the content of each essay in turn: Part One, on monotheism and the religious world of the New Testament, begins with Horbury's richly-detailed study. Horbury investigates the character of Jewish and Christian monotheism in the Herodian age as evidenced in ancient biblical interpretation and in Jewish and early Christian apologetic. He finds that these traditions witness to the strong influence of an 'inclusive' monotheism, where the supreme deity was envisaged in association with other spirits and powers. He suggests that this tendency was characteristically Herodian, even though it was concurrent with a rigorous 'exclusive' monotheism which was to gain the ascendancy in later rabbinic writings. In this context, the Christian approach to monotheism may be seen as having perpetuated some characteristically Jewish features of the Herodian age which became less prevalent in rabbinic teaching.

Stuckenbruck's essay also examines the cultural atmosphere in which early Christianity flourished by focusing specifically on the exalted status of angels in post-biblical Judaism. Passages discussed are those in which the language of worship is used in relation to angelic beings and are drawn from polemical literature directed against the practice of 'angel worship' as well as from sources which associate angels more positively with worship language. The study illustrates the degree to which some Jewish sources could tolerate venerative language directed to angelic beings while retaining a wholly monotheistic focus. Stuckenbruck concludes that, while the status accorded to Christ went beyond that ascribed to angelic mediatorial figures, the capacity within Judaism to accommodate honorific language towards angels into worship of the one God helped shape the ways in which earliest Christians who extolled Christ were able to insist that they were nonetheless not compromising their devotion to the unique God of Israel.

Fletcher-Louis' contribution tackles the issue of precedent within Judaism for early Christology from a different perspective. He maintains that Jewish cultic practice allowed, under certain circumstances, for the worship of a human being as God's idol and that this was based on the principle, set out in Gen. 1, that the legitimate cult object of the one creator God is true humanity. With this in view, he presents and then undertakes a detailed examination of evidence concerning Alexander the Great's worship of the Jewish high priest in Josephus' *Jewish Antiquities* and parallels. He concludes from Josephus' version of the story that the high priest is worshipped as the true divine human ruler because in that office he serves Israel's God in the same way a pagan idol would serve a pagan god. A late-attested appendix to the Alexander story further confirms that the earlier tradition relies on Israel's image-of-God-in-man theology.

Part Two, on the New Testament, begins appropriately with Dunn's essay in which he asks whether Jesus himself was a monotheist. Dunn examines three types of evidence: first, what may be inferred regarding Jesus' upbringing; second, the explicit 'God-talk' of his teaching; and third, what may be deduced from the impression he left on his disciples by the character of his mission. In the case of the first two types of evidence, Dunn concludes that the answer to his question must be unequivocally in the affirmative; Jesus was indeed a monotheist. As regards type three, Dunn asks whether the more controversial material reviewed there, which points to an awareness on Jesus' part of a special relationship with God, necessitates a qualification of that affirmative answer. Certainly it may be argued from such evidence that subsequent developing perceptions of Christ are well-rooted within the Jesus tradition. The data also indicate that something of the same tensions which characterize Christian monotheism, in which the affirmation that God is one is maintained alongside a more complex apprehension of the deity, are apparent in the earliest phases of the Jesus tradition.

The essay by Capes moves the investigation forward in time to the writings of Paul. Capes analyses Paul's use of YHWH texts, that is Old Testament texts that refer directly to the divine name, as a means of understanding the apostle's monotheism and Christology. Following a preliminary investigation into the state of Greek and Hebrew texts in Paul's time, Capes isolates 13 instances in Paul's writings where the apostle quotes YHWH texts and offers a detailed analysis of two which have Christ as referent (Rom. 10.13, cf. Joel 2.32; Rom. 14.11, cf. Isa. 45.23). He finds that Paul deliberately and unambiguously applies to Jesus scriptural language originally reserved for YHWH and includes Jesus within the divine name. Paul's use of YHWH texts thus suggests that he holds a 'high' Christology, a conclusion which calls into question any developmental scheme whereby New Testament Christology is seen as evolving from 'low' to 'high' with the passage of time. On the issue of Paul's Christology in relation to his monotheism, Capes is most in sympathy with the work of Richard Bauckham on the concept of divine identity.

Hayward's essay explores the issue of monotheism in the gospel of John by approaching the gospel's theme of unity from the perspective of the proclamation, 'the Lord is one' in the *Shema'*. Devout Jews of the period, he notes, were disturbed by the existence of more than one Jewish Temple, a plurality which was perceived as a threat to the uniqueness of God, of his name, and of the chosen tabernacle of his name on earth. The main part of the essay is taken up with a detailed investigation of the concept of unity at Qumran, whose members saw their own establishment as constituting the true Temple, and a number of parallels with the gospel are drawn. Hayward concludes that there is a *prima facie* case for arguing that Johannine formulations of unity which relate to Jesus and the Father and to Jesus as shepherd are concerned with the identity of the legitimate Temple and with the unity of God as required by the *Shema'*. Finally, he asks whether the hostility towards the Pharisees shared by Qumran and the gospel was due to the Pharisees' support of the Jerusalem Temple.

North contributes a further essay on monotheism in John which also tackles the issue from a Jewish perspective. Noting that it made theological sense to John to present Jesus as the Word which was God and yet retain a monotheistic standpoint, North seeks to understand John's thinking by investigating the gospel's background in Judaism. What the gospel reveals of difficulties with Judaism at the time of writing includes an awareness of certain non-hostile 'Jews' who believe in Jesus but remain low-profile in the synagogue. By focusing on John's presentation of this group, who appear to represent the middle ground between the Johannine Christians on the one hand and the hostile 'Jews' on the other, it becomes possible to establish that their faith in Jesus was based in a kind of Jewish piety in which Moses the lawgiver was central and accorded an exalted status in relation to God. In light of gospel evidence which indicates that Moses and the Law were also fundamental to the position of the hostile 'Jews' and were highly influential in John's own presentation of Jesus, it is suggested that John's Christology constitutes one element in a spectrum of responses to Jesus, all similarly rooted in the Judaism he knew. While his own response emerges as the most radical, John is unlikely to have regarded his own application to Jesus of the exalted status reserved for Moses and the Law in Judaism as in breach of monotheism.

Bauckham's study of monotheism and Christology in Hebrews 1 presupposes his general argument for a Christology of divine identity. This assumes that Jewish monotheistic understanding of God in the second Temple period was framed in terms of identity rather than of divine nature and therefore that early Christianity, by including Jesus in the unique identity of the one God of Israel, created a kind of christological monotheism. Bauckham regards Hebrews 1 as particularly important for understanding christological monotheism, for it not only brings the main components of Jewish definition of the uniqueness of the divine identity into christological service but also illustrates the extent to which early Christology deployed currently accepted methods of Jewish scriptural exegesis. He defines the role of the first two chapters of the epistle as one of rehearsing familiar themes of the exaltation and humiliation of Christ in preparation for the freshly creative exegesis to come later, while fulfilling the christological aim of affirming the divinity and humanity of Jesus in distinction from the angels. In a detailed structural analysis, the exordium in 1.1–4 is seen as setting out the narrative identity of the Son, in which his inclusion in the unique divine identity is made fully clear, and the catena of scriptural texts in vv. 5–13 as making the overall point that as Son Jesus participates in the exercise of the divine sovereignty, by contrast with the angels. On this basis, Bauckham suggests not only that Hebrews 1 envisages the personal pre-existence of the Son, but also that the first two chapters, taken together, are perhaps the closest the New Testament comes to the two-natures Christology of Chalcedon. Even so, however, they are more adequately interpreted in terms of human and divine narrative identity.

North's essay, which brings the New Testament section to a close, concentrates on the *realia* of προσκύνησις. The historically conditioned nature of language obliges one to argue not from modern but from as nearly contemporary understandings of προσκύνησις as possible and always to consider its social context(s). Here two of these are introduced. There are several Hebrew words which the rabbis used to denote the different *physical* aspects of 'worship': bowing from the waist, kneeling on one knee or both, prostration on knees of the upper body, and prostration on the face. Second, the Iconoclast controversy in the eighth century generated a fresh concern about the precise use of language involving προσκύνησις. John of Damascus defined and subdivided it, with ever further analysis, to show his concern to get it as right as possible. These comparative materials confirm the impression, already gained from the New Testament, that 'worship' is too imprecise a word to point necessarily to the conclusion that Jesus is divine. There is evidence in both the Jewish and Graeco-Roman *milieux* that it was sacrifice to, rather than προσκύνησις of, the deity that was the differentia of divinity. Since sacrifice, literal or metaphorical, was never said in New Testament or earliest Christianity to be offered to Christ, and 'worship' has been shown to be an unsatisfactory guide, another explanation for claims about the deity of Christ has to be sought.

The essays by Moberly and MacDonald in the final section raise questions related to the origin and definition of the term 'monotheism'. Moberly's contribution investigates whether use of the term 'monotheism' is appropriate to the discipline of biblical interpretation. He observes that modern scholarly study of biblical monotheism seems in practice to have internalized a modern account of deity as a human projection in which questions about God are really questions about human beliefs and practices, a context in which issues relating to the nature of religious truth and epistemology need not be addressed. In fact, to bring to the text the term 'monotheism' and related expressions is to use language freighted with conceptualizations rooted in the seventeenth century, a practice which is likely to force the biblical tradition into inappropriate moulds. Furthermore, traditional 'historical-critical' approaches to the Bible, which follow evolutionary models, may be less illuminating for believers today than 'canonical' approaches, which can show that belief in the one God is the normative pattern within which Israel's history should be understood and appropriated. In an exegesis of the *Shema'*, Moberly shows that to confess YHWH as 'one' is to affirm something that is inseparable from Israel's need to respond to YHWH. This is an affirmation which, he claims, is the clearest expression of what is consistently understood in the Old Testament as a whole. In his conclusion, he suggests that, rather than use 'monotheism' and related terms, a renewed attempt should be made to articulate how the Bible conceives the relationship between God who is 'one' and human life. Keeping this concept in focus in relation to certain New Testament passages may bring us closer to understanding why early Christians incorporated Jesus Christ into Israel's confession of the one God.

MacDonald's essay explores in detail the origin of the term 'monotheism' and the intellectual and philosophical atmosphere of the early Enlightenment that gave it meaning. He argues that 'monotheism' brings with it a conceptual framework constructed from seventeenth century interests which continues to have a significant effect on scholarly debate today. In particular, the developmental approach to monotheistic thought, which largely governs modern discussions of monotheism in the biblical texts, reflects the same interests in the nineteenth century, when the vocabulary of 'monolatry' and 'henotheism' was introduced. In conclusion, MacDonald observes that the ideal in Old Testament scholarship still seems to be to define 'monotheism' *correctly* and then to approach the biblical texts historically in order to ascertain when 'monotheism' first arose. However, the key question raised by his investigation into the origin of the term is whether we really know what 'monotheism' means.

As our summary makes apparent, the present volume is marked by contributions that espouse a diversity of views. Every effort has been made herein not to 'sweep' these differences of approach and perception 'under the carpet'. In this way, it is hoped that the book not only provides some gauge for the present state of research and discussion, but also provides a stimulus to engage in further lines of inquiry.

As editors, we would like to thank members of the New Testament postgraduate Seminar in Durham, whose participation in discussions (originally given as papers in the seminar) contributed to refinement and improvement of several of the essays appearing in this volume.[19] In addition, and especially, we thank the editors of the series Studies of the New Testament and its World, Professors John Barclay and Joel Marcus, for accepting this volume in the series and for their valuable advice in preparing the manuscript for publication.

---

19. In addition to the contributors to this volume, Larry Hurtado also gave a paper to the Seminar entitled 'The Origin and Development of Christ-Devotion: Forces and Factors', which has now been incorporated into his most recent monograph, *Lord Jesus Christ: Devotion to Jesus in Earliest Chrisianity* (Grand Rapids: Eerdmans, 2003).

Part I

MONOTHEISM AND THE RELIGIOUS WORLD OF THE NEW TESTAMENT

Jewish and Christian Monotheism in the Herodian Age

William Horbury, University of Cambridge

Loyalty to one God among Jews in the Greek and early Roman periods has an almost Protean image in current study. It can appear as strict anti-polytheistic monotheism, or as acknowledgement of a supreme deity with a subordinate mediator amid other angel-divinities, or as an anticipation of Christian Trinitarianism, or simply as showing some polytheistic features, despite its tenacious adherence to the One.[1] The earliest Christian monotheism, likewise, can seem primarily remarkable either for its anti-idolatrous zeal, or on the other hand for its gentilizing tendencies.[2] These divisions in contemporary opinion of course in part continue long-standing differences in biblical interpretation that reflect theological debate between Jews and Christians and within Christianity.[3] All these faces of Jewish and Christian monotheism had already emerged, however, as is noted below, in Jewish and Christian apologetic in the ancient world.

This polymorphic image then probably reflects not merely the variation in modern opinion, but also something of the complex character of Jewish and Christian monotheism in antiquity. Thus the importance of differentiating between various types of monotheism attested in Jewish literature of the Hellenistic age has been underlined by M. Mach.[4] Hence it remains necessary to ask what features stood out in a given period, not least in the time of Christian origins.

1. See for example P.M. Casey, 'Monotheism, Worship and Christological Development in the Pauline Churches', in *JRCM*, pp. 214–18 and R.J. Bauckham, 'The Throne of God and the Worship of Jesus', in *idem, Christological Monotheism*, pp. 43–48 (strict monotheism); C. Rowland, *The Open Heaven* (London: SPCK, 1982), pp. 94–113 (supreme deity and exalted angel); J.C. O'Neill, *Who Did Jesus Think He Was?* (Leiden: E.J. Brill, 1995), pp. 94–114 (Trinitarianism anticipated); E.P. Sanders, *Judaism: Practice and Belief, 63 BCE–66 CE* (London: SCM Press; Philadelphia: Trinity Press International, 1992), pp. 242–47 (monotheism with some acknowledgement of other divine beings in theory and practice).

2. For examples see, respectively, Y. Kaufmann, *Christianity and Judaism: Two Covenants* (trans. C.W. Efroymson [Heb., 1929–1930]; Jerusalem: Magnes Press, 1988), pp. 12–16 and O. Skarsaune, 'Is Christianity Monotheistic?', *SP* 29 (1997), pp. 359–61; H. Maccoby, *Paul and Hellenism* (London: SCM Press, 1991), pp. 59–63.

3. An influential early modern instance of Trinitarian interpretation, worked out with an eye to both inner-Christian and Christian-Jewish debate, is P. Allix, *Judgment of the Ancient Jewish Church against Unitarians* (London: Richard Chiswell, 1699), on the Old Testament Apocrypha, Philo, and the Targums.

4. M. Mach, 'Concepts of Jewish Monotheism during the Hellenistic Period', *Christological Monotheism*, pp. 21–24.

In what follows attention is concentrated on a period delimited by special political conditions, the Herodian age. Elsewhere I have tried to show that the conditions
of this age helped to keep in being, within loyalty to the one God, a messianism
and a remembrance of the righteous which echoed Greek and Roman ruler-cult and
hero-cult.[5] The present study explores some indications of Herodian monotheism
that arise from the prominence of monotheism as a topic in ancient biblical interpretation and in Jewish and early Christian apologetic. These sources have perhaps
been less to the fore recently in this discussion than the Old Testament Apocrypha
and pseudepigrapha. It is argued overall that the interpretation of Judaism as a
rigorous monotheism, 'exclusive' in the sense that the existence of other divine
beings is denied, does less than justice to the importance of mystical and messianic
tendencies in the Herodian age – for these were often bound up with an 'inclusive'
monotheism, whereby the supreme deity was envisaged above but in association
with other spirits and powers. Christianity would then have perpetuated some
features of Jewish monotheism that were characteristically Herodian, but became
less obvious in much rabbinic teaching – although they by no means completely
disappeared.

1. *The Herodian Age and Herodian Monotheism*

The Herodian age is taken in what follows to comprise the period of nearly two
centuries during which the house of Herod was dominant or influential in Jewish
public life at home and abroad. Antipater and his son Herod were already eminent
in the last years of the Hasmonaeans, but the Herodian age can best be said to
begin when the Roman senate designated Herod the Great as king of the Jews in
40 BCE. The end of the Herodian age came at least in principle with the death of
Herod's great-grandson Agrippa II, probably in 100 CE.[6] Judaism bearing what
may be called a Herodian stamp will not, however, have vanished overnight in 100.
Perhaps then the revolts against Roman rule that broke out in the diaspora in 115
and in Judaea in 132, and issued ultimately in the pre-eminence of the house of
Judah ha-Nasi, can be taken to signal the final departure of the Herodian age.

Geographically, the Herodian heartland is Syrian, running from Idumaea in the
south to the region of Damascus and the southern Lebanon in the north, where the
kingdom of Chalcis remained in the hand of Agrippa II. From this Syro-Palestinian
base Herodian influence extended throughout the Roman diaspora, as is vividly
shown by the acclamation accorded to real or supposed Herodian princes by the
Jews of Alexandria and Rome.

The Herodian heartland, however, also overlapped with the heartland of the
Aramaic language. Herodian Judaism and Christianity are now known predomi-

---

5. W. Horbury, 'Herod's Temple and "Herod's Days"', in *idem* (ed.), *Templum Amicitiae*
(JSNTSup, 48; Sheffield: JSOT Press, 1991), pp. 103–149, reprinted with revisions in *Jewish
Messianism and the Cult of Christ* (London: SCM Press, 1998); and 'The Cult of Christ and the
Cult of the Saints', *NTS* 44 (1998), pp. 449–69, reprinted with revisions in *Jewish Messianism*.

6. N. Kokkinos, *The Herodian Dynasty* (JSPSup, 30; Sheffield: Sheffield Academic Press,
1998), pp. 396–99.

nantly through Greek and some Hebrew literature, but their expression through Aramaic will have stood out in the Herodian age itself. Hints of its former prominence are given by the Aramaic renderings of Leviticus and Job attested in the Qumran discoveries, with the Aramaic texts of such books as Enoch and the Genesis Apocryphon, and by the importance in the LXX, Philo, Josephus and the New Testament of transliteration from Aramaic when Jewish institutions and groups are named. The specifically Herodian and Judaean importance of both Greek and Aramaic is confirmed by Murabba'at papyri relating to the Jewish villages of Judaea, as F. Millar has shown.[7]

The joint Jewish-gentile participation in Aramaic and Greek recalls an aspect of the Herodian Jewish community which was of importance in interpretation of loyalty to one God, the communal penumbra in the form of a 'mixed multitude' (Exod. 12.28, Neh. 13.3) consisting of people of mixed Jewish-gentile descent, and of non-Jewish adherents and sympathizers. These classes are named together by Philo (*Vit. Mos.* 1.147) in his description of the 'mixed multitude' which accompanied the exodus. Josephus, similarly, when noting (*War* 2.463) that the gentile cities of Syria at the outbreak of revolt against Rome in 66 included not only Jews but gentile Judaizers (ἰουδαίζοντες), also mentions people of mixed Jewish-gentile descent (μεμιγμένος). Thus the convergence of conflicting ancestral traditions of religion was to some extent an inner-Jewish concern as well as an aspect of Jewish-gentile relations.

From the literature, inscriptions, art and architecture of the Herodian age an impression can be gained of a characteristically Herodian version of the ancestral Jewish culture. However it should be more closely defined, it was at once both Jewish and Greek and Roman. Writings which breathe a Herodian atmosphere include the works of Philo, in which Agrippa I is a hero; the *Assumption of Moses*, in which Herod the Great is viewed with detachment as the staff of God's anger; and Luke–Acts, interested especially in Antipas, Agrippa I and II, and Berenice. Similarly Josephus, although he insists on his own Hasmonaean descent and loyalty, is also a Herodian author; he submits his literary work to Agrippa II, he takes over writings by Herod the Great's court historian Nicholas of Damascus, and he carries on the history of the Herodian house. There is a case for Herodian connection in other influential texts that circulated in the Herodian diaspora in Greek. Thus the Pauline corpus probably alludes to Aristobulus, brother or son of Herod of Chalcis, at Romans 16.10, and at the same time discloses a relative of Paul with the name Herodion.

In the Qumran texts, by contrast, the historical personages mentioned by name are strikingly concentrated in the Hasmonaean period, down to the 50s of the first century BCE Similarly, the Qumran discoveries seem not to include any of the major apocalypses or other literary works of the Herodian period, such as the

---

7.   J.T. Milik, in P. Benoit, J.T. Milik and R. de Vaux (eds.), *Les Grottes de Murabba'at* (DJD, 2; Oxford: Clarendon Press, 1961), nos. 18 and 115 (an Aramaic acknowledgement of debt dated 55–56, and a Greek contract of re-marriage dated 124, respectively), discussed in a review of communal self-representation in Herodian Judaea by F. Millar, *Roman Near East 31 B.C.–A.D. 337* (Cambridge, MA; London: Harvard University Press, 1993), pp. 351–74.

Assumption of Moses, the apocalypses of Ezra (*2 Esdras* 3–14 or *4 Ezra*) and Baruch (*2* [Syriac] *Bar.*), and the *Similitudes* of Enoch (*1 En.* 37–71). Qumran material thus seems more particularly relevant to late Hasmonaean times. Nevertheless, like the late Hasmonaean *Psalms of Solomon*, the writings attested by the Qumran finds probably often represent circumstances or outlooks which continued at the beginning of the Herodian age.

Last but not least, although the Old Greek (LXX) translation of Hebrew scripture goes back in the Pentateuch to the third century BCE, and in other books too is mainly pre-Herodian, it remains of first-rate importance as a formative influence on Herodian Judaism. The Herodian age indeed saw early Jewish revision of the LXX, as shown especially by the Greek Minor Prophets scroll from Nahal Hever (Wadi Habra) and the Theodotion-like Old Testament quotations in the New Testament. It was also, however, the age of Philo's encomium on the LXX Pentateuch as an inspired sister-writing rather than a translation, and of Josephus' reproduction of the compliments to the Septuagint translators in the *Letter of Aristeas* – although, here differing in emphasis from the *Letter of Aristeas*, he significantly allows for correction of corrupt texts (Philo, *Vit. Mos.* 2.40; Josephus *Ant.* 12.107–110).

Against this literary background, note should be taken first of the clear expressions of an inclusive monotheism in pre-Herodian biblical and post-biblical texts which continued to be influential in the Herodian age in Greek as well as Hebrew: Deut. 32.8–9 (discussed further in section 4, below), Dan. 10.13–21, Sir. 17.17, and *Jub.* 15.31. All these envisage Israel as the Lord's portion (with the celestial prince Michael as the Lord's representative in Daniel), but the gentiles as allotted to lesser sons of God, princes, spirits or angels. The pattern is that of the divine council depicted in Ps. 82, the book of Job, and elsewhere.

Then, in the Herodian age itself, some Jewish expressions of loyalty to one God appear to reflect Herodian conditions in ways that a rigorous monotheist might avoid. First, expressions of monotheism by gentiles in this period, in the sense of recognition of one deity as supreme, can sometimes be closely paralleled in the modes of describing Judaism employed by their Jewish contemporaries. An influential instance of gentile monotheistic tendency, at the end of the first century BCE, is formed by Virgil's depiction of Jupiter in the closest connection with fate; both are mentioned together in the *Aeneid*, in such a way as to suggest that destiny is effectively identical with the divine will and providence.[8] Somewhat comparably, the Stoic-like Pharisees in Josephus 'attribute everything to fate (εἱμαρμένη) and to God' (*War* 2.162). Both writers use a conjunction over which a strict monotheist might hesitate, but Josephus will intend, as it appears that Virgil also does, to save the significance of the highest deity, and to hint at a philosophical theism.

---

8.   C. Bailey, *Religion in Virgil* (Oxford: Clarendon Press, 1935), pp. 141–43 and 204–234, quoting lines such as *Aen.* 8.398 'neither the almighty father nor the fates forbade Troy to stand' for longer, *nec Pater omnipotens nec fata vetabant | stare*. A Stoic view such as appears to influence Virgil's presentation should be recognized as genuine belief in one God, according to M. Frede, 'Monotheism and Pagan Philosophy', in P. Athanassiadi and M. Frede (eds.), *Pagan Monotheism in Late Antiquity* (Oxford: Clarendon Press, 1935), p. 55; Bailey, *Religion in Virgil*, p. 141, perhaps with exclusivity more strongly in view as a criterion, calls it 'almost monotheistic'.

Secondly, there is a case for interpreting the conceptions of an exalted messiah current in this period against the background of contemporary monarchy. Thus the apocalypses of the later Herodian age – notably the *Similitudes* of Enoch, the apocalypses of Baruch (*2 Bar.*) and Ezra (*2 Esdras* 3–14), and the Fifth *Sibylline Oracle* – characteristically depict a godlike and spiritual messiah in association with the one God; and an often comparable depiction is found in the New Testament. This godlike messianic figure arises from the mingling of human and divine traits in Old Testament royal texts, and the perpetuation of this mingling as it occurs in the LXX; but it also seems to reflect contemporary ruler-cult, in specifically Herodian as well as Ptolemaic and Roman form.[9] Thus the appearances of the Son of Man in the *Similitudes* of Enoch (*1 En.* 46.1; 48.5; 62.9) recall the brilliance of imperial and Herodian epiphanies, and a famous echo of Herodian ruler-cult preserved by Philo also resembles contemporary Christian messianism; for the Alexandrian mob satirize Jewish acclamation of the Herodian king Agrippa I by hailing a beggar in Aramaic as *Marin* (Philo, *Flacc.* 39). This royal title '(our) lord' appears in Herodian inscriptions in both Aramaic and Greek.[10] Christians in Corinth, however, are familiar with the comparable Aramaic acclamation and prayer *Maranatha* (1 Cor. 16.22), addressed to Christ, and with the Greek *Kyrios* as a title of Christ (1 Cor. 12.3). Once again a rigorous monotheism might balk at the association of a godlike king-messiah with the supreme deity, despite the biblical link between the Lord and his anointed (Ps. 2.2). At the end of the Herodian period, accordingly, negative reaction to association of an exalted messiah with God seems to be perceptible in the opposition which is said to have been aroused by Akiba's suggestion that the plural 'thrones' of Dan. 7.9 are for God and for 'David' – a suggestion which seems to perpetuate what may be called, in the light of the texts cited above, a typically Herodian outlook (so the *baraitha* in *b. Hag.* 14a; *b. Sanh.* 38b).

Thirdly, some titles reflecting an inclusive monotheism and given to the one God by writers of the Herodian age were biblically based and of long standing; but they can be judged characteristic of this age inasmuch as, despite their biblical basis, they were no longer favoured in rabbinic literature, and are noticeably curtailed in the later of the ancient biblical versions. The examples in question here associate the one God with other divine beings, spirits or powers in a way that further attests the inclusive monotheism picked out above. Thus the Deuteronomic title 'God of gods' (Deut. 10.17), which was taken up in the rolling corpus of biblical writings down to Maccabaean times (Ps. 136.2; Dan. 2.47; 11.36; Ps. 50 [49].1 LXX), is developed in Hebrew hymnody attested at Qumran, and connected with Ps. 95.3 'a great king above all gods', in such titles as 'king of gods' (4Q 400 frg. 2, line 5) or 'prince of gods and king of the glorious ones' (1QH^a col. xviii [x], line 8). This Hebrew usage finds correspondence in 'king of gods' in Greek (Esther's prayer in *Additions to Esther* 14.12), including Herodian literature (Philo, *Conf.* 173, βασιλεὺς τῶν θεῶν, in a paraphrase of Deut. 10.17 to show that the astral deities of the gentiles are beneath the supreme deity).

---

9. Horbury, *Jewish Messianism and the Cult of Christ*, pp. 102–108, 126–27 and 134–36.

10. Examples from Sia in the Hauran (Philip, *marana*) and Sanamayn in Batanaea (Agrippa II, *kyrios*) are cited by Millar, *Roman Near East*, p. 62 (see n. 7).

Comparably, the similar divine title 'God of spirits' flourished and was adapted from the time of the LXX Pentateuch down to and including the Herodian period. In the LXX Pentateuch it is found in the phrase 'God of the spirits and of all flesh' at LXX Num. 16.22 and 27.16 (where the Hebrew consonantal text of MT corresponds rather to 'God of the spirits of all flesh'); compare 'ruler of the spirits' (2 Macc. 3.24, in Hasmonaean times; *1 Clem.* 64.1, towards the end of the Herodian age); 'lord of spirits and all flesh' (Rheneia inscription, c. 100 BCE); 'lord of every spirit and ruler of every work' (1QH[a] col. xviii [x], line 8, immediately after the title 'prince of gods and king of the glorious ones' quoted above from this line); 'father of spirits' (Heb. 12.9); and 'lord of spirits', used repeatedly in a Herodian apocalypse, the *Similitudes* of Enoch (*1 En.* 37.2; *passim*).[11]

The 'gods' and 'spirits' saluted in these titles can be interpreted as angels, but they continue the biblical conception of a pantheon or divine council presided over by a supreme deity, and retain the majesty of lesser gods to an extent which 'angel' may not always convey.[12] Thus in the prayer of Esther and in Philo, as quoted above, the 'gods' of whom the Lord is king include the gods of the gentiles (cf. *Additions to Esther* 14.7); and in hymnody known from Qumran texts the group of greater ones among the gods are themselves honoured by the lesser, 'honoured in all the camps of the gods and feared by the companies of men' (4Q 400 frg. 2, line 2).[13]

On the other hand, the rabbinic titles of God surveyed by A. Marmorstein strikingly avoid the biblically-based 'God of gods' or 'God of spirits', and eschew any presentation of the deity as ruler of lesser divinities or angels.[14] Similarly, 'the Holy One, blessed be he' supersedes older titles such as 'the holy one of Israel' in Isaiah or the later 'great holy one' of the Genesis Apocryphon (col. xvii, line 17 and elsewhere), for these suggest one who is singled out among other divinities ('holy ones'). The rabbinic titles tend instead to present what M. Pesce called 'a God without mediators', and this presentation, famous from the Passover Haggadah on 'not by the hand of an angel and not by the hand of a seraph and not by the hand of a legate', likewise has pre-rabbinic antecedents at least from the time of the LXX Isaiah, 'not an envoy or a messenger, but the Lord himself saved them' (Isa. 63.9 LXX).[15] It is characteristic of the concurrence of this tendency with a

---

11. On the further comparable title 'God of the powers' see Horbury, *Jewish Messianism and the Cult of Christ*, pp. 120–21; on the pre-exilic pantheon as part of a group of Near Eastern traditions that influenced the depiction of a similar Greek pantheon in Homer and Hesiod, see M.L. West, 'Towards Monotheism', in *Pagan Monotheism*, pp. 42–49 (see n. 8). The address to the all-seeing Lord and the angels of God in the Rheneia text is discussed by L.T. Stuckenbruck in this volume, '"Angels" and "God": Exploring the Limits of Early Jewish Monotheism', Section 3.

12. Thus the 'gods' are treated with an almost exclusive stress on their ministerial rôle as 'angels' in H. Ringgren, *The Faith of Qumran: Theology of the Dead Sea Scrolls* (New York: Crossroad, 1995 [1963]) , pp. 82–84 (including comment on 1QH[a] col. xviii [x], line 8).

13. 4Q 400 frg. 2, line 2 is more fully discussed by Stuckenbruck in this volume, '"Angels" and "God": Exploring the Limits of Early Jewish Monotheism', Section 3.5.

14. A. Marmorstein, *The Old Rabbinic Doctrine of God*. I. *The Names and Attributes of God* (London: Oxford University Press, 1927), pp. 54–107.

15. M. Pesce, *Dio senza mediatori* (Brescia: Paideia, 1979), pp. 203–205, discussed in connection with messianism by Horbury, *Jewish Messianism and the Cult of Christ*, pp. 78 and 81.

more 'inclusive' monotheism that both figure in the longer Greek text of Sirach, where wisdom's mediation is expressed in the title 'mother of fair love and fear and knowledge and holy hope', but soon afterwards comes the slogan 'the Lord almighty is God alone, and beside him is no other saviour' (Sir. 24.18, 24). Although the most widely-attested rabbinic objection is to 'two powers in heaven', *minim* are also envisaged in the Mishnah (*Sanh.* 4.5) as ready to say 'there are many powers in heaven' – and it is suggested that a reason for the creation of one man only was to rule out this view.[16] This Mishnaic wariness has a precedent with regard to 'God of gods' in particular at Jos. 22.22 LXX, which like MT here excludes any rendering of the Hebrew *el ᵉlohim* in this sense; but contrast Ps. 50.1, where the same Hebrew is rendered 'God of gods' in LXX, as noted above. Similarly, the Targums of Numbers avoid any understanding of Num. 16.22 and 27.16 which would lead to the title 'God of spirits'.[17]

Avoidance of these particular titles is indeed part of a more general caution over depicting the one God in connection with many gods, in accord with the *soli Deo gloria* tendency already exemplified through the slogans on unmediated divine help and the Mishnaic objection to 'many powers'. This caution appears in revision of the LXX and in other later biblical versions, for instance with regard to the questions:

> Who is like unto thee among the gods? Who is like unto thee, glorified in holiness, fearful in praises, doing wonders? (Exod. 15.11).

For this verse LXX may be translated:

> Who is like unto thee among the gods, O Lord? Who is like unto thee, glorified in the holies (*or*, among the holy ones [ἐν ἁγίοις]), wonderful in glories (ἐν δόξαις), working marvels?

Here 'gods', 'holy ones' and 'glories' can all be taken as terms for the celestial host; compare 'glorious ones' in 1QHᵃ xviii [x], line 8, quoted above, and an interpretation of 'fearful in praises' by Psalm 89.8 'a God greatly to be dreaded in the council of the holy ones', which is preserved in the *Mekhilta*.[18] Many later versions, however, either restrict any such reference to the initial 'gods', or exclude it altogether (Peshitta), most stridently in Targum Onkelos 'There is none but thee; thou art God, O Lord'.[19]

---

16. The saying would have strengthened reserve about language associating the one God with other powers, whatever group was primarily in view here (A.F. Segal, *Two Powers in Heaven* [SJLA, 25; Leiden: E.J. Brill, 1977], pp. 109–115, thinks of Gnostics and Jewish Christians); Gnostics are favoured in many other treatments of the passage cited by J. Maier, *Jüdische Auseinandersetzung mit dem Christentum in der Antike* (Darmstadt: Wissenschaftliche Buchgesellschaft, 1982), p. 233 n. 309.

17. A. N. Chester, *Divine Revelation and Divine Titles in the Pentateuchal Targumim* (TSAJ, 14; Tübingen: J.C.B. Mohr [Paul Siebeck], 1986), p. 358 nn. 77–80.

18. *Mekhilta de-R. Ishmael, Beshallah, Shirata* 8, on Exod. 15.11, in J.Z. Lauterbach, *Mekilta de-Rabbi Ishmael* (3 vols.; Philadelphia: Jewish Publication Society, 1933), II, p. 63.

19. On the versions see A. Le Boulluec and P. Sandevoir, *La Bible d'Alexandrie*, p. 2: *L'Exode* (Paris: Les Éditions du Cerf, 1989), p. 174, and A. Salvesen, *Symmachus in the Pentateuch* (*JSS* Monographs, 15; Manchester: University of Manchester, 1991), pp. 93–94.

The extent to which rabbinic caution in this area is shared and anticipated in the ancient biblical versions was brought out especially by A. Geiger, and emphasis on it can aid depiction of ancient Jewish monotheism as characteristically rigorous and 'exclusive'. The point being stressed at present is a complementary one, which Geiger also noted on occasion: the extent to which the LXX and the earlier versions, together with Jewish writers of the Herodian age as cited above, still perpetuate that 'inclusive' view of the supreme deity as a king of gods which many later interpreters sought to erase.[20]

2. Monotheism in Jewish and Christian Apologetic

The concurrence of 'exclusive' and 'inclusive' interpretations of monotheism, and the abiding importance of an 'inclusive' interpretation in the Herodian age, are indicated in another way by the treatment of monotheism in ancient apologetic. Jewish and Christian apologetic directed towards the gentile world, Christian polemic against Judaism, and Jewish reaction against Christianity all appear to reflect a background of divergent Jewish understandings of monotheism.

This background is suggested, first of all, by aspects of the commendation of Judaism in a gentile setting. It is true that in ancient Judaism and Christianity, as in modern scholarship, the broad general contrast between biblical monotheism and pagan polytheism was often stressed. Thus Abraham leaves home in Philo to remove himself from the influence τῆς πολύθεου δόξης, 'of polytheism' (Philo, *Virt.* 214); and in a modern statement of this contrast by A. Momigliano, 'To be a Jew was to consider oneself separated from the surrounding world. This separation was altogether easier because monotheism faced polytheism.'[21] On the other hand, when the biblical inheritance was being commended in antiquity, a resemblance between Judaism and paganism was sometimes asserted for good or ill.

In general, this apologetic claim for resemblance can find support in the observations just made on links between Herodian Judaism and its gentile setting, and on the 'inclusive' Jewish monotheism which hailed a 'God of gods'. It is of course important that the independence ascribed to the many pagan deities, even when they were regarded as subordinate to a supreme god (see below), should not be underrated; this point is brought out, through a protest of Plutarch (born 46 CE) against Stoic reduction of the gods to forces of nature, by J. Teixidor.[22] This pagan

---

20. A. Geiger, *Urschrift und Uebersetzungen der Bibel in ihrer Abhängigkeit von der innern Entwicklung des Judenthums* (Breslau: J. Hainauer, 1957), pp. 279–82 (rabbinic and versional treatment of *ᵉlohim, el*) and 444 (at Deut. 4.19, discussed here further below, LXX retain a sense which was later excluded).

21. A. Momigliano, 'On Hellenistic Judaism', in A. Momigliano, *Nono contributo alla storia degli studi classici* (ed. R. Donato; Storia e letterature, 180; Rome: Edizioni di storia e letterature, 1992), p. 764; the pervasiveness of the cults of the many gods, vividly suggested by K. Hopkins, *A World Full of Gods* (London: Weidenfeld & Nicolson, 1999), pp. 7–42, also emerges from the ancient sceptical polemic cited from Cicero below.

22. Plutarch, *De defectu oraculorum*, 426BC, discussed by J. Teixidor, *The Pagan God: Popu-*

outlook finds correspondence in Judaism, however, in the concern with celestial 'princes' or 'holy ones' as powers with a comparable measure of independence that is manifest in Daniel, *1 Enoch*, and *Jubilees*, and forms part of the background of the Jewish divine titles which have just been considered. If then this kind of Jewish monotheism is presupposed, it can indeed be said with due caution, in the words of M. Mach, that 'There is no great difference between the duality of Zeus and the minor gods, on the one hand, and the duality of the biblical god and the angels, on the other'.[23]

Perhaps the most famous instance of what can be called an apologetic claim for resemblance made by a Jewish author occurs in the probably second-century BCE *Letter of Aristeas*, considered further below. Here Aristeas the Greek is imagined as saying to Ptolemy Philadelphus 'the god whom the Jews worship is he whom all worship, and we too, O king, though we address him by other names as Zeus and Dis' (*Letter of Aristeas* 16). A similar statement on the God whom 'both they and we worship' is comparably prominent in the version of this narrative given towards the end of the Herodian age by Josephus (*Ant*. 12.22), also considered further below.[24]

These claims, which are of considerable significance for the view of Judaism as well as paganism which they imply, were not without basis. The polytheistic Greek and Roman piety of the Herodian age indeed sometimes acquired a monotheistic air, as when one supreme god was held to be raised over lesser deities – a picture presented with abiding effect in Homer and Hesiod and Virgil, as noted already – or when one deity such as Isis was praised as the summation of all others, or when mediators between humanity and one supreme deity become important.[25] This tendency manifests itself not only through Greek and Latin sources, but also through Aramaic inscriptions reflecting non-Jewish Syrian religion with reference to a divine assembly or to messengers of a supreme god.[26] Later in antiquity it would be possible for Samaritans, Jews, pagans and Christians all to use, with varying connotations, the epigraphic formula ΕΙΣ ΘΕΟΣ.[27] The importance of one possible connotation stressed in the present study, the recognition of a supreme deity over

lar Religion in the Graeco-Roman Near East (Princeton: Princeton University Press, 1977), pp. 15–16.

23. Mach, 'Concepts of Jewish Monotheism during the Hellenistic Period', p. 36.

24. These passages are reviewed in a broader consideration of Jewish identification of the biblical deity with Greek conceptions of divinity by M. Hengel, *Judaism and Hellenism* (2 vols.; London: SCM Press, 1974), I, pp. 264–66.

25. A.B. Cook, *Zeus: A Study in Ancient Religion* (3 vols.; Cambridge: Cambridge University Press, 1914–1940), III/1, pp. 944–54; M.P. Nilsson, *Geschichte der griechischen Religion* (2 vols.; Munich: Beck, 1961, 2nd edn), II, pp. 569–81; the closeness of Philo to the philosophical expressions of gentile monotheism in Dio Chrysostom (c. 40–112) and Maximus of Tyre (*fl*. c. 180) is brought out by H. Chadwick, *Origen*: Contra Celsum (Cambridge: Cambridge University Press, 1953, repr. 1965), pp. xvi–xix.

26. Teixidor, *Pagan God*, pp. 13–15.

27. E. Peterson, *ΕΙΣ ΘΕΟΣ* (FRLANT, 41; Göttingen: Vandenhoeck & Ruprecht, 1926); W. Horbury, 'A Proselyte's *Heis Theos* Inscription near Caesarea', *PEQ* 130 (1997), pp. 133–37, with note of some instances from the fresh review by L. Di Segni of Palestinian examples.

lesser gods, emerges in the attestation from pre-Christian times onward of another such formula used by Jews, Christians and pagans, ΥΨΙΣΤΟΣ.[28]

Moreover, even the biblical idol-satire, with its tendency towards an exclusive rather than an inclusive monotheism, could find non-Jewish counterparts. Thus ruler-cult combined itself with due reverence for the gods above when the monarch was associated with a particular deity, but it could also bring a potentially impious contrast between the monarch as 'living god' or 'present god', and the ineffective or lifeless gods of ancestral tradition; both approaches were continued in the Herodian age from Hellenistic antecedents, in the praise of Augustus and his successors.[29] In philosophy, similarly, sceptics could mock the multitude of deities, an argument exemplified just at the beginning of the Herodian age in Cicero's depiction of debate on the divine nature: if the cosmos is divine, as the Stoics assert, why then do we add more gods? – and what a lot of them there are, 'quanta autem est eorum multitudo!' (Cicero, *N.D.* 3.16.40–42). Perhaps more typical of the philosophy of this age, however, M. Frede suggests, was monotheistic interpretation of the many deities as derivative from or at least subordinate to the one great god; but one should note the pious gloss on such interpretation made by Plutarch, who accepted it, in the passage cited above.[30]

In Christian apologetic, on the other hand, as represented in the second century by the apocryphal *Preaching of Peter* (or *Kerygma Petrou*) it is claimed that the Jews, 'thinking that they alone know God, do not understand, worshipping angels and archangels, month and moon' (*Preaching of Peter*, frg. 4, as quoted by Clement of Alexandria, *Strom.* 6.5.41).[31] The antecedents of this claim in the Pauline corpus (Gal. 4.8–10; Col. 2.18) confirm that polemists in the Herodian period could portray Judaism as including a polytheistic trend, picked out in all these passages as service to the sun and moon, the heavenly bodies which govern sabbaths and monthly observances.[32] Angelolatry was likewise an anti-Jewish charge in pagan polemic as represented towards the end of the second century by Celsus (Origen, *c. Celsum* 1.26; 5.6). This polemic sets in the worst light some famous features of Herodian Judaism as described by Josephus, the Essene prayers to the rising sun, and the depiction of the heavens on the temple veil (Josephus *War* 2.128; cf. 148 'the rays of the god'; 5.212–214; cf. *Ant.* 3.179, on the slanders occasioned by the sanctuary furnishings).

28. S. Mitchell, 'The Cult of Theos Hypsistos between Pagans, Jews, and Christians', in *Pagan Monotheism*, pp. 81–148 (see n. 8).

29. Horace, *Od.* 3.5.1–3, on Augustus as *praesens divus*, a 'present divinity' by contrast with Jupiter, and Statius, *Silvae*, 5.1.37–8, on Domitian as *propior Iove*, 'nearer than Jupiter', are among examples discussed, together with Hellenistic royal praises expressly damning other gods as absent or lifeless, in Horbury, *Jewish Messianism and the Cult of Christ*, pp. 73–74.

30. Frede, 'Monotheism and Pagan Philosophy in Later Antiquity', pp. 51–55.

31. An almost identical quotation is given by Origen, *Comm. in Ioann.*, 13.17, on Jn 4.22 'Ye worship ye know not what', with the statement that Heracleon had drawn his comment on this Johannine text from the *Preaching of Peter*.

32. T.C.G. Thornton, 'Jewish New Moon Festivals, Galatians 4.3–11 and Colossians 2.16', *JTS* NS 90 (1989), pp. 97–100, confirms that, despite relatively late attestation of στοιχεῖα in the sense of the sun and planets, this sense best fits the Pauline context.

In this Christian and pagan polemic the 'inclusive' tendency in Jewish mono-theism is viewed negatively as an angel-cult. At the same time, of course, the Christians claimed that the Jewish scriptures anticipated and taught the specifically Christian form of Jewish monotheism. Then, however, a more favourable view of the 'inclusive' tendency was implied, given the importance for early Christian doctrine of the angelic spirits surrounding 'the father of spirits'. Thus the media-tory wisdom in Sirach and the Wisdom of Solomon is a spirit, God's initiated asso-ciate in the making of the universe and partner of his throne (Wis. 7.22; 8.4; 9.4, 10), great both in the divine council (Sir. 24.2) and as angelic guide of the exodus (Sir. 24.4; Wis. 10.16–17); and under all these aspects wisdom was understood by many Christians as the pre-existent Christ, following an interpretation which is presupposed by Justin Martyr on 'another god' in scripture beside the maker of all (*Dial.* 56.4, 11), a reasonable Power (*Dial.* 56.1) begotten as a Beginning and called Glory, Son, Wisdom, Angel, Lord, Word, and Commander-in-chief (Jos. 5.13). This line of thought is already attested in the Herodian age (Jn 12.41; cf. 10.35; 1 Cor. 10.4, 9). O. Skarsaune points out that here only in the dialogue is Trypho portrayed as fully convinced by Justin's argument.[33] This striking feature suggests, as he shows, a Jewish understanding of monotheism related to Philonic understanding of the Logos as a 'second god' (Philo, *Quaest. Gen.* 2.62).

In these Christian sources the Christians rather than the Jews are presented as the true heirs of biblical monotheism; but their non-Christian Jewish contemporaries, as represented by Justin's Trypho, appear in their turn to have judged the Chris-tocentricity of Christianity as a decline from monotheism: 'for one who has for-saken God, and placed hope on a man, what kind of deliverance is left?' (*Dial.* 8.3, echoing Jer. 17.5 LXX ἐπικατάρατος ὁ ἄνθρωπος ὡς τὴν ἐλπίδα ἔχει ἐπ' ἄνθρωπον...καὶ ἀπὸ κυρίου ἀποστῇ ἡ καρδία αὐτοῦ).[34]

Here again the polemic is not insubstantial, for the Christian cult of Christ some-times gave rise to ways of speaking in which Christ seems effectively to replace God, just as the bitter comment ascribed to Trypho the Jew might suggest. Thus Christ can appear as sole executor of the power of the Highest, rather as in ruler-cult a monarch might be sole executor of the power of Zeus or Jupiter here below (as in Horace on Augustus, quoted above); so the Father has given all judgment to the Son (Jn 5.22–23). The praise of Christ could take a different but equally striking form when he was envisaged rather as a mode of the manifestation of the one divine king. Second-century instances of this modalist monarchianism are found in Melito of Sardis and the apocryphal acts of the apostles, where Christ is hailed as father and

33. Skarsaune, 'Is Christianity Monotheistic?', pp. 357–59.

34. Skarsaune, 'Is Christianity Monotheistic?', pp. 360–62, differentiates this, as an objection to divine incarnation, from a charge that Christians fail in monotheistic loyalty. He seems to me right in underlining the shared monotheism of Jews and Christians, even in respect of a 'second god' (see nn. 2 and 30 above), but more questionable in separating Jewish objections to claims for Christ (which he recognizes behind the Fourth Gospel and some of the 'two powers' texts) from zeal for monotheism. Forsaking God, the taunt ascribed to Trypho here, suggests a charge of apostasy from the Lord (Jer. 17.5).

as God alone.[35] Their Herodian-age antecedents include New Testament passages such as Tit. 2.11–13 or Heb. 13.8, which when heard in their larger context may allow for acknowledgement of one God working through Christ, but individually are wholly Christocentric. These two contrasting approaches to Christology, subordinationist and monarchian respectively, represent an inner-Christian conflict between inclusive and exclusive forms of monotheism, as R.M. Hübner has argued.[36] One could perhaps also associate with this conflict, on the 'exclusive' side, the Ebionite Christology described by Eusebius, which included differing views on the natural or supernatural birth of Christ, but united in rejecting his divine pre-existence as Logos and Wisdom (Eusebius, *Hist. Eccl.* 3.27.3).

Such conflict among contemporary Jews seems to be reflected in one further Christian apologetic statement, found in the second- or early third-century Tripartite Tractate known from Nag Hammadi Codex I, 5, and speaking of the schools of thought (αἱρέσεις) among the Jews. 'Some say that one God only proclaimed the ancient scriptures. Others say that there are many of them.'[37] This description shows special concern with the unity of inspired scripture, but it also suits the difference which has appeared in various elements of Jewish and Christian apologetic and polemic, a difference between the 'inclusive' monotheism of a 'God of gods' and that 'exclusive' approach which is attested in the later ancient versions and the preferred rabbinic divine titles.[38]

This difference clearly marked both Herodian and later Judaism and Christianity. 'Inclusive' monotheism, however, emerges from review of apologetic as particularly characteristic of the Herodian age. This type of monotheism formed a basis for both Jewish and Christian apologetic claims, and a target for anti-Jewish polemic, in sources ranging from the first to the second century.

3. *Jewish Acknowledgement of Gentile Monotheism*

Herodian Judaism was further characterized by some readiness to recognize Gentile monotheism, and some willingness to accord a degree of legitimation to gentile

35. S.G. Hall, *Melito of Sardis On Pascha and fragments* (Oxford: Clarendon Press, 1979), pp. xl–xli, xliii–xliv (citing passages including *Peri Pascha* 9–10 'inasmuch as he begets, Father; inasmuch as he is begotten, Son' and *Acts of John* 77 'Jesu, thou alone art God, and no other'); E. Junod and J.-D. Kaestli, *Acta Iohannis*, ii (Turnhout: Brepols, 1983), pp. 680–81; A. von Harnack, *History of Dogma* (7 vols.; London: Williams & Norgate, 1894–1899, 2nd edn), I, p. 196 n. 1 draws attention to the rejection of this viewpoint by Justin, *Dial.* 128.2–4.

36. R.M. Hübner, *Der Paradox Eine: Antignostischer Monarchianismus im zweiten Jahrhundert* (Supplements to *VC*, 1; Leiden, Boston, Köln: Brill, 1999), pp. 209–10. Christian reflection of divergent Jewish approaches seems to me more likely than the interpretation of such conflict as simply inner-Christian, offered with reference to Tertullian *adversus Praxean* by Skarsaune, 'Is Christianity Monotheistic?', p. 359.

37. Col. 112, ll. 22–27, in E. Thomassen (ed. with introduction and commentary, trans. jointly with L. Painchaud), *Le Traité Tripartite (NH I, 5)* (Bibliothèque Copte de Nag Hammadi, Section 'Textes', 19; Québec: Les Presses de l'Université Laval, 1989), pp. 198–99.

38. Thomassen, *Le Traité Tripartite* , pp. 418–19, argues, especially on the basis of *m. Sanh.* 4.5 on 'many powers' (see n. 16 above), that a position in contemporary Judaism is reflected here.

polytheism. Both attitudes bring Jewish monotheism into connection with gentile religion, and modify that straightforward opposition between biblical monotheism and pagan polytheism which also retained strength. Recognition of gentile monotheistic tendencies will be considered first; it was of course aided by the resemblances between gentile and Jewish monotheistic argument which were exemplified in section 1, above.

Jews, followed by Christians, argued in the Herodian age that the gentiles had at least vestiges of the knowledge of the one God, and that these were ultimately derived from the biblical revelation. It became a Jewish and then a Christian commonplace that the Greek poets and philosophers indicated a true theology, which polytheistic practice blindly ignored. This argument continued and adapted the appeal to the poets together with the philosophers which was favoured by Stoics like Chrysippus, and is often found in Hellenistic debate on the nature and form of the gods.[39]

Herodian Jewish and Christian apologetic on these lines can be exemplified from Philo, on Moses rather than Hesiod as the father of Platonic and Aristotelian doctrine on the cosmos as originate yet imperishable (Philo, *Aet.* 17–19); Josephus, on the theological wisdom known to the Greek philosophers but imparted only to the few (Jos. *c.Ap.* 2.168–169, 281); and Luke–Acts, on the theological testimony of 'your own poets' for divine generation of humanity and against the likening of the divine to works of art (Acts 17.28–9). In the second-century Christian apologists the citation of poets jointly with philosophers reappears regularly in Aristides, Justin Martyr, and others.[40] Their witness confirms the favour enjoyed by this argument among Jews and Christians at the end of the Herodian age.

Yet of course the employment of this argument cannot simply be described as apologetic. It also reflects an approach which arises naturally from Greek education. Thus Philo reasserts the sole divine monarchy, in comment on Pentateuchal verses where in self-reference the deity speaks of 'us' (Gen. 1.26, 3.22, 11.7), by quoting not Moses himself but the lines of Homer on kingship which Aristotle (*Metaph.* 12.1076a.3) had applied to theology:

οὐκ ἀγαθὸν πολυκοιρανίη·
εἰς κοίρανος ἔστω, εἰς βασιλεύς.

It is not good that many lords should rule:
Let there be one lord, one king.

---

39. On the joint appeal to poets and philosophers as an apologetic *topos* see J. Geffcken, *Zwei griechische Apologeten* (Leipzig and Berlin: Teubner, 1907), pp. 77 and 171; from Hellenistic philosophy he cites among other passages Cicero, *N. D.* 1.15–16, 41–2; 3.38, 91 on Stoic appeal to the poets, and Plutarch, *Isis and Osiris*, 45, 369B.

40. Aristides, *Apology*, 13 (Syriac) 'their poets and philosophers assert and say that the nature of all their gods is one'; Justin Martyr, *I Apol.*, 20.3 'if we say some things which are like what is said by the poets and philosophers who are honoured among you'; Athenagoras, *Leg.* 5–7, 24 (poets and philosophers not been reputed atheists for inquiring concerning God; if poets and philosophers did not acknowledge that there is one God, there might be some reason for our harrassment); Theophilus, *Aut.* 1.14 (poets and philosophers stole from the scriptures), 2.37–38 (prophets, poets and philosophers alike teach divine judgment).

(Philo *Conf.* 170, quoting Homer *Il.* 2.204–205). On this subject, as has often been noted, the literary Hellenism enthusiastically embraced by Jews and Christians could bring with it a measure of religious Hellenism; loyalty to the one God could be envisaged on Greek lines, and Greek religion as well as literature could be evaluated with closer attention.

The link between literature and religion is displayed clearly in the argument that Zeus is a name for the biblical deity who made heaven and earth. It was illustrated above from the Letter of Aristeas on the translation of the law of Moses into Greek, including the form of the Letter reproduced by Josephus. The widespread currency of this argument is confirmed by the witness of Varro in Rome, just before the beginning of the Herodian age, to a corresponding Latin-language connection of the name Jupiter/Jove with the name of the Jewish deity in the form Iao (fragments from Varro, *Ant. r. d.* 1).[41] In the *Letter of Aristeas* as presented by Josephus the Greek spokesman (here 'Aristaeus') states that both Greeks and Jews worship 'the God who constructed all things, calling him *Zena* because he breathes life into all' (Josephus *Ant.* 12.22). Here this form of the *Letter of Aristeas* takes up the traditional etymology of Zeus as life-giver, whereby 'Zeus gets his name *Zêna* as being the giver of "life" to all things, and *Día* as being the cause "through" which they came to be'.[42] Jews were aware of the potential contact with their ancestral books offered by this widespread Greek interpretation of Zeus.

The same apologetic alignment of Zeus with the biblical tradition makes another well-known pre-Christian appearance in the second-century BCE Jewish philosopher Aristobulus, who addressed an allegorical exposition of the Mosaic law to Ptolemy Philometor. This work is likely to have been known throughout the Herodian period, for Clement of Alexandria could still quote it in the second century CE (*Strom.* 1.22.150, itself quoted by Eusebius, *Praep. Ev.* 9.6). The continuation of the passage quoted by Clement and Eusebius is preserved because Eusebius quotes from the same place more fully a second time. Here Aristobulus refers, like the *Letter of Aristeas*, to the making of the Septuagint translation; and he goes on to argue that the divine origin and governance of all things, which is attested by Moses, is also witnessed by the Orphic verses and Aratus. Both are quoted at some length, including those lines in praise of Zeus at the beginning of Aratus' *Phenomena* from which a quotation was later to be made at Acts 17.28. 'I think it has been clearly shown', Aristobulus then says, 'that the power of God pervades all things' – for what was said of *Zena* and *Dia* indeed refers to God (Eusebius, *Praep. Ev.* 12.12.7). Here there is perhaps again an allusion to the traditional etymology noted above. Irrespective of this point, however, it is clear that the Greek praises of Zeus are taken as a witness to biblical theology, just as in both forms of the *Letter of Aristeas* the Greek spokesman is allowed to claim that both Greeks and Jews worship the Maker of all.

---

41. The relevant fragments are printed with translation and comment by M. Stern, *Greek and Latin Authors on Jews and Judaism* (3 vols.; Jerusalem: Israel Academy of the Sciences and Humanities, 1974), I, pp. 209–212, nos. 72b–d (from Augustine, *De Consensu Evangelistarum*, 1) and, for the name Iao, 75 (in Greek, from Lydus, *De Mensibus*).

42. Cook, *Zeus*, 3.1.947–948.

It was thus possible for Jews to envisage Greek religion as not wholly without shadows of the truth. Of course a great point of the Letter of Aristeas and Aristobulus is to strengthen Jewish distinctiveness and pride, as J.M.G. Barclay and E.S. Gruen have emphasized.[43] These writings are also, however, implicit endorsements of the Greek literary tradition, which was admired and promoted in the Greek-speaking Jewish community not only through philosophical prose, like that of Aristobulus, but also through poetry in the classical metres, like that of Ezekiel Tragicus, Philo Epicus, and the funerary epigrams sponsored by Jews. Approval extends not just to form, but also to content, in this case a content which includes the acknowledgement and praise of Zeus.

The *Letter of Aristeas* does indeed go on (131–138), like later Jewish and Christian apologists, to contrast the one God set forth by Moses with the many gods vainly venerated in human or bestial form by Greeks and Egyptians, respectively; but even this characteristically biblical attitude has analogies in philosophical debate on the divine nature and form, as noted already from Cicero, and the critique of apotheosis in the *Letter of Aristeas* has a relatively mild presentation comparable with that found in the Wisdom of Solomon (14.12–21). Moreover, when it is claimed in the sequel that non-Jews cannot be called 'men of God', there is the not insignificant qualification 'unless anyone reverences the one who is truly God' (εἰ μὴ τις σέβεται τὸν κατὰ ἀλήθειαν θεόν, 140).[44] The vocabulary used here sets this saving clause beside the group of texts in Acts and Josephus concerning 'those who reverence God', σεβούμενοι τὸν θεόν, considered as a special class of gentiles who indeed honour the one God, and to be associated with the 'godfearers' attested in other literary sources and inscriptions.[45] This passage in the *Letter of Aristeas* therefore hints at the penumbra of the Jewish community mentioned in section 1, above, and should not be taken to cancel the measure of approval of Greek theology implied in the earlier passage on Zeus.[46]

The approval of gentile monotheistic doctrine and censure of gentile polytheistic practice will then coexist here in the *Letter of Aristeas* as they do in other instances of this apologetic commonplace (Acts 17.22–29 forms a concise example), and to

43. J.M.G. Barclay, *Jews in the Mediterranean Diaspora* (Edinburgh: T. & T. Clark, 1996), pp. 138–58 (on the *Letter of Aristeas* and Aristobulus); E.S. Gruen, *Heritage and Hellenism* (Berkeley, Los Angeles, London: University of California Press, 1994), pp. 213–22 (on the *Letter of Aristeas*), pp. 243–53 (on Aristobulus), and pp. 295–97.

44. The possibility that this saving clause envisages gentiles is surely rightly allowed for by Barclay, *Jews in the Mediterranean Diaspora*, pp. 144–45, although he would himself prefer to restrict it to Jews.

45. Acts 13.43, 50; 16.14 (Lydia); 17.4, 17; 18.7 (Titius Justus), reviewed with comparable epigraphic references to θεοσεβεῖς, I. Levinskaya, *The Book of Acts in its Diaspora Setting* (The Book of Acts in its First Century Setting, 5; Grand Rapids: Eerdmans and Carlisle: Paternoster, 1996) 51–82; Josephus, *Ant.* 14.110; 20.41 (τὸ θεῖον σέβειν), reviewed with other passages including *Test. Jos.* 4.4 by L.H. Feldman, *Jew and Gentile in the Ancient World* (Princeton, NJ: Princeton University Press, 1992), pp. 349–53.

46. Gruen, *Heritage and Hellenism*, p. 216 tends in this direction; but Hengel, *Judaism and Hellenism*, I, p. 265, rightly notes the relative mildness with which the folly of apotheosis is censured.

some degree in its gentile philosophical background (compare again Cicero as quoted above). It is in the atmosphere of Jewish recognition of elements of truth in Hellenic theological tradition that Philo can quote Homer and Plato with delight and reverence. The particular argument just considered will have been most readily accessible to those who knew some Greek, but that does not mean that it was restricted to Alexandria or the diaspora; in the Herodian age it was taken over without fuss by the Jerusalemite Josephus.

Greek and Roman tendencies towards the recognition of one supreme deity, such as were noted above, could then be saluted by Jews in the Herodian age as glimpses of the biblical revelation. This measure of approval inevitably affected the way in which biblical loyalty to one God was itself understood by Jews. Homer and the poets as well as the philosophers were taken as exponents, here and there at least, of true religion. The importance of inclusive monotheism, of intermediaries, and of divine immanence in and communion with humanity and nature was thereby strengthened, and any tendency to make an absolute separation between the supreme deity and the cosmos was mitigated. The approving salute to the glories of the Greeks was regularly followed, however, as noted already, by a regretful shake of the head over polytheism. It is therefore important that Jewish as well as Christian sources can occasionally suggest at least some excuse for or even legitimation of ancestral polytheism.

4. *Legitimation of Polytheism*

This legitimizing trend can be traced to the sacred books, as is noted below, but it emerges strikingly in Artapanus' *Concerning the Jews*, an account quoted through Alexander Polyhistor by Eusebius. In this Greek Jewish narrative the Greeks are said to know Moses as Musaeus, who is here described as the teacher rather than the pupil of Orpheus; Moses gives the Egyptians their rites, founds Hermoupolis, and is hailed by the Egyptian priests as Hermes (Eusebius, *Praep. Ev.* 9.27.3–9). This aspect of the legend corresponds to the veneration of Thoth under the name of Hermes in the Hellenistic age (Philo of Byblos in Eusebius, *Praep. Ev.* 1.9.19; Cicero, *N.D.* 3.56). Artapanus is probably pre-Herodian, but, like the *Letter of Aristeas* and Aristobulus, was still read in the Herodian age, at least in extracts; for his work was excerpted by Alexander Polyhistor in the first century BCE, and quoted through Alexander by Clement of Alexandria in the second century CE.

The playful inventiveness which Artapanus shares with Hellenistic retellings of myth does not preclude narrative contact with versions of the stories of Joseph and Moses preserved by Philo and Josephus.[47] These suggest that a life of Moses on the

---

47. On Artapanus' inventiveness, see Gruen, *Heritage and Hellenism*, p. 160 and n. 97; on his contacts with Philo and Josephus, see J. Freudenthal, *Hellenistische Studien*, Heft 1–2: *Alexander Polyhistor und die von ihm erhaltenen Reste judäischer und samaritanischer Geschichtswerke* (Breslau: Skutsch, 1875), pp. 169–71; M. Braun, *History and Romance in Graeco-Oriental Literature* (Oxford: Basil Blackwell, 1938), pp. 27–31 and 99–102; E. Bammel, 'Das Judentum als eine Religion Ägyptens', in *idem, Judaica et Paulina: Kleine Schriften II* (ed. P. Pilhofer; WUNT, 91; Tübingen: J.C.B. Mohr [Paul Siebeck], 1997), pp. 116–20.

lines relatively favourable to Egypt which Artapanus follows will not have been altogether exceptional in Jewish tradition. Of special note in the present connection, however, are the contacts between Artapanus and apologetic themes. Thus Moses is identified with Musaeus, here viewed as the founder of the Orphic tradition which was drawn on by Aristobulus and others to commend Judaism; this Moses-Musaeus is honoured as Hermes-Thoth, by one of those apotheoses of mortal benefactors which are criticized in the *Letter of Aristeas* 135–137; and he lays down those very Egyptian rites involving 'cats and dogs and ibises' which are picked out for mockery by others, as in the *Letter of Aristeas* 138.

In all this there is a note of the glee which is inseparable from such claims that our neighbours' ancestral religion has been, all unbeknown to them, founded by one of ourselves; but there is also, by contrast with the *Letter of Aristeas*, a calm acceptance of the Egyptian rites, and even some endorsement of them as prescribed by Moses for the sake of peace and order. As J. Freudenthal noted, however, the manner of this endorsement of Egyptian rites as somehow Jewish is indeed recalled by the confidence of the claim in the *Letter of Aristeas* 16 that the deity revered by the Jews is the same whom all honour, as is the case with the Greeks, although they call him by a different name.[48] In each case there is at least a qualified endorsement of gentile cult. Thus the approval of Greek approaches to monotheism which is explicit in the Letter of Aristeas is probably implied in Artapanus' identification of Moses with Musaeus, given the monotheistic interpretation of Orphic verses; and Artapanus adds to this a depiction of Egyptian polytheism not only as Mosaic but also as useful – and the utility of ancestral religion could figure among gentiles too as a rationale of reverence for the gods.

The background of Artapanus' striking concession includes an at least equally striking inner-biblical tension. Within the Hebrew scriptures the prophetic expectation of an end to idolatry (Isa. 2.20), when the gentiles will see the falsehood of their ancestral tradition (Jer. 16.19, cf. 1 Pet. 2.18),[49] stands in some contrast with Pentateuchal passages which suggest divine appointment of gods for the gentiles. Most notable among these are Deut. 4.19 on the apportionment of sun, moon and stars to the nations and Exod. 7.1 on Moses as a god for Pharaoh (cf. Exod. 4.16, where Moses is 'for a god' for Aaron). Both texts often became subject to interpretation that modified or removed the sense which on the face of it they suggest, but the interpretative tradition also shows that this prima facie sense was not altogether lost.[50]

48. Freudenthal, *Hellenistische Studien*, p. 163; the positive evaluation of Egyptian religion in Artapanus is underlined by Barclay, *Jews in the Mediterranean Diaspora*, pp. 130–32.

49. The forsaking of ancestral error as a topic in early Christian apologetic is illuminated by W.C. van Unnik, 'The Critique of Paganism in I Peter 1.18', in E.E. Ellis and M. Wilcox (eds.), *Neotestamentica et Semitica: Studies in Honour of Matthew Black* (Edinburgh: T. & T. Clark, 1969), pp. 129–42; he views it as Christian rather than Jewish in origin, but earlier Jewish thought on these lines (already sketched in Jer. 16.19) is exemplified at Philo, *Spec.Leg.* 1.52–53, on incomers to the Jewish community as having denounced their ancestral error – but as not entitled, on that account, to revile gentile gods with a convert's zeal. (Juvenal [14.96–100] later comparably expects Judaizers to honour no other gods and despise Roman customs.)

50. The importance of Deut. 4.19 LXX as pre-rabbinic evidence for tolerance of gentile paganism

Thus the two texts were cited together by Irenaeus to show that Paul will have had in mind these deities, rather than the special cosmic powers envisaged by the Valentinians and others, when he writes (1 Cor. 8.5) of 'those who are called gods, whether in heaven or on earth' (Irenaeus, *Haer*. 3.6.5). The joint influence of the two Pentateuchal passages can probably already be detected in Artapanus. There Moses is indeed made 'a god for Pharaoh' (Exod. 7.1) at Hermoupolis (his status as 'god' in Exod. 7.1 was also taken up in the perhaps roughly contemporary Sir. 45.2, as noted below); and when he lays down the Egyptian rites he can do so, although they descend to theriomorphism, to some extent on the analogy of the divine appointment of higher celestial deities for the gentiles in general (Deut. 4.19).

The potential influence of these passages in Exodus and Deuteronomy is underlined not only by the fact that they come from the Pentateuch itself, but also by the coherence of Deut. 4.19 with other passages in the same fifth book of Moses. 'The vision of the end of idolatry in the world which is so prominent in the prophets is completely missing in Deuteronomy.'[51] The book of Deuteronomy indeed indicates divine authorization of gentile star-cult not just in passing but through a group of texts (4.19; cf. 29.25[26]; 32.8). Particularly notable among these is of course 4.19 itself, a declaration, in the speech introducing the recital of the Ten Commandments, according to which the people are to guard their souls vigilantly lest they be led away to worship sun, moon, stars and the celestial host – 'which the Lord thy God apportioned (חלק; LXX αἱρένειμεν) to all the nations that are beneath the whole sky'. Comparably, towards the end of Deuteronomy (29.25 [26]), Israel are said to have worshipped 'gods whom they knew not, and whom he had not apportioned to them' (חלק; LXX διένειμεν). Indeed, in the greater Song of Moses which had its own separate circulation but soon follows in the book as it stands, 'Israel is the Lord's portion', but 'he fixed the bounds of the nations according to the number of the sons of God', the heavenly beings who can be identified with the stars (Deut. 32.8 [4QDeut^j and LXX]; cf. Job 38.7; Sir. 17.17).[52] When bowing down 'to the sun and moon and the host of heaven, which I have not commanded' is condemned in Deut. 17.3, this can be understood as a prohibition for Israel rather than the nations.

outside the Land is brought out by M. Goodman, *Mission and Conversion: Proselytizing in the Religious History of the Roman Empire* (Oxford: Clarendon Press, 1994), pp. 52 and 116. Ancient versions and early commentators on Exod. 7.1 and Deut. 4.19, discussed further below, are surveyed by Salvesen, *Symmachus in the Pentateuch*, pp. 78–79 and 147–49.

51. M. Weinfeld, *Deuteronomy and the Deuteronomic School* (Oxford: Clarendon Press, 1972), p. 294.

52. J.A. Duncan in E. Ulrich, F.M. Cross *et al.* (eds.), *Qumran Cave 4, IX* (DJD, 14; Oxford: Clarendon Press, 1995), p. 79 (on the use of Deut. 32 in Hebrew), p. 90 (the text of v. 8); C. Dogniez and M. Harl, *La Bible d'Alexandrie, 5: Le Deutéronome* (Paris: Les Éditions du Cerf, 1992), pp. 319–20 (use of Deut. 32 in Greek) and pp. 325–26 (variation in Greek text between 'sons' and 'angels'). The Greek text with 'angels' shows, like some renderings of divine titles noted at the end of section 1, above, a wariness of 'inclusive' expressions; 'angels' also replaces 'sons', by contrast with 4QDeut^j, in the Qumran Aramaic version of Job 38.7 (11Q10, col. xxx, line 5).

In Deuteronomy, therefore, the nations are allotted to the celestial sons of God, but Israel to the Lord himself (Deut. 32.8); and although the gentile worship of planets and stars is forbidden to Israel (Deut. 4.19a; cf. 17.3), to whom it has not been apportioned (Deut. 29.25[26]), the astral deities have indeed been divinely apportioned to the gentiles (Deut. 4.19b). This teaching emerges equally from the Hebrew text and from the LXX of Deuteronomy.[53]

Hence, even in the Herodian-age arguments against idolatry attested in Wisdom and Philo, the astral cult is set on a higher plane than the worship of images.[54] Wisdom of Solomon 13.6–8 judges that those who took the elements or the stars for gods have but small blame, for they may have erred precisely because they were seeking for God and wanting to find him (cf. Acts 17.27), and were persuaded by the beauty which they saw – even though they are still not to be pardoned (cf. Rom. 1.20), for having been able to know so much, how did they not find him more quickly?

Philo, similarly, in the discussion of plural divine speech which was quoted above, contents himself with saying that some have called not only the whole cosmos but also the sun, moon and heaven 'gods' (cf. Deut. 4.19); and that Moses, seeing their opinion (ἐρίνοια), says 'Lord, Lord, king of the gods' (cf. Deut. 10.17), so as to show the difference between God the ruler and the gods who are his subjects (*Conf.* 173). Here Deut. 10.17 'God of gods and lord of lords' is quoted in a form mixed with that of the current phrase 'king of gods', based on Ps. 95.3, which was quoted above from Greek and Hebrew sources. The conjectural emendation ἀρόνοια 'delusion' was preferred by P. Wendland in his edition to the relatively colourless ἐρίνοια 'opinion' given by the MSS., but this conjecture is perhaps an example of that accentuation of the rigour of ancient Jewish monotheism which is sometimes found in modern scholarship. The less judgmental word which more probably represents Philo's text at the same time suggests that some influence has been exerted by the degree of acceptance of gentile worship displayed in Deut. 4.19. In a comparable passage on the divine monarchy, *Spec. Leg.* 1.13–20, Deut. 4.19 is explicitly quoted, and again combined with Deut. 10.17 to show that the error against which Israel are warned in 4.19 is to take these subordinate gods as supreme (see *Spec. Leg.* 1.15,20). In Acts, correspondingly, in a passage which is close to Wisdom of Solomon as just cited, the gentiles fall into idolatry in the differing conditions that have been allotted to them (cf. Deut. 4.19) so that they may seek God, but hitherto he has been able to overlook their ignorance (Acts 17.26–30).

In Wisdom of Solomon and Philo, then, the astral cult is at least partly excusable, but the supreme deity should have been acknowledged over and above these subordinate gods. In Acts, however, the excuse goes further, and also covers the making of images of the gods. The divine appointment of gentile worship which Deut. 4.19 suggests seems correspondingly to have been more fully affirmed by some Jews in the Herodian age.

---

53. That LXX makes no attempt to paraphrase (by contrast with later Greek versions) was emphasized by Geiger, *Urschrift*, pp. 444–45.

54. This point is made by Dogniez and Harl, *Le Deutéronome* , p. 139.

Thus Justin Martyr ascribes to Trypho the Jew a 'plain' interpretation of Deut. 4.19, in the sense that the cult of the heavenly bodies has indeed been divinely allotted to the gentiles; but his paraphrase includes an implied explanation, for 'it is written', says Trypho, 'that God permitted (συγκεχωρηκέναι) the gentiles to bow down to sun and moon as gods' (Justin, *Dial.* 55.1). Here apportionment is interpreted as permission for, rather than establishment of, the gentile rites. Later on, however, Justin again summarizes the verse, this time in a speech in his own name, and here he makes no qualification; with special reference to the gentiles and to sun-worship, he now says simply that God 'formerly gave the sun, as it is written, that they might bow down to him' (*Dial.* 121, ἐδεδώκει). The difference between these two paraphrases should perhaps be regarded as one of the lifelike touches in Justin's presentation; the Jewish spokesman understands gentile worship of the heavenly bodies to have been permitted rather than ordained by the one God, but the gentile Christian takes it to have been divinely appointed for the nations.[55]

The interpretation of Deut. 4.19 as attesting divine allotment of the astral cult to the gentiles reappears in Clement of Alexandria (*Strom.* 6.14.110) and Origen (*Comm. in Ioann.* 2.24–27, on John 1.1), and in later Christian authors.[56] 'Our holy scriptures teach…that in the beginning the worship of the visible luminaries had been assigned to all the nations, and that to the Hebrew race alone had been entrusted full initiation into the knowledge of the God who made and shaped all things' (Eusebius, *Praep. Ev.* 1.9.15). As in Trypho's speech, the apportionment is understood as a concession, and now its purpose is often spelt out – either to raise them to perceive the true God (Clement; compare Wisdom of Solomon and Philo, as cited above) or at least to keep them from idolatry (Origen).

This interpretation of Deut. 4.19 as declaring a concession of astral deities to the gentiles was taken by Wilfred Knox to be Jewish in origin.[57] His view receives confirmation from the Hebrew and LXX texts of Deuteronomy and from Artapanus and Justin Martyr, as discussed above. It can perhaps also appeal to two contrasting aspects of rabbinic biblical interpretation. What has been regarded as a lenient attitude to idolatry emerges on the one hand, but on the other there is a wide-ranging attempt to interpret the Pentateuch in a way that excludes divine appointment of gods for the gentiles.

Thus, on the side of leniency, the often-repeated command to break down the gentile altars (Deut. 12.3, cf. Exod. 34.13, Deut. 7.5), which was expressly connected with monotheism in Josephus' explanatory paraphrase (*Ant.* 4.201, 'for God is one'), is none the less clearly restricted to the land of Israel (*Sifre Deut.* 61, on

55. These passages can be added to the material for Justin's view of the origin of pagan religion which is discussed by O. Skarsaune, *The Proof from Prophecy* (Supplements to *New Testament*, 56; Leiden: E.J. Brill, 1987), pp. 368–69; the Deuteronomy-based notion of the heavenly host as a concession to gentiles then appears as a parallel to the notion of sacrifice as a concession to Israel (Skarsaune, *The Proof from Prophecy*, p. 368; cf. also pp. 313–24).

56. Comments by Eusebius, Isidore of Pelusium and an anonymous commentator are summarized by Salvesen, *Symmachus in the Pentateuch*, p. 149 n. 15.

57. W. L. Knox, *St Paul and the Church of the Gentiles* (Cambridge: Cambridge University Press, 1939), p. 100 n. 3.

12.3); and a contrary injunction 'do not pull down their high places' (lest you should find yourself rebuilding them) is attributed to a Herodian-age authority, Johanan ben Zaccai (*Aboth de-Rabbi Nathan*, version B, 31), in contrast with the command to destroy the high places at the entry into the land (Num. 33.52).

These lenient interpretations in turn cohere with the LXX rendering of Exodus 22.27 'Do not revile the gods', a commandment understood by Philo (see n. 45 above) and Josephus to forbid blasphemy of the gods revered by others; Philo (*Vit. Mos.* 2.203) also understands Leviticus 24.15 in this way, and Josephus (*Ant.* 4.207) connects Exodus 22.27 with Deuteronomy 7.25, understood as a commandment not to rob foreign temples. Characteristically of the lenient tendency which is being traced, this prohibition of sacrilege in gentile sanctuaries is derived here in Josephus from the second clause of Deut. 7.25 – a prohibition against plundering the gold and silver from images of the gods – without any reference to the first clause – a commandment to burn such images.

A comparable degree of tolerance of images and their ornaments emerges in rabbinic teaching of the second and third centuries, as E.E. Urbach has shown.[58] According to a ruling in the name of Eliezer b. Hyrcanus (Lydda, early second century), Jewish craftsmen may make necklaces and ornaments for idols, if the work is done for payment (*m. Ab.Zar.* 1.8). Again, the maxim was current that an idol is not forbidden unless it has been worshipped (*baraitha* in *b. Ab.Zar.* 51b). In the view attributed to R. Ishmael, this maxim applies to the idol of a gentile, whereas a Jew's idol is at once forbidden (*tos. Ab.Zar.* 5.4, expressly restricting the scope of the first clause in Deut. 7.25); in R. Akiba's view, on the other hand, it applies to a Jew's idol, whereas a gentile's is at once forbidden (*m. Ab.Zar.* 4.4). Similarly again, an image in one's house for decoration is pure (*tos. Kel.*, *tos. Bab. Mez.* 4.8).

This lenient tendency was treated by Urbach as a new development, to be contrasted with earlier Jewish rejection of idols, and to be associated with a closer proximity of Jews to Palestinian gentiles which was newly brought about in the period after the destruction of Jerusalem by Titus.[59] Aniconic principle and iconoclastic zeal in and before the First Revolt against Rome is indeed made evident by Philo and Josephus, as the contrast drawn by Urbach would lead one to expect; but these Herodian-age authors also show, as noted above, that this zeal coexisted uneasily with a lenient tendency. The leniency to be seen at the end of the Herodian age in the tannaitic rulings discussed by Urbach was therefore continuous with one tendency already known (together with its opposite) in the Herodian age itself.

On the other hand, the trend in rabbinic Pentateuchal interpretation towards excluding any suggestion of divine appointment of gods for the gentiles itself indicates that this suggestion was a live interpretative option. The trend against it is

58.   E.E. Urbach, 'The Rabbinical Laws of Idolatry in the Second and Third Centuries in the Light of Archaeological and Historical Facts', *IEJ* 9 (1959), pp. 158–65, 229–38, reprinted with additional material in E.E. Urbach, *Collected Writings in Jewish Studies* (ed. R. Brody and M.D. Herr; Jerusalem: Magnes Press, 1999), pp. 153–93 (here, see pp. 160–77).

59.   Urbach, 'The Rabbinical Laws of Idolatry', pp. 156–57 = Urbach, *Collected Writings in Jewish Studies*, pp. 158–59.

also evident in the later biblical versions from antiquity – by contrast with the retention of the 'plain' sense in the LXX, from the third century BCE, and the Peshitta Pentateuch, probably not later than the mid-second century CE.

The persistence of the unwelcome option is particularly clear in the case of Exod. 7.1, whence the giving of the name 'god' to Moses was taken up in Sirach (45.2, where 'god' is indicated by the fragmentary Genizah Hebrew), and again in the Herodian age by Philo (*Vit. Mos.* 1.158, 'he was named god and king of the whole people').[60] It was also probably taken up in 4Q374, a Hebrew fragment on the exodus and conquest (line 6, 'he set him for a god over mighty ones, and a cause of reeling to Pharaoh').[61] In the ancient versions, the sense 'a god for Pharaoh' or 'a god of Pharaoh' remains not only in the LXX and the Peshitta but also in later Jewish or Jewish-influenced versions and interpretations, including Aquila, Symmachus, and the Vulgate. This sense survives too, but now with an added explanation which can modify the understanding of deity, in part of the Targumic tradition (*Ps.-Jonathan* 'a fear [deity] for Pharaoh, as if his god') and in the midrash (*Exod. R.* 8.1–2, on 7.1).[62] The attempt to exclude any suggestion of divine appointment of gentile worship gains more foothold, however, in the targumic paraphrase *rabba* – 'great one' or 'master' – 'for Pharaoh', which is given in *Onkelos* and *Neofiti*, and readily suggests a human 'master'; but even this paraphrase can still recall the rendering 'god for Pharaoh', for *rabba* was sometimes a divine title (as in *I En.* 91.13 'the temple of the kingdom of the Great One'; Aramaic text in 4Q212, col. iv, line 18).

This attempt to exclude the view that God appointed gentile worship is represented still more strongly in the interpretation of Deut. 4.19 and related Deuteronomic texts. Thus in the name of R. Jose the Galilaean, who was teaching before the Bar Kokhba revolt, the following exegesis of Deut. 4.19 is preserved in *Sifre* (148, on Deut. 17.3): 'From *which the Lord thy God apportioned to all the nations* [4.19] one could infer that he apportioned them to the gentiles, but the biblical teaching says *gods which they did not know and he did not apportion to them* [29.25(26)]'. Here 29.25(26), although it refers to Israel, is taken as a second reference to the gentiles and a sign that 4.19 cannot bear its prima facie sense of divine appointment of gods for the the gentiles; for 17.3 has also been taken just

---

60. In Sir. 45.2 the Greek 'made him like to the glory of the ἅγιοι [holy ones]', shows that *ᵉlohim* in the Hebrew (where the preceding words are lost) has been taken in the sense of the 'gods' of the divine council, as in Ps. 82.1 'in the midst of gods'; see J.J. Collins, 'Ecclesiasticus', in J. Barton and J. Muddiman (eds.), *The Oxford Bible Commentary* (Oxford: Oxford University Press, 2001), 694b, *ad loc*, who contrasts a merely angel-like Moses in Sirach here with a divine Moses depicted by Philo under the influence of Exod. 7.1, but both Ben Sira and Philo appear to allude to Exod. 7.1.

61. The application to Moses is expounded, with comparison of 4Q377, frg. 1 recto, col. ii, ll. 10–11 on Moses speaking 'as an angel from his mouth', by Fletcher-Louis, 'The Revelation of the Sacral Son of Man: The Genre, History of Religious Context and the Meaning of the Transfiguration', in F. Avemarie and H. Lichtenberger (eds.), *Auferstehung-Resurrection* (Tübingen: J.C.B. Mohr [Paul Siebeck], 2001), pp. 250–52.

62. The versions and the midrash are discussed by Salvesen, *Symmachus in the Pentateuch*, pp. 78–79.

beforehand as a general prohibition against associating the host of heaven with God in worship (see below).[63]

In this comment on Deuteronomy 4.19, from the end of the Herodian age, the unwelcome option is clearly stated. The systematic reinterpretation of Deuteronomy which lies behind the exegesis which avoids it is made evident by additions to the Hebrew text which figure in rabbinic tradition as changes which the translators into Greek made 'for king Ptolemy', although they do not appear in the LXX as now known. With these additions, Deut. 4.19 reads *apportioned to all the nations – to give light* (as in Gen. 1.15, 17); and Deuteronomy 17.3, which in its context is a command to Israel, now reads *or all the host of heaven which I did not command – the nations to worship*.[64]

Reinterpretation in this sense is especially clear in the later of the ancient versions and in mediaeval Jewish commentary, but the rejected 'plain' sense does not entirely disappear from Jewish interpretation. Its capacity for survival or reintroduction in mediaeval Jewish exegesis, noted below, should be borne in mind in assessment of its significance in the Herodian age. Perhaps the strongest instance of reinterpretation away from the 'plain' sense in the later versions is the Vulgate of Deut. 4.19 *quae creavit Dominus Deus tuus in ministerium cunctis gentibus*, 'which the Lord thy God *created for service* to all nations'.[65] Apportionment is replaced by the emphatic 'created'; and the addition 'for service' is on the lines of the rabbinic 'to give light', but is a more comprehensive phrase – recalling 2 Esd. 6.46 'thou commandedst them to serve [*ut deservirent*] humankind that was to be formed', and perhaps meant to cover all the various services of the heavenly bodies which are mentioned in Gen. 1.14–18 – and a clearer limitation of rank.

It is not surprising that in mediaeval Jewish exegesis this Vulgate interpretation of 4.19 can appear side by side with the rabbinic addition, as in twelfth-century northern France in Joseph Bekhor Shor: '*which the Lord apportioned* to give light *to all the nations*; which were created to minister to the children of the world'.[66] On the other hand, in the same region in the following century the excluded option of divine appointment of gods for the gentiles reappears as an alternative exegesis of Deut. 4.19, immediately after a comment very close to that of Bekhor Shor, in the commentary *Hizquni* of Hezekiah b. Manoah: 'another interpretation: *which he apportioned to all the nations* to be their fear [deity]; for God is not concerned with them, but you has he taken to be the people of his inheritance – and how should you bow down to them? Hence you are not permitted to serve any other deity save

63. L. Finkelstein (ed.), *Siphre ad Deuteronium* (Berlin, 1939, repr. New York: Jewish Theological Seminary, 1969), p. 203; the passage is explained in this way by Geiger, *Urschrift*, pp. 445–46.

64. Babylonian Talmud, *Megillah*, 9b, and *Sopherim*, 1.8, with other witnesses assembled by G. Veltri, *Eine Tora für den König Talmai* (TSAJ, 41; Tübingen: J.C.B. Mohr [Paul Siebeck], 1994), pp. 92–97.

65. The versions of 4.19 and 27.25 (26) are surveyed by Salvesen, *Symmachus in the Pentateuch*, pp. 147–49.

66. Y. Nebo (ed.), *Perushe Rabbi Yoseph Bekhor Shor 'al ha-Torah* (Jerusalem: Mossad Ha-Rav Kook, 1994), p. 314.

him.'[67] Here the emphasis is on the fidelity required of God's own people, but it is assumed that the nations, for whom God does not care, are permitted to worship the heavenly host – as in the ancient interpretation illustrated above.

Interpretation which preserves the sense of a Pentateuchal authorization or concession of pagan cult thus spans the Herodian period, and reappears in mediaeval Jewish exegesis. It has been traced above from the LXX and Artapanus to the opinion that was sponsored by Justin's Trypho and rebutted at about the same time in the exegesis preserved in Sifre. Thus at least from the end of the Herodian period, and probably earlier, such interpretation was flanked by strong rebuttal. Somewhat comparably a degree of tolerance for paganism was flanked throughout the Herodian period by strong monolatrous and aniconic zeal, and by a welcome for non-Jewish adherents that continues very strongly in the later Roman period. M.D. Goodman has urged that, although rejection and tolerance of gentile religion are both attested in rabbinic teaching, a shift away from tolerance and towards antagonism to gentile paganism can be detected in the later Roman period – although tolerance continues to be evident, notably in respect of godfearers, and within rabbinic circles in the opinion ascribed to Hiyya bar Abba that gentiles outside the land are not idolaters, but simply follow their ancestral customs (*b. Hull* 13b).[68] Such a shift would correspond to the trend observed above in the later ancient biblical versions and in rabbinic divine titles towards excluding connection between the one God and other powers. It then seems likely that opposition was increasingly encountered in the later Roman period by the Jewish attitudes that have just been discussed – a recognition of gentile tendencies to monotheism, and a measure of legitimation of gentile polytheism. They can accordingly be considered as more characteristic of the Herodian age than of the later period, even though strictness and leniency are both attested together before, during and after the Herodian age.

Lastly, however, it should be stressed that although legitimation of gentile worship well fits an inclusive Jewish or Christian monotheism, the legitimizing attitude is not a *conditio sine qua non*, a condition without which inclusive monotheism cannot be present. Inclusive monotheism can embrace a negative as well as a more concessive attitude. This point emerges clearly from Origen's answer to Celsus. Celsus' second-century claim that 'the different parts of the earth were allotted to different overseers' – the subordinate deities – was appropriately matched by Origen with a quotation of Deuteronomy 32.8–9 LXX, discussed above, from the greater Song of Moses, on the bounds of the nations set according to the number of the angels (Origen, *c. Celsum* 5.25–32). Origen affirms (29) that Greek and even Egyptian tradition and poetry, when presenting the idea that territories are allotted to particular gods, allude to truths which are outlined in the Pentateuch and the Wisdom of Solomon, not only through the Song of Moses but also through the narrative of the tower of Babel (understood by Origen somewhat as it is in Philo and, with its sequel concerning Abraham, in Jubilees); but the biblical teaching in fact is that the rulers of the nations are angels appointed for punishment, and of

67. H.D. Chavel (ed.), *Hizquni* (Jerusalem: Mossad Ha-Rav Kook, 1981), p. 532.
68. Goodman, *Mission and Conversion*, pp. 111–20.

varying character. Moreover, those subject to them were given over to a reprobate mind, as Paul says (Rom. 1.28), and should therefore break the customs current in their territories and adopt the more divine laws of Jesus, who delivers us from the rulers of this world (Gal. 1.4; 1 Cor. 2.6). Origen here continues the early Christian zeal against idolatry noted above (n. 2), which likewise combines with inclusive monotheism in Paul and other Christian writers; but the same combination is of course also found, with a degree of concession, in Philo and the Wisdom of Solomon, as cited in this section above, and (with the sole concession that the gentiles are led astray by the spirits who rule them) in *Jubilees* (15.31–2, cf. 11.4–5). In these anti-idolatrous examples, however, the subordinate spirits retain, as Origen notes, a varying character; as with Plutarch's lesser gods (see n. 22 above), their individuality for better or worse is not erased by the supremacy of the One.

From changes in divine titles and from themes of apologetic it emerged above (see sections 1–2) that inclusive monotheism continued to be of importance in the Herodian age. This impression has received confirmation from Herodian continuance of a recognition of gentile monotheism (section 3) and now from evidence for some legitimation of gentile polytheism (section 4). This degree of acceptance of gentile rites will have fitted well into an inclusive rather than an exclusive monotheism. Such acceptance could extend, as Artapanus and treatments of Exod. 7.1 showed, to a form of apotheosis; under the supreme deity, mortals could be given the glory of a lesser 'god', as was thought to have occurred with Moses. The legitimation of gentile worship here recalls the resemblance between Herodian messianism and ruler-cult which was sketched in section 1, above.

It is of special note, however, that this legitimizing tendency in general can appeal to the Pentateuch, as shown above. This appeal would not simply be to one or two verses, but to a coherent Deuteronomic theology which rabbinic exegetes sought to reinterpret through textual adaptation as well as comment. Thus that respect for the ancestral rites of gentiles which external conditions usually encouraged need not have been regarded simply as a matter of convenience. Appeal could be made with justification to the Pentateuch, and Deuteronomy in particular could be and was understood as Mosaic teaching on inclusive monotheism.

5. *Modern Reconstruction of Ancient Jewish and Christian Monotheism*

The differing views of monotheism sketched at the beginning of this essay (see n. 1 above) in part reflect the long-term influence of the handbooks of ancient Judaism by W. Bousset and G.F. Moore, both covering the Herodian age. Broadly speaking these books recall, respectively, the divergent Christian and Jewish interpretations of biblical monotheism (n. 3 above). They sometimes also recall, respectively, the 'inclusive' and 'exclusive' approaches to monotheism which have been presented above as concurrent, with the suggestion that the 'inclusive' approach was characteristically Herodian. Bousset, concentrating on the period from the Maccabees to the Bar Kokhba revolt, saw monotheism as evincing the diversity which, anticipating many more recent interpreters, he regarded as typical of the Judaism of this period in general. The Pharisaic and rabbinic movements, for him, were by no means necessarily representative. He entitled the relevant section of his book (1926, 3rd edn) 'Monotheism, and the Undercurrents which restrict Monotheism'. These 'undercurrents' include angelology and demonology, dualism, and speculation on hypostases.[69] Their study was taken further by E.R. Goodenough and others, and its efflorescence is at the heart of current interpretation of monotheism with reference to angels and divine beings.

G.F. Moore's grand description of Jewish monotheism, on the other hand, written with reference to the period from Herod the Great to Judah ha-Nasi, belongs to a work (issued 1927–30) which in part was intended as a corrective to Bousset, and excludes from monotheism those 'undercurrents' which Bousset brought to the fore.[70] Moore showed the importance in the history of religion of conceptions like those reflected in Deut. 4.19, but he presented the rabbinic tendency to move away from them towards an exclusive monotheism as the great characteristic of Judaism. A series of mordant epigrams drove home his point: a 'solution, which made God himself the author of polytheism, could not permanently satisfy' (I, p. 226); 'it must, I fear, be confessed that the Jews had never thought of the advantages of a limited monarchy as a form of divine government... the autocracy of God is in fact their rejection of the limited monarchy of the supreme god in organized polytheisms' (I, p. 432 and n. 2); indeed, 'for demigods Jewish monotheism had no room' (II, p. 349). Thus he displays one great stream of rabbinic theology, although the interpretations of Deut. 4.19 and Exod. 7.1 noted above show that none of these epigrams is fully valid for the Herodian age.[71]

The difference between Moore and Bousset partly lies in the primacy of rabbinic texts for Moore, and of the LXX, the Old Testament Apocrypha and pseudepigrapha, Philo and Josephus for Bousset. Moore regarded apocalypses as unrepresentative of Judaism, whereas for Bousset they might indeed sometimes be marginal, but were still of value as indicators of widespread pious opinion.[72] Behind Moore and Bousset, however, there is also, as hinted already, the long history of Jewish-Christian debate on the doctrine of God in the biblical books, Moore basing himself on ancient Jewish works handed down in Jewish tradition, Bousset on those which had been preserved by the church.

Moore had deliberately distanced himself from the older Christian writers on Judaism and their apologetic emphasis on intermediaries in Jewish theology – an emphasis which had enabled them to elicit from 'the ancient Jewish church', as P. Allix put it (n. 3, above), a 'judgment...against unitarians' and contemporary

---

69. W. Bousset, *Die Religion des Judentums im späthellenistischen Zeitalter* (ed. H. Gressmann; Tübingen: J.C.B. Mohr [Paul Siebeck]), pp. 4 and 302–357.

70. G.F. Moore, *Judaism in the First Centuries of the Christian Era: The Age of the Tannaim* (3 vols.; Cambridge, MA: Harvard University Press, 1927–30). On Moore's outlook and aims see R. Deines, *Die Pharisäer* (WUNT, 101; Tübingen: J.C.B. Mohr [Paul Siebeck], 1997), pp. 374–81.

71. Deines, *Die Pharisäer*, p. 378 notes that Moore's aim, to describe ancient Judaism 'as it presents itself in the tradition which it has always regarded as authentic' (*Judaism*, i, vii), leads to an idealized presentation.

72. Concerning Bousset's defense of his range of sources as reflecting a manifold Jewish piety which would not fully emerge just from rabbinic texts see Deines, *Die Pharisäer*, pp. 131–32.

Jews. Within this Christian argument, a long-standing appeal to the complex monotheism of the Zohar as a witness to ancient Judaism gradually lapsed when the mediaeval origin of the Zohar was recognized in the nineteenth century (and the newly-published *Ethiopic Enoch* had provided, as its first editor Richard Laurence urged, a better Trinitarian argument on the same lines).[73] The Targumic term *memra* had also been widely understood, as it was by Allix, to signify a Logos-like intermediary Word; but Moore urged that it was 'purely a phenomenon of translation, not a figment of speculation' (I, pp. 417–20). Similarly, Moore regarded Shekhinah in rabbinic literature as a reverent equivalent of God, not an independent being (I, pp. 436–38).

These judgements, largely shared by the equally influential Paul Billerbeck, have been reviewed in later study and in the light of new Targumic texts;[74] but they meant that for Moore (I, pp. 415–17) the possible intermediary figures were restricted to wisdom in Ecclesiasticus and the Wisdom of Solomon (here he found personification rather than a personal agent), and the Logos of Philo (here he found an intermediary indeed, but one envisaged under philosophical influence which was not central in Judaism).

Moore's stress on exclusive monotheism and his minimizing of intermediaries gave his work some affinity with a series of studies that have linked a rigorous monotheism with ancient Jewish rejection of Christian doctrines of God.[75] Presentation of monotheism on lines which broadly recall these emphases in Moore has continued, especially in connection with Christian origins.[76] In general it is open to the criticism that, although the one God is indeed considered supreme, reverence for him among both Jews and Christians in the Herodian age also allows, as noted above, for due honour to lesser divine beings and to human beings who receive a godlike glory.[77]

73.　R. Laurence, *The Book of Enoch the Prophet* (Oxford: Parker, 3rd edn, 1838), p. liv, with reference to the Son of man and the divine spirit in the *Similitudes* of Enoch, which he judged to have been completed in the Herodian age.

74.　See Chester, *Divine Revelation and Divine Titles*, pp. 293–324.

75.　For example K. Kohler, *Grundriss einer systematischen Theologie des Judentums* (Leipzig: G. Rock, 1910), pp. 40–45 and 61–68, closely followed in *idem, Jewish Theology, Systematically and Historically Considered* (New York: Ktav, 1968, repr. from 1918), pp. 52–58 and 82–91; Marmorstein, 'Unity', pp. 101–104; Kaufmann, *Christianity and Judaism*, pp. 22–24 (urging however that the true cause of separation lay in claims for the authority of Jesus); H.J. Schoeps, *Paul* (London: Lutterworth, 1961), pp. 162–63 and 166–67.

76.　L.W. Hurtado, *One God, One Lord: Early Christian Devotion and Ancient Jewish Monotheism* (Edinburgh: T. & T. Clark, 2nd edn, 1998), pp. vii–xxii reviews work (representing varying points of view) from 1988 onwards; see also n. 58, above; examples of an emphasis on exclusive monotheism which recalls Moore include Hurtado, *One God, One Lord*, pp. 36–39 (acknowledging diversity, but minimizing mediation and stressing exclusivity); Bauckham, 'The Throne of God and the Worship of Jesus', *Christological Monotheism*, p. 48 (traces of less strictly monotheistic loyalty are 'only rarely and weakly discernible, and can usually be seen to have been subordinated and neutralized by the dominant tendency').

77.　The presentation of an emphasis on absolute divine uniqueness as the overwhelming tendency in the Second-Temple period by Bauckham, *God Crucified: Monotheism and Christology*

This point emerges in a different way from the treatment of monotheism by E.P. Sanders, whose sense for unity in ancient Judaism and sober admiration of ancient Jewish religion recall other very notable aspects of Moore. Sanders is reviewing the mainly Herodian period from Pompey to the First Revolt against Rome in Judaea.[78] Jews of this time, he says, had come to the view that other gods were not real gods, and so had clearly attained to monotheism; on the other hand, few of them would have thought other gods to be non-existent. St Paul is characteristic of the period when he writes of servitude 'to those that by nature are not gods', yet do exist (Gal. 4.8, on the στοιχεῖα [see n. 32 above]). Sanders also allows for a measure of practice and belief of a kind that would later be thought pagan, particularly (as noted in section 2, above) in the prayer to the sun described as such by Josephus, and the depiction of heavenly bodies on the temple veil and elsewhere.

The argument offered above has drawn on different sources, but coheres with Sanders' outline. Like Sanders, it suggests the survival of a conception of lesser divine beings; and the reverent treatment of the celestial host noticed above in the ancient versions and in apologetic is entirely consistent with the prayer to and depiction of the heavenly bodies picked out by Sanders, in sectarian and non-sectarian settings respectively.

To summarise, it has been urged here that exclusive monotheism was not clearly the dominant tendency in the Herodian age. Rather, exclusive and inclusive types of monotheism were concurrent, and the inclusive type was also influential. This point emerged from the treatment in the interpretative tradition of biblically-based divine titles (section 1), Christian polemic against and appropriation of Jewish monotheism (section 2), Jewish recognition of gentile monotheism (sections 2 and 3), and Pentateuchal texts on divine appointment of lesser deities (section 4).[79]

Jewish apologetic justifiably built (sections 2 and 3) on the resemblance between Jewish and non-Jewish views of a 'God of gods', for Jews, Greeks and Syrians were alike indebted to ancient Near Eastern conceptions of a divine council. This line of argument, notable for its recognition of gentile monotheism (section 3), itself tended to strengthen the inclusive view of Jewish monotheism. It was also consistent with the Herodian and earlier tendency to legitimize gentile rites (section 4), not only through legendary presentations like that of Artapanus but also through the Pentateuchal texts just mentioned; their prima facie sense of divine appointment of deities for the nations shows a striking capacity for survival.

Christian apologetic, by contrast with Moore's dismissal of it, rightly perceived in the inclusive Jewish monotheism some antecedents of Christian 'subordination-ist' understanding of the pre-existent Christ as a great divine spirit (section 2). This perception was consistent with Christian polemic against what were stigmatized as

---

in the New Testament (Grand Rapids: Eerdmans, 1998); and 'The Throne of God and the Worship of Jesus' is considered more fully in Horbury, *Messianism among Jews and Christians.*

78. E.P. Sanders, *Judaism: Practice and Belief, 63 BCE–66 CE* (London: SCM Press; Philadelphia: Trinity Press International, 1992), pp. 242–47.

79. Toleration of prayer and praise addressed to angels, and a 'resilient' monotheistic framework, are comparably discerned in a study of the question of angel-veneration by Stuckenbruck in this volume, ' "Angels" and "God": Exploring the Limits of Jewish Monotheism'.

Jewish declensions from monotheism (section 2). Christians like Jews were affected also by the exclusive tendency (section 2), which probably encouraged the
otherwise contrasting Christian phenomena of modalist monarchianism and Ebionite
christology. The conditions of the Herodian age, however, were suited to interpretation of Jewish monotheism in ways that rigorous monotheists might have
avoided, and did later seek to avoid (section 1).

This argument has been drawn mainly from the interpretative tradition of the
Hebrew scriptures and from the Jewish and Christian apologetic literature in
Greek. The interpretative tradition has been understood in the past especially as a
witness to the power of exclusive monotheism, but it also shows the strength of
inclusive views (sections 1 and 4, above). The early apologetic literature has been
regarded as marginal or misleading, but its treatment of monotheism, whether in
the Jewish or the Christian interest, coheres convincingly with impressions gained
from the interpretative tradition of the biblical books. These sources together suggest not only the concurrence of exclusive and inclusive interpretations, but also
the importance of an inclusive interpretation in Herodian Jewish and Christian
monotheism.

'ANGELS' AND 'GOD':
EXPLORING THE LIMITS OF EARLY JEWISH MONOTHEISM

Loren T. Stuckenbruck, University of Durham

1. *Introduction*

In the following essay, I would like to revisit an area of debate to which in 1995 I initially devoted part of a monograph-length study.[1] There the main question asked was: How much, if at all, did the exalted status of angelic beings in post-biblical Judaism contribute to the origin of the worship of Jesus; to what extent may this have shaped ongoing developments in Christology within and beyond the New Testament? At the time, I could only conclude that Jewish angelology shed some, albeit limited, light on the origins of Christology. Here, however, I shall be more exclusively concerned with angelology in the Jewish context *per se*. Thus the problem to be considered here is how monotheistic proclivities in antiquity could be sustained among Jews (and Jewish Christians) despite the logical difficulties created when activities of God could be attributed to other beings allied with God's purposes. This problem presents itself in texts that, nominally or otherwise, include expressions of devotion or honour addressed to 'angelic beings'. While it has become axiomatic to recognize that Jesus was being worshipped alongside God in Christian circles during the first century CE,[2] it is less clear that angelic beings could be the recipients of such worship in non-Christian Judaism of antiquity.[3] Nevertheless, it seems significant that the language of worship is directed at angels in literary contexts that otherwise underscore the pre-eminence of God.[4] It is on an

---

1.   *Angel Veneration and Christology: A Study in Early Judaism and in the Christology of the Apocalypse of John* (WUNT II/70; Tübingen: J.C.B. Mohr [Paul Siebeck], 1995).

2.   This is the view, whether or not one regards the worship of Jesus as an activity among the earliest Christians or one that developed at a later point during the first century.

3.   As I have argued, there is very little evidence for the kind of 'angel cult' posited by Wilhelm Bousset as a crucial development in Judaism during the pre-Christian period. Bousset's thesis was largely built on a mirror-reading of polemical texts containing accusations against Jews (whether by other Jews or non-Jews) of such a practice; see, correctly, Larry W. Hurtado, *One God, One Lord: Early Christian Devotion and Ancient Jewish Monotheism* (Edinburgh: T. & T. Clark, 2nd edn, 1998 [Philadelphia: Fortress Press]), pp. 23–35 and, with some modifications of Hurtado's critique, Stuckenbruck, *Angel Veneration*, pp. 51–149.

4.   This is not to deny a significance to texts in which worship language is directed towards human priestly or royal representatives of God or even towards the idealized righteous community, as has been argued, for example, by Crispin H.T. Fletcher-Louis in *Luke–Acts: Angels, Christology and Soteriology* (WUNT II/94; Tübingen: J.C.B. Mohr [Paul Siebeck] 1997); 'The Worship of

assessment of several passages among the early Jewish sources containing such worship language that the present discussion shall be focused.

This topic seems once again appropriate to consider, as I have benefited through ongoing dialogue with and further study of recent scholarly literature. Specifically, Larry Hurtado has continued to defend his view that the 'worship' of Jesus in early Christianity, without any substantive analogy in ancient Judaism, remains the decisive point at which a Jewish 'monotheism' 'mutated' into a 'binitarianism' that accommodated Christ into the worship of the one God.[5] Furthermore, others, most notably Margaret Barker and Crispin H.T. Fletcher-Louis, have argued that the worship of Jesus – indeed his apotheosis and deification – took over and adapted an already existent and widespread religiosity towards royal-priestly representatives of God among Jews whose worldview was dominated by a temple ideology.[6] Finally, in addition to offering further reflections on a limited number of early Jewish materials that I have previously discussed, it is now possible to do so by drawing attention to additional evidence in which worship language is applied to angelic beings, evidence which does not necessarily uphold the notion that 'worship' is itself a decisive criterion for divinity.

While a focus on 'angelic beings' is in some respects rather narrow, it nonetheless provides a conduit into a much larger problem in our study of Jewish antiquity and early Christianity. It is thus important to recognize from the outset that, despite the focus of the present discussion, a study of 'angels' should not be isolated within the broad spectrum of ideas regarding mediation in Jewish antiquity. Other categories of mediator figures with which divine activity was associated have been identified and discussed, categories that cannot be completely distinguished from either 'angelic beings' on the one hand or, in some cases, from one another, on the other hand. A listing of these illustrates how fluid a typology of mediator figures can actually be: divine attributes (e.g. Logos, Sophia, Glory); patriarchal personages (e.g. Enoch, Jacob, Moses); priestly and royal figures in the literature (e.g. the idealized monarch and high priest); and eschatological ideal figures (e.g. 'Messiah', 'Son of Man', Melchizedek).[7] While illustrating the problem of nomenclature,

Divine Humanity as God's Image and the Worship of Jesus', in *JRCM*, pp. 112–28; and, most recently, *All the Glory of Adam: Liturgical Anthropology in the Dead Sea Scrolls* (STDJ, 42; Leiden: E.J. Brill, 2002). Nor does the present article proceed on the assumption that humans and angels can, strictly speaking, always be distinguished among the texts. At the same time, for all the functions and activities attributed to both mediatorial figures (whether angelic and/or human) and God, it remains that many of the texts retain cosmological distinctions that should not be glossed over.

5.   See the lengthy Foreword in the 2nd edition of Hurtado's *One God, One Lord* and *idem*, 'First Century Jewish Monotheism', *JSNT* 71 (1998), pp. 3–26.

6.   See the bibliography and comment in n. 4 above. In addition see, though with some differences, Margaret Barker, e.g., in *The Great Angel: A Study of Israel's Second God* (London: SPCK, 1992); 'The High Priest and the Worship of Jesus', in Newman, *et al.* (eds.), *JRCM*, pp. 93–111; and *The Risen Lord: The Jesus of History as the Christ of Faith* (Edinburgh: T. & T. Clark, 1996).

7.   The list as given is adapted from the discussions of Hurtado, *One God, One Lord*, pp. 17–92 ('personified divine attributes', 'exalted patriarchs', 'principal angels'); James R. Davila, 'Of Methodology, Monotheism and Metatron', in *JRCM*, pp. 3–18 (esp. 4–6, in which are added 'charismatic prophets and royal aspirants' and 'ideal figures'); and Charles Gieschen, *Angelomorphic*

this list also suggests that to treat the question of 'angels' in relation to 'worship' in the literature may be one way of entering into the wider network of religious ideas, perhaps even practices, current amongst Jewish circles around the turn of the Common Era. Indeed, in a number of polemical traditions, it is precisely the worship of angels – that is, of heavenly beings allied with God, whether named or generally so designated – of which Jews are accused. This is significant: for all the ambiguities associated with 'angels', there is hardly any evidence which suggests that vigorous anti-Jewish polemic in antiquity was in any sense an accurate reflection of practices devoted to the exaltation of figures in any of the other categories mentioned above. Nevertheless, it is equally wrong to suppose that such anti-Jewish claims bore *no relation at all* to a religious self-understanding of at least some Jewish groups.

Thus, while attempting to retain an awareness of the problem of devising descriptive categories, I shall proceed with the discussion as follows. First, I shall review briefly and reflect upon the polemical literature directed against the practice of 'angel worship'. What is the nature of such accusations? Allowing for the problems inherent in mirror reading, can we learn anything from such sources about the 'worship' language associated with angelic beings? Second, I shall look in more detail at those sources that actually associate angels more positively with the language of worship. Does or can any of this literature serve as a background to the polemical texts against 'angel worship'? More importantly, what do such texts suggest about patterns of accommodating mediatorial figures alongside God?

2. Polemical Traditions Regarding 'Angel Worship'

It is not necessary herewith to conduct a thorough analysis of the polemical materials, as this has been done elsewhere.[8] However, with the present question in mind, we may find ourselves in a better position to reflect on the significance of these sources in relation to the question of Jewish ideas. This is possible in at least three ways.

Firstly, a review of the polemical materials concerned with 'angel worship' reveals that they were generated out of a variety of tradition- and socio-historical contexts. It is not unlikely, therefore, that at least some of the accusations arose independently and were relatively widespread. Briefly, common motifs among the sources allow us to classify at least six traditions through which objections to 'angel worship' were being expressed.[9] The first four, which are primarily found in

Christology: Antecedents and Early Evidence (AGAJU, 42; Leiden: E.J. Brill, 1998), pp. 51–151 ('angelomorphic God', 'angelomorphic divine hypostases', 'principal named angels', and 'angelomorphic humans'). Gieschen's categories correctly reflect the 'angelomorphic' overlap among these mediator figures. However, the usefulness of the 'angel of the Lord' traditions in denoting figures of exalted status which attracted interest among Jews at the turn of the Common Era is limited, and it is still not clear, despite Gieschen's arguments to the contrary, that the term 'hypostasis' is an appropriate way to describe divine attributes.

8.   See Stuckenbruck, *Angel Veneration and Christology*, pp. 51–149.

9.   Due to uncertainties in relation to the question of worship directed towards angels, I am not

rabbinic and related literature, are as follows: (1) proscriptions including angels among the objects to whom sacrifices would be inappropriately directed (*tos. Hull.* 2.18//*b. Hull.* 40a; *b. Ab. Zar.* 42b–43a); (2) prohibitions against making images of angels, that is, against angel idolatry (*Mek. R. Ishmael* at *BaHod* chs. 6 and 10; *Tg. Ps.-Jon.* to Exod. 20.23); (3) prohibitions against praying to or petitioning angels (*j. Ber.* 9.13a–b; *b. Yom.* 52a; *Exod. Rab.* 32.4; *b. Sanh.* 38b; *b. R. Shan.* 24b); and (4) rejections of the notion of 'two powers' (*b. Hag.* 15a; *3 En.* 16.1–5; cf. *b. Sanh.* 38b). Moreover, and among some Christian sources as well, there are (5) second-century accusations by Christian apologists and others broadly claiming that Jews worship angels (*Ker. Petrou* [=*Preaching of Peter*; in Clement of Alexandria, *Strom.* 6.5.41.2–3]; Aristides, *Apol.* [Syriac]; Heracleon in Origen, *Comm. in Ioann* 13.17; Celsus in Origen, *c. Celsum* 1.26 and 5.6–9) and (6) early Jewish and Jewish-Christian texts in which angels playing a prominent role in a vision or narrative reject a human being's misguided behaviour, whether through prostration or an inappropriate form of address (esp. *Apoc. Zeph.* 6.11–15; *Asc. Isa.* 7.18–23; 8.1–10, 15; Rev. 19.10; 22.8–9; cf. also Tob. 12.16–22; *2 En.* 1.4–8; *3 En.* 1.7; Cairo Genizah A/2,13–16; *Apoc. Gos. Mt.* 3.3).

Secondly, it is important to note the sorts of beings with which each of these traditions are concerned. The proscriptions in the rabbinic texts focus on angelic beings 'in heaven above' (cf. Exod. 20.4–5). These are either named (e.g. Michael, Gabriel, Metatron) or are referred to collectively. While the heavenly nature and the subservient status as God's allies of the angels Michael and Gabriel are undisputed among the early Jewish sources, the generic references to 'angels', on the one hand, and to Metatron, on the other, require comment. Because of their association with the nations in some sources,[10] it might be argued that the rejection of angels alongside celestial bodies as worthy of worship is not so much concerned with a potential threat within Judaism as it is an attempt to belittle so-called deities of other nations.[11] However, in the rabbinic passages that explicitly reject any form of worship towards angels there is no indication that any of these angels are evil; in relation to the God of Israel they are understood as subordinate, yet independent, beings.[12] Thus the traditions seem to have functioned less as propaganda against

including a discussion of Col. 2.18 here; see Stuckenbruck, *Angel Veneration and Christology*, pp. 111–19.

10.　So *Midr. Tann.* (in D. Hoffmann, *Midrasch Tannaim zum Deuteronomium* [Berlin: Poppelauer, 1908–1909], pp. 190–91); *Deut. Rab.* 2.34; and *Lam. Rab.* 3.8. In this midrashic tradition, Israel and the nations are reported to have reacted differently to God's descent to Sinai. Whereas Israel chose the Lord as her 'portion', the nations selected angels to rule over them. Significantly, in *Deut. Rab.* Michael and Gabriel are identified among the angels.

11.　See Gershom Scholem, e.g., in *Jewish Gnosticism, Merkabah Mysticism and Talmudic Tradition* (New York: Jewish Theological Seminary, 2nd edn, 1965) and Ioan P. Culianu, 'The Angels of the Nations and the Origins of Gnostic Dualism', in R. van den Broek and M.J. Vermaseren (eds.), *Studies in Gnosticism and Hellenistic Religions: Festschrift for G. Quispel* (EPRO, 91; Leiden: E.J. Brill, 1981), pp. 78–91.

12.　The notion of angelic rule over the nations was, of course, early on, subjected to a dualistic interpretation going back to Deut. 32.43, according to which the notion of conflict among angels (and eventually, therefore, between angels and God) could be entertained as a possibility; see esp.

'outsiders' than as instructions for insiders that underscore for Jews the incomparability of Israel's God to anything or anyone else.[13] The case of Metatron is of special interest, as in the much later *3 Enoch* this figure is presented as the one into whom the mystic visionary Enoch has been transformed – this is much like the earlier tradition in the *Similitudes* of *1 Enoch* 71.14–15 according to which Enoch the seer is told that he himself is the Son of Man who has been the subject of the foregoing visions.[14] Though here the distinctions between an idealized or exalted patriarch and a prominent angelic figure seem to break down, it is that figure's *heavenly* status that is regarded as posing a real or potential threat to exclusive worship of God.[15]

The second century Christian and pagan critiques of Judaism, which caricature Jewish religiosity as involving the worship of angels, do not reveal explicitly what sort of angels the Jews were supposed to have in view. Since angel worship is linked closely to the observance of feasts in the *Kerygma Petrou* (or *Preaching of Peter*) and Aristides' *Apology* (Syr. version), it would seem safe to infer that these angels are understood as subservient allies of God. Not too much should be made of this, however, as such polemical sources cannot be expected to reveal anything about nuanced beliefs of those on the 'inside'.

The angelic refusals to be worshipped characteristically have in view *heavenly* angelic figures who have served as guides in a story or apocalyptic vision. There is no reason to suspect that, as emissaries of God, the angels in each of the texts are thought to have been anything other than subservient to God's purposes. Again, the overriding concern seems to have been a strict interpretation of the injunction against bowing down to or serving 'anything in heaven above' as specified in the Second Commandment (Exod. 20.4–5). Indeed, a refusal by one who is the target of worship reflects a more widespread form of piety that could, for example in the New Testament, be attributed to Peter (Acts 10.25), Paul and Barnabas (Acts 14.13–15), and even Jesus (Mk 10.17–18//Lk. 18.18–19).[16] Given the passages just mentioned, it may be suggested that the rejection of worship by angels and humans alike should not be attributed to a worldview that simply regarded humans and angels as interchangeable with respect to nature. If anything, the emphasis of the tradition, when adapted in the case of humans refusing worship, is that here they

Dan. 10.13, 20–21 and the Jewish-Christian *Clementine Recognitions* 8.50. Even in the *Recognitions*, however, the assignment of angels over the nations at Sinai is not a matter of their being rebellious or insubordinate; rather, the emphasis is on the inappropriateness of designating them (as any other created beings) as 'gods'; cf., along these lines, Deut. 32.8 [LXX]; Sir. 17.17; *1 En.* 60.15–21; 89.70–76; *Jub.* 35.17; *Shep. Herm. Vision* 3.4.1–2.

13. It would have been taken for granted that any worship of evil angels or demons is forbidden; cf. e.g. *1 En.* 19.1; *Ps.-Philo* 34.1–5.

14. Cf. Davila, 'Of Methodology, Monotheism and Metatron', esp. pp. 7–17.

15. That is, it is Metatron's position 'sitting on a great throne' before the denizens of heaven that makes the conclusion of 'Aher' that there are 'two heads' *in heaven* so heretical and leads to Metatron's punishment by 'sixty fiery lashes' (cf. *b. Hag.* 15a).

16. The parallel in Mt. 19.16–17 retains, though with less emphasis, Jesus' word on God being the only one who is 'good'. See further the contribution by J.D.G. Dunn in this volume, 'Was Jesus a Monotheist?', section 3.2.

are *not divine* in any sense, but – just as the angels of the apocalyptic visions – merely instruments of God.[17] There is therefore no reason to argue that the authors of the literature wished to distinguish categorically between the human visionaries and the angels refusing their worship. Indeed, the angelic guides in Rev. 19.10 and *Asc. Isa.* 8.2–3 could stress that, like the seers, they are 'fellow servants' of God. To some extent, moreover, the attribution of angelic characteristics or even nature to righteous humans would have been a natural way of emphasizing the extent of the latter's piety. But the stress in the refusal tradition falls so much on exclusive devotion to the unique transcendent God that a sorting out of ontological distinctions between God's creatures and servants was, by and large, a matter of less urgency for the writers of the documents.

Third, what can be learned from these polemical traditions? Hurtado[18] has rightly questioned the view advanced by Wilhelm Bousset and Marcel Simon that the traditions point to the existence of an 'angel cult' in Judaism at the turn of the Common Era.[19] In addition, I am convinced that Hurtado is correct in maintaining that there is little evidence that the undeniable, exalted status accorded to angelic beings in early Jewish literature lay behind developments that could explain the rise of the worship of Jesus. However, is Hurtado right in supposing that nothing regarding the worship of angels in any form may be inferred from these sources?[20]

Clearly, the polemical nature of the materials does not allow for a mirror-reading that throws direct light on an actual practice of worshipping angels among Jews. Briefly, though, we nevertheless learn something about the sorts of religious attitudes, beliefs, and modes of behaviour that the exponents of the literature deemed objectionable. Specifically, the traditions listed above refer to *proskunesis* before an angel, confusion of an angel with God, overenthusiastic reliance on angelic mediation as a means of access to God, prayer directed at an angel, and other, more obvious, ways of honouring angels, such as through the offering of sacrifices and the making of images. While there is no evidence of religious rites being organized around heavenly angelic beings or that there was ever an attempt to fashion images

17. *Contra* Fletcher-Louis, who in relation to Luke–Acts is too quick to collapse the human and angelic categories into 'a thoroughly Jewish view of humanity as angelomorphic, and in that sense "divine"'. The claim that in Acts 28.6 'a divine Paul is left unchallenged' fails to take into account that by this time in the narrative the reader is expected to be aware of what has transpired in 14.13–15, namely, that Paul is *not* divine.

18. *One God, One Lord*, pp. 28–35.

19. Bousset, with Hugo Gressmann, *Die Religion des Judentums im späthellenistischen Zeitalter* (HNT, 21; Tübingen: J.C.B. Mohr [Paul Siebeck], 3rd edn, 1926), pp. 302–357, esp. 330 and 343; M. Simon, 'Remarques sur l'Angélolâtrie Juive au Début de l'Ère Chrétienne', in *idem, Le Christianism antique et son contexte religieux* (WUNT, 23; Tübingen: J.C.B. Mohr [Paul Siebeck], 1981), pp. 450–64 (esp. 454). See further literature cited in Stuckenbruck, *Angel Veneration and Christology*, p. 53 n. 10. Peter Schäfer, *Rivalität zwischen Engeln und Menschen* (SJ, 8; Berlin: W. de Gruyter, 1975), pp. 67–72, has argued that the rabbinical sources constitute evidence for 'das tatsächliche Vorhandensein eines Engelkultes im rabbinischen Judentum' (p. 67).

20. At the most, he is only able to surmise that the apocalyptic and rabbinic prohibitions may relate to 'indications that Jews as well as others involved themselves in the ancient quasi-religious phenomena commonly called magic' (*One God, One Lord*, p. 35).

of them, the other accusations may have more of a basis in reality. On a case-by-case basis, one may weigh the following possibilities: were the attitudes or practices criticized actually adopted in some form by any Jews or Jewish Christians, are the criticisms proactive rather than reactive towards these activities, or do they more generally derive from a pool of religious literary-rhetoric that reflected the respective writers' ways of understanding the world? Below, without embarking on a detailed analysis,[21] it is helpful to consider briefly the rabbinic materials and the angelic refusal tradition.

A study of the rabbinic sources yields several tradition-historical conclusions that suggest something about attitudes towards angels among some Jews during the Tannaitic and Amoraic periods. First, the proscriptions that elaborate 'things above and on the earth' in the Second Commandment are comprised of various lists: some refer to celestial bodies and natural phenomena only, others mention only angels, and yet others apply the prohibition to both. The existence of lists referring to one or the other suggests that the Second Commandment was being applied to celestial bodies and angels separately before they were combined. Given that each probably had a pre-history of its own, it would be misleading to infer that the mention of angels in these texts was a novel element inserted into a previously existing tradition primarily concerned with celestial phenomena. This distinction between prohibitions against worshipping natural phenomena, on the one hand, and against angels, on the other, is underscored by the fact that the angels in view (for example, Michael) – in contrast to mountains, animals, and even stars – are perceived as independent beings who function actively as God's servants.[22] Second, the tradition in *j. Berakot* 13a,b objects to the possibility of calling upon angels in a time of trouble (עת צרה). Here, though the notion of angelic mediation is not in itself discarded, apotropaic petitions of angels may have been thought to undermine or detract from the special relationship between God and God's people. Third, the passages that focus on objectionable attitudes towards angels (as in *b. Sanh.* 38b; *Exod. Rab.* 32.4; *j. Ber.* 9.13a-b) assume a milieu in which the objectors and those being criticised were both heirs to common traditions, such as an interest in explicating the Torah (e.g. as it relates to Ezekiel's vision of the *merkabah*), and not least the names of angels. This combination of ideas, assumed even among those who generated the polemical tradition, suggests that there were serious attempts to curb possible practical ramifications of speculation on the *Ma'aseh Merkabah* within Jewish circles. One should be wary, then, of any assumption that no religious attitudes towards angels held among Jews could have lay behind rabbinic prohibitions against the worship of, or even an overemphasis on angels. While there is a lack of data that supports any general or widespread existence of cultic organization around a heavenly angel (or angels), the polemical texts seem to sug-

---

21. This has been done in Stuckenbruck, *Angel Veneration and Christology*, esp. pp. 51–103, though my reflections here below go beyond the conclusions reached there.

22. This view is different from the identification of stars as angelic beings, which sometimes (though not always) availed in the earlier Jewish apocalyptic literature. See, e.g., the early Enochic traditions at *1 En.* 18.15; 21.6; 82.9–20; 86.1–4; 88.1; 90.24.

gest that attitudes and devotional practices relating to them were not only a hypo-thetical possibility but also posed a practical problem that was subject to internal debate. Perhaps the perspectives represented by early Christian accusations in the *Kerygma Petrou* and Aristides reflect distorted caricatures that grew out of their unsympathetic, one-sided hearing of such a debate.

The 'angelic refusal tradition', in contrast to the rabbinic polemical traditions, is attested in sources composed during the Second Temple period. Allowing for variation among the sources, the primary components of this tradition consisted of a narrative containing (1) a description of a prominent angel or angelic guide, (2) the visionary's venerative posture or address towards the angel, (3) the angel's censure of the visionary's behaviour, and (4) the angel's emphasis on God who alone is worthy of such high esteem. The rhetorical thrust of these scenes cer-tainly involves an attempt to reinforce monotheistic devotion in the face of specu-lative interest in angels. The angelic refusals are never accompanied by a denial of the angels' glorious appearance; thus their exalted status is likely to have been an assumption shared by authors and readers alike. Both, moreover, would have assumed – despite the angelic self-demotion – that beings having special proximity to the divine throne quite naturally reflect its glory.[23] Thus it is not misleading to infer that the apocalyptic writers knew of dangers that speculation about the function and appearance of angels could pose for proper religious devotion to God. Analogous to some rabbinic proscriptions, the tradition seems at times, when interpreted within its literary context, to operate as an *internal* corrective which recognized the problem that an inappropriate esteem of angels would have fol-lowed naturally from speculation about angels who performed special mediatorial deeds on behalf of the human recipients of God's activity. The objectionable form of veneration could, as described, have been behaviour observed by the writers among individuals or groups within their respective communities. Or, alterna-tively, they could have been avoiding possible implications within their own liter-ary presentations; the narratives themselves could generate inappropriate attitudes among audiences who as they participated in the vision or storyline through hearing and reading. As argued below, I believe the latter is illustrated by consid-eration of the angelic refusals in the Book of Tobit and *Ascension of Isaiah*.

Since it is unwise to assume on the basis of the polemical traditions against angel worship that they have little or no basis in reality, what positive evidence is there for venerative attitudes towards angels in early Jewish and Jewish Christian sources? In the discussion below the focus on language of 'praise' and petition in relation to angels shall mark an attempt to address this question.

3. The 'Worship' of Angels

While there is certainly a lack of data that supports the existence of cultic organi-zation around any single heavenly angel, a number of sources suggest that angelic

---

23. To have denied such glory to angelic mediators would have called God's own glory into question and undermined the communicative force of the angelic refusals.

beings could on occasion be regarded with an esteem analogous to that attributed to God. In some passages humans call upon angels for assistance in relation to a particular request, while in another series of texts interaction, participation, even functional identification with angelic beings could at times inspire the faithful human community to express its relationship with them in terms of 'praise'. Though such traditions do not necessarily lie directly behind all or any of the polemical sources mentioned above, I think it is appropriate for two reasons to present and discuss them here: (1) they demonstrate the sorts of ideas that in another context could have been conveniently construed by outsiders as reprehensible practices that contravene proper devotion to the God of Israel and (2) they show how the use of worship language in relation to beings allied with, yet subordinate to, God was not regarded as a problem for exclusive, monotheistic devotion to God.

The sources referring to angels conveying prayers to God on behalf of humans are widespread,[24] and should not be confused with prayer addressed directly to angels. The latter, though perhaps a logical development from the former, is unambiguously extant in only one source, a double inscription from Rheneia.

The much discussed epigraph from Rheneia, confidently dated to the 2nd century BCE,[25] was discovered on two stones near Delos. The text belongs to a prayer for vengeance against the murderers of two girls and contains an address to the 'Lord who sees all things and angels of God'. Hurtado, following the judgement of Adolf Deissmann, argues that the thought reflected here does not essentially go beyond what is already expressed in Ps. 103.20.[26] This is simply not true. Whereas the psalmist calls upon '[all: LXX] his [God's] angels' to 'bless the Lord', the inscription invokes both the angels and God together, expressing the hope that the petition will be carried out on behalf of those seeking vengeance. This inclusion of angels in the prayer is conspicuous, as it goes beyond the motif of angelic participation in divine vengeance known elsewhere (cf. *1 En.* 99.3; 104.1; cf. 47.1–2). Neither, however, is the expression 'angel cult' an appropriate description of what the text represents. Significantly, the inscription is otherwise monotheistic in tone. It opens with an appeal directed only to 'the Most High, the Lord of the spirits and of all flesh'. In addition, text following the address that includes the angels is formulated in the singular: 'before whom (sg.) all souls on this day humble themselves with a supplication, that you (sg.) avenge the innocent blood and render

---

24. Such texts ascribe an intercessory role to angels, whether it is assumed to have been a general function (*1 En.* 15.2; Tob. 12.12,15 – Raphael; *T. Levi* 3.5–7; *T. Dan* 6.2; *3 Bar.* 11–16; *Ps.-Philo* 15.5; *Vit. Ad. et Ev.* 9.3; cf. Rev. 8.1–3) or occurs in response to the request of righteous or victimised human beings, as interceding to God (*1 En.* 9.1–11 – Michael, Sariel/Uriel, Raphael, Gabriel; 40.6,9; 47.1–2; 99.3; 104.1; *T. Levi* 5.5–6; cf. *T. Sol.* 5.5).

25. See esp. Adolf Wilhelm, 'Zwei Fluchinschriften', *Jahrhefte des österreichischen Archäologischen Institutes in Wien* 4 (1901), pp. 9–18; Adolf Deissmann, 'Die Rachegebete von Rheneia', in *idem, Licht vom Osten* (Tübingen: J.C.B. Mohr [Paul Siebeck], 4th edn, 1923), pp. 351–62; and Pierre Roussel and Marcel Launey, *Inscriptions de Delos* (Paris: Librairie Ancienne Honoré Champion, 1937), no. 2532.

26. *One God, One Lord*, pp. 28–29.

account (for it) quickly'. Thus, despite the unusual inclusion of angels in the invocation, the writer(s) of the text seem to have made every effort to retain, at least formally, an emphasis on *God*.

More common, though again not numerous or necessarily widespread, are sources in which praise and/or blessing are directed towards angels alongside God. Identifying such texts is not, however, a straightforward matter. For one thing, where the language of 'blessing' is used, one cannot assume that venerative language towards angels is in play, especially since throughout the Hebrew Bible and early Jewish literature, humans may be 'blessed' as well. Therefore, it is the context, if possible, that determines the particular direction the language is to be construed. With this in mind, the following passages are discussed: *Testament of Levi* 5.5–6; *Joseph and Aseneth* 15.11–12; Tobit 11.14–15; 11Q14 (= 11Q*Berakot* or 11Q*Milhamah*) frg. 1 col. ii, lines 2–6; *Shirot 'Olat ha-Shabbat* at 4Q400 frg. 2, lines 1–9 and 4Q403 frg. 1 col. i, lines 31b–33a; 4Q*Instruction* at 4Q418 frg. 81, lines 1–15; and *Pseudo-Philo* 15.6.

3.1. *Testament of Levi 5.5–6*

The seer, the priestly patriarch Levi, recounts being assisted by an angel when he defeated the sons of Hamor (vv. 3–4). Levi's success is guaranteed by the angel's promise that 'I shall be with you, for the Lord sent me' (v. 3b). Levi, in turn, addresses the angel as 'Lord' and requests to learn the angel's name 'so that I may call on you in the day of tribulation' (v. 5). Thereupon the angel identifies himself as the one 'who makes intercession for the nation Israel, that they might not be beaten' (v. 6). This encounter marks the conclusion of a dream vision from which the seer awakens. In response, Levi blesses (εὐλόγησα) God 'the Most High'. One family of manuscripts at this point adds that Levi also blesses 'the angel who intercedes for the nation Israel and all the righteous' (v. 7). It is not clear that the inclusion of angels in Levi's praise of God is original to the text.[27] Whatever the case, there is at least no indication of anything distinctively Christian in this verse. If Levi's praise of angels derives from a Jewish stage of the document, then the author of the text has the intercessory angel praised alongside God for his protective activity. The phrase 'day of tribulation' (ἐν ἡμέρᾳ θλίψεως), which is formally paralleled by the similar phrase in *j. Berakot* 13a-b (עת צרה; see above), is reminiscent of petitions to God on such an occasion as, for example, in LXX Ps. 49.15 and the thanksgiving song in Sir. 51.10.[28] In this context, it is not apparent whether Levi hopes for the angel's help 'in the day of trouble' to be apotropaic in the present age or to avail for him in the eschatological future.

---

27. The translation by Howard Clark Kee in J.H. Charlesworth (ed.), *Old Testament Pseudepigrapha* (hereafter *OTP*) (2 vols.; Garden City, NY: Doubleday, 1983–1985), I, p. 790 omits this addition, but it is supplied in the margin as a later addition by R.H. Charles (ed.), *Apocrypha and Pseudepigrapha of the Old Testament* (2 vols.; Oxford: Clarendon Press, 1913), I, p. 307 (among text families β, A^β, S¹).

28. See H.W. Hollander and Marinus de Jonge, *The Testaments of the Twelve Patriarchs* (SVTP, 8; Leiden: E.J. Brill, 1985), p. 145.

3.2. *Joseph and Aseneth 15.11–12x*[29]

The encounter between Joseph's bride-to-be and a heavenly 'man' occurs after the latter has announced that Aseneth's repentance has been accepted. Of concern here is the nature of Aseneth's response. Hurtado has argued that in v. 12 (i.e. 12x in Burchard's verse numeration; see below) the angel refuses to divulge his name to Aseneth who has asked to know it 'in order that I may praise and glorify your name forever'. Hurtado goes on to describe the angel's reluctance as a 'refusal to cooperate with Aseneth's desire to offer him cultic devotion' and emphasizes that the text wishes to underscore that it is only God who deserves such attention.[30] There is, however, a text-critical problem here; the part of v. 12 that contains the angel's reluctance to accede to Aseneth's wish belongs to the longer recension of the document,[31] that is, it is not found in the shorter Greek recension published by Marc Philonenko.[32] The angel's lack of cooperation in the longer text is preceded by the description of Aseneth's response to his announcement. The text states that Aseneth 'fell at his feet and prostrated (προσεκύνησεν) before him on (her) face to the ground' (v. 11), that she uttered a two-fold blessing (εὐλογημένος/ν) to 'the Lord your God the Most High' and to 'your' [shorter version: 'his'] name forever'. Finally, in the longer version Aseneth requests to learn the angel's name 'in order that I may hymn (ὑμνήσω) and glorify (δοξάσω) you forever' (v. 12x). Without the addition in verse 12x, the text allows, without qualification, the angel to be praised alongside God. Even if Burchard's longer recension in verse 12x is accepted, the reason for the angel's lack of co-operation with Aseneth's request is *not*, as might be expected, the appropriateness of her venerative activity for God alone, nor does it have anything to do with the angel's unworthiness or subordinate status. Rather the angel refuses to divulge his name because it is secret, as are 'all names recorded in the book of the Most High', names that are 'exceedingly great and wonderful and praiseworthy'. In other words, Aseneth's intention to praise the angel is itself not unambiguously rejected, and this pertains (though with different emphases) to both recensions. The tradition-historical complications of the passage aside, the document probably describes several acts of devotion directed towards the heavenly 'man' since he is 'chief of the house of the

---

29. The antiquity of *Joseph and Aseneth* as an early Jewish composition has recently been challenged by Ross Kraemer, *When Aseneth Met Joseph: A Late Antique Tale of the Biblical Patriarch and his Egyptian Wife, Reconsidered* (New York: Oxford University Press, 1998), who has revived the thesis of Christian provenience argued by E.W. Brooks, *Joseph and Asenath* (TED, 2/7; London: SPCK, 1918). While the absence of historical allusions in the document has made the composition difficult to date, the absence of specifically Christian allusions strengthens the argument for its Jewish provenience. Most scholars have thus dated the document to sometime between 100 BCE and the early second century CE.

30. *One God, One Lord*, p. 81.

31. The longer recension (Greek) is published by Christoph Burchard, *Untersuchungen zu Joseph und Aseneth* (WUNT, 8; Tübingen: J.C.B. Mohr [Paul Siebeck], 1965), pp. 68–73 (15.12x), the versification of which is followed by his translation in 'Joseph and Aseneth', *OTP*, II, pp. 202–247 (here p. 227).

32. *Joseph et Aséneth* (SPB, 13; Leiden: E.J. Brill, 1968), whose versification is indicated by parentheses in Burchard's *OTP* translation.

Most High' (v. 12x; cf. also 14.8) and has come 'to rescue' her 'from the darkness' and to wrest her 'from the foundations of the abyss' (v. 12). Aseneth does *proskunesis* before the angel that is not refused,[33] she blesses him alongside God (in Burchard's recension),[34] and she declares her intention to praise him forever.[35]

3.3. *Tobit 11. 14*
The passage in question is a prayer recited towards the end of this fictive narrative about a pious Jewish family living in the diaspora. Just prior to the prayer, Tobias has returned to his father Tobit from abroad where, with the help of the angel Raphael, he has retrieved his inheritance money, found Sarah to be his wife, and acquired the means through which to heal his father's blindness. When his sight is restored, Tobit utters a doxology that that includes angels alongside God (v. 14). Here the versions and recensions of the text diverge: whereas the Vulgate does not mention the angels at all,[36] the shorter recension (Codices Alexandrinus and Vaticanus) mentions them once, and the longer recension (Codex Sinaiticus) contains two doxologies each of which refers to the angels. Though the fragments from five manuscripts of Tobit among the Dead Sea documents (4Q196–199 Aramaic and 4Q200 Hebrew) correspond most often to the longer recension, not enough of this passage is preserved therein to offer clues about which of the recensions at this point may be dated to before the Common Era. Hence a translation of both these Greek recensions is given below in synoptic format:

(Sinaiticus)	*(Alexandrinus, Vaticanus)*
(14) And he said,	
'Blessed (be) God,	'Blessed are you, O God,
and blessed (be) his great name,	and blessed (be) your great name,
and blessed (be) all his holy angels;	and blessed (be) all your holy angels;
may his name be great over us,	
and blessed (be) all the angels	
unto all ages,	
for he has afflicted me,	for you have afflicted me
and had mercy on me;	
but now I see my son Tobias.'	behold, I see Tobias my son.'

33. Given a mild refusal of this posture in 14.9–11, one might have expected the same to occur here.

34. Here the text of the shorter recension is more innocuous, in that the second part of the blessing is made to refer, repetitively, to the name of God. It seems more likely that the longer version has been corrected in the transmission of the book in order to avoid excessive veneration being directed towards the angel.

35. In 19.8 Joseph states that Aseneth's name is to be 'blessed for ever'. The difference in context, however, is apparent; Aseneth's blessedness follows upon Joseph's declaration that Aseneth is 'blessed…by the Most High God'; cf. also 22.8.

36. The same is true of the third Greek recension, the medieval Aramaic Bodleian text published by A. Neubauer (*The Book of Tobit* [Oxford: Clarendon, 1878]), and the so-called Münster Hebrew text in the British Museum published by M. Gaster (*Two Unknown Hebrew Versions of Tobit* [London: Harrison and Sons, 1897]).

The texts allow for several observations. First, the benedictions here are not to be confused with those pronounced in 11.17 (Cod. Sin.; absent in Cod.'s Alex. and Vat.), according to which Tobit, Tobias, and Sarah are all 'blessed' as those who have enjoyed God's mercy in response to their faithfulness. The context makes it clear that the sense of the doxology in v. 14 is unmistakably different. In contrast to v. 17, the 'blessedness' of God and God's angels marks Tobit's response of thanksgiving to the events that have transpired in the book.

Secondly, the inclusion of the angels in the benediction reflects a touch of irony. The readers and hearers of the story certainly know that the man 'Azariah' who has accompanied Tobias on his journey is in fact the angel Raphael (cf. Tob. 5.4, 16). In the narrative, however, Tobit does not know this as he recites the benediction, as Raphael does not identify himself as an angel to the characters of the story until 12.12–15. For this reason, the mention of 'angels' (plural), though thematically appropriate, does not *strictu sensu* fit well with the narrative. The story has focused on the help of only one, not more, of God's emissaries. It is possible, therefore, that the blessing formula in v. 14 was not generated by the author(s) for the sake of the storyline itself, but rather was imported into the text as a benediction that may already have been familiar to some readers. This point is strengthened by the existence of a similar series of blessings in 11Q14 (see section C.4 below).

Thirdly, the inclusion of angels in the blessing is not meant to distract from the ultimate focus on God in the story. The doxology is ultimately formulated in terms of *God*'s activity; it is God who has afflicted Tobit and at the same time has made is possible for him to see again. The author's awareness of Raphael's importance for the story and the need to clarify the angel's role in relation to God is reflected in chapter 12 by means of a mild form of the angelic refusal tradition (12.16–22). Raphael's self-revelation in verses 12 (as intercessor), 13 (as God's emissary), and 15 (Cod. Sin. – as one of the seven angels who stand in God's presence; Cod.'s Alex., Vat. – as intercessor again) inspires fear in Tobit and Tobias who prostrate themselves before him (v. 16). Raphael's response, however, takes the form of an exhortation that they praise God for what has happened (vv. 17–18; so also v. 20). In this way, Raphael's refusal to accept undue devotion by the human characters ensures that his prominence in the story (as protector and counsellor of Tobias) does not detract from or substitute for God's preeminence.

Thus in Tobit we have evidence for a form of religiosity, perhaps already known beyond the story, in which God's angels could be praised. Within the story itself, therefore, lie the seeds for a confusion that could follow from the benediction. The possibility that this confusion might not have been merely hypothetical would be strengthened if the formula reflects wider practice known to the author(s). In any case, the author(s) took measures (11.14b; 12.16–22) to ensure that an essentially monotheistic outlook in the telling of the story was not be compromised. There is no indication that the use of worship language in relation to angels was intended to substitute or undermine the worship of God.

3.4. *11Q14 (Berakot or Serek ha-Milhamah) frg. 1 col. ii, lines 2–6*
Before discussing the passage itself, a brief comment is necessary about the nature of the document in which it is contained. This fragmentary passage, edited ini-

tially by A.S. van der Woude and then together with Florentino García Martínez and Eibert J.B. Tigchelaar, overlaps with an even more fragmentary text in 4Q285 frg. 8, lines 1–4.[37] By virtue of this overlap, 11Q14 has plausibly been ascribed to the *War Rule*; however, the matter remains ultimately uncertain, as neither 11Q14 nor 4Q285 overlap directly with contents preserved among the 1Q and 4Q *Milhamah* materials. If 11Q14 does not, strictly speaking, preserve part of the same document as the *War Rule*, one may at least observe that the eschatological, post-war context of the 11Q14 passage coheres well with the *War Rule* setting. Within such a framework, the blessings in lines 2–6 in 11Q14 column ii likely belong to a benediction to be pronounced by a priestly figure (a specially appointed one – 1QM col. xv, line 7: הכוהן החרוץ; or, more likely, the high priest – 1QM col. xvi, line 15: הכוהן הראש) over the victorious eschatological Israel after the Kittim have been defeated.

The fragmentary blessings are introduced by the words 'and he shall bless them in the name of [the God of I]srael…' (lines 2–3). These blessings consist, as may be argued, of four benedictive formulae which are either fully or partially preserved. These are listed below, along with comparisons to analogous texts:

(1)   'Blessed (plur.) are y[ou (plur.] in the name of God Most High (lines 3–4).'
       Given the preceding introduction on lines 2–3, this benediction is probably directed at the victorious community of Israel. The epithet for God is followed, before a lacunae, by two dots that correspond to what may be remnants from the bottom of *aleph*. Plausibly, therefore, the lacunae – the width of which is approximately 17–18 letter spaces – originally contained a relative clause that describes God further.

(2)   'And blessed be his (God's) holy name for eternal ages (lines 4–5).'
       This formula is paralleled in Tobit, for which the shorter recension reads 'Blessed be your name for ever' and the longer recension has the 3rd person 'blessed be his great name'.[38]

(3)   'And blessed (plur.) be […]his (line 5).'
       The unknown plural predicate allows, according to the DJD 23 editors (see n. 37), for a space of approximately 12 letters. Here we may restore something like 'all the sons of] his[truth (אמ[ת]ו)/covenant (בר[י]תו).'[39]

37.   See the edition of 11Q14 and 4Q285, respectively, by F. García Martínez, E.J.C. Tigchelaar, A.S. van der Woude, *Qumran Cave 11. II: 11Q2–18, 11Q20–31* (DJD, 23; Oxford: Clarendon Press, 1998), pp. 243–51 and P. Alexander and G. Vermes, *Qumran Cave 4. XXVI: Miscellanea, Part 1* (DJD, 36; Oxford: Clarendon Press, 2000), pp. 228–46. See also esp. B. Nitzan, 'Benedictions and Instructions for the Eschatological Community (11QBer; 4Q285)', *RevQ* 16 (1993–1995), pp. 77–90 and W.J. Lyons, 'Possessing the Land: The Qumran Sect and the Eschatological Victory', *DSD* 3 (1996), pp. 130–51.

38.   While the 2nd person formulation in Cod. Alex. and Cod. Vat. of Tobit has integrated the blessing more fully into the story-line (so that it is spoken by Tobit who directly addresses God while referring indirectly to the angels) – and therefore in this respect is less original – this recension may nonetheless preserve an earlier element in the phrase εἰς τοὺς αἰῶνας, lost to the longer version (or displaced there to the second blessing of angels near the end of the verse: πάντας τοὺς αἰῶνας).

(4) 'And blessed be all his holy angels (lines 5–6).'
This formula is exactly (and exclusively) paralleled in the Tobit longer
recension: 'blessed[40] be all his holy angels' (Cod. Sin.).

Two points may be made on the basis of my reconstructed text of 11Q14 (i.e. the
second blessing formula) and its parallels with Tob. 11.14. First, both 11Q14 and
Tobit adapt a similar benediction which at the core would at least have contained
(1) a blessing of God's name and (2) a blessing of all God's holy angels. Among
Jewish documents from antiquity, this doubling is exclusively shared by 11Q14
and Tobit; in addition, it is reminiscent of the two-fold formula spoken by Aseneth
in the longer recension of *Joseph and Aseneth* 15.12 (see above). Secondly, given
the focus of the blessings in 11Q14 on faithful Israel, we may suggest that Tobit
preserves (variously the so-called longer and shorter versions) a less developed, or
more original, form of the benediction. On the other hand, 11Q14 seems to have
preserved a more original priestly context for the formulae. If there is any tradition-
historical link between the two texts, there may thus be reason to conjecture that
they have adapted a liturgical fragment that enjoyed independent use.

The formulation of the blessings in 11Q14, as mentioned above, is made to
reflect the literary context. After the defeat of the Kittim, a priest blesses Israel in
the first blessing and, perhaps, in the third one as well; these blessings upon the
eschatological community have been introduced into the more traditional benediction. The convergence of benedictions on Israel, God, and the angels thus
raises a question about the sense in which each of the blessings is to be understood: are they, for example, all of the same sort? An answer to this question
would have to be 'no'. Israel is surely not being blessed in the same way in which
God is being blessed.[41] Lines 7–14 clearly show that Israel's blessing is being
understood in terms of her well-being as recipients of blessings from God (cf. line
8). This distinction throws into sharp relief the problem of what to infer about the
angels: are they 'blessed' in the same way as the 'Israel' (after all, both formulae

39. See, respectively, 1QM col. xvii, line 8 and 1QH col. xiv, line 29. The DJD 23 editors'
suggestion that either עד[תו] or נחל[תו] be restored is, by contrast, not based on any existing parallel amongst the Dead Sea document if 'sons of' is included in the formula. Lyons ('Possessing
the Land', p. 138) argues that, since this blessing comes between blessings of God and the angels,
the doxology could have referred to 'archangels' (as mentioned e.g. in 1QM col. ix, lines 15–16).
Though hypothetically possible, however, Lyons' reconstruction would be without contemporary
analogy.

40. The term εὐλογημένοι (pass. ptc.) is used instead of the adjective εὐλογητοί (as later
for the angels in the verse) and instead of εὐλογητός applied to God at the beginning of the
benediction. These forms all, however, go back to the same term in an Aramaic or Hebrew
Vorlage.

41. Hence van der Woude is correct to distinguish the first benediction with the word 'gesegnet'
while translating the second (and fourth) one with 'gepriesen'; so in 'Ein neuer Segensspruch aus
Qumran (11QBer)', in H.S. Wagner (ed.), *Bibel und Qumran* (Berlin: Evangelische Haupt-
Bibelgesellschaft, 1968), pp. 253–58. I assume here that the text presupposes – despite the use of the
same terminology – a cosmological distinction between God, on the one hand, and God's people, on
the other.

are given in the plural) or are they being 'blessed' in analogy to the way God's name is praised?[42]

Two reasons may be offered to strengthen the view that the blessedness of God's angels and that of the sons of Israel are to be distinguished in meaning. First, the weaker argument of the two: form. First, though there is a shift in person from the first to the subsequent blessings, in 11Q14 the series of blessings, in terms of its structure, consists of two doublets. The first of them opens with a blessing of Israel followed by a blessing of God's name, while the second one – if the third blessing has been correctly restored – combines a blessing of the faithful community with a subsequent one of God's angels. The placement of the holy angels in the second part of the doublet may suggest an analogy to the blessedness of God's holy name in the second part of the first. In effect, the angels are, like God, to be praised. Such an interpretation does not require that the angels are being worshipped in the same way or to the same degree as God, but does reflect the conviction that their function in some (subordinate) way reflects God's activity on faithful Israel's behalf.

The second and stronger argument in favour of this interpretation emerges as the remainder of column ii is read. Here the reason for the blessedness of God's 'holy angels' in distinction to the congregation of Israel is not hard to find. In lines 7–14, the blessing conferred upon the community in the name of God (line 3) is elaborated through language reminiscent of Num. 6.24–26 (cf. further 1QSb frg. 1, line 3 and frg. 3, line 25). In lines 8b–14a, the divine blessings for the community are described (cf. Deut. 11.13–15) in terms of favourable weather, good harvest, and protection from a variety of mortal and unclean dangers. These blessings in the passage are not given to the angels; on the contrary, they are described on the basis of the belief that 'God is with you and [his holy] angels ar[e positioned] in your congregation' (lines 13–14).[43] The function of the angels as protectors whose presence contributes to the community's well-being is analogous to what is ascribed to God. In this way the parallel sense of the second and fourth benedictions in the series of lines 2–6 is matched in the column below by the analogy between God and the angels.

3.5. *Shirot 'Olat ha-Shabbat (4Q400 frg. 2, lines 1–9 and 4Q403 frg. 1 col. i, lines 31b–33a)*

The case for identifying the language of worship directed towards angelic beings is more difficult to make in this document. The language of the *Shirot*, though not rich in vocabulary, is characterized by a frequency of participial forms, paucity of verbs, and chains of nouns in construct, resulting in a text that is difficult to break down into meaningful sense units. In addition, the particular meaning of a word

---

42. See Fletcher-Louis, *All the Glory of Adam*, p. 186 n. 102, who argues against distinguishing the angels' blessing from that associated with Israel.

43. The column then concludes with the phrase 'and his holy name is called over you', which may be thought to begin a new sentence or thought continued on the (now lost) third column of the fragment. Concerning significance of the notion of the angels' presence in the community in other Dead Sea texts, see e.g. Maxwell J. Davidson, *Angels at Qumran* (JSPSup, 11; Sheffield: Sheffield Academic Press, 1992), esp. pp. 166–70, 185–86, 194–96, 198–200 and 230–31.

such as אלוהים, whether referring to God or to angelic beings, is sometimes difficult to infer. Nevertheless, interpreters of the document, preserved among some ten
manuscripts from Caves 4 (4Q400–407) and 11 (11Q17) and from Masada,[44] may
be reasonably assured about its structure. The composition consists of thirteen
songs each of which corresponds to a sabbath within a thirteen-week period, that is,
to three months within the 364-day reckoning of the solar calendar. With regard to
the present discussion, two passages come into consideration.

The passage in 4Q400 frg. 2, lines 1–9 belongs to the second of the *Shirot*. After
referring to the praise of God's glory among 'the elim of knowledge' and the
praiseworthiness of God's kingship 'among the most holy ones' (line 1), the text
(lines 2–4) states:

(2)   They are honoured[45] among all the camps of the *elohim*
      and revered[46] by councils of humans;
      more w[ondrously] (3) than the *elohim* and humans,
      they declare the splendour of his kingship according to their knowledge,
      and they exalt[…] (4) the heavens of his realm.

If this translation is correct, these lines contain a reference to elite angelic beings
(that is, either the 'elim of knowledge' [cf. line 7] and 'most holy ones' in line 1,
on the one hand, or 'the chiefs of realms' before line 1 restored from 4Q401 frg. 14
col. i, line 6, on the other). Their superior worship of God (lines 2–3) is held in awe
among both other angelic beings (*elohim*) and humans alike (line 2). This is, of
course, not the only way to read the text,[47] and as interpreters have recognised, it is
important not to consider it in isolation from the remainder of the fragment. The
interpretation hinges on what one makes of the relationship of several elements in
the passage: (a) the role of angelic praise of God (lines 3–4); (b) the worship
offered by the human community (lines 6–7); (c) the comparison drawn between
human and exemplary worship of God; and (d) the degree to which the human
community participates in angelic worship.

---

44.   The *editiones principes* are published by Carol Newsom in *Qumran Cave 4* (DJD, 11;
Oxford: Clarendon Press, 1998) 4Q400–407 and the Masada manuscript, and by F. García Martínez,
E.J.C. Tigchelaar and A.S. van der Woude in *Qumran Cave 11* (see n. 37 above) 11Q17. The
materials are all conveniently re-edited by Newsom in *Angelic Liturgy: Songs of the Sabbath
Sacrifice* (Princeton Theological Seminary Dead Sea Scrolls Project, 4B; Tübingen: J.C.B. Mohr
[Paul Siebeck]; Louisville, KY: Westminster John Knox, 1999).

45.   It is possible (so Fletcher-Louis, *All the Glory of Adam*, p. 306) to read this and the next
participle as substantives: 'glorious ones' and 'feared/revered ones'. However, this possibility does
not materially affect the meaning of the phrase.

46.   Given the parallelism with the foregoing phrase, the most natural sense for נוראים is
reverence rather than the fear 'before the divine judge' (so Fletcher-Louis, *All the Glory of Adam*,
p. 306 n. 2) about which there is no hint in the passage. Fletcher-Louis' argument that many of the
'angelic' beings in the *Shirot* are actually humans who consider themselves angelic or divine is
overstated, and plays down the importance of the distinction between the human and angelic
priesthood in 4Q400 frg. 2, esp. lines 6–7. See James R. Davila, *Liturgical Works* (Eerdmans
Commentaries on the DSS; Grand Rapids: Eerdmans, 2000), p. 102.

47.   See Fletcher-Louis, *All the Gory of Adam*, pp. 306–309.

Significantly, the passage allows for an analogy between the human community and the angelic *elohim*; both accord honour and reverence to a class of angels who perform their worship in an exemplary fashion. It is with *these* elite angels, and not with all angels in general, that the human community compare the unworthiness of their 'priesthood' to be 'among their dwellings' (line 6). Thus the analogy between the human and angelic communities is not vitiated by the comparison. The lowliness of the human worshippers does not preclude their privileged participation in the worship described. They are, however, reminded that there is a worship which, apparently for the time being, outclasses their own worship.

The passage, as is true of many others throughout the *Shirot*, is overwhelmed by highly differentiated vocabulary in relation to angelic beings. Nevertheless, it should be remembered that the special status accorded a special group of angelic beings is not meant to take away from the whole thrust of the passage, indeed, the document as a whole: the worship of God whose rule is incomparable.

The interpretation of the other passage (4Q403 frg. 1 col. i, lines 31b–33a), from the climactic seventh song, depends on how one chooses to interpret four occurrences of the substantive ת(ו)שבחות; the term could either be a plural form meaning 'praises' or an abstract noun with the ending *-ut*. Both possibilities are given below:

(31) ...O chiefs of the praises	(31) ...O praiseworthy chiefs
(32) praise the God of	(32) praise the splendorously
splendorous praises	praiseworthy God
for in majesty of praises is	for in praiseworthy majesty is
the glory of his rule,	the glory of his rule,
in it are the praises	in it is the praiseworthiness
of all (33) *elohim*	of all (33) *elohim*
together with the majesty of	together with the majesty of
[his] whole king[dom	[his] whole king[dom

It is possible to consider whether for the author(s) the praises of the chiefs contribute anything to God's rule or, better, help bring God's rule to expression. The view is problematic, given the strong emphasis in the document on the transcendence of God as suggested in the heaping of divine titles and repetitive descriptions in lines 33–35 ('the height of the highest heights', 'the one exalted above all', 'God of gods', 'King of kings'). If one adopts the view that in the second song (discussed under 4Q400 frg. 2 above) it is the 'chiefs' who are held in reverential awe for their exemplary worship, then the translation here 'praiseworthy' is not so remote a possibility.[48] In this case, the expression 'in it' (line 32), in referring back to the feminine substantive 'rule' that immediately precedes, does not regard the chiefs' status at the expense of God: it is in God's rule that any praiseworthiness of the *elohim* is grounded (line 32). In the end, however, the text of the seventh song remains difficult to interpret with precision; the case for worship language directed towards angels in 4Q400 frg. 2 is stronger than in the present passage.

48. This is the view adopted by Anna Marie Schwemer, 'Gott als König in den Sabbatliedern', in M. Hengel and A.M. Schwemer (eds.), *Königsherrschaft Gottes und himmlischer Kult im Judentum, Urchristentum und in der hellenistischen Welt* (WUNT, 55; Tübingen: J.C.B. Mohr [Paul Siebeck], 1991), p. 100 n. 153.

3.6. *4QInstruction at 4Q418 frg. 81, lines 1–15*

A growing number of publications have been devoted to this document, also some-times referred to as *Sapiential Work A* or *Musar ha-Levin*.[49] In fragment 81, there are two possible references to praise towards angelic beings. The relevant passages for this are found, respectively, in lines 1–5 and 11–14:

'…your lips he has opened (as) a spring (מקור) to bless the holy ones (לברך קדושים). And you as an eternal spring (מקור עולם) praise (הלל) .[…]. he has separated you from every (2) spirit of flesh. And you, keep separate from everything that he hates and abstain from all the abominations of the soul, [fo]r he has made everyone (3) and has given each their inheritance. And he is your portion and your inheritance in the midst of the sons of Adam, [and] he has caused them to rule [over] their [in]heritance. And you (4) honour him (כבדהו) in this: by consecrating yourself to him, just as he has placed you as a holy of holies [for all]the world, and among all [*e*]*lim* (5) he has cast your lot and made exceedingly great your glory…'

(11) '… Before you take your inheritance from his hand, honour his holy ones קדושיו כבד)… (12) open a [sp]ring (מ]קור)[50] for/of all the holy ones (כול קדושיו). And everyone who is called by his name (will be) holy […] (13) during all times his splendour, his beauty for the eter[nal] plantation […] (14) …world. In it shall walk all who inherit the land, for in heaven…

---

49. See the *editio princeps* by D. Harringon and J. Strugnell, *Qumran Cave 4. XXIV: Sapiential Texts, Part 2. 4Q Instruction (Mûsar l^e Mevîn): 4Q415 ff.* (DJD, 34; Oxford: Clarendon Press, 1999). See also, in particular, the introductory discussions and analyses by Armin Lange, *Weisheit und Prädestination: Weisheitliche Urordnung und Prädestination in den Textfunden von Qumran* (STDJ, 18; Leiden: E.J. Brill, 1995), pp. 45–92; D. Harrington, 'Wisdom at Qumran', in E. Ulrich and J. VanderKam (eds.), *The Community of the Renewed Covenant: The Notre Dame Symposium on the Dead Sea Scrolls* (Notre Dame: University of Notre Dame Press, 1994), pp. 137–52 and *Wisdom Texts from Qumran* (The Literature of the Dead Sea Scrolls; London/New York: Routledge, 1996), pp. 40–59. Of particular interest here are, further, the following articles (among many) by Torleif Elgvin: 'The Mystery to Come: Early Essene Theology of Revelation', in F.H. Cryer and T.L. Thompson (eds.), *Qumran between the Old and New Testaments* (JSOTSup, 290; CIS, 6; Sheffield: Sheffield Academic Press, 1998), pp. 113–50; and 'Wisdom and Apocalypticism in the Early Second Century BCE – The Evidence of 4QInstruction', in Lawrence H. Schiffman, Emanuel Tov and James C. VanderKam (eds.), *The Dead Sea Scrolls: Fifty Years after their Discovery. Proceedings of the Jerusalem Congress, July 20–25, 1997* (Jerusalem: Israel Exploration Society and The Shrine of the Book, Israel Museum, 2000), pp. 226–47.

50. Restoring פתח [מ]קור (see the same expression on line 1 in the context of blessing 'the holy ones') instead of פתח [ב]שור, as e.g. F. García Martínez and E.J.B. Tigchelaar, *The Dead Sea Scrolls Study Edition. 2. 4Q274–11Q31* (Leiden/Boston/Köln: Brill, 1998), p. 872. Reading this text at all depends on whether the tiny fragment containing these words has been correctly joined within fragment 81 (cf. Harrington and Strugnell, DJD 34, p. 308 to lines 11–12; see the photo on Plate XVIII). If this placement may be granted, several considerations favour מקור over בשור as a restoration: (1) the ligature atop the left vertical stroke of a letter following the lacunae is more consistent with a ק than with ש; (2) *contra* Strugnell and Harrington, the lacunae on line 12 and the varying shape of the tail of ק in the manuscript make it possible to restore [מ]קור; and (3) a ש would require the foregoing space after פתח to be wider than spaces between any of the other words in the column.

The question arises: who are the 'holy ones' referred to in lines 1 and 11–12? Are they the faithful human community[51] and/or angelic beings?[52] The precise meaning in both passages of fragment 81 is hard to infer. Nevertheless, an argument can be put forward on the basis of context. Questioning the assumption that the holy ones are angels *per se*, Fletcher-Louis has noted that 'there are weighty theological considerations which would have dissuaded Jews from such a potentially polytheistic activity'.[53] To support this claim, he argues that primary texts for the 'veneration of angels' in early Jewish literature are hard to find. His own interpretation for this passage is that here an angelomorphic priest, who is distinct from the 'understanding one' otherwise addressed in the document, is being asked to 'bless' and 'glorify' the faithful of the community. He is right, of course, that the mere use of the terms 'bless' and 'glorify' do not in themselves indicate that the text is concerned with angels; as, for example, observed in 11Q14 above, humans could just as well be in view.[54]

The possibility that the one addressed is a priest cannot be discounted, as it is hard to construe the phrase 'he has placed you as a holy of holies' otherwise (line 4). However, to distinguish between the 'understanding one' (addressed elsewhere in the document) and a priestly figure (who is addressed here) is misleading.[55] If a priest is being told to bless the holy ones here, we may have an analogy to the benediction of 11Q14, in which a priest is to utter a blessing *inter alia* for God's holy angels.[56] More important, however, is the wording of the passage itself. The beginning of line 1 refers to the opening of the addressee's lips; the opening of lips is activity whose subject is likely to be God. In the Hebrew Bible[57] and the Dead Sea documents[58] the opening of lips (or even the use of lips) – when the language of blessing and praise occurs – is restricted to instances that refer to praise of God, that is, not to a blessing of the human community. By inerence, then, the benedictive activity referred to in line 1 does not proceed from the one addressed to the righteous faithful so much as it is directed 'upwards', in this case towards angelic

---

51. So Fletcher-Louis, *All the Glory of Adam*, pp. 176–87.

52. So, without making a case for this, Harrington and Strugnell, DJD 34, pp. 304 and 308; see Elgvin, 'The Mystery to Come', p. 143.

53. *All the Glory of Adam*, p. 186.

54. *All the Glory of Adam*, p. 186. For this Fletcher-Louis thus adduces parallels from, e.g., *Jub.* 31.14–15, according to which the angelomorphic priesthood, separated from all flesh (parallel to 4Q418 frg. 81, line 1b), are expected, with 'the blessing of the Lord…in their mouth', to 'bless all the seed of the beloved'. Similarly, 1 Macc. 3.3 (Judas Maccabee, in celebration, 'made glory great for his people') and Sir. 50.

55. Thus, whereas Elgvin ('The Mystery to Come', p. 150) misleadingly excludes a priestly vocation from the addressee in 4Q418 frg. 81 lines 1–14, Fletcher-Louis's identification of this individual as one who is different from the 'understanding one' referred to in the next passage (lines 15ff.) falls prey to the very distinction between sage and priest of which he is critical.

56. This is admitted, though dismissed as a relevant parallel, by Fletcher-Louis (*All the Glory of Adam*, p. 186 and nn. 101–102).

57. See esp. Ps. 51.15 ('O Lord, open my lips and my mouth shall show forth your praise'); also, Ps. 59.12; 63.3, 5; 71.23; 119.171.

58. See 1QS col. x, line 6; 1QH col. ix, lines 27–31; and 4Q511 frgs. 63+64 col. iii, 1–2.

'holy ones'. If this construal is correct, then lines 11–12 may be thought to resume some of the language from line 1: the priestly addressee is told to honour God's holy ones (line 11), and the content of line 1 is further taken up in line 12 ('open a spring for/of all the holy ones'). While it is possible to suppose that line 12 simply reiterates the sense of line 1 – so that line 12, in effect, means 'open (your lips as) a spring (of blessing for) all the holy ones' – it is preferable to attempt an interpretation that adheres more strictly to the economy of words as they appear in line 12.

If, however, we take the ambiguous text as reconstructed with the tiny fragment (cf. n. 50), two interrelated problems for understanding the passage emerge. First, we may ask: is the one addressed being asked to open a fountain *for* all God's holy ones, or is he to open the fountain *of* all God's holy ones? Secondly, how are these holy ones related to the 'eter[nal] plantation' in line 13?

With respect to the first question, if the fountain is to be opened *for* 'all his holy ones', then we may consider whether this watering metaphor extends to the 'plantation'. In this way, the fountain (perhaps referring to the instruction given to the addressee) would be that which feeds or waters the eternal plantation (i.e. the human community of 'holy ones' called by God's name). In this case, the 'holy ones' to be honoured could be readily identified as the righteous congregation of the elect. If the fountain, however, is *of* the holy ones, then it becomes more difficult to identify them straightforwardly with the plantation that follows.

This latter rendering of מ[קור כול קדושים would signify that the chosen community (the eternal plantation) is being allowed to receive or participate in the fountain which belongs to the angels. Indeed, in 4Q418 frg. 55, the vigilant 'angels of holiness' (line 8 – מלאכי קודש) who pursue 'after all the roots of understanding' (line 9) are contrasted with a lazy and sedentary proclivities of humankind (line 11).[59] It is *these angels*, also called 'sons of heaven' (4Q418 frg. 69 col. ii, lines 12–13), who will (in the future) become heirs of an 'eternal holding' (4Q418 frg. 55, line 12 – עולם אחזת) and who will inherit 'eternal life' (4Q418 frg. 69 col. ii, lines 12–13 – חוום עולם).[60] Significantly, this contrast between righteous humanity and angels does not function so much to differentiate between the human and angelic spheres as it holds out the activities of the angels as exemplary.[61] In fragment 81 the watering from the fountain may thus signify the participation of the community in the activities that characterize God's holy ones in heaven. In turn, it would not be misleading to think that for the author(s) of 4Q*Instruction* the 'eternal

---

59. A similar contrast is in 4Q418 frg. 69 col. ii, lines 10–15.

60. Fletcher-Louis insists that the 'sons of heaven' are the angelomorphic congregation of the righteous, arguing that nothing connects the notion of 'inheritance' to angels, while it is commonly applied to human beings (*All the Glory of Adam*, pp. 119–20). A fragmentary text in the first song of the *Shirot 'Olat ha-Shabbat* (4Q400 frg. 1 col. i, lines 10–13) refers to the 'princes' (line 12), apparently a class of angelic beings. If the pronominal suffixes in the phrases 'in their territories and in their inheritance' refer to them, there is indeed evidence – and among the Dead Sea documents – that links inheritance to a (privileged) class of angels. See further 11Q13 col. ii, line 5, in which 'the inheritance of Melchizedek' is referred to twice; cf. Davila, *Liturgical Works*, p. 99.

61. The implication of 4Q418 69 col. ii, lines 12–14 is that since the angels do not slacken in their pursuit of insight and knowledge, neither should the human elect.

plant(ing)' is, in principle, the elect community *insofar as it participates in the angelic community* in anticipation of eternal life. The association of the metaphor with the angelic 'holy ones' is picked up again in the Qumran *Community Rule* (1QS col. xi, lines 7–9) and *Hodayoth* (1QH col. xiv, lines 12b–16a),[62] though now in relation to a more clearly defined group in the present.

If this interpretation is correct, then 4Q*Instruction* fragment 81 preserves further evidence for a veneration of angels. This veneration would be based on the function attributed to the holy angels as beings who serve God in an exemplary manner.[63] Despite directing the language of praise towards angelic 'holy ones' in line 1, the text goes on to emphasize that 'he has separated' the addressee 'from every spirit of flesh' (line 2). In other words, the special position given to the addressee is due to the activity of God (the likely subject of the verb), and not to the angelic beings just mentioned.

This convergence of praise towards angels and focus on God's activity accords with the pattern that has been observed in a number of the other documents discussed above (*T. Levi* 5.5–6?; *Jos. Asen.* 15.11–12x; Tobit 11.14; 11Q14; 4Q400; 4Q403).

3.7. *Pseudo-Philo 15. 6*

The meaning of this text in relation to angels has recently been debated. Here the Festival of Trumpets at Rosh ha-Shanah is referred to as an 'offering' (*oblationem*) for God's 'watchers' (*speculatoribus*).[64] Both Hurtado and Fletcher-Louis have argued that any worship of 'good' angels as the likely meaning of the text.[65] Both appeal to another passage in the document (34.1–5) in which a Midianite magician, named Aod, is said to have been able to do his magic tricks through 'angels' (*angelii*) 'because he had been sacrificing to them for a long time' (v. 2).[66] Do these words amount to an 'unambiguous' condemnation of an 'angel-cult'? In interpreting the sense of this passage, it is important to consider the following verses 3–4, in which four things are communicated about the angels worshipped by Aod: (1) there was a time when angels taught magic to humans (cf. esp. *1 En.* 8.3); (2) this magic, if gone unchecked, would have threatened to undermine the eschatological

---

62. See the discussion of these texts in Tiller, 'The "Eternal Planting" in the Dead Sea Scrolls', pp. 328–31.

63. The combination of reverence and sense of unworthiness before angelic beings would have its closest parallel in the *Shirot* at 4Q400 text (see above).

64. The manuscripts read 'for' with the 'watchers' as one word: *prospeculatoribus*. Since the term is a *hapax legomenon* and given the wording of the previous verse (v. 5 – *oblationem pro fructibus vestris*, 'an oblation for your fruits'), one might think it best to read the preposition separately. Unfortunately, in the absence of any *Vorlage*, we cannot infer whether – as e.g. in Greek – 'for your fruits' took a preposition while 'for your watchers' did not (i.e. was simply in the dative, so that the Latin translator inserted a separate preposition to create a parallelism in the text).

65. Hurtado, 'First-Century Jewish Monotheism', p. 363; Fletcher-Louis, *Luke–Acts: Angels, Christology and Soteriology*, pp. 5–6 n. 23.

66. See further the discussion of difficulties in the Latin text by H. Jacobson, *A Commentary on Pseudo-Philo's Liber Antiquitatum Biblicarum: With Latin Text and English Translation* (2 vols.; AGAJU, 31; Leiden, New York, Köln: Brill, 1996), II, pp. 512–13.

age; (3) these angels, however, had been stripped of their power due to their transgression; and (4) these angels are still active, though only in a restricted sense, that is, through magicians who deceived people through the practice of 'magic'. Unequivocally, the angels in ch. 34 are, therefore, 'bad' angels, not 'good'. There could be no question for the author of *Pseudo-Philo* of the faithful of Israel showing anything remotely honorific towards such angels. In 13.6, however, the 'watchers', who are linked to the Feast of Trumpets, are assumed to be functioning in cultic service to God. Fletcher-Louis would seem to add a further, more compelling, objection to a straightforward reading of the festival as 'an offering to watchers': the preceding phrase ('an offering for your fruits') leads him to suggest that the most natural way to take the parallel phrases is as an offering *to God* for the fruits and for the watchers, respectively. Despite the parallel structure, it should be remembered that the offering for the fruits is related to a different feast, that is, the Festival of Weeks. Hence, although Fletcher-Louis' reading is plausible, it remains possible that the preposition 'for' does not bear the same sense in both feasts. Finally, Howard Jacobson, who, due to a lack of connection between angelic 'watchers' and the New Year holiday, plays down any possibility that the text can have anything to do with 'watcher angels', suggests alternatively that the passage may be referring to the 'watchmen' who blow the trumpets in the event of danger. In such a case, Jacobson argues, as a corollary, that 'offering' should be understood simply as 'on behalf of' or 'as thanks for', that is, rather than in the sense of 'offering *to*'.[67] This interpretation is, however, overly categorical and ends up reducing the obvious sense of 'sacrifice' behind the term *oblatio* to a meaning that is more innocuous.

In the end, the text remains difficult. If, however, the text does denote a venerative posture towards God's angels during the New Year Festival, one may ask why this may have been so. A clue, albeit very uncertain, may be inferred from *Pseudo-Philo* 15.4–6. The passage describes how God informs Moses that he will withdraw his angels of protection (*custodes*, v. 5) because of the Israelites' complaints in the wilderness. The significance of this action is that Israel no longer had angelic advocates who intercede before God on their behalf. The text regards this angelic function as bearing a special potency; without such intercession, the promises of God to the patriarchs can no longer apply and the punishments against Israel can take effect. The bearing of this passage on 13.6 is unclear. However, one may ask whether the offering to 'your [Israel's] watchers' in 13.6 presupposes their function as effective intercessors whose activity guarantees Israel's privileged status before God.

---

67. Jacobson, *Commentary on Pseudo-Philo*, II, pp. 512–13, supports his suggestion by referring to the blowing of trumpets in Num. 10.9 during an attack, in which God is reminded to rescue the people, and to Ezek. 33.2–6 according to which the prophet's message is portrayed as a blast of a trumpet by a watchman. The connection between this metaphor (as in Ezek. 33) and the New Year is elaborated in a Sabbath homily between Rosh ha-Shanah and Yom Kippur (so *Pes. DeRav Kahana* 24) and, more generally, references to Ezek. 33 are made in the Rosh ha-Shanah liturgy itself.

Conclusions

The foregoing review allows for the following conclusions. First, in none of the passages discussed is there any hint that in Judaism a *cultus* was being organised around angelic beings. I am thus convinced that Hurtado's thesis is essentially correct that the sometimes exalted position of angels did not directly contribute to the *inception* of early Christian devotion to Christ alongside God.

But this is nowhere near the end of the matter. At the same time, the Jewish sources containing language in which angels are venerated cannot be pressed so neatly into a *non-cultic* category. It is thus important to understand first what is meant by 'cultic' devotion when it is used. Here the polemical sources, which express what was *perceived* as objectionable forms of worship, may provide some clue. Is one to regard the *proskunesis* rejected in the angelophanic traditions as 'cultic'? Since in some of the apocalyptic texts this posture is perceived as a contravention of God's prerogative to be worshipped, this may be thought in such instances to have constituted reprehensible devotion in a 'cultic' sense. Moreover, one may ask, is 'cultic' devotion expressed when, in an angelophanic context, Aseneth declares a desire to 'hymn and glorify' the angelic emissary 'forever' (*Jos. Asen.* 15.11–12x)? This behaviour is at least considered by Hurtado to be 'cultic devotion'[68] and, therefore, for the sake of consistency he is constrained to conclude that precisely *this* is what the angel wishes to reject. Finally, is 'cultic devotion' operative when, for reasons supplied in a given story, the 'blessedness' of angels is asserted alongside that of God, as in Tobit 11 and *Jos. Asen.* 15, or when their 'blessedness' next to God reflects a community's conviction that the presence of angels in their midst functions as a guarantee for their well-being (as in 11QBerakot; perhaps, though uncertain, *Ps.-Philo* 13.6; 15.4–6)? The question becomes all the more acute if we are to suppose that Tobit 11 and 11QBerakot preserve portions of a similar liturgical fragment.

These questions lead to the suggestion that there is some evidence in early Jewish texts that allows for the 'cultic' worship of angels, if by this is meant reverence-honour-praise directed at angelic beings within the setting of the worshipping community. To the extent that the evidence adduced above reflects such veneration, it becomes misleading to conclude that 'cultic devotion' in the broad sense functioned as the decisive criterion that determined the boundaries of early non-Christian Jewish monotheistic belief.[69] Nevertheless, if 'cultic devotion' is more

68. Hurtado, *One God, One Lord*, p. 81.
69. Thus it is possible that in the Enochic *Similitudes* (*1 En.* 46.5; 48.5; 61.11; 62.9) the language of worship is used to describe the position of honour given to the angelomorphic (cf. 46.1) Son of Man without intruding in any sense into what the author regards as the exclusive prerogative of 'the Lord of the spirits' who alone is 'the Most High'.

Similarly, I have argued that the praise directed towards angels in the Christian *Ascension of Isaiah* (early 2nd century CE) is not considered a breach of the author's monotheistic proclivities, despite the angel's rejection of the honour shown by the seer (7.21–22; 8.4–5). Though God, Christ, and the Holy Spirit are all worshipped in the *Ascension*, the monotheistic framework for the author is ultimately retained through a spatially stratified cosmos. God alone assumes the tran-

narrowly conceived as cultic organization, it is hard to find anything in Jewish sources that suggests Jews had ever assimilated inclusion of angels alongside God in worship into an organized cult, that is, into their temple-centred sacrifices and offerings. Honorific and worship *language* could, on occasion, be ascribed to angelic beings, but to have sacrificed to them would have gone too far.[70]

Secondly, and following from the first point, it becomes useful to distinguish between 'veneration' and 'worship', the former referring to honorific reverence, even praise towards an angel or angels in the language of the worshipping community, while 'worship' is organized in practice and expresses itself in terms of sacrifice.[71] This distinction should not, however, be pressed without qualification. What counts in one document as inappropriate behaviour may in another be regarded as acceptable. Sometimes, even in single documents there is little terminological distinction made between these categories, and it is left to a reading of the context to determine the religious significance of this or that form of address or activity.[72]

Third, in 'insider' literature, that is, writings composed for fellow-adherents of small or large communities, certain liberties could be taken, for example, to extol an angel or angels. This was possible in stories or narratives in which visionaries were interacting with heavenly figures in God's cosmos. Significantly, whether vehemently (as in the angelic refusal tradition) or subtly (as in the use of the singular following the praise of angels alongside God), such instances betray an awareness of the problem. Potential or real, the problem of fitting heavenly figures into a larger cosmological framework in which the God of Israel remains at the top was recognized and thus had to be dealt with in a number of ways. Even where the venerative language towards angelic beings is allowed, the authors ensure that it does not come at the price of reflection and focus on God. The logical tension remains, but the uniqueness of God continues to be asserted against any other possibility.

In compositions functioning as propaganda, the distinctions between Judaism and other religions would be drawn more sharply. Conceptual categories such as idolatry, on the one hand, and the worship of God alone, on the other, are held as far apart as possible.[73] With respect to angels, the Jewish polemic against 'polythe-

---

scendent position in the seventh heaven. See Stuckenbruck, 'Worship and Monotheism in the *Ascension of Isaiah*', in *JRCM*, pp. 70–89.

70. See the contribution by Lionel North in this volume.

71. Although among the Dead Sea documents angels could be the object of honorific language, no 'cultic' language, even when used metaphorically, is ever directed towards them. The passage in *Ps.-Philo* considered above, if it does preserve 'cultic' language in relation to Israel's 'watchers', does not provide sufficient evidence that cultic practice was (re-)structured to accommodate it.

72. In addition to *Joseph and Asenath*, Tobit, 11Q*Berakot*, and 4Q*Instruction*, so also, for example, the *proskunesis* in John's Apocalypse (cp. 19.10 and 22.8–9, e.g., with 3.9) and the venerative language in *Ascension of Isaiah* (cf. Stuckenbruck, 'Worship and Monotheism', bibl. in n. 67).

73. On this, see Michael Mach, 'Concepts of Jewish Monotheism in the Hellenistic Period', in *JRCM*, pp. 21–42 (esp. pp. 24–32 – referring to Deutero–Isaiah, *Epistle of Jeremiah*, Judith, *Jubilees, Pseudo-Aristeas, Sibylline Oracles* Book 3).

istic' or idolatrous religions could be turned around, as some asserted (mistakenly) that at least some Jews were vulnerable when measured against the strict adherence to God they could claim for themselves.

This study of angelic beings in Early Judaism forms only a small part of the question of 'worship' in relation to mediatory figures. However, it is hoped that it illustrates the degree to which some early Jewish sources could tolerate language of prayer and praise as directed towards angels and, in addition, how resilient a monotheistic framework could remain in such cases. As far as the significance for early Christology is concerned, it is not the 'worship' of angels itself that left its mark on earliest formulations of Jesus' exalted status. Rather, it is *how* such honorific language towards angels was accommodated into worship directed ultimately towards God which established a pattern that helped to shape ways Christians extolled Christ during the first century, as they insisted that their devotion to the one God of Israel was not being compromised.

Alexander the Great's Worship of the High Priest

Crispin H.T. Fletcher-Louis, University of Nottingham

Recent discussion of the origins and shape of early Christology has focused much attention, reflected in several other essays in this volume, on the precedents, or lack thereof, for a worship offered to Jesus of Nazareth. In several earlier treatments of this question I have argued that, contrary to the opinion of some,[1] there was a well-established precedent in mainstream Jewish cultic practice for the worship of a human being.[2] There is much primary textual evidence that *under certain circumstances* Jews believed it right that peculiarly righteous individuals (e.g. the king, the high priest, Moses, the Enochic Son of Man) should receive literary or communal praise, cultic prostration and even sacrifices.[3]

Of course, many aspects of this evidence, its interpretation and precise significance are contested. This, as I have argued, is because the shape of Jewish monotheism has been predetermined by modern commentators so as to exclude any form of veneration of a divine humanity prior to a proper historical assessment of the primary sources. One of the most important possible witnesses to a Jewish belief that a human being can, and should, be 'worshipped' is the account of the worship of the high priest by Alexander the Great in Josephus' *Jewish Antiquities* and its parallels. In this paper I examine this tradition, its interpretation, and the theological rationale it offers for Alexander's worship of the high priest.[4]

---

1.   E.g. L.W. Hurtado, *One God, One Lord: Early Christian Devotion and Ancient Jewish Monotheism* (Philadelphia: Fortress Press, 1988); R. Bauckham, *God Crucified: Monotheism and Christology in the New Testament* (Carlisle: Paternoster Press, 1998).

2.   *Luke–Acts: Angels, Christology and Soteriology* (WUNT, II.94; Tübingen: J.C.B. Mohr [Paul Siebeck], 1997); 'The Worship of Divine Humanity and the Worship of Jesus', in *JRCM*, pp. 112–28; cf. also *All the Glory of Adam: Liturgical Anthropology in the Dead Sea Scrolls* (STDJ, 42; Leiden: E.J. Brill, 2001).

3.   King: Ps. 45; 1 Chron. 29.20; High Priest: Hecataeus of Abdera (in Diodorus Siculus, *Bibliotheca Historica* 40.3.3–8); Josephus, *Ant.* 11.331–335 (*par*. Scholion to *Megillath Ta'anith* 21st Tislev and *b. Yoma* 69a); *T. Reub.* 6.12; Sirach (44–)50; XIIIth of the *Songs of the Sabbath Sacrifice* (4Q405 frg. 23 col. ii); so Fletcher-Louis, *All the Glory of Adam* (pp. 356–94); *1 En.* 48.5; 62.6–9 (cf. also 46.5; 52.4); *3 En.* 12–16; and Pharaoh's prostration before, and blessing of, Levi in *Joseph and Aseneth* 29.6; Moses: Ezekiel the Tragedian's *Exagoge* line 81. For a recognition of the significance of this kind of evidence as well as of further material that implies conformity of Jewish practice to the conventions of the Graeco-Roman Ruler Cult, see W. Horbury, *Jewish Messianism and the Cult of Christ* (London: SCM Press, 1998).

4.   Most discussions of this passage have focused on its historicity and literary tradition history.

I have argued in an earlier study that because Jewish monotheism is not, as has traditionally been thought, utterly an-iconic, the worship of a human being is both possible and, in fact, a logical response to the anthropomorphic form of Israel's god.[5] As a number of recent Old Testament commentators have seen, at least in the priestly tradition (represented by P and Ezekiel), the worship of man-made images of the divinity or other aspects of creation is prohibited because it is only humanity that truly represents the form of God.[6] By using the language of the cult object for the creation of humanity in God's 'image (צלם)', Gen. 1 sets up the pre-lapsarian humanity as the legitimate cult embodiment of the one creator God, in a way that is analogous to the relationship between pagan gods and their idols. And if the true humanity is God's idol then it stands to reason that where that true humanity is found it should be given the same kind of cultic devotion that pagans give to their idols. Our principal contention in what follows will be that it is this theological vision that justifies Alexander's worship of the high priest in Josephus' version of our story.[7]

The Texts

In his account of Jewish history, the aristocratic high priest Josephus records the following story of a meeting between Alexander of Macedon and the Jews of Jerusalem led by their high priest Jaddua (*Ant.* 11.326–338).[8]

> [326] When the high priest Jaddua heard this [of the approach of Alexander the Great], he was in an agony of fear, not knowing how he could meet the Macedonians, whose king was angered by his former disobedience. He therefore ordered the people to make supplications, and, offering sacrifice to God together with them from the dangers that were hanging over them. [327] But, when he had gone to sleep after the sacrifice, God spoke to him in his sleep, telling him to take courage and <u>adorn the city with wreaths and open the gates and go out to meet them, and that the people should be in white garments, and he himself with the priests in the robes prescribed by the Torah,</u> and that they should not look to suffer any harm,

---

5. Fletcher-Louis, 'Divine Humanity'.

6. Besides the secondary literature for this view cited in Fletcher-Louis, 'Divine Humanity', see now I. Provan, 'To Highlight All our Idols: Worshipping God in Nietzsche's World', *Ex Auditu* 15 (1999), pp. 19–38 (esp. pp. 25–26); Ulrich Mauser, 'God in Human Form', *Ex Auditu* 16 (2000), pp. 81–100 (esp. pp. 90–92); S. Dean McBride, 'Divine Protocol: Genesis 1.1–2.3 as Prologue to the Pentateuch', in W.P. Brown and S.D. McBride (eds.), *God Who Creates: Essays in Honor of W. Sibley Towner* (Grand Rapids: Eerdmans, 2000), pp. 3–41 (esp. pp. 15–17); and R.E. Watts, 'On the Edge of the Millennium: Making Sense of Genesis 1', in H. Boersma (ed.), *Living in the Lamb Light: Christianity and Contemporary Challenges to the Gospel* (Vancouver: Regent College, 2001), pp. 129–51.

7. For a discussion of the role of this theology in the story of the worship of Adam by the angels (i.e. in *Vit. Ad. et Ev.* 12–16 and parallels), see Fletcher-Louis, *All the Glory of Adam*, pp. 69–70 and 99–103.

8. A slightly modified version of the translation may be found in the LCL edition. The date of the meeting would have been 332 BCE. The underlined and dotted underlined text represent formally distinct aspects of the story that are discussed below.

for God was watching over them.[328] Thereupon he rose from his sleep, greatly rejoicing to himself, and announced to all the revelation that had been made to him, and, after doing all the things that he had been told to do, awaited the coming of the king.

[329] When he learned that Alexander was not far from the city, he went out with the priests and the body of along thought to themselves that the king [i.e. Alexander] in his anger would naturally permit them to plunder the city and put the high priest to a shameful death, but the reverse of this happened.citizens, and, making the reception sacred in character and different from that of other nations, met him in a certain place called Saphein...[330] Now the Phoenicians and the Chaldaeans who followed.

[331] For when Alexander while still far off saw the multitude in white garments, the priests at their head clothed in linen, and the high priest in a robe of hyacinth-blue and gold, wearing on his head the mitre with the golden plate on it on which was inscribed the Name of God, he approached alone and worshipped the Name and hailed the high priest first [i.e. before the high priest greeted him] (προσελθὼν μόνος προσεκύνησε τὸ ὄνομα καὶ τὸν ἀρχιερέα πρῶτος ἠσπάσατο).[332] Then all the Jews together hailed Alexander with one voice and surrounded him, but the kings of Syria and the others were struck with amazement at his action and supposed that the king's mind was deranged.[33] And Parmenion [Alexander's second in command] alone went up to him and asked why indeed, when all men prostrated themselves before him, he had prostrated himself in worship before the high priest of the Jews (τί δήποτε προσκυνούντων αὐτὸν ἀπάντων αὐτὸς προσκυνήσειε τὸν Ἰουδαίων ἀρχιερέα), whereupon he replied, 'It was not before him that I prostrated myself but the god of whom he has the honour to be high priest (οὐ τοῦτον προσεκύνησα τὸν δε θεόν, οὗ τῇ ἀρχιερωσύνῃ οὗτος τετίμηται),[334] for it was he whom I saw in my sleep in the form that he is now (ἐν τῷ νῦν σχήματι), when I was at Dium in Macedonia and, as I was considering with myself how I might become master of Asia, he urged me not to hesitate but to cross over confidently, for he himself would lead my army and give over to me the empire of the Persians.[334] Since, therefore, I have beheld no one else in a garment, and on seeing him now I am reminded of the vision and the exhortation, I believe that I have made this expedition under divine guidance and that I shall defeat Darius and destroy the power of the Persians and succeed in carrying out all the things which I have in mind.'[336] After saying these things to Parmenion, he gave his hand to the high priest and, with the Jews running beside him, entered the city. Then he went up to the Temple, where he sacrificed to God under the direction of the high priest and showed due honour to the priests and to the high priest himself (αὐτὸν δε τὸν ἀρχιερέα καὶ τοὺς ἱερεῖς ἀξιοπρεπῶς ἐτίμησεν).

[337] And, when the book of Daniel was shown to him, in which he had declared that one of the Greeks would destroy the empire of the Persians, he believed himself to be the one indicated; and in his joy he dismissed the multitude for the time being, but on the following day he summoned them again and told them to ask for any gifts which they might desire.[338] When the high priest asked that they might observe their country's laws and in the seventh year be exempt from tribute, he granted all this. Then they begged that he would permit the Jews in Babylon and Media also to have their own laws, and he gladly promised to do as they asked.

This story is retold in Jewish, Samaritan and Christian literature in many, slightly different, forms. These are principally four in number and they offer potentially reliable evidence of the 'original' Second Temple version of the story.[9] (1) one in the Judaizing (γ) recension of Pseudo-Callisthenes' *Alexander Romance* (ii. 24), (2) a Talmudic version (*b. Yoma* 69a *par.* Scholion to *Megillath Ta'anith* ch. 9 for the 21st of Tislev),[10] (3) the account in Josippon and lastly (4), a version in the Samaritan Chronicles. Because these are not widely known or readily available and in the interests of a comprehensive analysis of the tradition, it is as well that these be given in full here.

The relevant section of the Alexander Romance version reads.[11]

> When their [the Jews'] leaders heard this [of Alexander's threatening approach], they decided to submit to Alexander, and so their priests put on their priestly robes and went out to meet Alexander with all their host. When Alexander saw them he was awed by their appearance (ἐδεξίει τοῦ σχήματος αὐτῶν) and told them not to come any nearer to him but to remain in the city. Then he summoned one of the priests and said to him, 'How divine is your appearance (ὡς θεοειδες ὑμῶν τὸ σχῆμα)! Tell me, I pray, what god you worship. For I have never seen so seemly an array (εὐταξαν) of priests among those of our gods.' The priest then said, 'We serve one God who created heaven and earth and all things in them. But no man is able to expound/translate him (αὐτὸν ἑρμηνεῦσαι).' Thereupon, Alexander said, 'As servants of the true God go in peace. For your God shall be my God. And I will make peace with you and will not invade your country as I have done those of other nations, because you have served a living God.' Then the Jews took an abundance of money in gold and silver and brought it to Alexander. But he refused to take it, saying, 'Let this, together with the sum set apart by me, be tribute to the Lord God. But I will not take anything from you.'

Of the almost identical two versions in rabbinic literature the one in the Babylonian Talmud tractate *Yoma* reads:

> The 25th of Tebeth is the day of Mount Gerizim, on which no mourning is permitted. It is the day on which the Cutheans demanded the House of our God from Alexander the Macedonian so as to destroy it, and he had given them the permission, whereupon some people came and informed Simeon the Just. What did the latter do? He put on his priestly garments, some of the noblemen of Israel went with him carrying fiery torches in their hands, they walked all the night, some walking on one side and others on the other side, until the dawn rose. When the dawn rose he [Alexander] said to them [the Samaritans]: 'Who are these?' They answered: 'The Jews who rebelled against you'. As he reached Antipatris, the sun having shone forth, they met. When he saw Simeon the Just, he descended from

---

9. For a fuller list of witnesses, see Moses Gaster and B. Schindler, *The Exempla of the Rabbis: Being a Collection of Exempla, Apologues and Tales Culled from Hebrew Manuscripts and Rare Hebrew Books* (2 vols.; London: The Asia Publishing Co., 1924), I, pp. 232–33.

10. See also *Lev. Rab.* 13.5 and *Pesiq. Rab.* 14.15.

11. For the text, see Ursula von Lauenstein, *Der griechische Alexanderroman: Rezension [G] Buch I* (Meisenheim am Glan: A. Hain, 1962), p. 218. For a good commentary on this story, see G. Delling, 'Alexander der Grosse als Bekenner des jüdischen Gottesglaubens', *JSJ* 12 (1981), pp. 1–51 (esp. pp. 3–11).

his chariot and bowed down before him (והשתחוה לפניו). They said to him: 'A great king like yourself should bow down before this Jew (זה ישתחוה ליהודי)?' He answered: 'the likeness of his image (דמות דיוקנו)[12] it is which wins for me in all my battles'. He said to them: 'What have you come for?' They said: 'Is it possible that star-worshippers should mislead you to destroy the house wherein prayers are said for you and your kingdom that it be never destroyed!' He said to them: 'Who are these?' They said to him: 'These are the Cutheans [i.e. Samaritans] who stand before you'. He said: 'They are delivered into your hand'.

The Jews proceed to raze to the ground the Shechem sanctuary and make the day a festival in perpetuity. The story in Josippon (10.3–51) assumes the same narrative setting as the others. Alexander is on his way to defeat Darius, he has conquered the communities of the Asiatic and Mediterranean coastlines and now makes for Jerusalem:

So he set out from Gaza with all his army, advancing until he came near to some resting place on the road where he encamped together with all his army. [10] That night as he lay on his bed in the tent, he saw a man (איש) standing at his head garbed in white linen (לבוש בדים) and a drawn sword in his hand (חרבו שלוחה בידו). And the appearance of the sword was like the appearance of the likeness of lightning that flashes on a rainy day (cf. Ezek. 1.13, 28); and he raised his sword over the king's head. The king was greatly alarmed and said to him: 'My Lord, why should you smite your slave?' And the man answered: 'Because God sent me before you to subdue great kings and many peoples, for I am he that goes before you in order to aid you (cf. Exod. 23.20, 22) [15] Now I would have you know that you will most assuredly perish because your heart has led you to go up to Jerusalem and do evil to the priests of the Lord and His people.'

But the king said, 'I pray you, pardon the transgression (שא נא פשע) of your servant (cf. Exod. 23.21)! I entreat you, my Lord, if it seems evil in your eyes, I shall turn about.' But the man answered: 'Have no fear, for I forgive you, go your way to Jerusalem! When you come to the gateway of Jerusalem, you will see a man clothed in white linen like me (איש לבוש בדים כמוני), and he will have precisely my form and my likeness (כתוארי וכדמותי). Quickly, fall to your face and prostrate yourself before him (נפול על פניך והשתחוית לאיש),[20] and whatever he may tell you, that you should do, and do not transgress his command (אל תעבור את פיו; cf. Exod. 23.21), otherwise you will assuredly perish on that day'.

So the king rose and proceeded to Jerusalem. And when the (high) priest heard that Alexander the king was coming against Jerusalem in furious anger, he and all the people were greatly afraid, and they cried out unto the Lord and proclaimed a fast. After the fast the Jews went out to meet him and make entreaty before him that he should not destroy the city. And so the (high) priest went forth [25] from the gateway, he and all the people and the priests; and the high priest stood at their head clothed in white linen (הבדים לבוש). As soon as Alexander the king saw the priest, he swiftly descended from his vehicle and fell on his face and prostrated himself before the priest (וישתחוו אל הכהן ויפול על פניו) and greeted him. All the kings who served Alexander were greatly disturbed at this and said to him:

---

12. Cf. *b. Bath.* 58a. For instances where דיוקנו refers to a statue of some sort, see *Tanh. Vayesh* 9; *b. Shab.* 149a; *j. Ab. Zar.* 3.42b. Concerning דיוקנו in relation to Gen 1.26, see *b. Moed Qatan* 15b and דיוקנא in *Tg. Ps-Jon.* to Gen. 1.26.

'Why are you prostrating yourself to a man who has no power for waging war?' And the king explained to his royal servants: 'because the man who goes before me [30] to subdue before me all the peoples has the likeness and appearance (דמות ותוארו) of this man to whom I have just prostrated myself.'

After this the priest and King Alexander came to the Temple of our God. There the priest showed him the *hekhal* and the house of the Lord and its courts and its treasuries and its vestibules and the place (מקום) of the Holy of Holies and the place (מקום) of the altar and the place (מקום) of the burnt offering.[13] And the king said: [35] 'Blessed is the Lord God of this House, because now I know that he is lord of all and his dominion is over all and the life of all that lives is in his hand to put to death and to bring to life, and blessed are you his servants who minister before him in this place.

Now, behold, I shall make for myself a memorial, and I shall give gold in abundance to artists, so that they shall construct my image (צלמי) and erect it between the Holy of Holies and the house and it will be my *golem* as a memorial in the house of this great god'.

But the priest said to the king: 'the gold which you so generously offer, [40] give it for the support of the priests of the Lord and poor of his people who come to prostrate themselves to him in this house. And I shall make you a memorial far better than the one you propose: all the boys of the priests who will be born during this year in the whole of Judah and Jerusalem will be given your name Alexander. And that will be your memorial when they come to perform their service in this house. Because it is not permitted for us to accept graven image or any form (פסל וכל תמונה) in the house of our god.' And the king obeyed him and gave gold abundantly to the house of the Lord [45] and great gifts to the priest.

Then the king requested the priest to question God on his account whether he should go to war against Darius or refrain? And the priest said to him: 'Go, for he will certainly be given into your hands.' And he brought the Book of Daniel before him and showed him what was written there regarding the ram with the horns that was victorious in all directions, and the he-goat that charged at the ram and trampled him to the ground (Dan. 8). Then the priest said to him: [50] 'You are the he-goat and Darius is the ram, and you will trample him and take his dominion from him.' And the priest strengthened him to go against Darius.[14]

The Samaritan version is also almost identical to that of Josephus, with the expected substitution of Samaritans and Shechem for the Jews of Jerusalem.[15] The version in Samaritan *Chronicle II* reads (Folio 129B–130B):[16]

---

13. The threefold reference to the 'place' perhaps alludes to Exod. 23.20: 'an angel…to bring you to the *place* (המקום) that I have prepared'.

14. The translation is taken from the edition of David Flusser, *Sefer Yosippon* (2 vols.; Jerusalem: Bialik Institute, 1978–1980), I, pp. 54–57.

15. For the later medieval versions dependent on the older Josephus, the Talmudic literature and the rabbinic texts, see I.J. Kazis, *The Book of the Gests of Alexander of Macedon* (Cambridge, MA: The Mediaeval Academy of America, 1962).

16. The translation given here is by C.H.R. Martin ('Alexander and the High Priest', *Transactions of the Glasgow Oriental Society* 23 [1969–70], pp. 102–114) on the basis of Ms H2 (i.e. Ms 1168 of the Gaster collection in the John Rylands Library, Manchester). Parallels in the Samaritan *Chronicle of Abu'l Fath* and the *Arabic Book of Joshua* ch. 46 are probably later.

[129B] ...At the time of his appearance he was set on making war on King Darius. Now, it is said that when he was engaged in the war against him, he saw, as it were, an angel descending from heaven clothed in linen garments (לבוש בגדים בדים) and wearing a turban of the type a priest wears. The angel went up to him and began to speak to him. 'Do not be afraid, Alexander,' he said, 'for the LORD has put the inhabitants of the earth into your power.' When he saw this vision in his dream and heard this good news, he was encouraged. He fought Darius fiercely and defeated him, subduing the inhabitants of his cities and his forces.

He came to the city of Tyre, the villages around which had Samaritan people living in them. He asked them to help him, but they refused to do so, because they and the Tyrians had made a special agreement. He was furiously angry with them.

[130A] Later he came to Shechem and the leaders of his Kingdom reminded him of how the Samaritans had treated kings before him. 'They have no fear of us and now they are paying no heed to you.' They deceived him about them so that he would destroy them. His anger was inflamed and he planned to destroy the Samaritans and not to spare any of them.

When the Samaritan inhabitants of Shechem heard of his coming they assembled and went out to meet him carrying the Holy Books and the Laws, that they might find favour with him. In front of them walked the High Priest Hezekiah in the perfection of his fullness (בתם מלאו),[17] turbaned and clothed in linen garments. When Alexander saw him and the magnificent display of the headgear he was wearing, he dismounted from his horse and prostrated himself on the ground (וישתחוה ארצה). His anger melted and he kissed his right hand, saying, 'My Lord, I ask you to bless me, Your Excellency, for when I saw you my breastplate gleamed (אתניר חשני) and light dazzled my eyes (ואתונסיף נור עיני)'. When his military leaders, officers, and servants saw this, they hastily descended from their chariots and prostrated themselves on the ground before the High Priest whom the LORD filled with His Glory (דמלא יהוה כבודו). They were amazed at the king and said to him, 'This is nothing but sorcery (כשף). The Samaritans have utterly bewitched you. Quickly they have done it.' 'The matter is not as you say,' answered the king. 'The Samaritans have not bewitched me, but they have honoured me. I shall now tell you the truth of the matter which is that when I was besieging King Darius, [130B] I saw this man in my sleep with my own eyes, as he gradually descended to confront me. He descended on me and brought me good news. With his glorious mouth (פמו ההדר) he spoke to me. "Alexander", he said, "do not be afraid, for the LORD, praised be His Name, is with you, and all the peoples of the earth will fear you and every one of your enemies will fall before you". Things turned out just like the good news that he brought me. It was for this reason that I had to bow to his glory (לכבודו) and his glory dwelt in my heart (ואיקרו בלבי אשכין).' All his men expressed approval of this.

Alexander met with the High Priest Hezekiah and treated him kindly. He gave him valuable gifts and he also gave presents to the community of the Samaritans whom he liked very much, more than words can tell. 'Now I know', he said to them, 'that the LORD your God is most just and powerful in all places.'

---

17. This is my translation. Martin ('Alexander', p. 106) renders the phrase 'in all his perfection'. The language evokes the Urim and Thummim (תמים) and anticipates the statement that the LORD filled the high priest with his Glory in what follows.

After several Alexander legends – which happen to have Talmudic parallels – this Samaritan version then records a parallel to Josippon's story of the children named after Alexander:

> [131B] King Alexander then returned to Shechem from where he ascended Mount Gerizim and met with the High Priest Hezekiah. 'My Lord priest', he said to him, 'I wish you, by your honour, to build for me on this mountain a place named after me with a form of my image (ותמונה צלמי), just as other nations have done at my command, so that when I return from Egypt I may find done all that I have said.'
>
> Now this command embittered the Samaritan community and when the king had left them they ascended the Holy Mountain and fasted and prayed. All of them besought the LORD in anguish of spirit. The High Priest asked the LORD for guidance to save them from the king's oppression of them, because of what he demanded of them. The Lord, Holy is He, told them to call everyone born to them, whether male or female, by the name of Alexander instead of the image which he had ordered them to make. When the king returned to Shechem after an absence of three years, he made his headquarters in Shechem and ascended the Holy Mountain of the LORD… [132A] There he found neither picture nor image such as he had ordered the priest (to have made). His anger was inflamed against the Samaritans and he summoned the High Priest and the leaders who were with his warriors and spoke to them as follows: 'Have I not shown more regard for you than for all the rest of the world, whether near to or far from you? Why, then, have you not done as I ordered you before I left you?'
>
> The High Priest answered the king, 'We have not disregarded your orders. What you ordered us to do we have done. We have set up pictures and statues (ומציבות תמונות) the like of which no other nation has made for you. They set up for you pictures and statues (תמונות ומציבות) which neither speak nor see. But we have provided for you, by the power of our God, pictures which move perfectly and beautifully and which speak and understand perfectly by themselves and which distinguish good from evil on the face of the ground.'
>
> The king said to him, 'My lord, I wish you now to let me see with my own eyes what you have spoken of.' Then the priest called for everyone to whom the LORD had granted a child since the day the king had given his command. Their names were written down in a document in the priest's possession that was established by him. The children came holding their father's hand. He ordered them to bring forward the children that had been born to them, [132B] and the priest called out to the children, both male and female in a beautiful and dignified voice, 'Alexander!' Each of them thought that he meant him. When the king saw that his joy was great, and the priest told him that the reason for calling them after him was that the making of pictures and images was forbidden to them by the LORD in His Holy Laws and in this way they were keeping the commandments. After this the king recounted to the priest the dream that he had earlier.
>
> The High Priest said to king Alexander, 'Your Majesty, now listen to what I have to say. Believe in the LORD my God and my Lord, and do not take for Him a partner. Do not make for yourself any picture or image and do not believe in false gods.'

All versions of the main story have the same basic narrative setting – a delegation of Jews meets Alexander in fear at his army's approach – and have at their centre Alexander's awe at the appearance of the priesthood. In all five versions, as we shall see, the (high) priesthood is divine. In the *Alexander Romance* the divinity of the priesthood is explicitly stated, in the rabbinic, Josippon and Samaritan versions the worship offered by Alexander is straightforward and, apparently, accepted. In the last two the high priest is identified with the Angel of the LORD and God's Glory.

In the Josephus version, matters are far from straightforward. The casual reader is justifiably puzzled by the narrator's, and the various actors', intentions and puzzlement increases once the other versions are compared and the story's religious and political setting is examined. At first it might seem that Alexander simply and straightforwardly worships the high priest. Given the conventions of the ancient Ruler Cult, his approach, the imagined location of his *proskunesis* before the high priest and the fact that it receives no rebuttal all conform to the straightforward accounts of worship by prostration (*proskunesis*) in the rabbinic, Josippon and Samaritan versions. Certainly, his fellow Macedonians, represented by Parmenion, think that Alexander has done to the high priest what others did to him. But then, on the other hand, Josephus tells us only that Alexander directed his *proskunesis* to 'the Name', presumably, of God. And, in response to Parmenion's objection that his action ill-befits his superior political and religious position, Alexander gives two reasons for his action. First, he says, 'It was not before him that I prostrated myself but the God of whom he has the honour to be high priest'. This sounds like a flat denial of any inclusion of the high priest in the worship offered by Alexander and, thus, the end of the matter. But, then again, the continuation of Alexander's explanation throws the reader into confusion. He says, secondly, that the high priest is the visible image of a god who had appeared to him in a dream announcing his future world dominion when he first crossed the Hellespont. If the high priest is the visible manifestation of the god who leads him in all his battles, how does he, the high priest, not himself participate in the reception of *proskunesis* that Alexander offers? And, finally, we are told that, on entering the Jerusalem temple, Alexander 'showed due honour (ἀξιοπρεπῶς ἐτμησεν) to the priests and to the high priest himself' (11.336). Showing of 'honour (τιμή)' is itself highly ambiguous, but the cultic context and contemporary Jewish parallels to the language here encourage the lingering suspicion that Alexander does in fact somehow venerate the Jewish priesthood itself.[18] Josephus himself, in an earlier part of his *Antiquities,* uses exactly the same language to describe how Nebuchadnezzer held Daniel (and his friends) 'worthy of this highest honour (πάσης ἀξιούμενοι...τιμῆς)' after he had 'fallen (before Daniel) on his face, hailed (ἠσπάζετο) him in the manner in which men worship God (ᾧ τρόπῳ τὸν θεὸν προσκυνοῦσι) ...and...commanded that they should sacrifice to him as a god' (10.211–12, 15, cf. Dan. 2.46). In that early passage Josephus in no way qualifies the account of Nebuchadnezzar's cultic veneration of Daniel.

---

18. This honouring of the priest recalls Sir. 7.27–31, according to which gifts to the priests fulfill the call to love God in the *Shema'* (see Fletcher-Louis, 'Divine Humanity', p. 118). Moreover, S.J.D. Cohen ('Alexander the Great and Jaddus the High Priest according to Josephus', *AJS Review* 7–8 [1982–1983], pp. 41–68 (esp. pp. 56–57) rightly compares this with the cultic veneration of Daniel in Dan. 2.46–47.

What then for Josephus, whose version is the earliest datable, is this story all about? And what does Josephus (and/or its original author) think Alexander does? What does Alexander's comment about the high priest looking like the god who had appeared to him mean? Can the tensions in the story be reconciled or are they, perhaps, simply a sign of poor editorial skill in the use of sources?[19] How does Josephus' version relate to that in rabbinic literature and the *Alexander Romance*? Should, perhaps, those comments which deny that worship is directed to Jaddua be treated as a response to the affirmation of such worship in a tradition now represented by the rabbinic and Samaritan versions?[20] What, in any case, does *proskynesis* mean? And if here *worship*, in some sense, is directed to the high priest, how would the veneration of the high priest by a gentile ruler relate to the author's understanding of the cultic practice of Jews themselves? These are the questions that a satisfactory interpretation of our text needs to address.

Despite confusing impressions, Josephus' story is, in fact, an exquisite piece of literary and theological creativity. *It is both a carefully woven tapestry of antique religious motifs, especially those associated with Alexander, and a profound critique of the pagan Ruler Cult from the perspective of a radically anthropomorphic Jewish monotheism.* In what follows I shall try to solve the text's literary and conceptual conundrums through a careful analysis of its literary and conceptual life setting and demonstrate two theses which also apply more widely than this particular text: (1) *Israel's high priest is the appropriate recipient of worship because he is to Israel's one God what a pagan idol or statue is to their god*, and (2) *it is not so much the private person, here Jaddua, as the office of high priest of which Jaddua is the bearer, that is worshipped.*

The Tradition's Life Setting: Preliminary Observations

The more one ponders the relationship between, and peculiarities of, the various witnesses to this Alexander-meets-High Priest story, the more a confident picture of the story's exact provenance and the tradition history of its various witnesses appears a vain hope. There are innumerable variables and uncertainties which preclude confident historical judgements. The Josephus version is the only one that can be confidently dated (to the 90s CE). As such, it is also the earliest.[21] The rabbinic version is obviously centuries older, but is more likely to preserve an old pharisaic-rabbinic or popular story than to be dependent on Josephus.[22] Whilst

19. For other tensions in the text and a source critical hypothesis see Cohen, 'Alexander'.

20. This, in addition to the assumption that Josephus himself was embarrassed by any suggestion that Alexander worshipped the high priest, was the view I took in my earlier treatment of the passage (Fletcher-Louis, *Luke–Acts*, pp. 124–25). As is clear from the discussion below, I am now convinced that Josephus is neither embarrassed by Alexander's actions, nor does his version respond to a simpler account of Alexander's action attested in the other versions.

21. R. Gnuse, *Dreams and Dream Reports in the Writings of Josephus: A Traditio-Historical Analysis* (AGJU, 36; Leiden: E.J. Brill, 1996), p. 243 has suggested that Acts 16.9 knows, and reverses, a version of Alexander's dream vision. If this is the case, then Acts would be a slightly earlier witness to the popularity in Jewish circles of Josephus' story, or at least part of it.

22. So, e.g., Kazis, *Gests of Alexander*, pp. 7–8; *pace* Cohen, 'Alexander', p. 65 who thinks it

various Alexander stories circulated in rabbinic circles (cf. *b. Tamid* 32a–b; *Gen. Rab.* 41.7), it is hard to see how this one, with its unashamed veneration of the human high priest, could have entered the haggadah at a late date.[23] The existence of a version in the *Alexander Romance*, albeit substantially different, attests the popularity of the story in a variety of ancient Jewish communities. The text of the *Alexander Romance* version cannot be dated earlier than the 3rd century CE, but on other grounds the Judaising recension of which it is a part has been plausibly dated to the first century CE.[24] The earliest attestation of the Samaritan version is a fourteenth century CE text and an assessment of its provenance is bound up with the intractable difficulties inherent in the study and dating of the mediaeval Samaritan corpus.[25] Theoretically, the Samaritan story could be simply dependent on Josephus (or Josippon). But other Alexander tales that accompany it in the Samaritan Chronicles have parallels in rabbinic literature,[26] and it exhibits enough features independent of both Josephus and Josippon to suggest it derives from a separate, (native Samaritan?) source.[27]

Even with only Josephus' text before us we would assume that the Jewish historian is recording for his Gentile readership an older and, to him, well-known oral or written tale. All in all, there can be no doubt that these diverse sources are witness to a tradition which is much older than its first, late first century CE, attestation.[28]

But how early – how near in time to the historical Alexander – is the story? There are numerous historical difficulties that mean the tale must have developed, or been composed, some time after Alexander's original occupation of Coele-Syria. Some have felt that there is a chronological difficulty in fitting in a visit to

---

'likely that all post-Josephan authors who retell this material depend upon Josephus either directly or indirectly'. Cohen's judgement at this point is not entirely in accord with his literary-critical attempt to find an earlier 3rd–2nd century BCE origin for the story. If Josephus knew so well a three-hundred-year old or even older story, it must be that others near the close of the Second Temple period also knew the story and are likely to have had slightly different versions of it. This best explains the diversity of detail amongst the witnesses.

23. For the Talmudic material see Kazis, *Gests of Alexander*.

24. E.g. Kazis, *Gests of Alexander*, p. 11.

25. For the date of Samaritan *Chronicle II*, see J.M. Cohen, *A Samaritan Chronicle: A Source-critical Analysis of the Life and Times of the Great Samaritan Reformer, Baba Rabbah* (SPB, 30; Leiden: E.J. Brill, 1981), p. 176.

26. See J. Bowman, *Samaritan Documents: Relating to their History, Religion, and Life* (Pittsburgh Original Texts and Translation Series, 2; Pittsburgh: Pickwick Press, 1977), p. 67.

27. Distinctive features of the Samaritan story that are not obviously explained simply as the Samaritans' own adaptation of the Josephus text are (1) the comparison of the high priest to an angel (though this has a partial parallel in Josippon); (2) the tradition that the Samaritans were in league with the citizens of Tyre to oppose Alexander, which may recall genuine Samaritan opposition to Alexander's takeover; (3) the omission of Parmenion's point that the high priest ought to worship Alexander; (4) the accusation that the Samaritans are guilty of sorcery; and (5) the reference to the gleaming of Alexander's breast piece in the high priest's presence.

28. F. Pfister, *Eine jüdische Gründungsgeschichte Alexandrias* (Heidelberg: Carl Winters, 1914), pp. 23–25. The New Schürer thinks Josephus is witness to a lost pseudepigraphon which it entitles *A History of the Visit to Jerusalem of Alexander the Great*; see E. Schürer, G. Vermes, F. Millar and M. Black, *The History of the Jewish People in the Age of Jesus Christ (175 B.C.–A.D. 135)* (3 vols.; Edinburgh: T. & T. Clark, 1973–87), III, p. 557.

the Levantine hinterland between Alexander's sieges of Tyre and Sidon in 332 BCE and his march on to Egypt. This has led many to conclude that the whole notion of Alexander paying a visit to Jerusalem (or Shechem) is an apologetic fabrication.[29] Even if we grant the probability of some contact with these inland city-states we then have to judge between the competing Samaritan and Judaean accounts.[30] Was the story's historical core originally in fact Samaritan, not Jewish?[31] And there are also several details of Josephus' version that are historically anachronistic. The *universal* worship of Alexander by his followers of which Parmenion speaks was not a reality until a much later stage in his life.[32] The role of Parmenion as interlocutor and foil to Alexander's authority is an instance of a stereotype that owes more to later conventions of Alexandrian (romantic) historiography than history itself.[33]

Despite these historical difficulties nothing prevents the story from being created as early as the third or second centuries BCE The reference to the Book of Daniel is neither anachronistic nor does it require a second century date since a form of that book containing the essential chapters pertaining to the Macedonian conquest of the East (chs. 2–6 plus an earlier version of ch. 7[?]) was in circulation long before the final, post-Maccabean, redaction of the work.[34] In fact, whilst in several respects

29. E.g. A.D. Momigliano, 'Flavius Josephus and Alexander's Visit to Jerusalem', *Athenaeum* 57 (1979), pp. 442–48 and R. Stoneman, 'Jewish Traditions on Alexander the Great', *Studia Philonica Annual* 6 (1994), pp. 37–53.

30. For a defense of the historical core behind the text, see I. Abrahams, *Campaigns in Palestine from Alexander the Great* (Schweich Lectures 1922; London: Oxford University Press, 1927), p. 8 onwards.

31. Concerning Samaritan opposition to Alexander's takeover, which may have provided an appropriate historical context for the story, see Quintus Curtius Rufus *Alex.* 4.8.9 and evidence from the Wadi Daliyeh papyri; cf. Menachem Mor, 'Samaritan History: The Persian, Hellenistic and Hasmonaean Period', in Alan D. Crown (ed.), *The Samaritans* (Tübingen: J.C.B. Mohr [Paul Siebeck], 1989), pp. 1–18 (esp. pp. 9–10) which provides reasons why the Samaritans would have been opposed to Alexander's takeover.

32. Though already after his initial defeat of Darius at Issus, orientals were greeting Alexander in this way (Cohen, 'Alexander', p. 52 n. 29).

33. On Parmenion's literary role in the histories, see R. Lane Fox, *Alexander the Great* (London: Allen Lane, 1973), p. 121; cf. also the famous dialogue in Plutarch *Alex.* 29. There may also be here a historical memory of Parmenion's tenure as governor of Coele-Syria (Curtius Rufus, *Alex.* 4.1.4). Further anachronisms exist in the rabbinic version: (a) the high priest could not have been either Simon the first or Simon the Just, both of whom officiated later; (b) the destruction of the Samaritan temple by the Jews did not occur until the reign of John Hyrcanus and the end of the second century BCE; and (c) the location of the meeting at Antipatris is probably based on a confused memory of the location at Mount Scopus (see Kazis, *Gests of Alexander*, p. 7).

34. *Pace* e.g. F.-M. Abel, 'Alexandre le grand en Syrie et en Palestine', *RB* 43–44 (1934–35), respectively, pp. 528–45 and 42–61 (esp. p. 54); Cohen, 'Alexander', p. 44. Dan. 2.31–45; 7.1–7 (minus the phrase 'and it had ten horns') are all that Alexander need have read. Cohen's view (p. 64) that Josephus has added the Daniel reference to his material is also unconvincing. Given the priestly orientation of Daniel and its interest in the divine high priest (see Fletcher-Louis, 'The High Priest as Divine Mediator in the Hebrew Bible: Dan. 7.13 as a Test Case', in E. Lovering [ed.], *SBL Seminar Papers* [Atlanta, GA: Scholars Press, 1997], pp. 161–93), the Daniel reference is quite plausibly an early, or 'original', part of the story which Josephus received.

the Alexander story is close in form and theology to those older chapters in Daniel the later chapters, 7–12, look well beyond the appearance of Alexander on Israel's political stage and contain material that he is not likely to have enjoyed reading, such as the bestial decline of his empire and its overthrow by Israel's own 'one like a son of man'. The positive portrayal of Alexander and the warm appreciation of his religious and constitutional patronage would have served many a Jewish community well in its political and apologetic struggles throughout the late Second Temple period.[35] But the text's irenic view of foreign, Hellenistic, rule, which reminds us of the portrayal of pagan power in Dan. 2–6,[36] is best suited to the third century BCE or the early post-Maccabean periods.[37] It is also in the early Hellenistic period when, by contrast to the later Maccabean and, more especially, the Roman periods, that the thoroughly hierocratic portrayal of the Jewish state fits: it is Israel's high priest accompanied by his fellow priests and the people who meet Alexander. There is no royal figure anywhere to be seen.[38] The story's assumed priestly hegemony suits the early Hellenistic (and late Persian) period since it was not until Maccabean claims to kingship, the later Pharisaic and Essene belief in the importance of royal messianism and Herodian claims to kingship that Israel's simpler, more narrowly priestly, constitution was lost. The text's early Hellenistic dating also accords well with indications that the story is Palestinian rather than Alexandrian in provenance.[39]

Whatever the exact date of composition, as our study of the story proceeds it will be clear that its Josephan form fits best a Judaism which is both fully cognizant of the cultural and religious world to which Judaism was introduced at the end of the fourth century BCE and also sophisticated in its theological response to the new

35. See generally Delling, 'Alexander der Grosse'.

36. See Cohen, 'Alexander', pp. 56–57. With respect to Alexander's recognition of Israel's god compare Dan. 2–6 with Bel and the Dragon 41; 2 Macc 3.36–39; and *3 Macc.* 7.6–9.

37. Here I concur with Cohen, 'Alexander', pp. 66–67 who thinks the literary core (the Adventus) is a third century BCE story. However, I see no justification for his view that Josephus added the Daniel material or for his confidence in dating the dream epiphany to a later second century BCE development of the tradition. Contrary to Cohen's view that 'the Jaddus story has nothing to do with the Samaritans' (p. 65), the larger narrative setting of a conflict between Jews and Samaritans (*Ant.* 11.302–47) also suits very well a time of composition between the late fourth and second century's BCE when other priestly oriented anti-Samaritan polemic was composed (see Fletcher-Louis, *All the Glory of Adam,* pp. 20–27 on the *Book of Watchers*; Sir. 49.14–50.23; the *Original Testament of Naphtali*; *T. Levi* 2–7; and *Jub.* 30). In all these texts the true, and usually divine, priesthood of the Jews is set over against the Samaritan priesthood and temple).

38. Delling, 'Alexander der Grosse', p. 11, rightly compares the portrayal of the Jewish constitution with the view that the high priest is the cause of awe and wonder to gentiles in *Aristeas* (92–99). We should compare, more widely, the account of Judaism and the role of the high priest in the late fourth century BCE Hecataeus of Abdera (Diodorus Siculus, *Hist.* 40.3), the vision for priestly hegemony in Sirach (esp. chs. 44–50) and those texts inherited by the Qumran community in which the king is thoroughly subordinate to the priest (see previous note). Concerning the thoroughly priestly, rather than royal, orientation of the Daniel tradition, see Fletcher-Louis, 'High Priest as Divine Mediator', and the literature cited there.

39. See Cohen, 'Alexander', pp. 67–68 for convincing arguments against an Alexandrian provenance.

Hellenistic *Zeitgeist*. For now, as an orientation to what follows, we should note those ways in which Josephus' version is finely attuned to the religious shock-waves sent through the Mediterranean world by Alexander's rise to power.

A Jewish Response to Hellenistic Ruler Cult

Alexander's ascent to a position of world dominion was accompanied by a no less epoch-making rise in Alexander's own self-consciousness. Early in his career he was named the son of Zeus and by the end of it there was founded a religious cult the members of which believed his accomplishments were those of a god. The form and development of the Alexander cult are disputed by modern historians.[40] In his own time the cult was a matter of controversy because the degree of divinity accorded Alexander, and the fact that he and his successors demanded its recognition, was unprecedented. Before him there was little warrant for Greek kings claiming divinity in their own communities. But then Greek kings had always had only parochial power. Alexander aspired to and won world power. In the process he encountered a Persian royal ideology according to which the king was superhuman even if not fully divine. In Egypt he encountered an established and fully developed divine kingship that he and his Ptolemaic successors would naturally inherit. As a founder of cities, a benefactor to states and a saviour of those who felt under Persian oppression Alexander naturally received heroic cult status in individual city-states. But his divine status went beyond these voluntary devotions. The decisive issue was *proskynesis,* a gesture (of full genuflection or more minimal bowing and the blowing of a kiss) that in the Persian world was given to the king as a matter of course by all his subjects. It did not, in that cultural context, necessarily mean the recipient was divine. But in a Greek context *proskynesis* was only given to the gods. In a famous incident in Bactria in 327 BCE, when he had defeated Darius and assumed his throne, Alexander insisted that all his subjects, including his own Macedonian countrymen greet him with *proskynesis*. The matter offended many of his Greek and Macedonian compatriots. Whether Alexander himself meant by this demand to claim divinity or to simply acculturate the two parts of his empire, Greek and Persian, is debated. That Alexander demanded *proskynesis* in recognition of his divinity was the view of ancient commentators

---

40. For differing opinions and the details see, e.g., E. Badian, 'The Deification of Alexander the Great', in Charles F. Edson (ed.), *Ancient Macedonian Studies in Honor of Charles F. Edson* (Thessaloniki: Institute for Balkan Studies, 1981), pp. 27–71; S.R.F. Price, *Rituals and Power: The Roman Imperial Cult in Asia Minor* (Cambridge: Cambridge University Press, 1984), pp. 23–40; D. Fishwick, *The Imperial Cult in the Latin West: Studies in the Ruler Cult of the Western Provinces of the Roman Empire* (Leiden: E.J. Brill, 1987), pp. 8–11; A.B. Bosworth, *From Arrian to Alexander: Studies in Historical Interpretation* (Oxford: Oxford University Press, 1988), pp. 113–23; E. Badian, 'Alexander the Great between Two Thrones and Heaven: Variations on an Old Theme', in A. Small (ed.), *Subject and Ruler: The Cult of the Ruling Power in Classical Antiquity. Papers Presented at a Conference Held in the University of Alberta on April 13–15, 1994, To Celebrate the 65th Anniversary of Duncan Fishwick* (Ann Arbor: Journal of Roman Archaeology, 1996), pp. 11–26.

and the precedent that it set for Greek and Roman Ruler Cults meant its propriety continued to be a matter of much debate for the next 500 years.[41]

For the purposes of our interpretation of the Jewish (and Samaritan) story the precise form of the Alexander Ruler Cult is less significant than the fact that Josephus' version locates the worship of the high priest by Alexander in this specific Greco-Roman conceptual context; of the heated debates surrounding the rights and wrongs of Ruler Cult. For any reader aware of the Hellenistic political and religious context this is one obvious function of the exchange between Alexander and Parmenion.

Many Jews, of course, rejected, mocked and died in the fight against the Ruler Cult tradition that Alexander started.[42] But their response to it was not necessarily, or always, black-and-white or wooden.[43] On the one hand, obviously, this Jewish story is a polemic against Hellenistic claims for divine kingship inasmuch as Alexander venerates the high priest and not *vice versa*. Subtle, and slightly humorous polemic against the Alexander cult is perhaps also in view in Parmenion's claim that all individually in the world prostrate themselves before Alexander. Alexander never actually enjoyed this universal reception of *proskynesis*.[44] So, either the Jewish author is a naïve observer of Hellenistic custom or, much more likely, placing a touch of self-condemning irony on the lips of the obsequious Macedonian general. But, on the other hand, one significant element of the Hellenistic Ruler Cult is accepted. When Alexander has greeted Jaddua, then 'all the Jews together hailed Alexander with one voice (ὁμοῦ πάντων μιᾷ φωνῇ...ἀσπασαμένων)' (332). This acclamation mirrors Alexander's own greeting of the high priest. Alexander, like Josephus' Nebuchadnezzar who had hailed (ἠσπάζετο) Daniel as though he were God (see above), had just 'worshipped the Name and hailed (ἠσπάσατο) the high priest'. This language is stereotypical of the acclamation of the Ruler Cult and *might* imply that the Jewish delegation acknowledge Alexander's divinity to a limited degree.[45]

Does the story reject the non-Jewish Ruler Cult outright? Or does it concede, in part, its validity? Just how our text views the Jewish constitution and its understanding of divinely legitimated authority will become clearer as we proceed. For now, these preliminary considerations establish that the text is carefully situated in

41. See Arrian, *Anabasis* 4.11.1–9; Quintus Curtius Rufus, *Alex.* 8.5.5–6; Justin, *Historiae Philippicae* 12.7.2–3; and Bosworth, *From Arrian to Alexander*, pp. 113–23 for the way in which these later historians relate the issue to debates in their own time.

42. For protestations against Alexander's divinity in Jewish circles, see *Sib. Or.* 5.7 ('not truly descended from Zeus or Ammon'); cf. also 11.197.

43. Concerning Jewish openness to the conventions of Graeco-Roman Ruler Cult, see Horbury, *Jewish Messianism*.

44. See the recent conclusion of the study by Badian, 'Alexander the Great between Two Thrones', p. 26: 'Alexander was never universally recognized as a god, nor even universally as "equal" to one'.

45. Cohen, 'Alexander', p. 48 n. 18 and note esp. 1 Macc 7.33 and 11.6. For the willingness of Jews to recognize the divinity of non-Jewish rulers, see especially, in addition to the material in Horbury's *Jewish Messianism*, the LXX Addition to Est. 15.4–19, a text that is probably pre-Maccabean.

a wider Hellenistic context of debates about the propriety of Ruler Cult in general and, following the achievements of Alexander, of *proskunesis* in particular.

Dressing as a God

Another detail of Josephus' account that, at least in part, reflects the story's orientation to the Hellenistic Ruler Cult context, is the visual identity between high priest and Israel's god. In his priestly attire the high priest is the visual image of the god who has appeared to Alexander. In essence, as we shall see, this is a fundamentally Jewish understanding of the high priestly office. However, the notion that a human being can dress as a god is a familiar one for the emerging Hellenistic Ruler Cult.

According to the historians, Alexander liked to take on the guise of the gods. According to Ephippus, at banquets he would dress up as Hermes, Artemis and Ammon.[46] That he did, in historical fact, dress up as Ammon is supported by the fact that after his death his successors minted coins bearing his image not just in the likeness of the hero Herakles but also with the horns of Ammon.[47] Pliny (the Elder) tells us that already during his life time, the court painter Apelles painted Alexander as Zeus, thunderbolt in hand, in the temple of Artemis in Ephesus (*NH* 35.92–93, cf. Plutarch, *Alex.* 4.2).[48]

Like Parmenion's comment on Alexander's *proskunesis,* the fact that Alexander recognizes the high priest as Israel's god by his attire is, therefore, ironic.[49] Alexander hereby acknowledges that it is not he who can claim by his dress to be a manifestation of the highest god of the pantheon, but Israel's high priest.[50] The force of the polemic is all the more poignant when one purpose of this divine cross-dressing is understood. Alexander's sartorial incarnations support his claim to be world ruler: his conquests are those of the thunderbolt wielding Zeus and his exploits comparable to the deified Herakles. The Jews, by the same token, believed

---

46. Athenaeus, *Deip.* 12.537d–f; cf. the story of his imitation of Dionysus in Carmania: Quintus Curtius Rufus, *Alex.* 9.10.24–27; Plutarch, *Alex.* 67; Diodorus, *Hist.* 17.106.1; and Arrian, *Anabasis* 6.28.1–2.

47. A.B. Bosworth, *Conquest and Empire: The Reign of Alexander the Great* (Cambridge: Cambridge University Press, 1988), p. 287. For examples of the coins, mostly minted by Lysimachus, see R. Lane Fox, *The Search for Alexander* (London: Allen Lane, 1980), pp. 200–201 and 207.

48. Cf. the coins minted at Babylon during his reign showing him grasping a thunderbolt, so in P. Goukowsky, *Essai sur les origines du mythe d'Alexandre (336–270 av. J. C.)* (Nancy: Universite de Nancy II, 1978), I, p. 62; A.R. Bellinger, *Essays on the Coinage of Alexander the Great* (Numismatic Studies, 11; New York: The American Numismatic Society, 1963), p. 27. Note also the apocryphal but amusing story of Alexander dressed as Hermes visiting Darius before battle in the *Alexander Romance* (2.13–15).

49. The sartorial pretensions of Alexander were retained by the Diadochi. Note especially the cosmic clothing (like that of the Jewish high priest) worn by Demetrius Poliocrates (Athenaeus, *Deip.* 12.535f–536a).

50. Concerning Josephus' knowledge of a tradition that Alexander had a divine warrior-like power over the sea, see *Ant.* 2.348; cf. further Callisthenes, in *FGrH* 124 F 31.

their high priest played the human part of the divine warrior Yahweh, and there is evidence that his garments (especially the *ephod* and sash), and his bloody ordination (Exod. 29), were intended to make him the visual image of Israel's god *precisely in his manifestation as divine warrior in creation and history.*[51] The high priest's ephod is probably the same kind of garment which Ba'al wears when he slays Leviathan (*CTA* 5.I.1–5). A passage in Josephus (*Ant.* 3.154–6) suggests his sash was worn to evoke the image of a slain Leviathan hanging limp at its conqueror's side. The pomegranates and golden bells of the hem of his garments evoke the thunder and lightning of the divine warrior (*War* 5.231; *Ant.* 3.184). The splattering of Aaron's garments with a ram's blood at Sinai (Exod. 29.19–21) makes him the image of the bloodstained warrior marching through the wilderness to the promised land (Isa. 63.1–6; cf. Deut. 33.2–3; Judg. 5.4–5; Ps. 68.8–9, 18). All this is probably in the author's mind when he says that it is the high priest who is the one who leads Alexander's army and gives the Persians into his power.[52] Jaddua marches forth from Jerusalem to meet Alexander with his priestly entourage just as the divine warrior marches forth from his heavenly house to do battle surrounded by his angelic host. And, so, whilst the historical Alexander dressed as Zeus-Ammon, for the Jewish author of Josephus' story it is only Israel's high priest who is worthy of the costume of the god who holds sway over human history.

Alexander's Worship of the Name

What does it mean that Alexander worships the Name as he greets Jaddua? And why is this detail included in Josephus' account where the Samaritan and rabbinic versions are happy to have a straightforward *proskunesis* to the high priest? Part of the answer to that question will come later when we consider the difference between Hellenistic Ruler Cult and Israel's divine priesthood. But, for the most part, the matter can be explained by a consideration of the role of the Name in Israel's priestly theology.

'The Name' to which Alexander offers *proskunesis* must be the Name of God, the Tetragrammaton emblazoned on the forehead of the high priest. We have just been expressly told that Jaddua is all dressed up in his high priestly clothing and that he is 'wearing on his head the mitre with the golden plate on it on which was inscribed the Name of God' (11.331). This Name is a prominent feature of the high priest's garb in post-biblical descriptions (cf. *Aristeas* 98; Philo *Vit. Mos.* 2.115; Josephus *War* 5.235; 4.164).

Does this mean that the high priest and the Name of God are wholly separate and that worship of the latter at the place and (ritual) time of the former's presence

---

51. For this see Fletcher-Louis, 'High Priest as Divine Mediator', pp. 186–92; 'The Temple Cosmology of P and Theological Anthropology in the Wisdom of Jesus ben Sira', in C.A. Evans (ed.), forthcoming volume; and, more generally on the high priest as divine warrior, see M. Barker, 'The High Priest and the Worship of Jesus', in *JRCM*, pp. 93–111 and Fletcher-Louis, *All the Glory of Adam*, chs. 3, 6, 7 and 11.

52. *T. Reuben* 6.12 provides a particularly important parallel: 'prostrate yourselves before his [Levi's] posterity, because (his offspring) will die in your behalf in *wars visible and invisible*'.

is simply coincidental? Does the statement that Alexander worshipped the Name of God (worn by the high priest) mean, categorically, that the high priest himself was excluded from the reception of divine honours? With confidence we can answer 'no' to both these questions.

Wider considerations of the function of the high priestly clothing in Exod. 28–29 and in later interpretation – for which there is not space here for discussion – indicate that the high priest wears the divine Name *precisely because he is the visible and ritual embodiment of Israel's god*. In his gold and jewel-studded garments he *is* (ritually and dramatically) Yahweh. His garments have a designer label, with *the* designer's (the creator's) Name emblazoned on his headgear because in his official duties he plays the role of the creator and saviour.[53]

We don't know whether Josephus himself contributed the reference to *proskynesis* to the Name to the tradition he passed on.[54] But we do know from another passage that Josephus would have assumed that the high priest himself received Alexander's veneration inasmuch as the nation's leader was himself the embodiment of the divine Name.

In his *Jewish War* book 4 Josephus reports a speech made by the high priest Ananus to the revolutionaries during the Great War with Rome. Ananus begins his speech:

> It would have been best for me to have died before I had seen the house of God laden with such abominations and its unapproachable and hallowed places crowded with the feet of murderers. But wearing the high priest's vestments and *being called the most honoured of revered names* (ἀλλὰ περικείμενος τὴν ἀρχι-ερατικὴν ἐσθῆτα καὶ τὸ τιμιώτατον καλούμενος τῶν σεβασμίων ὀνο-μάτων), I am alive and fond of life, instead of braving a death which would shed lustre on my old age (163–164).

The Greek is straightforward: Ananus is *called* (καλούμενος) the Name. He does not, as Thackeray in the *Loeb Classical Library* translation would have it, *bear* the Name as though he and the Name were separate entities. This would have required the verb φέρω and is an unprecedented translation of the verb καλέω. Thackeray recognises that the name is God's. Whiston tries to avoid the plain – if puzzling – sense by making the name be 'high priest'.[55] But where else and on what grounds might Josephus regard the title 'high priest' 'the most honoured of revered names'? Contemporary Jewish texts do not describe that title in this way. On the other hand,

53. For a fuller explanation of these claims, see Fletcher-Louis, *All the Glory of Adam* and 'The Temple Cosmology of P'.

54. Since Josephus does not otherwise use the absolute form 'the Name (τὸ ὄνομα)', the balance of probability favours Josephus' retention of wording from the tradition as he received it. Elsewhere he avoids 'the Name' (so *Ant.* 3.178 'the title [ἡ προσηγορία]'; *Ant.* 8.93 'the crown onto which Moses inscribed God [εἰς ἣν τὸν θεὸν Μωυσῆς ἔγραψε]'; and *War* 5.235 'whereon were embossed the sacred letters [τὰ ἱερὰ γράμματα]') or uses a more elaborate form (*War* 4.164 'the most honoured of revered names [τὸ τιμιώτατον τῶν σεβασμίων ὀνομάτων])'.

55. W. Whiston, *Josephus: Complete Works* (London: Pickering & Inglis, 1960). So also A. Pelletier, *Flavius Josèphe: Guerre des Juifs. III. Livres IV et V* (Paris: Belles Lettres, 1982), pp. 35 and 217 n. 4.

the Name of Israel's God, about which there was much speculation in its own right,[56] is very appropriately so described.[57] And, in any case, coupled with a statement that Ananus wears the high priest's *vestments* the implied author and reader are bound to have in mind the Tetragrammaton-bearing headdress.[58] So, Josephus' Ananus reminds his audience that as high priest he is called the Name of God. Or, leaving aside the reverential circumlocution, he is called Yahweh.[59]

This important passage in an earlier of Josephus' works must guide our interpretation of his account of Alexander's meeting with the high priest. When Josephus says that Alexander offers *proskynesis* to the Name as he greets the high priest this, at least for Josephus, must mean that the high priest is, in some not clearly defined way, included as a recipient of that act of veneration *because the high priest himself 'is', or is 'called', the Name.*

If this is the case, then we are bound to ask what justification there is for the worship of a human being. Even if the high priest is the peculiar manifestation of the Name of Israel's god then is that not a transgression of the biblical proscription against the making of an image of Israel's otherwise invisible god? Does this not entail a transgression of the absolute qualitative difference between creator and creation that modern commentators assume is fundamental to Israel's faith?

To date the most perceptive discussion of Josephus' Alexander story is that of Shaye D. Cohen who has shown that it relies on two generic conventions – the Adventus and an epiphanic vision report.[60] When we consider the text's relationship to these generic conventions it is clear that the author makes the explicit claim that *Israel's high priest is worshipped because he is to the one true God what a pagan idol is to its god.*

The Adventus

In an *Adventus* the emperor or king comes to visit a city. Its inhabitants come out to meet him with pomp and ceremony, the leaders dressed in their religious finery, offering libations and a welcome appropriate to their saviour and benefactor. The city is decked with wreaths and the emperor is taken into the city where he and/or

---

56. See J.E. Fossum, *The Name of God and the Angel of the Lord: Samaritan and Jewish Concepts of Intermediation and the Origin of Gnosticism* (WUNT, 36; Tübingen: J.C.B. Mohr [Paul Siebeck], 1985).

57. Compare *Jub.* 36.7: '...by the glorious and honoured and great and splendid and amazing and mighty Name which created heaven and earth and everything together'. Apart from a reference to the veneration of the laws of Moses (*Ant.* 3.88) and a veneration of the altar in Jerusalem (*War* 5.17), Josephus always uses σεβασμ- for the veneration of God, gods and their images.

58. Concerning the high priest's headdress and its theophanic significance, see Fletcher-Louis, *All the Glory of Adam*, pp. 93–94 and 223–48.

59. In the description of the Name as 'the most honoured of *revered* (τῶν σεβασμίων) names' there is, no doubt, an allusion to the use of the same language in the Roman Ruler Cult for the Caesars. This does not, however, affect in either way our assessment of the principal referent of the expression.

60. Cohen, 'Alexander', who is followed in detail by Gnuse, *Dreams and Dream Reports*, pp. 186–89 and 236–45.

the priesthood make(s) an offering, there is feasting, followed by the practical business of the affairs of state. The visiting ruler makes administrative and political decisions for the city's constitution. The people ask for certain privileges and it is expected that some of these will be granted. *One key element in this ceremony and its literary form is the bearing by the welcome party of the host community of images of its gods. In this manner the gods are also brought out to greet the emperor.*

The (Latin) Adventus (in Greek a παρουσία) and its conventions were well-known and ubiquitous in Graeco-Roman antiquity.[61] That the Jews knew it well is clear from the number of references Josephus himself makes to the scene.[62] For example, Antiochus III was received in this way by the Jews of Jerusalem in 199 BCE (*Ant.* 12.138).[63] With the exception of the prominent role played by the cult statues in the welcoming party's reception, nothing in Jewish religious practice or belief would prevent, in principal, the adoption of these conventions. Indeed, ancient Israel had its own processions and ceremonies designed for the welcome of its rightful king which could very well be adapted to the Hellenistic fashions.[64]

Clearly the essential features of the Adventus are present in Josephus' Alexander story as the underlined text indicates. Form critically the main structure of this story is an Adventus. But the genre is subverted in two ways: in the first place the Jews do not initiate the reverence to the emperor which would be expected of them. Rather he pays homage to their cultic representative. And secondly, as Cohen points out, *the role which is normally played by the statue of the god is now taken by the high priest bearing the Name of God.*[65] Indeed, the narrative is quite self-conscious about these generic subversions. Jaddua and the Jews make 'the reception sacred in character and different from that of other nations' (11.329). That is, they make the reception conform to the social and religious conventions of an Adventus, yet at the same time in several important ways they give their own religious definition to those cultural expectations.

The Epiphany

That the high priest here functions as Israel's god's idol is also a natural conclusion for the ancient reader of Alexander's vision report. Cohen rightly identifies Alexander's account of his dream vision as a clear example of an epiphany in which a god appears to a human to warn, exhort or otherwise direct them in social and political affairs (see the dotted underlined text).[66] Cohen compares many examples of

---

61. See, e.g., G.A. Deissmann, *Light from the Ancient East: The New Testament Illustrated by Recently Discovered Texts of the Graeco-Roman World* (London: Hodder & Stoughton, 1927), pp. 368–73; F. Millar, *The Emperor in the Roman World* (London: Gerald Duckworth, 1977), pp. 31–40.

62. *War* 7.63–74, 119; 7.100–102; *Ant.* 12.138; 16.14; and 18.122–123.

63. Note also Alexander's reception at Babylon and his sacrifice to Bel (Quintus Curtius Rufus, *Alex.* 5.1.17–23; Arrian, *Anabasis* 3.16.3–5).

64. See, e.g., 2 Sam. 6; Ps. 118; and Jdt. 1.15–16.

65. Cohen, 'Alexander', p. 48.

66. Cohen, 'Alexander', pp. 49–55.

this form.[67] Of these the nearest parallel is an allegedly 5th century BCE epiphany recorded in Justin's *Historiae Philippicae* 43.5–7:

> By general consensus the chieftain Catumandus was chosen general [of the Gauls in their war against Massilia]. When he was besieging the enemy city with a large army of select soldiers, Catumandus was terrified in his sleep by the figure of a fierce woman who said that she was a goddess. [As a result] he voluntarily established peace with the Massilians. After requesting permission to enter the city and to worship (*adorare*) their gods, he arrived at the citadel of Minerva and, seeing the image of the goddess in the colonnade, exclaimed suddenly that it was she who had terrified him at night, that it was she who had ordered him to withdraw from the siege. Congratulating the Massilians because he realised that they belonged to the care of the immortal gods, he donated a golden necklace to the goddess and concluded with the Massilians a friendship treaty in perpetuity.

The setting is slightly different from that of Alexander's vision and his meeting with the Jews. But, again, it is clear that by comparison with this story the Jewish high priest plays the role of cult statue in relation to its god. He is the visible, physical manifestation and form of Israel's god: his clothes the kind one might otherwise see adorning an idol. And in this light Catumandus' donation of a necklace to the goddess, to be worn by her statue, is equivalent to Alexander's prostration before the Jewish high priest and his subsequent honouring of the priesthood when they retire to Jerusalem.

Alexander's Visit to the Sanctuary of Ammon at Siwah

Besides the Adventus and Epiphany forms adduced by Cohen, Josephus' story is partly modelled on, and a polemic against, the famous visit by Alexander to the sanctuary of the god Ammon in the Libyan desert, as several commentators have noted.[68] Having passed through the Levant, Alexander proceeded to Egypt which acceded to his cause and authority without resistance. From there he continued west and braved the desert heat and sands to visit the sanctuary and oracle of the god Ammon at Siwah. The god, though originally distinct from the Egyptian Amun-Re, became fused with that principal god of Pharaonic religion. Ammon had already been identified with Zeus in the Greek pantheon. Both for the historical Alexander and the Alexander of later, popular history the visit was of seminal significance for the development of Alexander's self-belief and for the cult of his

---

67. See also Gnuse, *Dreams and Dream Reports*, pp. 228–45. Comparison is also frequently made with the story that, when Alexander was besieging Tyre, he had a vision of the city's god Herakles-Melqart beckoning him into the city (Arrian, *Anabasis* 2.18.1; Quintus Curtius Rufus, *Alex.* 4.2.17; Plutarch, *Alex.* 24.3). The comparison is appropriate, as there it is also assumed that the statue of the god in the city's temple is its real presence.

68. Delling, 'Alexander der Grosse', p. 15; J.M. Modrzejewski, *The Jews of Egypt from Rameses II to Emperor Hadrian* (Edinburgh: T. & T. Clark, 1995), pp. 54–55. Cohen ('Alexander', p. 64 n. 69) denies the formative role of the Siwah incident. His comparison with the dream in which Serapis grants Alexander world dominion in the *Alexander Romance* (1.33.7–11) is no doubt significant. But the story of his visit to Siwah had a far greater popularity and biographical prominence in the life of Alexander.

divinity. Diodorus Siculus' first century BCE account of Alexander's encounter with the god and the end of Quintus Curtius Rufus' first century CE version are worth citing.[69]

> [50.6] The image of the god is encrusted with emeralds and other precious stones, and answers those who consult the oracle in a quite peculiar fashion. It is carried about upon a golden boat by eighty priests, and these, with the god on their shoulders, go without their own volition wherever the god directs their path. [7] A multitude of girls and women follows them singing paeans as they go and praising the god in a traditional hymn. [51.1] When Alexander was conducted by the priests into the temple and had regarded the god for a while, the one who held the position of prophet, an elderly man, came to him and said, 'Rejoice, son, take this form of address as from the god also.' [2] He replied, 'I accept, father; for the future I shall be called your son. But tell me if you give me the rule of the whole earth.' The priest now entered the sacred enclosure and as the bearers now lifted the god and were moved according to certain prescribed sounds of the voice, the prophet cried that of a certainty the god had granted him his request, and Alexander spoke again: 'The last, O spirit, of my questions now answer; have I punished all those who were the murderers of my father or have some escaped me?' [3] The prophet shouted: 'Silence! There is no mortal who can plot against the one who begot him. All the murderers of Philip, however, have been punished. The proof of his divine birth will reside in the greatness of his deeds; as formerly he has been undefeated, so now he will be unconquerable for all time.' [4] Alexander was delighted with these responses. He honoured the god with rich gifts and returned to Egypt. (Diodorus Siculus, *Hist.* 17.50.6–51.4).

> Then, after sacrifice had been offered, gifts were given both to the priests and to the god, and the king's friends also were allowed to consult Jupiter [i.e. Zeus]. They asked nothing more than whether the god authorized them to pay divine honours to their king. The prophets replied that this also would be acceptable to Jupiter (Quintus Curtius Rufus, *History of Alexander* 4.7.28).

What was revealed to Alexander at Jerusalem is identical to the oracular guidance given by Ammon; in both stories, Alexander is given imperial rule by the supreme god. The role played by priest and prophet (the book of Daniel) in the Jewish tale is equivalent to that played by cult statue and prophet (the elderly man) in the Ammon story. As is expected from such a story, both scenes end with an appropriate sacrifice and Alexander's bestowal of gifts to the sanctuary.

With the parallels between the two accounts there are also, crucially, some prominent differences. In the Jewish story Alexander is not, in any peculiar sense, the son of the god and, though he is promised world dominion, the silence on such matters implies that the legitimacy of his deification and of Ruler Cult is either denied or at least subordinated to the superiority of Israel's cult and her high priest.[70]

---

69. See generally Diodorus, *Hist.* 17.49.2–17.51.4; Strabo, *Geog.* 17.1.43; Quintus Curtius Rufus, *Hist.* 4.7.22–28; Plutarch, *Alex.* 27; and Justin, *Hist. Phil.* 11.11.2–12.

70. The fact that Alexander's own sacrificing in Jerusalem is stressed (*Ant.* 11.336) is perhaps meant to emphasize his own humanity and further direct the reader away from any acceptance of Alexander's divinity.

We would expect an 'orthodox' Jewish text to call into question Alexander's cult in this way. But there are no grounds in this literary comparison for thinking that the Jewish text rejects, *in principle*, the notion that a human being can be divine and worthy of cultic devotion. On the contrary, the most striking antithetical parallelism between the two stories is the fact that Israel's high priest is dressed in precisely the kind of materials (multi-coloured, jewel-studded, golden garments) that clothe the image of Ammon. Whereas the Jerusalem high priest is accompanied by other priests in their pure white festal garments, Ammon is carried by a large body of priests and serenaded by the voices of a female choir. Whereas it is the emerald and gem encrusted idol that manifests the presence of Ammon, it is the Jewish high priest who, as Alexander recognizes, manifests the presence of the god who truly had the power to give him world dominion. Just as the idol of Ammon's ouija-like movements convey the answer to Alexander's questions, so it is Israel's high priest who had revealed, in a dream vision, the future of Alexander's dealings with Darius. The point of the similarity of scenes is obvious: once more, *Israel's high priest plays the role otherwise played by the pagan idol*. And so it is fitting that when he goes off to Jerusalem to sacrifice to Israel's god he simultaneously 'showed due honour (ἀξιοπρέπως ἐτίμησεν) to the priests and to the high priest himself'. As the *image* of Israel's god the priesthood deserves to be treated as well as any cult statue.

So, then, by comparison with the foundational myth of the Alexander Ruler Cult, Josephus' story provides a radically alternative theology. It is not that Alexander's position on the world stage is entirely indebted to the one true God of Judaism or that only in Jerusalem one can have a genuine encounter with that god. No, much more than that, the text says that where the rest of the Hellenized world thinks Alexander of Macedon or his successors are divine and worthy of worship the Jews believe that only their high priest, as the bearer of the true humanity and the one God's *image,* is worthy of anything akin to the Graeco(-Roman) Ruler Cult.

The contrast here is not just between competing claims to possess the true divine ruler – though that is part of the matter since Israel's Torah prescribes so distinct an ethical vision of true human identity and political power. We must also compare the different *forms* taken by pagan Ruler Cult and Israel's hierocratic cult. We can see that, for example, in the common use of particular clothing to claim divine identity the two are similar. Just as Alexander dons the garb of his divine parents, Zeus, Ammon *et al.*, so too, Israel's high priest is dressed in her god's garb. But a closer examination of the issue of identity in the two environments reveals a radical disjuncture between the two forms of worship; that of Alexander and that of the high priest.

In the first instance we should note that throughout the presentation of the high priest as God's idol there is implicit a rejection of all forms of man-made images. The Hellenistic cult of the hero and then Ruler Cult entailed the making of paintings, statues and images on coins. Israel has none of these. Only the human being – the high priest being the true instance of the genus – is able to represent and embody divine presence. This, of course, is an essentially biblical view adopted long before the appearance of Hellenism.

Whilst the Jewish view of the matter is radical and uncompromising on the rejection of man-made images its insistence on *humanity's* bearing of divine presence would, nevertheless, have been entirely *comprehensible* for a Hellenized reader. There is a famous hymn sung for Alexander's successor Demetrius Polyocretes in 290 BCE in gratitude for his delivering of Athens from the tyrant Lachares. The Atheneans exclaimed:

> O son of the most mighty god Poseidon and of Aphrodite, hail! For the other gods are either far away or do not have ears, or do not exist or do not pay attention at all to us, but you we see present, not of wood or stone but real. And so we pray to you.[71]

These sentiments are similar to those on which Israel's image-of-God-in-humanity theology relies in its critique of non-Israelite idolatry. Once again our Josephus text emerges as a carefully constructed response to Ruler Cult in terms appropriate to the Hellenistic context. The new Hellenistic view of kingship as divine accords with Israel's own theological anthropology: a human being is a more accessible manifestation of divinity than man-made idols which have neither ears, eyes, speech nor movement.

But, of course, Israel's theology entails in several respects a more thoroughgoing critique of pagan idolatry. First, for Israel, the idols' inferiority to their human creators means their use is categorically rejected. By contrast, the Atheneans' sentiments did not mean statues, paintings, images on coins and the normal paraphernalia of the cult of gods and heroes were abandoned. Secondly, Jews believed that the divinity of their head – the high priest – was grounded in a more fundamental *anthropo*logical vision, expressed in the cosmology of Gen. 1: the high priest is the true Adam and as such the bearer of God's image, his idol. Thirdly, and on the basis of this second point, the Jews believed that *they*, by virtue of their Temple and Torah constitution, and *not Alexander* or his successors had the true divine humanity.

The Divinity of the Person not the Office

Whilst so much of Josephus' story and Alexander's behaviour is now clear, we are still left wondering what the reader is meant to make of Alexander's comment that 'It was not before him that I prostrated myself but the god of whom he has the honour to be high priest' (*Ant.* 11.333). Does our contention that the high priest functions as the image or idol of Israel's god founder on Alexander's apparent denial that he worships the high priest?

In order to be able to understand Alexander's point we need to think ourselves out of modern notions of human identity and back into those of Jewish and Hellenistic antiquity. Fundamentally, Alexander's denial rests on the distinction between a private *person* and an *office* and, accordingly, it can be paraphrased; 'it was not before *Jaddua the private citizen* that I prostrated myself but the God whom *his high priestly office embodies*'.[72]

---

71. Athenaeus, *Deip.* 6.253e, citing Duris of Samos.
72. It might be tempting to compare this text with the Jewish institution of agency (*Shaliach*);

Alexander was hailed a god by his subjects because of his personal achievements, not because he attained to a position in the ancient ideology of kingship for which worship was an expected part. Before Alexander, Greeks and Macedonians had no developed understanding of a royal office that entailed divinity. Far from it, Alexander's rise to divine heights was a novelty in fact and, however much it had precedents in the Hellenistic, Persian and Egyptian worlds, in kind. To some extent – the matter is debated – Alexander's divinity, and that of the Ruler Cult which he inspired thereafter, was an extension of the cult of heroes.[73] A hero was granted superhuman status because of his own individual *achievements* as a founder (κτίστης) of a city, a benefactor (εὐεργέτης) to society or a saviour (σωτήρ) of threatened communities. Alexander was all of these. But his achievements and the universal scope of his power went far beyond the achievements of his heroic forebears. For him a new form of cult had to be tailor-made as Arrian has Anaxarchus argue at Bactria 'it would be far more just to reckon Alexander a god than Dionysus and Heracles...*because of the many great achievements of Alexander*' (*Anabasis* 4.10.6). Alexander further detached himself from established roles and tradition by nurturing the belief that his parentage was divine rather than simply human. Early on in his career the story developed – probably at the instigation of his mother Olympias – that Philip was not his real father, but that his mother had conceived during a divine visitation from Zeus in the form of a thunderbolt or a serpent.[74]

Alexander's divinity was not so much a matter of royal lineage but unique vocation demonstrated by heroic exploit. He was believed to come not from men but the gods.[75] As the oracle at Siwah said in Diorodus' account (above) 'the proof of his divine birth' lay 'in the greatness of his deeds'. Inasmuch as his divinity was understood on analogy with that of the Olympiads his apotheosis meant a numerical addition to the pantheon.[76] It is true that after him a dynastic form of Ruler Cult was established among his successors that lessened the significance of the ruler's personal qualities.[77] But the diadochi remained very much individuals with their reception of cult being dependent on their benefactions.[78] They did not, like the

however, whereas that entails a legal understanding of identity, here we are concerned with a cultic one.

73. Price (*Rituals and Power*, pp. 32–40) has argued against the role of the cult of heroes in providing a stimulus for Alexander's deification, preferring to see a Ruler Cult modelled on the worship of the gods themselves. That heroic honours played some part in his deification is clear from Diodorus, *Hist.* 18.28.4.

74. Plutarch, *Alex.* 2.2–3.4; see Bosworth, *Conquest and Empire*, p. 282; Badian, 'Alexander the Great between Two Thrones', p. 19.

75. Arrian, *Anab.* 4.9.9: 'For the tale goes that Alexander even desired people to bow to the earth before him, from the idea that Ammon was his father rather than Philip'.

76. Note the late tradition in Aelian (*Var. Hist.* 5.12) that he was made the thirteenth god.

77. See D. Fishwick, *The Imperial Cult*, pp. 11–13; F.W. Walbank, 'Monarchies and monarchic ideas', in F.W. Walbank *et al.* (eds.), *The Cambridge Ancient History.* VII. *Part 1. The Hellenistic World* (Cambridge: Cambridge University Press, 1984), pp. 62–100.

78. See, for example, the altar inscription to Antiochus I (and Stratonike and Antiochus II) written between 268 and 262 BCE (*OGIS* no. 222; C. Habicht, *Gottmenschentum und griechische Städte* [Munich: Beck, 1970], pp. 91–93).

later Roman emperors who followed in the footsteps of 'Caesar' Augustus, claim to be holders of an 'Alexander' office.[79]

All this is in sharp contrast to the rule of the Jewish high priest. The Zadokite Jaddua is only high priest when he is dressed in his appropriate garments and when he fulfills the prescribed rituals of the peculiar time and space prescribed by Israel's Torah and Temple. Many biographies of Alexander were written by both his contemporaries and later Graeco-Roman authors. These, especially that by Callisthenes, contributed to the cult of his personality. No Jew bothered to write and preserve a biography of Jaddua the Zadokite who, like his biblical model, Aaron, is a faceless character.[80] In contemporary parallels the Jewish high priest is worshipped in the context of his office.[81] This worship is natural because it is as the wearer of God's garments and as the actor who plays the part of the creator and saviour LORD God in the temple-as-microcosm that the high priest *'is'* Israel's God. The Israelite adoption of Hellenistic Adventus conventions is a novel, emergency measure, which, perhaps because it means the high priest must wear his garments outside of the temple (against Lev. 21.10–12; Ezek. 42.14; 44.19), requires a special divine revelation (*Ant.* 11.327). But it is precisely in those official garments that Jaddua meets Alexander. And, whilst Alexander would receive *proskunesis* wearing whatever garments he happened to fancy (his sartorial playfulness was well-known), it is in those garments which represent 'the God of whom he has the honour to be high priest' that Jaddua receives Alexander's *proskunesis.*[82]

It is, then, only in a highly attenuated sense that Jaddua himself receives worship and a satisfactory understanding of that sense would require a fuller exploration of the relationship between person and office in Jewish thought. That is a desideratum. But we can at least be confident that when, for example, Cohen says 'Alexander had the good sense to realize that the human figure who appeared to him was not God but the priest of God, and that obeisance was due not to the human figure but to God', that this short-circuits the intricacies of the text's theological anthropology.[83] Perhaps, at the very least we can say that Alexander worships the office

79. For this distinction compare Josephus, *Ant.* 8.157.

80. The conspicuous contrast in the Pentateuch between Moses the runaway anti-hero, sage, politician, prophet, king and omni-competent leader, on the one hand, and Aaron the characterless priest explains the distinction our post-biblical story assumes.

81. Sirach 50, given its cosmology and carefully structured ordering of Simon's actions according to the standards of his office prescribed by the Pentateuch, provides the closest parallel to the understanding of *official* identity in our text. The contrast between the Jewish focus on *office* and the contemporary Hellenistic interest in *persons* throughout Sir. 44–50 has been noted by B.L. Mack, *Wisdom and the Hebrew Epic: Ben Sira's Hymn in Praise of the Fathers* (Chicago: University of Chicago Press, 1985), pp. 11–36 and 47–52. See also Hecataeus of Abdera (in Diodorus Siculus, *Hist.* 40.3.3–8); XIIIth of the *Songs of the Sabbath Sacrifice* (4Q405 frg. 23 col. ii); and the worship of the king in a highly ritualized context in 1 Chron. 29.20.

82. Alexander's divinity is everywhere reflected in depictions of the beauty of his face (see H.P. L'Orange, *Studies on the Iconography of Cosmic Kingship in the Ancient World* [Oslo: H. Aschehong, 1953], pp. 28–53). Whilst physiognomy was important for Jews, the divinity of the serving high priest was less a matter of personal physical features than impersonal glorious garments.

83. 'Alexander', p. 52. Cohen's comment that Alexander 'did obeisance to the *person* who was

of which Jaddua is a holder. But that office is an essentially human one and the Torah's vision of human identity prescribes a quite *particular* kind of human identity for all eligible holders of the office. And so it is as the human person meeting those qualifications that Jaddua is qualified to hold the office that deserves the worship of the king of Macedon.

Conclusion to the Examination of Josephus' Version

We are now in a position to summarize the findings of our examination of Josephus' version of the story in its historical context. The following points have emerged: (1) throughout, Josephus' version is carefully designed for a Hellenistic cultural, religious and political context. Cohen, who has done most to locate the story in its appropriate historical context, concludes that 'the aim of the adventus story was to find a place for the Jews in Hellenistic history, to show that the conqueror of the world considered Jerusalem worthy of a visit and the Jews worthy of respect'.[84] We must now go further and say that the story is a carefully nuanced response to the central Hellenistic institution of royal Ruler Cult. (2) As such a response, the story claims that Israel's high priest is the true divine human ruler, the genuine manifestation of the one God, Lord of the whole world, who alone has the power to give to others, such as Alexander, human authority. (3) Not only is Jerusalem the home of this one supreme God, that god is also peculiarly manifest in Israel's high priest because this cultic official serves him as a pagan statue or idol would serve its god. (4) Unlike the personality cult of Hellenistic divine kingship Israel's divine humanity is peculiarly sacral and therefore a matter of divine office rather than divine persons. Where Alexander's rise to divinity was a matter of promethean achievement, charisma and prowess, Israel's humanity is summed up in a life humbly submitted to a carefully circumscribed divine office.

Self-evidently Josephus' version is not only the oldest but also the one that best fits the historical context of its alleged origin. Neither the version in the rabbis nor the *Alexander Romance* have the complexity or neatness of historical fit that Josephus' demonstrates. They are testimony, nevertheless, to the political and religious power of the story and its enduring vitality for the Judaism(s) of Late Antiquity. Although they each accept without question the high priest's divinity and (in the rabbinic version) the propriety of Alexander's worship of him, neither of those versions is as sharply focused a response to the Hellenistic Ruler Cult as Josephus'. Besides their greater distance in composition from the 'original' 3rd–2nd century BCE story, both have an intramural, Jewish readership, which will partly explain their lack of attention to the differences between the Jewish and the Hellenistic Ruler Cults. We do not know for whom exactly the original (Josephan) version was composed, but obviously Josephus himself has in mind a Graeco-Roman readership. Like the *Letter of Aristeas*, Ezekiel the Tragedian's *Exagoge*, Aristobulus

---

the vehicle for the manifestation of divine power, but his real obeisance was to God, not the *minister*' (p. 57, italics added) senses the different categories of identity, but does not grasp their proper place in the story.

84. 'Alexander', p. 66.

and so much other extant Jewish Greek literature from the Hellenistic period the original would have been composed for a readership (of Jews and/or Greeks) on the cultural frontline between Israel and Hellenism.

Obviously the Josippon and Samaritan versions are also written for insiders and so it is not surprising that they too do not so obviously play with Hellenistic conventions (the Adventus and epiphany) or motifs associated with Alexander's life. But, turning now to a detailed consideration of these two versions, we find that both record intriguing details of their own and a sequel to Alexander's initial encounter with the high priest which corroborates our contention that the tradition was based on the Jewish image-of-God-in-humanity theology.[85]

The Josippon and Samaritan Versions

Both the Josippon and Samaritan versions identify the high priest with the angel of the LORD. Both, also, it seems want us to see in the high priest a peculiar manifestation of the Glory of the LORD, though each makes the point in different ways.

The Samaritan account simply has an angelophany where Josephus had an epiphany. The angel is dressed as is the high priest. Angel and priest share, in particular, the same headgear. In Josippon, again, the angel and high priest are visually identified though nothing is made of any headdress. This angel–high priest relationship reminds us of Second Temple tradition. For example, in several Qumran texts human priests are called angels (4Q511 frg. 35, line 4; 4QVisions of Amram[(a+c)], cf. 1QSb, 4/11QShirShabb) a designation which is reflected in wider non-Essene tradition (e.g. Hecataeus of Abdera [Diodorus Siculus, _Hist._ 40.3.5]; _Jub._ 31.14; _T. Mos._ 10.1).[86]

In Josippon the angelological form of the high priest is richer in several respects. The way the angel stands at Alexander's head, unsheathed sword in hand, recalls the appearance of the angel of the LORD with drawn sword to Joshua (Josh. 5.13–15). In this case the allusion perhaps suggests that the _worship_ that Alexander then offers to the high priest is equivalent to the worship that Joshua made at the appearance of the angel of the LORD (Josh. 5.14). Still more suggestive is the use of the language specific to the Name-bearing angel of Exod. 23.20–22. There, God promises to send an angel before Israel to aid them as they enter the promised land. They are warned, however, to listen attentively and obey the instructions of that angel since it carries God's Name and it has the power to punish their transgression. At several points in Josippon Exod. 23.20–22 is clearly evoked and both angel and high priest are identified with this Name-bearing angel: the angel tells Alexander that he is the one who _goes ahead of him to help him_ and that he must listen to and obey the words of the high priest.

---

85. Josippon's independence from Josephus in this material and the likelihood that he preserves more reliable traditions have been noted by L.L. Grabbe ('Josephus and the Judean Restoration', _JBL_ 106 [1987], pp. 231–46, esp. p. 242).

86. On these texts see Fletcher-Louis, _All the Glory of Adam_. Concerning the parallelism between angel and priest see, respectively, Wis. 18.14–20 and 18.21–25. See also _Jos. Asen._ 5 and 14 for the homology between principal angel and the (angelomorphic) Joseph.

This subtle identification of high priest with the Name-bearing angel is not altogether surprising. Already Zech. 12.8 had identified David with this angel in a similar way,[87] and an identification between that angel and the high priest who wears God's Name probably explains the identification of the angel of the LORD with Enoch(-Metatron), the *Urpriest* and the Lesser Yahweh in *merkabah mysticism* (*3 En.* 12, cf. *b. Sanh.* 38b and *1 En.* 48). There are good grounds for thinking that here Josippon recalls an old, Second Temple, tradition.

In Josippon we are also told that the sword of the angel who appears to Alexander was 'like the appearance of the likeness of lightning that flashes on a rainy day (כמראה דמות ברק אשר יבריק ביום הגשם ומראה החרב)'. This is a deliberate allusion to the statement in Ezekiel 1.28 that the 'appearance of the likeness (דמות כמראה)' of the Glory of the LORD was like a bow in a cloud 'on a rainy day (ביום הגשם)'. The lightning has probably been drawn from Ezek. 1.13 where lightning issues from among the four living creatures of God's throne.[88] If this vignette makes the angel a manifestation of God's Glory then that Glory is probably also manifest in the high priest who has precisely the same form and 'likeness' as the angel. Given that several other ancient Jewish sources identify the high priest with the Glory of Ezek. 1, that is probably also implicit here.[89]

The Samaritan version is less interested in Josippon's angelological themes, but it accentuates the identification of the high priest with God's Glory.[90] The encounter is introduced with the statement that Hezekiah led the procession 'in the perfection of His fullness (בתם מלאו)'. What does that mean? It appears to introduce two ideas that are then developed in what follows. The fullness is God's since the LORD is said to have 'filled' Hezekiah, the Samaritan high priest, 'with His Glory (דמלא יהוה כבודו)'. This is an obvious allusion to the Qedushah of Isa. 6.3 where heaven and earth are full of God's Glory. To my knowledge, there is no *exact* semantic parallel extant for this bold statement. But, again, Second Temple texts similarly identify the high priest with the *fullness* of God's Glory. In particular, we should compare *Aristeas* 99 where, wearing his light-giving garments and the Name-bearing diadem, the high priest is said to be 'the fulfillment of Glory (δόξης [some MSS: δόξῃ] πεπληρωμένον)'. This is a nice example of a much wider and well-established theme: the true high priest is the embodiment of God's Glory, the receptacle of its fully manifest presence.[91]

The second aspect of the Samaritan version introduced by the expression 'in the perfection (בתם) of His fullness' is perhaps the role of the Urim and Thummim in

---

87. See Fletcher-Louis, *Luke–Acts*, p. 112 and *idem*, *All the Glory of Adam*, pp. 9–10.

88. Ezekiel 1.13 and 28 are combined in the praise of the high priest in the Synagogue's *musaph* prayer for Yom Kippur, according to which 'the appearance of the priest' is both 'as lightnings going out from the splendour of the living creatures' and 'as the bow in the midst of a cloud'.

89. See Sir. 50.7; 4Q405 23 ii 9; and the מראה כהן of the *musaph* prayer for Yom Kippur.

90. The lack of an allusion to Josh. 5 in the Samaritan version is unsurprising given that that text is not a part of the Samaritan canon.

91. See generally Fletcher-Louis, *All the Glory of Adam* and 'The Temple Cosmology of P'. On the use of Isa. 6.3 here compare 1QM col. xii (*All the Glory of Adam*, pp. 437–42).

what follows. As I have demonstrated elsewhere, the divinity of Israel's high priest was bound up with mystical speculation surrounding the light-giving properties of his breastpiece, the stones on his shoulder and the mysterious Urim and Thummim.[92] In this speculation the Urim (אורים) are assumed to be related somehow to the light (אור) that is reflected off and pours fourth from the high priest's garments. In the same context the Thummim (תמים) appears to have been taken to refer to the 'perfection' or 'completeness' (תם?) of the high priest's divine appearance. Now, although there is no mention of Urim (אורים) in our text Alexander's statement that when he saw the high priest his breastplate 'gleamed' and 'light dazzled his eyes' suggests he encounters the fully operating Urim and Thummim of the true high priest.

This possibility is further supported by the suitability of the Urim and Thummim's operation for the political context. The high priest in visionary form has promised Alexander military success against the Persians. According to Num. 27.20 Israel's military exploits were guided by the Urim and Thummim, and the civil leader of the people had to stand before the high priest whilst his operation of this oracle was made. According to both Josephus (*Ant.* 3.215–218) and texts from among the Dead Sea Scrolls (1Q26; 4Q376; and 4Q408[?]) this procedure entailed the shining of the high priest's stones when God was present to give the people victory. In our Samaritan text the angel's verbal promise of Alexander's victory is now supported by the oracular operation of the Urim and Thummim.

Obviously, both Josippon and our Samaritan Chronicle are dated much later than Josephus and the original Alexander story. Using texts from the tenth (Josippon) and fourteenth (*Chronicle II*) centuries to inform the world of the Second Temple is a precarious enterprise. However, there are here, in the above observations, indications, that in their versions of our tale they preserve ancient traditions surrounding Israel's high priest that are plausibly located in Second Temple versions of the Alexander story.[93] In the case of the Samaritan text a later portion of *Chronicle II* must be considered in assessing the role of Alexander's worship of the high priest in Samaritan self-definition. In the section of the Chronicle dealing with the third-fourth century reforms of Baba Rabba there is the following passage describing the expectation that with his Adventus others should so treat the priest Baba Rabba as Alexander treated the high priest Hezekiah.[94]

> Concerning the priests – before this time any man who inspired awe and respect was called 'priest' by the people. With the advent of Baba Rabbah, the priest, they were merely called 'Sages'; and the priestly title was removed from many priests.

92. *All the Glory of Adam*, pp. 150–61, 222–51 and 356–94.

93. In the rest of his work, in the interests of his Graeco-Roman readership, Josephus avoids biblical angelological language and imagery (see M. Mach, *Entwicklungsstadien des jüdischen Engelglaubens in vorrabbinischer Zeit* [TSAJ, 34; Tübingen: J.C.B. Mohr (Paul Siebeck), 1992], pp. 306–10). Thus it is conceivable that Josephus has omitted the angelology and allusions to Josh. 5 and Exod. 23.20–21 from the tradition he knew.

94. The date for Baba Rabbah's career is debated, though some time in the third or fourth centuries CE is certain (see B. Hall, 'Samaritan History: From John Hyrcanus to Baba Rabba' in A.D. Crown [ed.], *The Samaritans* [Tübingen: J.C.B. Mohr (Paul Siebeck), 1989], pp. 32–54, esp. p. 53).

He likewise removed many people from their priestly rank. The cause of this was that when the priest Baba Rabbah came to Bashan the priests who were there did not come forth to meet him, neither did they fulfill their obligation to accord him honour and glory (H1 להכבידו ולאיקרו, H2 למוקרא). However, when he arrived at the city and assumed his rightful position then they came to greet him in their customary manner with all the people. Because of this act he removed from them their positions, because they did not journey out of the city to meet him. In their place he appointed ordinary individuals to discharge their supervisory functions, with the exception of the responsibility (to teach) Holy Scripture.[95]

If this story is reliable (which itself is uncertain) then at the time of Baba Rabbah's reforms there was a shared understanding that the Adventus, including the worship ('honouring and glorifying') of the high priest was the expected recognition of his divine authority and identity in the Samaritan community.[96] (Since Baba Rabbah's position as *high* priest was not accepted by the people of Bashan, he was not given the welcome he thought he deserved). If, at this time, the Samaritans had their own version of the Alexander Adventus story, then *Chronicle II* is an important witness to the role of that story not just as a myth of origins but as a model of political and religious etiquette in the Judaisms of Late Antiquity.[97]

Bearing in mind the likelihood that both our Samaritan and Josippon versions contain very old material we come to the story that both versions append to the main account of Alexander's meeting with the high priest. Alexander expects the trappings of the new Ruler Cult to be established in Jerusalem: he demands that his physical likeness, a statue, be built and placed in the Temple. Here we are once again in the very real world of the Hellenistic Ruler Cult and this is precisely what some did do for Alexander as our story of Apelles' Ephesus painting (above) illustrates. The request could reflect a genuine expectation of the new western rulers anytime from the reign of Alexander himself onwards. It obviously recalls the crisis in the Roman period when Gaius Caligula expected the Jews to allow the erection of his statue in their Temple. But the story could equally be much older. The Jewish response to the request is an ingenious strategy based on their image-of-god-in-humanity theology. As the Samaritan high priest Hezekiah explains to Alexander in response to his request for 'a picture of my image (צלמי)', they have no pictures or statues like the other nations. The nearest, moreover the *better,* likeness of his divine image which they can offer are their own children who, being made in the image of God, can move, speak and discern between good and evil, unlike pagan idols which can neither speak nor see. Alexander obviously is then himself an image of God, in that sense. The Jews (in Josippon) are willing at the very least to have some memorial of him in their sanctuary. And, in recognizing

95. §5.4–10. Translation is that of J.M. Cohen, 'A Critical Edition of the Baba Rabbah Section of the Samaritan Chronicle No. II: With Translation and Commentary' (PhD thesis; Glasgow, 1977), p. 67.

96. In his discussion of this section of *Chronicle II* (*Critical Edition*, pp. 423–26), J.M. Cohen thinks it is a secondary addition but recognizes that it may well preserve historically reliable tradition.

97. Cf. also perhaps 1 Macc. 11.6 according to which Jonathan meets the king at Joppa with pomp (lit. 'with Glory [μετὰ δόξης]').

the limited extent to which Alexander himself has a divinity arising from his own creation in the image of God, the Samaritans (and the Jews in Josippon) name their children after him. This compromise position might seem to us to undermine fundamentally the image-of-God-in-humanity theology; the naming of children after Alexander might suggest that they bear his image and not that of Israel's creator God. But that the Jewish and Samaritan strategy is based on their native image-of-God-in-humanity theology is clearly the view of the texts.[98]

Although it is not entirely clear what degree of recognition of Alexander's divinity is intended here, we are obviously back in the world of nuanced affirmation and polemic that characterizes Josephus' story's response to the Hellenistic Ruler Cult. But, most importantly of all, the late attested appendix to this Alexander story confirms our conclusion that the earlier tradition (to which Josephus witnesses) relies on the fundamental, and biblical, belief that the divine image – God's idol – is only truly present in humanity.

98. Again, this has the ring of historical verisimilitude in as much as it was a common element of the Hellenistic Ruler cult for a tribe to be named after a benefactor and divine Ruler. This story hardly fits with the later crisis under Caligula and so may well emanate from the earlier, pre-Maccabean, period during which Jewish-Hellenistic cultural relations were less fraught.

Part II
MONOTHEISM AND THE NEW TESTAMENT

WAS JESUS A MONOTHEIST?
A CONTRIBUTION TO THE DISCUSSION OF CHRISTIAN MONOTHEISM

James D.G. Dunn, University of Durham

1. *Introduction*

The question, 'Was Jesus a Monotheist?', has a slightly shocking ring for those brought up in the Christian tradition. It conjures up fanciful pictures of Jesus engaged in the great debates of the fourth and fifth centuries on God as Trinity, and the possibility of him refusing to affirm the Nicene Creed, or even siding with Jews and Muslims of later centuries in accusing Christians of tri-theism. But after the initial jolt, the appropriateness of the question in reference to a first century Jesus soon asserts itself.

More serious is the issue of the appropriateness of the term 'monotheism' itself, given the caveats and strictures already raised earlier in the volume, including not least the distinction between monotheism and henotheism, and the more difficult concept of 'oneness' or 'unity' when talking of divine reality.[1]

Nevertheless, the question can be posed legitimately and meaningfully to the extent of asking whether Jesus would have shared the common beliefs of his fellow Jews of the time and would have said the *Shema'* with good heart and conscience. Or if the suggestion that a twenty-first century student of the Gospels could somehow penetrate into the mind and conscience of the first century Jesus is to point down a path largely abandoned by those in 'quest of the historical Jesus', let us at least allow as a legitimate and important question whether Jesus affirmed that 'the Lord our God is one Lord' (Deut. 6.4). And if we can further inquire into Jesus' teaching in reference to God and draw legitimate inferences in this connection from the Jesus tradition, we will be well on the way to answering the question to the extent that an answer is possible at this distance in time.

My current work in joining the quest of the historical Jesus has given me opportunity to pursue this more limited question and I draw on it for the purposes of this paper.[2] I offer first some inferences regarding Jesus' upbringing, then examine the explicit God-talk of his teaching as attested in the Jesus tradition, and finally probe what further deductions may be drawn from the impression he left on his disciples by the character of his mission.

---

1.   Cf. the contribution in this volume by R.W.L. Moberly, 'How Appropriate is "Monotheism" as a Category for Biblical Interpretation?'.

2.   I refer to my *Christianity in the Making* I. *Jesus Remembered* (Grand Rapids: Eerdmans, 2003).

2. *Inferences from Jesus' Upbringing*

2.1. There need be little doubt that recital of the *Shema'* was an established practice within Second Temple Judaism at the time of Jesus. The obligation laid down in Deut. 6.4–9 was clear beyond demur, and the inference from 6.7 that the *Shema'* should be said twice a day ('when you lie down and when you rise') was probably already long established. Certainly the Mishnah presupposes a long established practice. And the prominence given in the Mishnah's opening tractate to clarifying what recital 'in the evening' and 'in the morning' meant in practice, and in what circumstances the *Shema'* should or should not be said, attests its prime importance for a long period before the Mishnah's publication (*m. Ber.* 1–3). That 'God is one' was a defining confession for all Jews is affirmed by both *Letter of Aristeas* 132 and Josephus, *Ant.* 5.112 ('owned by all Hebrews alike').

Similarly, the basic statement of Jewish obligation, the ten commandments, begins with the clear charge: 'You shall have no other gods besides (or before) me' (Exod. 20.3). According to *m. Tamid* 5.1 these too were to be recited daily, in public worship. And even if that ruling may reflect later practice, we need not doubt that the first of the ten commandments was deeply ingrained in Jewish faith and praxis. Philo brings his exposition of the first commandment to a climax thus:

> Let us, then, engrave deep in our hearts this as the first and most sacred of commandments, to acknowledge and honour one God who is above all, and let the idea that gods are many never even reach the ears of the man whose rule of life is to seek for truth in purity and goodness (*Decal.* 65).

We may deduce with similar confidence that the second commandment, 'You shall not make for yourself an idol' (Exod. 20.4–5a; Deut. 5.8–9a), was a defining characteristic of first century Judaism. The antipathy to man-made idols is clear beyond doubt in Israel's sustained prohibition and polemic.[3] And the fact that Paul, for all his liberty in regard to the law, was equally unyielding in his hostility to idolatry,[4] gives no encouragement to any suggestion that Jesus might have been less resolute on the point. The mood of Jesus' immediate contemporaries is probably well illustrated by their violent reaction to Pilate's misguided attempts to bring Roman standards perceived as idolatrous into Jerusalem (*Ant.* 18.55–59) and to the subsequent attempt of Caligula to have his own statue set up within the Temple (*Ant.*18.261–272). The former episode most probably took place in the early years of Pilate's governorship (26–36/37 CE), that is, immediately prior to Jesus' own mission (usually dated 27–30). And the latter was notable as involving Galilean peasants (including, no doubt, villagers who had heard Jesus teaching) in the protest (*Ant.* 18.271–272).

The complementary conviction in God's un-image-ableness ('invisible') is late and Hellenistic in formulation.[5] But that God cannot be seen, not even by Moses, is

---

3. Classically Isa. 44.9–20; Wis. 12–15; Ep. Jer.; *Sib. Or.* 3.8–45; *m. Ab. Zar.*
4. Rom. 1.23; 1 Cor. 5.10–11; 6.9; 10.7, 14; Gal. 5.20; similarly 1 Jn 5.21.
5. ἀόρατος ('invisible') appears only in the New Testament (Rom. 1.20; Col. 1.15; 1 Tim. 1.17; Heb. 11.27) and nowhere else in biblical Greek (but note *Ps.-Philo* 35.3 and *Test. Abr.* 16.3–4).

a theologoumenon which runs through the whole Jewish and Christian tradition.[6] Here again, is exposed a central element in Judaism's nervous system, already well matured by the time of Jesus.

2.2. What can we deduce from all this in regard to Jesus himself? It is a commonplace of contemporary Jesus research that Jesus was a Jew; and given the diversity of first century Palestinian Judaism, more and more evident to us since the discovery of the Dead Sea Scrolls, there is every reason to locate Jesus firmly within that diversity.

To put more flesh on that initial affirmation, we can probably infer that Jesus was brought up by pious parents. Their piety is indicated by the names they gave their children (Mk 6.3) – James/Jacob (the patriarch), Joses/Joseph, Judas/Judah, Simon/Simeon. It can hardly be accidental that the latter three are the names of three of Jacob's twelve children, and heads of the resultant tribes. Nor need we hesitate to draw a similar inference from the name given to Jesus himself – Jesus/Joshua.

A pious upbringing would include the tradition of reciting the *Shema'* regularly; we can return below to the explicit references to the *Shema'* in the Jesus tradition (see 3.1). The same inferences can be drawn regarding a practice of daily prayer, twice a day (Josephus, *Ant.* 4.212) or even three times a day (*m. Ber.* 4.1).[7] As Joachim Jeremias observes, 'It is hardly conceivable that the earliest community would have observed the hours of prayer had Jesus rejected them'.[8]

Likewise, we can probably assume that Jesus was brought up to attend the local synagogue sabbath by sabbath. Whether the word συναγωγή refers to the assembly itself, or to a building set apart, or to a communal meeting place (village hall), or to meetings in a private house, and whether Nazareth had its own 'synagogue', are matters of some dispute.[9] But the references to 'synagogues' in the Jesus tradition (Mk 12.39 and parallels; Lk. 11.43; Mk 13.9/Mt. 10.17) and to Jesus' regular practice of teaching and preaching in Galilean 'synagogues'[10] should be sufficient to confirm both that such assemblies were an established feature of Galilean village life and that Jesus was a regular participant in such assemblies from childhood.

However, it is common in Philo, and especially of God (e.g. *Sac.* 133; *Mut. Nom.* 14; *Som.* 1.72); and worth noting is Juvenal's characterization of Jewish belief in God (*Sat.* 14.97 – 'worship nothing but the clouds…').

6.   Exod. 33.17–23; Deut. 4.12; Ps. 97.2; *1 En.* 14.21; *Apoc. Abr.* 16.3; Philo, *Spec. Leg.* 1.45; Jn 1.18; 6.46. Exod. 24.9–10 is qualified by Deut. 4.15; and the extreme reservation shown in 1 Kgs 19.11–12 and Ezek. 1.26–28 indicates the sensitivity on the issue, even if it is less evident on other occasions (Isa. 6.1–2; Amos 9.1; Dan. 7.9–10).

7.   J. Jeremias, *The Prayers of Jesus* (London: SCM Press, 1967), pp. 66–81; E.P. Sanders, *Judaism: Practice and Belief 63 BCE–66 CE* (London: SCM Press, 1992), pp. 196–97 and 202–208.

8.   *New Testament Theology*. I. *The Proclamation of Jesus* (London: SCM Press, 1971), pp. 186–91 (here p. 188), referring to Acts 3.1; 10.3, 30; *Did.* 8.3.

9.   Full details in my *Jesus Remembered*, ch. 9, section 7.

10.   Mt. 4.23/Mk 1.39/Lk. 4.44; Mt. 9.35; Mt. 13.54/Mk 6.2/Lk. 4.16; Lk. 4.15; Lk. 6.6; 13.10; Jn 6.59.

Whether Jesus could read for himself or not,[11] his knowledge of and familiarity with scripture indicated in the Synoptic tradition (e.g. Mk 2.25–26; 7.6–8; 10.5–8; 12.26) is entirely plausible, even for the son of an artisan. Josephus affirms that Jews generally 'give every seventh day over to the study of our customs and law' (Josephus, *Ant.* 16.43), and again there is no good reason to think that Jesus was exempted, or exempted himself from such praxis, even allowing for a degree of idealization in Josephus' description. The references to the 'tassels' of Jesus' garment (Mt. 9.20/Lk. 8.44; Mk 6.56/Mt. 14.36) strengthen the impression that he himself was a pious Jew who took his religious obligations seriously.[12]

At least some pilgrimage to Jerusalem for the great feasts can be assumed. Luke's report that Jesus' parents 'went to Jerusalem every year (κατ᾽ ἔτος) at the feast of the Passover' (Lk. 2.41) may be exaggerated (*every* year?), but otherwise is entirely plausible.[13] The story of Lk. 2.41–51 suggests that (preparation for) Jesus' transition to manhood would have been regarded as a particularly appropriate occasion for a pilgrimage.[14] At any rate, he would have been familiar with the Temple and its functionaries, priests who served locally as teachers and magistrates (Mk 1.44 and parallels),[15] and the requirements of tithing (Mt. 23.23/Lk. 11.42)[16] and purity.[17]

Most of this is circumstantial, but the overall picture that emerges is certainly coherent and is entirely consistent with the affirmation of Jesus' belief and practice as a devout Jew. That this included the conviction and regular affirmation that 'God is one' is a corollary hard to escape.

3. *Jesus' God-talk*

Scot McKnight notes how strange it is that so little has been written in scholarship about the God of Jesus, even though scholars like T.W. Manson have emphasized that 'in the teaching of Jesus his conception of God determines everything'.[18]

11. The fact that Jesus' literacy is a matter of dispute should not be ignored (see again my *Jesus Remembered*, ch. 9, section 9b).

12. With reference to the instructions of Num. 15.38–39 and Deut. 22.12 (note also Zech. 8.23).

13. Sanders estimates that between 300,000 and 500,000 would attend the Passover (Herod's temple could accommodate 400,000 pilgrims) out of a Palestinian Jewish population of between 500,000 and 1,000,000 (*Judaism*, pp. 127–28).

14. Mishnah tractate *Niddah* 5.6 implies that the thirteenth birthday marked a boy's transition to adult responsibility in legal and religious matters. *Hagiga* 1.1 may imply an older custom of taking boys on pilgrimage at a younger age to accustom them to the obligation (J.A. Fitzmyer, *Luke* [2 vols.; AB, 28; New York: Doubleday, 1981–1985], pp. 440–41).

15. Sanders, *Judaism*, p. 177.

16. On tithing, see Sanders, *Judaism*, pp. 146–57.

17. Mk 1.40–44 and parallels; Mk 7.15–23/Mt. 15.11–20; Mt. 23.25–26/Lk. 11.39–41. Noteworthy is the presence of a large ritual bath adjacent to the Gamla synagogue above the north-east corner of the Sea of Galilee.

18. S. McKnight, *A New Vision for Israel* (Grand Rapids: Eerdmans, 1999), p. 15, citing T.W. Manson, *The Teaching of Jesus* (Cambridge: Cambridge University Press, 1939), p. 211; in the same connection he also cites Adolf Schlatter and Adolf Harnack.

Presumably a large part of the reason for this is that, as with Paul,[19] God is the chief axiom on which the whole religious system is predicated. As the foundation of a great structure is 'fundamental' to it, but is mostly hidden from view, so God, as the axiomatic presupposition for both Judaism and Christianity, need be little named but was always to be assumed. In Jesus' case, we may further infer, the little he is recalled as saying about God *expressis verbis* is, in consequence, all the more significant.

3.1. Of first importance is the fact that the Jesus tradition includes the explicit recollection of Jesus drawing upon the *Shema'* for his own teaching. The tradition is carried by all three Synoptic Gospels (Mk 12.28–31 and parallels).

Matthew 22.35–40	Mark 12.28–31	Luke 10.25–28
35 ...one of them [Pharisees], a lawyer,	28 One of the scribes came near and heard them disputing with one another, and seeing that he answered them well, he asked him,	25 Just then a lawyer stood up to test him, saying.
asked him a question to test him. 36 'Teacher, which commandment in the law is the greatest?' 37 He said to him,	'Which commandment is the first of all?' 29 Jesus answered, 'The first is, "Hear, O Israel: the Lord our God, the Lord is one; 30 and you shall love the Lord your God with all your heart, and with all your soul, and with all your mind, and with all your strength."	'Teacher, what must I do to inherit eternal life?' 26 He said to him, 'What is written in the law? What do you read there?' 27 He answered, '"You shall love the Lord your God with all your heart, and with all your soul, and with all your strength, and with all your mind;
'"You shall love the Lord your God with all your heart, and with all your soul, and with all your mind." 38 This is the greatest and first commandment. 39 The second is like it: "You shall love your neighbour as yourself." 40 On these two commandments hang all the law and the prophets.'	31 The second is this, "You shall love your neighbour as yourself." There is no other commandment greater than these.'	and your neighbour as yourself."' 28 And he said to him, 'You have given the right answer; do this, and you will live'.

The tradition itself comes to us in different versions. Matthew and Mark sum up the significance of the teaching in regard to the law in different but complementary words (Mt. 22.40; Mk 12.31b). Somewhat surprisingly it is Mark (rather than Matthew) who takes the opportunity to include the beginning of the *Shema'* (Mk 12.29), though the citation of Deut. 6.5 in all three versions (Mk 12.30 and parallels) shows that Mark's elaboration simply makes explicit what was anyway implicit. And Luke has given the teaching an intriguing twist by having the key command uttered by a lawyer (νομικός), with Jesus approving (Lk. 10.27–28). But the key consideration is that the focus on the fundamental teaching of the

---

19. See my *The Theology of Paul the Apostle* (Grand Rapids: Eerdmans; Edinburgh: T. & T. Clark, 1998), pp. 28–33.

Shema' is constant. It is precisely characteristic of oral tradition that what is deemed important remains stable, while variation of detail attests the adaptability of the tradition as it was 'performed' in differing contexts of the early churches.[20]

The point, then, is that Jesus is remembered in earliest Christian tradition not simply for putting the love commandment ('love your neighbour as yourself') at the heart of his teaching. The influence of that teaching on the first Christians is clear enough from first century Christian writings,[21] and there are no grounds for denying that the inspiration for that focus in early Christian teaching is to be attributed to Jesus. For such a consistent singling out of just this commandment (Lev. 19.18) can hardly be coincidental.[22] More to the point, Jesus is remembered as also putting the love command second to the primary command, to love *God* with all one's being (Mk 12.30 and parallels).[23] For Jesus the *Shema'* was indeed fundamental, fundamentally determinative of the whole orientation of life. It is not the case that Jesus' ethic can be boiled down to 'love of neighbour'. On the contrary, the implication is that the two go together,[24] and perhaps also that the second is only possible in long-term reality as the corollary to the first.[25]

The conclusion is strong, then, that the *Shema'* continued to be of central importance for Jesus during his mission and in the teaching he both gave and lived out. Which also means that the conviction that God was one continued to be a basic axiom for Jesus, a core principle from which he drew his inspiration and instruction. To that extent at least, in other words, we have to answer the question of our title with a clear afffirmative.

3.2. Additional strength is provided by three other passages in the Synoptic tradition. The first is the opening of Mark's report of Jesus' encounter with the rich young man (Mk 10.17–18). The Matthean parallel is also instructive.

20. A central thesis of my *Jesus Remembered*; see particularly chapter 8.

21. Rom. 13.8–10; Gal. 5.14; Jas. 2.8; *Did.* 1.2; 2.7; *Ep. Barn.* 19.5; *Gos. Thom.* 25; cf. Jn 15.12. In the same spirit is the consistent Pauline exhortation to consideration for others (as in Rom. 12.9–10; 15.1–2; Phil. 2.1–5).

22. Explicit references to Lev. 19.18 are lacking in Jewish literature prior to Jesus, and such allusions as there are give it no particular prominence, though subsequently the opinion is attributed to Rabbi Akiba (early second century) that Lev. 19.18 is 'the greatest general principle in the Torah' (*Sifra* on Lev. 19.18). See further particularly A. Nissen, *Gott und der Nächste im antiken Judentum: Untersuchungen zum Doppelgebot der Liebe* (WUNT, 15: Tübingen: J.C.B. Mohr [Paul Siebeck], 1974) and K. Berger, *Die Gesetzauslegung Jesu I* (WMANT, 40; Neukirchen–Vluyn: Neukirchener Verlag, 1972), pp. 50–55 and 80–136. Data also in W.D. Davies and D.C. Allison, *Matthew* (3 vols.; ICC; Edinburgh: T. & T. Clark, 1988–1997), III, pp. 237–38; G. Theissen and A. Merz, *The Historical Jesus: A Comprehensive Guide* (London: SCM Press, 1998), pp. 384–90; and M. Reiser, 'Love of Enemies in the Context of Antiquity', *NTS* 47 (2001), pp. 411–27.

23. 'A wholly original conjunction of Deut. 6.4–5 and Lev. 19.18' (P. Stuhlmacher, *Biblische Theologie des Neuen Testaments*. 1. *Grundlegung von Jesus zu Paulus* [Göttingen: Vandenhoeck & Ruprecht, 1992], pp. 100–101). Note also that Luke's version of the saying on tithing (Mt. 23.23/Lk. 11.42) includes 'love of God' as part of the higher obligation.

24. See particularly V.P. Furnish, *The Love Command in the New Testament* (Nashville: Abingdon Press, 1972), pp. 27–28, 33 and 37.

25. See further W. Schrage, *The Ethics of the New Testament* (Philadelphia: Fortress Press, 1988), pp. 81–85.

Matthew 19.16–17	*Mark 10.17–18*
Then someone came to him and said, 'Teacher, what *good deed* must I do to have eternal life?' And he said to him, '*Why do you ask me about what is good? There is only one who is good.*'	A man ran up and knelt before him, and asked him, '*Good* Teacher, what must I do to inherit eternal life?' Jesus said to him, '*Why do you call me good? No one is good but God alone.*'

The clear implication of Mark's account is that Jesus declined the epithet 'good', because properly speaking only God is good. The response may come across as a rather heavy-handed, pedantic reply to a piece of well-meaning, innocuous flattery. But its theological rationale is obvious: God alone is worthy of such devotion, because God alone is the source and definition of all goodness. Equally interesting is the fact that nothing more is made of the opening exchange in the rest of the pericope. It is one of those incidental features, preserved by the tradition, not because it was important for that portion of tradition, but because it was part of the memory of how Jesus responded on the occasion. It is on such occasions that the modern reader is given a passing glimpse into the God-foundation of Jesus' whole mission.

Matthew's evident editing of the tradition is also illuminating. It would appear that he reacted against any suggestion that Jesus would have refused the epithet 'good'. Whether that was because he thought such a suggestion too ridiculous to be preserved (of course Jesus was good), or because on christological grounds he wanted to avoid any implication that Jesus denied an epithet appropriate only to deity,[26] we need not here decide. What is more relevant to the immediate issue is that his editing of the Markan version stayed so close to the Markan wording. That is to say, his respect for the tradition seems to have prevented him from omitting the initial exchange altogether or from editing it more thoroughly. In so doing he retained the crucial rationale of Mark's version ('There is only one who is good'), despite the fact that in Matthew's revised version the rationale is now a *non sequitur* and not really relevant to the revised version. In so doing Matthew joins with Mark in recording that Jesus affirmed as a matter of primary confession that God alone is (the) good; both no doubt drawing the corollary from the *Shema'*, since God alone is God; God is alone.

3.3. Without labouring the point, a similar deduction could be drawn, though as a more remote corollary, from the first petition of the Lord's Prayer: 'Hallowed (ἁγιασθήτω) be your name' (Mt. 6.9/Lk. 11.2). Basic to the idea of 'holiness', of the adjective 'holy' (ἅγιος) and the verb 'hallow/sanctify' (ἁγιάζω), is the thought of otherness, set-apartness from everyday usage.[27] As referred to God, holiness denotes the wholly otherness of God, and provides a further rationale for

---

26. The history of interpretation of the Markan version was much preoccupied with the christological problems it posed; see U. Luz, *Matthäus* (4 vols.; EKKNT, 1; Zürich: Benziger Verlag, 1985–2002), III, p. 122 n. 21.

27. Cf. O. Procksch, '*hagios*', in *TDNT*, I, pp. 89–94.

the rejection of all attempts to configure God as a projection of human ideals (a man-made idol). God's know-ability to humankind, that is, God in/as his name, depends on humankind according him/his name absolute respect; anything less will simply mean that his name is not apprehended, and God is not known.[28] This also is entirely of a piece with the affirmation that God is one, that Yahweh is alone Lord. For were there other worthy recipients of such devotion and commitment, the God of Israel could not demand such exclusive and total respect.

The point here is strengthened by the fact that this is the first petition of the prayer taught by Jesus to his disciples. The same inference can be drawn as with the love command: as love of neighbour depends for its empowering on the prior command and on the priority of the command to love God with all one's being, so the subsequent petitions of the prayer of Jesus' disciples depends on the prior petition and the priority of the petition that God's name should be properly reverenced. Here again we are afforded a glimpse into Jesus' conviction of the sole primacy of God and of God's sole worthiness of absolute reverence.

3.4. The second petition of the Lord's Prayer, 'May your kingdom come' (Mt. 6.10/Lk. 11.2), invites a further reflection. For no one disputes that the main emphasis of Jesus' preaching was 'the kingdom or kingship of God'. But few note the major corollary that in the kingdom of God, God is *King*, God alone. The reason, no doubt, is that Jesus is almost never recalled as referring to God as 'king', in any of the streams of Gospel tradition.[29] In contrast, in the worship of Jesus' time God would have been regularly addressed as 'king'; the idea of God as 'king (*melekh*)' over all the earth, over all the nations, over all the gods, was, after all, a familiar theme of worship in their psalm book.[30]

But we should not say 'in contrast'. For it is precisely this understanding of God as 'king' which the young Jesus would have been instructed in, and, more to the immediate point, which is assuredly reflected in the central motif of Jesus' teaching – the kingship of God, God's royal rule. And the same implication of God *alone* as king, the *only* God as ruler over all (including all other so-called gods), God as the only one worthy to command complete and singular loyalty and obedience, is clear. In the kingdom of God the (human) subject owes unconditional obedience to the king; a double allegiance is impossible (Mt. 6.24/Lk. 16.13/*Gos. Thom.* 47.1–2). The king, and the king alone has the power to determine the eternal destiny of his subjects (Mt. 10.28/Lk. 12.4–5).

---

28. The passive form of the verb ('be hallowed/sanctified') is a 'divine passive', no doubt corresponding to the Hebrew *qadash* (*Niphal*), and echoing the Hebrew Bible thought that it is God himself who demonstrates his holiness and sanctifies his name (Lev. 10.3; 22.32; Num. 20.13; Isa. 5.16; Ezek. 20.41; 28.20, 25; 36.23; 38.16; 39.27).

29. Only in Mt. 5.35, where the Jesus tradition calls Jerusalem 'the city of the great king', in immediate echo of Ps. 48.2. Otherwise the nearest examples are two parables in Matthew which feature a king (Mt. 18.23–35; 22.1–14) and one in Luke (Lk. 19.11–27).

30. Pss. 10.16; 22.28; 29.10; 47.2–3, 7–8; 95.3; 103.19 (*malkut*); 135.6 (as expanded at Qumran; see M.G. Abegg, P.W. Flint and E.C. Ulrich, *The Dead Sea Scrolls Bible* [San Francisco: Harper, 1999], p. 568). The data is summarized by K. Seybold, '*malkut*', in *TDOT*, VIII, pp. 365–66.

That the theme of God as *Father* is more prominent in Jesus' theology is not to be disputed. For Jesus is remembered as speaking of God quite regularly as 'your Father', the 'you' being his immediate disciples.[31] But the knowing of God as 'Father' only softens the harder outline of the understanding of God as King to an extent, since 'father' denoted authority as well as care. And anyway it does not undermine the primary point in this paper. For Jesus the Jew would presumably have assented with Paul to the confession that 'there is one God, the Father, from whom all things' (1 Cor. 8.6a). One God, one King, one Father were all equally aspects and expressions of Jesus' monotheism.

3.5. Although not part of the tradition of Jesus' own teachings, we should not ignore the tradition of Jesus' being tempted in its fuller Q form (Mt. 4.1–11/Lk. 4.1–13). For in Matthew's retelling, the climactic confrontation is the temptation for Jesus to abandon the first commandment. The devil offers Jesus 'all the king-doms of the world and all the glory of them…if you will (but) fall down and wor-ship me' (Mt. 4.8–9/Lk. 4.5–7). To which Jesus replies: 'It is written, "You shall worship the Lord your God and him only shall you serve"' (Mt. 4.10/Lk. 4.8).

Jesus' quotation is from Deut. 6.13: 'You shall fear the Lord your God, and you shall serve him…' Noteworthy is the addition of 'only' to the Synoptic quo-tation of Deut. 6.13. It is noteworthy, not because it changes the sense of the Deuteronomy passage. On the contrary, the addition simply brings out what is implicit in the original.[32] The significance rather is that the early Christian for-mulation of the tradition at this point evidently saw fit to emphasize that God alone is worthy of worship, and to show that that fundamental assertion of Jewish monotheism was affirmed also by Jesus. This is the more remarkable if by the time the fuller temptation tradition was first formulated, or was then used by Matthew, some sense of Jesus as the incarnation of God had already been attained (Mt. 1.23). For then Matthew would be reinforcing the memory of Jesus' own monotheism even while struggling to express the growing sense of Jesus' own divine significance. Within the higher christology of Matthew the recollection that Jesus himself refused to acknowledge the legitimacy of worship other than the worship of God only, God alone, the one God, has a weight of theological import insufficiently recognized.

In short, although the relevant data is hardly extensive, it is coherent within itself and in its ramifications within the Jesus tradition, and it is consistent with the circumstantial evidence adduced in section 2 above. In the light of the examination so far, then, it is hardly possible to avoid giving an affirmative answer to our initial question: Yes, Jesus was a monotheist.

However, there is still more to be said.

---

31. 'Your (singular) Father' – Mt. 6.4, 6, 18. 'Your (plural) Father' – Mk 11.25/Mt. 6.14–15; Mt. 5.48/Lk. 6.36; Mt. 6.32/Lk. 12.30; Mt. 7.11/(Lk. 11.13); Mt. 5.16, 45; 6.1, 8, 26; 10.20, 29; 18.14; 23.9; Lk. 12.32; Jn 20.17.

32. Davies and Allison, *Matthew*, 1.373.

4. *The Impression Jesus Made on his Disciples*

It was long ago recognized that for Jesus to *be* who he was it was not necessary for Jesus to *know* who he was. Such a reflection can easily become an apologia for the boldest of Christian claims regarding Jesus. But it can equally provide the basis for a more modest argument that the developing christologies of the next decades and centuries were firmly rooted in the reality of who Jesus was – more in the order of the unfolding of the great oak from the little acorn, than the evolution of one distinct species out of another.[33] There is bound to be a certain amount of unease about such an argument in dealing with an issue like the present one. For our question is whether Jesus himself was a monotheist. And the affirmation that, for example, Jesus was God incarnate, cannot ignore the possibility that Jesus as a devout monotheistic Jew would himself have denied that affirmation or even have found it ridiculous.

The problem can be eased, however, if we recall how difficult it is to penetrate into Jesus' self-consciousness. That was the difficulty which spelled the end of the nineteenth century quest of the historical Jesus, a quest which had focused precisely on the issue of Jesus' 'messianic self-consciousness'.[34] And subsequent questers have, for the most part, been duly chastened and much more hesitant to voice opinions on the issue. The more realistic objective for the quest is to inquire into the *impact* Jesus made on his first disciples, how they heard him, and to ask what their first century memories of him reveal when we pose our twenty-first century questions to these memories. After all, it is the impression made by Jesus on his first disciples which has ensured that there is a Jesus tradition in the first place and has provided the basic content of the tradition, however much that tradition has been subjected to subsequent reflection.[35]

There would probably be a substantial consensus among Life of Jesus researchers that if any answer is to be forthcoming which is of relevance to our question (Was Jesus a monotheist?), it will be found in three strands of the Jesus tradition: those passages which indicate in some way or other that Jesus envisaged himself as God's son; those where he is remembered as teaching with a surprising degree of self-asserted authority; and those in which he may have spoken of himself in terms of the Danielic 'one like a son of man'. For if Jesus was remembered as referring or alluding to himself in status terms beyond the ordinary, then that finding could certainly have a bearing on our question.

33. See, e.g., my 'The Making of Christology – Evolution or Unfolding?', in J.B. Green and M.Turner (eds.), *Jesus of Nazareth: Lord and Christ. Essays in Honor of I. Howard Marshall* (Grand Rapids: Eerdmans, 1994), pp. 437–52.

34. It was against the fruitless chase after this will-o'-the-wisp that Bultmann's famous dismissive judgment was delivered: 'I do indeed think that we can know almost nothing concerning the life and personality of Jesus, since the early Christian sources show no interest in either, are moreover fragmentary and often legendary; and other sources about Jesus do not exist...what has been written in the last hundred and fifty years on the life of Jesus, his personality and the development of his inner life, is fantastic and romantic' (R. Bultmann, *Jesus and the Word* [trans. Louise Pettibone Smith; New York: Charles Scribner's Sons, 1935; German, 1926], p. 8).

35. I here summarize my line of approach in *Jesus Remembered*.

There is no thought here, of course, of subjecting these passages to a full analysis; that would be impossible within the limitations of this paper. The challenge is simply this: let us grant for the sake of argument that these passages do indeed express an awareness or claim on Jesus' part to a special relationship with God, a special authority from God, a special status before God; what then are the consequences for our primary question, whether Jesus himself was a monotheist?

4.1. The case made by Jeremias that Jesus consistently and distinctively addressed God as *Abba* ('Father') has been surprisingly durable, despite some severe criticism.[36] So too with the conclusion Jeremias derived from that finding: that Jesus perceived his relationship with God as son to father in terms of the intimacy of a family relationship.[37] For my own part, the key consideration here is the repeated testimony of Paul (Rom. 8.15–17; Gal. 4.6–7) that the *abba*-prayer was a *distinctive* feature of earliest Christian worship, and distinctive not least as attesting a sonship and status of heirs which the Christian pray-ers *shared with Jesus* (συγκληρονόμοι Χριστοῦ). If Paul, who would have been no stranger to Jewish prayer, could regard the *abba*-prayer as such a distinctive feature of Christian prayer, and a sign of an inheritance shared with Jesus, then we can be confident that Jeremias' conclusion was basically sound.

How would that conclusion bear upon the question of Jesus' monotheism? The most obvious answer is: Not necessarily very much. For the sonship expressed in the *abba*-prayer is a relationship that was enjoyed also by Paul and the first Christians. And although there is a clear sense that the sonship of believers is *derived* from Jesus' sonship, is a sharing in *Jesus'* sonship, there is no clear implication that the sonship of believers is of a different order from Jesus' sonship. If anything, the thought is rather of Jesus as the eldest brother in a new family of God (Rom. 8.29). Of course, the theme of Jesus' divine sonship quickly became a major theme in developing christology. But our question focuses on Jesus' own sense of his relationship with God. And since it is the *abba* passages which provide the clearest reflection of Jesus' own prayer usage, it is difficult to press beyond the conclusion that Jesus probably experienced his relationship with God as son to father.

The one passage in the Synoptic Gospels which might call for some qualification of that conclusion is the famous Mt. 11.27/Lk. 10.22:

Matthew 11.27	*Luke 10.22*
All things have been handed over to me by my Father; and no one knows the Son except the Father, and no one knows the Father except the Son and anyone to whom the Son chooses to reveal him.	All things have been handed over to me by my Father; and no one knows who the Son is except the Father, or who the Father is except the Son and anyone to whom the Son chooses to reveal him.

---

36. E.g. F. Hahn, *Christologische Hoheitstitel* (Göttingen: Vandenhoeck & Ruprecht, 1963, [5]1995), p. 320; N. Perrin, *Rediscovering the Teaching of Jesus* (London: SCM Press, 1967), pp. 40–41; J.A. Fitzmyer, 'Abba and Jesus' Relation to God', in *A Cause de L'Evangile: Etudes sur les Synoptiques offertes à Jacques Dupont* (LD, 123; Paris: Éditions du Cerf, 1985), pp. 15–38.

37. Jeremias, *Proclamation*, pp. 63–68. For sympathetic restatements of Jeremias' argument

Not many are confident that the saying goes back to Jesus in its present form. It may be an elaboration of something Jesus did say, in some exceptional moment in which he reflected on his relationship with God as son to father – 'exceptional' because the saying is so exceptional within the Synoptic tradition.[38] It may also be an early indication of the way early Christian reflection on that relationship was to develop into the much extended Father-Son christology of the Fourth Gospel.[39] As it stands in the Synoptic account, however, it may indicate only that Jesus on one occasion spoke of his sense of sonship, and of his privileged revelation from God, in exalted terms. Whatever the status and privilege, it had been afforded him by God, the one God of Israel.

4.2. It was the *authority* of Jesus on which Ernst Käsemann famously focused in calling for the quest of the historical Jesus to be reopened.[40] And the argument that Jesus claimed an authority which rivalled or even outstripped that of Moses became something of a commonplace in the second or new quest. The argument is largely dependent on the ἐγώ δε λέγω ('But I say') formulation found in the antitheses of Mt. 5.21–48. It is usually accepted that the sixfold repetition of the formula (5.22, 28, 32, 34, 39, 44) owes at least something to Matthew's editing.[41] But it is maintained, nevertheless, that the formula reflects Jesus' own readiness to pronounce on the law and the tradition attributed to Moses and to do so with an astonishing sovereign freedom.[42]

We may at once add to this another of Jeremias' famous observations. Jesus is remembered for a characteristic use of 'Amen' to introduce a particular utterance.[43] The term is familiar in both Hebrew and Aramaic (*'amen*), as marking a strong solemn affirmation of what has been said, most typically in a formal liturgical context.[44] But Jesus' usage is quite distinctive. For whereas in regular usage 'Amen' affirmed or endorsed the words of someone else, in the Jesus tradition the

see B. Witherington III, *The Christology of Jesus* (Minneapolis: Fortress Press, 1990), pp. 216–21; and M.M. Thompson, *The Promise of the Father: Jesus and God in the New Testament* (Louisville, KY: Westminster/John Knox Press, 2000), pp. 21–34.

38. It will suffice for present purposes to refer to the discussion and bibliography in my *Jesus and the Spirit* (London: SCM Press, 1975), pp. 26–34.

39. See the contribution in this volume by Wendy North, 'Monotheism and the Gospel of John: Jesus, Moses, and the Law'.

40. E. Käsemann, 'The Problem of the Historical Jesus' (1954), in E. Käsemann, *Essays on New Testament Themes* (London: SCM Press, 1964), pp. 15–47 (here, pp. 37–45).

41. Bultmann's argument that 5.21–22, 27–28, and 33–37 have been drawn from pre-Matthean tradition and 'have given rise to analogous formulations, in which unattached dominical sayings have found a home' (*The History of the Synoptic Tradition* [trans. John Marsh; Oxford: Basil Blackwell, 1963; German, 1921], pp. 134–36) has proved very influential.

42. E.g. Käsemann, 'Problem', p. 40; M. Hengel, *The Charismatic Leader and His Followers* (trans. James Greig; Edinburgh: T. & T. Clark, 1981; German, 1968), p. 47.

43. E.g. Mk 3.28; 8.12; 9.1 pars.; 9.41 par.; 10.15 pars.; 10.29 pars.; 11.23; 12.43 par.; 13.30 pars.; 14.9 par.; 14.18 par.; 14.25; 14.30 pars.

44. Num. 5.22; Deut. 27.15–26; 1 Kgs 1.36; 1 Chron. 16.36; Neh. 5.13; 8.6; Pss. 41.13; 72.19; 89.52; 106.48; Jer. 11.5; 28.6. In the DSS the formula is usually the double 'Amen, Amen' (e.g. 1QS col. i, line 20; col. ii, lines 10 and 18).

term is used without exception to introduce and endorse Jesus' *own* words.[45] Here again, of course, we can hardly exclude the likelihood that in performances of the tradition the motif was extended within the tradition. But neither can it be seriously doubted that the usage began with Jesus and was a distinctive feature of his own teaching style. And an obvious corollary lies close to hand: that Jesus used this formula to call attention to what he was about to say and to give it added weight.[46]

The point could readily be elaborated in terms of the impact made by Jesus' teaching, summed up by Mark in the first public response to Jesus' mission: 'What is this? A new teaching with authority (κατ' ἐξουσίαν)' (Mk 1.27)! Or in terms of Jesus' authority in exorcism: 'I command' (Mk 9.25), rather than the usual, 'I adjure you by...' (that is, by some other authority).[47] Or in terms of C.H. Dodd's observation that the 'I say to you' seems to transcend the typically prophetic 'Thus says the Lord', just as, possibly, the 'I came' transcends the prophetic 'I was sent'.[48] Or even in terms that Jesus saw himself as the emissary of divine Wisdom[49] – that is, not just as a teacher of wisdom, but as the eschatological spokesman for Wisdom, acting in God's stead?[50] But what does it all amount to in terms of the question under discussion?

Certainly it can be argued that Jesus claimed to speak with divine authority,[51] as 'spokesman for God'.[52] But, once again, it is difficult to push the argument from difference in degree to difference in kind. In the end of the day we are still talking in terms of a Jesus authorized by God, of Jesus inspired by God's Spirit. This too is hardly inconsistent with a Jesus who confessed God to be one and who worshipped God accordingly.

4.3. In the latest phase of the quest of the historical Jesus one of the most interesting developments has been the reassessment of the tradition that Jesus spoke of himself as '*the son of man*' and the fresh attempt to argue that he did so by referring to the great vision of Dan. 7.9–14. I leave to one side two debates. One on whether the formulation *bar ʿᵉnasa* ('the son of man') was actually used by Jesus;

45. Jeremias, *Prayers*, pp. 112–15; see also Fitzmyer, *Luke*, pp. 536–37.

46. See also Theissen and Merz, *Historical Jesus*, pp. 523–24.

47. 4Q560 col. ii, lines 5–6; Acts 19.13; Josephus, *Ant.* 8.47; *PGM* 3.36–37; 4.289, 3019–20, 3046; and 7.242.

48. C.H. Dodd, 'Jesus as Teacher and Prophet', in G.K.A. Bell and A. Deissmann (eds.), *Mysterium Christi* (London: Longmans, 1930), pp. 53–66 (here p. 63).

49. Lk. 7.35/(Mt. 11.19); Mt. 11.25–27/Lk. 10.21–22; Lk. 11.49–51/(Mt. 23.34–36); see further my *Christology in the Making* (London: SCM Press, 1980, 2nd edn, 1989), pp. 197–204.

50. See further M. Hengel, 'Jesus as Messianic Teacher of Wisdom and the Beginnings of Christology', in M. Hengel, *Studies in Early Christology* (Edinburgh: T. & T. Clark, 1995), pp. 75–87.

51. 'Here is a consciousness of rank which lays claim to divine authority' (Jeremias, *Prayers*, p. 115).

52. Mk 9.37/Lk. 9.48; Mt. 10.40; Lk. 10.16; Sanders does not hesitate to affirm that 'Jesus claimed to be spokesman for God' (*Jesus and Judaism* [London: SCM Press, 1985], pp. 271 and 281); see also Witherington, *Christology*, pp. 142–43.

the testimony of the Jesus tradition (the phrase appearing only on Jesus' lips) should put that issue beyond doubt. And the second on whether the phrase referred to humankind generally or could include a self-reference; a rendering like 'one', 'someone', 'a man like me', probably catches its force as used by Jesus.[53]

The relevance of Jesus' use of 'the son of man' terminology for our question can be focused in a single passage – Mk 14.62 and parallels.

Matthew 26.63–66	*Mark 14.61–64*	*Luke 22.67–71*
Then the high priest said to him, 'I put you under oath before the living God, tell us if you are the Messiah, the Son of God.' 64 Jesus said to him, 'You have said so. But I tell you, From now on <u>you will see the Son of Man</u> <u>seated at the right hand of the</u> <u>Power and coming on the clouds of heaven.</u>' [65]	Again the high priest asked him, 'Are you the Messiah, the Son of the Blessed One?' [62] Jesus said, 'I am; and <u>you will see the Son of Man</u> <u>seated at the right hand of the Power, and coming</u> with <u>the clouds of heaven.</u>' [63]	[67] They said, 'If you are the Messiah, tell us'. He replied, 'If I tell you, you will not believe; [68] and if I question you, you will not answer. [69] But from now on <u>the Son of Man</u> will be <u>seated at the right hand of the power</u> of God.' [70] All of them asked, 'Are you, then, the Son of God?' He said to them, 'You say that I am'.
Then <u>the high priest tore his</u> garments, saying, 'He has blasphemed! <u>Why do we still</u> <u>need witnesses? You have</u> now <u>heard his blasphemy.</u> [66] <u>What is your</u> verdict?' They answered, 'He <u>deserves</u> <u>death.</u>'	Then <u>the high priest tore his</u> clothes and said, '<u>Why do we still need</u> <u>witnesses?</u> [64] <u>You have</u> <u>heard his</u> <u>blasphemy! What is your</u> decision?' All of them condemned him as <u>deserving</u> <u>death.</u>	71 Then they said, 'What further testimony do we need? We have heard it ourselves from his own lips!'

Leaving to one side problems which will be familiar to anyone who has studied the passage carefully,[54] we can focus the issue on the charge of blasphemy made by the high priest (Mk 14.64 par.). If that charge is indeed historical, though many doubt it,[55] what could have provoked it? The obvious answer in terms of the narrative itself is the preceding son of man saying, understood, presumably as a self-reference allusion to Daniel's vision. For in that case it could have been taken as a claim by Jesus to be the one who fulfilled the man-like figure's role (Daniel 7.13) in taking the second throne beside the Ancient of Days in heaven (7.9, 14).[56]

53. For fuller discussion see my *Jesus Remembered*, ch. 16 sections 3–5.

54. E.g. N. Perrin, 'Mark 14.62: The End Product of a Christian Pesher Tradition?', *NTS* 12 (1965–1966), pp. 150–55, reprinted with a postscript in *A Modern Pilgrimage in New Testament Christology* (Philadelphia: Fortress Press, 1974), pp. 1–22; R.E. Brown, *The Death of the Messiah: From Gethsemane to the Grave: A Commentary on the Passion Narratives in the Four Gospels* (2 vols.; New York: Doubleday, 1994), p. 496 (God as 'the Power') and 521–22 ('Son of the Blessed').

55. See again discussion in Brown, *Death*, pp. 522–26.

56. A recently popular view: e.g. J. Schaberg, 'Mark 14.62: Early Christian Merkabah Im-

There is more to be said for this suggestion than initially meets the eye. We know that a form of mysticism was being practised within late second Temple Judaism, focused particularly on the chariot throne of God (Ezek. 1).[57] We know that a century later even the great rabbi Akiba was accused of profaning the Shekinah for a similar speculation – that the second throne (of Dan. 7.9) was for the Messiah.[58] Also that Akiba was linked into the fascinating tradition of four who shared a mystical experience in which they entered paradise (*t. Hag.* 2.3–4). One of the other three was reported to have hailed the second enthroned figure as a second power in heaven; and for this he is condemned in rabbinic tradition as an arch-heretic, because he denied the Jewish axiom of the unity/oneness of God.[59] Could it be, then, that what Jesus said was heard in a similar way, as blasphemy, that is as claiming a status which belongs only to God, that is, as in effect denying the unity of God, denying the first principle of Jewish religion?

The problem with this line of argument is that it has to assume a sensitivity with regard to the oneness of God (monotheism in that sense) which is attested only for the period following the disaster of 70 CE. And this was a period when embryonic rabbinic Judaism was beginning to define (its) Judaism more narrowly to exclude other forms of Judaism that had previously flourished during the late Second Temple period. In that drawing of boundaries more tightly round a Torah-focused Judaism, the kind of speculation which we find in Jewish apocalypses regarding the deity and his heavenly agents was also ruled out. Conversely, the kind of speculation subsequently ruled out may well have been less unacceptable in the period prior to 70 CE.[60]

All this has direct bearing on the (albeit contested) argument that Jesus did indeed draw on Daniel's vision as a way of imaging his own confidence in God's vindication (the whole point of Dan. 7). For in that case, such a use of Dan. 7 might not have been so exceptional at the time of Jesus. More to the point, such a reference to

agery?', in J. Marcus and M.L. Soards (eds.), *Apocalyptic and the New Testament: Essays in Honor of J. Louis Martyn* (JSNTSup, 24; Sheffield: JSOT Press, 1989), pp. 69–94; C.A. Evans, 'In What Sense "Blasphemy"? Jesus before Caiaphas in Mark 14.61–64', in C.A. Evans, *Jesus and his Contemporaries: Comparative Studies* (Leiden: E.J. Brill, 1995), pp. 407–34 (here pp. 419–21); N.T. Wright, *Jesus and the Victory of God* (London: SPCK, 1996), pp. 642–44; Davies and Allison, *Matthew*, 3.534; D.L. Bock, *Blasphemy and Exaltation in Judaism and the Final Examination of Jesus* (WUNT, II/106; Tübingen: J.C.B. Mohr [Paul Siebeck], 1998), pp. 113–237.

57.   There are already hints to that effect in Sir. 49.8 and *1 En.* 14.18–20. The Qumran *Songs of the Sabbath Sacrifice* imply something to the same effect being practised in the worship of Qumran. Paul himself may have been a practitioner of such mysticism (2 Cor. 12.2–4) (J.W. Bowker, '"Merkabah" Visions and the Visions of Paul', *JSS* 16 [1971], pp. 157–73). The great rabbi Yohannan ben Zakkai, founder of the rabbinic school at Yavneh following the disaster of 70 CE, is also attested to have been a practitioner (*t. Hag.* 2.1).

58.   *b. Hag.* 14a; *b. Sanh.* 38b.

59.   *b. Hag.* 15a; *3 En.* 16. There is a direct line of thought between Dan. 7's 'one like a son of man', Enoch's identification with the Son of Man (*1 En.* 71.14), and Metatron in *3 En.* 3–16 (note particularly 4.2 and 16).

60.   See further my *The Partings of the Ways between Christianity and Judaism* (London: SCM Press, 1991), chs. 10–11.

Dan. 7 need not necessarily have rung so many alarm bells for those espousing a self-consciously monotheistic credo. And even if the argument is pressed that the utterance does express an out of the ordinary self-consciousness, it should not be forgotten that this is remembered as almost Jesus' last public utterance, and not necessarily any kind of qualification (or refutation) of the monotheism more clearly expressed earlier in his mission (see section 3 above). Nor should it be forgotten that the best attested utterance of Jesus subsequent to Mk 14.62 and prior to his death is Mk 15.34: '*Eloi, Eloi, lema sabachthani*; my God, my God, why have you forsaken me?'

5. *Conclusion*

So, what is the answer to our question: Was Jesus a monotheist? The obvious, indeed the only obvious answer to be given is, Yes: Jesus was a monotheist; he confessed God as one; he proclaimed the one God's royal rule; he prayed to and encouraged his disciples to pray to this God. The circumstantial evidence reviewed above (section 2) strongly disposes the questioner towards that answer. And the clearest evidence, in Jesus' own God-talk (section 3), can hardly be interpreted in any other way.

Do the data reviewed in section 4 necessitate a qualification of that answer? Such indications as there may be of Jesus' own self-understanding include some of the most contested material within the Jesus tradition (contested in terms of providing access to Jesus' own claims). It certainly can be argued that they indicate how well rooted within the Jesus tradition the subsequent developing Christian perceptions of Christ are; that is, both the roots that stretch back into Jesus' own lived-out but otherwise largely implicit claims for himself, and the roots already watered by earliest Christian reflection.

The point for us would then be that something of the same tensions which are a feature of *Christian* monotheism are already apparent in the earliest phases of the Jesus tradition. For Christians continue to assert that they are monotheists, that God is one, even if their sophisticated attempts to state what they mean (unity in trinity) leave both Jew and Muslim at best puzzled or simply unconvinced. We may be confident that Jesus himself would have wanted to make the same assertion ('The Lord our God is one Lord'), even if some of the claims implicit in his life and teaching can be taken to point to a more complex apprehension of divine reality and of his own relation to it than can easily fit within a simple definition of 'monotheism'. The same, of course, can be said of much of the speculation about divine reality in late Second Temple Judaism. But it was only in emerging Christianity that such speculation focused on a figure of such a recent past and with such far-reaching consequences in apprehension of the deity.

YHWH TEXTS AND MONOTHEISM IN PAUL'S CHRISTOLOGY

David B. Capes, Houston Baptist University, Texas

The following essay will consider Paul's use of Old Testament YHWH texts and offer some suggestions with regard to understanding his monotheism and Christology.[1] A YHWH text is one that refers directly to the divine name (יהוה) in the Hebrew Bible. Since Paul writes to his churches in Greek, the focus of this inquiry will be Old Testament quotations and allusions containing the *kyrios* predicate in which *kyrios* translates the divine name. This investigation will argue that Paul consciously and unambiguously applies to Jesus sacred words and texts originally reserved for YHWH, the unspeakable name of God. It will consider, furthermore, how it is that Paul includes Jesus within the name of God. This practice, along with other patterns of religious devotion, points to the existence of a high Christology in the first extant documents of the Christian movement.

The State of the Text at the Time of Paul

A natural question to ask at this point is: What is the state of the biblical text during the time of Paul? In particular, how would the divine name appear in the texts Paul encountered? Would there have been an opportunity for Paul to confuse the name of Israel's God with a title for a man in authority? Given Paul's own statement that he is a 'Hebrew of the Hebrews' (Phil. 3.5) and given that Paul wrote his letters in Greek, the focus here will be on the state of Greek and Hebrew texts of the Old Testament.[2] Earlier work on Paul has focused on whether Paul's Old Testament citations were closer to the Hebrew masoretic text or the Septuagint.[3] The assumption is, of course, that in existence were fixed Hebrew and Greek text traditions from which Paul drew. Any variations in the quotations are understood as Paul's own interpretative comments or possibly a memory lapse – assuming he quotes

---

1. I wish to thank Prof Loren Stuckenbruck for the opportunity to re-present some ideas I originally set out in *Old Testament Yahweh Texts in Paul's Christology* (WUNT II/47; Tübingen: J.C.B. Mohr [Paul Siebeck], 1992). The lecture, given to the New Testament Research Seminar at the University of Durham in March 2000, allowed me to rethink and respond to some of the work of others.

2. T.H. Lim, *Holy Scripture in the Qumran Commentaries and Paul's Letters* (Oxford: Clarendon Press, 1997), p. 148, concludes that Paul was tri-lingual, competent in Hebrew, Aramaic and Greek.

3. See for example E.E. Ellis, *Paul's Use of the Old Testament* (Grand Rapids: Baker Book House, 1957).

from memory. Recent assessments are challenging this assumption and show that the Hebrew and Greek biblical texts were not fixed at this period. In particular, the biblical manuscripts found among the Dead Sea Scrolls demonstrate the fluidity of the textual tradition within a single community's library.[4] It is reasonable to assume that a similar fluidity existed among other Hebrew and Greek Bible texts in the period. Indeed, manuscript evidence proves this to have been the case.

With regard to the divine name, scrolls found in the Judean desert present an interesting picture.[5] Among the Hebrew manuscripts the tetragrammaton (יהוה) is present in a number of biblical and non-biblical manuscripts. Most copies of Isaiah from cave four contain the tetragram written in Aramaic script (e.g. 4QIsa[a], 4QIsa[b], 4QIsa[d], 4QIsa[e], 4QIsa[f]). One copy, however, 4QIsa[c], contains the tetragram written in palaeo-Hebrew. In addition, it is peculiar that prepositions and prefixed conjunctions to YHWH are also written in palaeo-Hebrew. One should note as well that forms of *elohim* are written in the same archaic script within this manuscript.[6] The famous Isaiah scroll from cave 1 (1QIsa[a]) has the divine name in Aramaic script, but it also has the divine name written as four dots (text to 40.7; 42.6). In some places *adonay* is written above the Aramaic YHWH (to 28.16; 30.15; 65.13) as a gloss. The *Habakkuk Pesher*, although it is not strictly speaking a biblical manuscript, provides important evidence by representing YHWH in palaeo-Hebrew script (1QpHab col. vi, line 14). The sectarian document, the *Community Rule*, represents the divine name with a series of four dots in its quotation of Isaiah 40.3 in a practice similar to the great Isaiah scroll (1QS col. viii, line 14).[7]

Greek manuscripts from the period reveal a similar fluidity when dealing with the divine name. In 4QLXXLev[b] the divine name is written IAΩ with a space before and after the name; otherwise the manuscript is copied in *scriptio continua*. In 4QLXXNum the divine name is not extant among the extant fragments. Yet space would have allowed for either *kyrios* or YHWH (Aramaic script) to be written; IAΩ would appear to have been too short.[8] In 8HevXIIgr (a Greek Minor Prophets scroll from Nahal Hever, dated from the late first century BCE) the divine name is written in palaeo-Hebrew (twenty-eight examples altogether).

In *Papyrus Fouad* 266 the original scribe leaves large spaces framed by a dot on either side of the space. YHWH is added in Aramaic script, apparently by another hand, in the spaces indicated by the dots. In the course of copying, one space is left

4.   See, for example, E.C. Ulrich, 'The Qumran Biblical Scrolls – The Scriptures of Late Second Temple Judaism', in T.H. Lim (ed.), *The Dead Sea Scrolls in their Historical Context* (Edinburgh: T. &. T. Clark, 2000), pp. 67–87.

5.   For other representations of the divine name in the scrolls, see D.W. Parry, '4QSama and the Tetragrammaton', in D.W. Parry and S.D. Ricks (eds.), *Current Research and Technological Developments on the Dead Sea Scrolls* (STDJ, 20; Leiden: E.J. Brill, 1996), pp. 106–125.

6.   E. Ulrich et al, *Qumran Cave 4: The Prophets* (DJD, 15; Oxford: Clarendon Press, 1997).

7.   See Y. Yadin, *The Temple Scroll*. II. *Text and Commentary* (Jerusalem: Israel Exploration Society, 1983). The composer or copyist of the Temple Scroll has no qualms about writing out the divine name in Aramaic script like the rest of the document.

8.   P.K. Skehan *et al.*, *Qumran Cave 4: Paleo-Hebrew and Greek Biblical Manuscripts* (DJD, 9; Oxford: Clarendon, 1992), pp. 168 and 188.

blank. A similar procedure may be observed in *Papyrus Oxyr.* 656 where *kyrios* is added by a second hand.[9] There are also Greek manuscripts in which the divine name is represented by ΠΙΠΙ, [10] presumably because of its similar appearance to the Hebrew word.

To sum up the manuscript evidence, we have the following representations of the divine name:

In Hebrew texts

1. YHWH written in Aramaic script
2. YHWH written in Palaeo-Hebrew script
3. YHWH represented by four dots
4. YHWH in Aramaic script glossed by adonay

In Greek texts

1. YHWH written in Aramaic script (*Pap. Fouad* 266)
2. YHWH written in palaeo-Hebrew (8HevXIIgr)
3. YHWH transliterated as ΙΑΩ (4QLXXLev^b)
4. YHWH represented as ΠΙΠΙ
5. YHWH translated or written as κύριος (*Pap. Oxyr.* 656)

Philo also provides important evidence for the state of the text around the first century. Generally, the Alexandrian exegete writes the divine name as κύριος in his biblical quotations and his commentary. Some assume this provides evidence that the Greek manuscripts he employs contain the *kyrios* predicate for YHWH. The problem for this case, however, is that Christian scholars are responsible for copying and transmitting Philo's words to later generations. George Howard surveys the evidence and concludes: 'Although it is improbable that Philo varied from the custom of writing the Tetragram when quoting from Scripture, it is likely that he used the word κύριος when making a secondary reference to the divine name in his exposition'.[11] James Royse, however, redirects the issue from the state of the biblical texts to the 'custom' of quoting from Scripture.[12] Indeed Royse's careful analysis of the manuscript tradition and Philo's exposition indicates that (1) the exegete knows and reads biblical manuscripts in which the tetragram is written in palaeo-Hebrew or Aramaic script and not translated by *kyrios* and that (2) he quotes scripture in the same way he would have pronounced it, that is, by translating it as *kyrios*. As evidence Royse cites the practice mentioned by Origen that while the

9. E. Tov, *The Greek Minor Prophets Scroll from Nahal Hever (8HevXIIgr)* (DJD, 8; Oxford: Clarendon Press, 1990), p. 12.

10. E. Hatch and H.A. Redpath, 'ΠΙΠΙ', in *A Concordance to the Septuagint* (2 vols.; Grand Rapids: Baker Book House, 1983, repr. 1892–1906), II, p. 1135. See also H.A. Redpath, *Concordance to the Septuagint and Other Greek Versions of the Old Testament: Supplement* (Oxford: Clarendon Press, 1906), p. 126.

11. G. Howard, 'The Tetragram and the New Testament', *JBL* 96 (1977), p. 72.

12. J. Royse, 'Philo, ΚΥΡΙΟΣ, and the Tetragrammaton', in D.T. Runia (ed.), *The Studia Philonica Annual: Studies in Hellenistic Judaism*, Volume III (Atlanta: Scholars Press, 1991), pp. 167–83 (here p. 175).

tetragrammaton is written, κύριος is vocalized (Origen, *Selecta in Psalmos* 2.2 [PG 12.1104B4–9]). He also cites a sixth century Aquila manuscript from a Cairo genizah in which the tetragram is written by the *nomina sacra* κυ.[13] We should also add the more ambiguous statement made in Mishnah *Sotah* (*m. Sot.* 7.6) that when reciting the priestly blessing (Num. 6.24–26) in the Temple they pronounce the Name as written, but in the Diaspora, they substitute a word. The practice of substituting a word for the Name in the synagogues seems well attested. Thus the evidence suggests that (1) Greek biblical manuscripts employed by Philo contain the tetragram and (2) the Alexandrian exegete quotes scripture in his writings as it is customarily pronounced. Therefore Philo, not Christian copyists, is likely responsible for the presence of *kyrios* in his biblical quotations and exposition.[14]

A number of scholars take note of the variety of ways the tetragram is written in Greek manuscripts and offer some analysis for the extant manuscript evidence. In particular, P.W. Skehan reconstructs four stages in the development. First, in the oldest Greek manuscripts YHWH is represented by ΙΑΩ (4QLXXLev[b]). This may have been read 'Yaho' (= יהו), which is attested as early as the fifth century BCE. Second, the Name came to be written in Aramaic script (*Pap. Fouad* 266). Third, it was written in palaeo-Hebrew. Fourth, *kyrios* was used to translate YHWH in the final, Christian stage of development.[15] Martin Hengel offers a similar scheme for the use of *kyrios* for the divine name in the LXX tradition.[16] Albert Pietersma provides an alternative reading of the evidence and describes an 'archaizing process' in the writing of the divine name that takes place at Qumran. This may well coincide with reactions against the encroachment of Hellenistic ways. Indeed he notes: 'The palaeohebrew tetragram in Greek witnesses is not the oldest but apparently the youngest. Both in the Hebrew MSS from Qumran and in our earliest Greek MSS there is clear evidence that the divine name was the object of revisionary activity'.[17] Pietersma's own work focuses on Pentateuch manuscripts among the Dead Sea documents. Yet he thinks there is sufficient warrant to conclude that early on translators rendered the Name as *kyrios* and that later revisionary activities replaced it with the transliterations of Greek, Aramaic and palaeo-Hebraic renderings of the divine name in Greek manuscripts.

The above discussion allows us to venture several conclusions.[18] The examples cited – and there are others – indicate that there is no one way the divine name

13. Royse, 'Philo, ΚΥΡΙΟΣ, and the Tetragrammaton', p. 176.

14. Note the comment by N. Dahl and A. Segal, 'Philo and the Rabbis on the Names of God', *JSJ* 9 (1978), p. 1 n. 2: 'While preserved Jewish fragments of the Greek version have some form of transliteration for the tetragrammaton, Philo must have read *kyrios* in his texts'.

15. P.K. Skehan, 'The Divine Name at Qumran, in the Masada Scroll, and in the Septuagint', *BIOSCS* 13 (1980), pp. 238–44.

16. M. Hengel, 'The Interpenetration of Judaism and Hellenism in the pre-Maccabean Period', in W.D. Davies and L. Finkelstein (eds.), *The Cambridge History of Judaism*. II. *The Hellenistic Age* (Cambridge: Cambridge University Press, 1989), pp. 167–228 (here pp. 197–98).

17. A. Pietersma, 'KYRIOS or Tetragram: A Renewed Quest for the Original LXX', in A. Pietersma and C. Cox (eds.), *De Septuaginta: Studies in Honour of John William Wevers on his Sixty-Fifth Birthday* (Mississauga, ON: Benben, 1984), pp. 85–101 (here p. 99).

18. Earlier (Capes, *Old Testament Yahweh Texts*, pp. 37–43), I argued that the divine name was

was written in Greek or Hebrew biblical texts around the time of Paul. This would include entire scrolls held in synagogue collections or excerpts used for polemical, liturgical or devotional purposes.[19] What is evident, however, is that the divine name and in some cases the spaces and letters around the divine name are treated differently, with great reverence. The archaizing tendency of writing the Name in palaeo-Hebrew provides early material evidence for the reverence accorded the divine name. Other evidence for this reverence is provided by (1) the prostration of supplicants when the High priest speaks the divine name on the Day of Atonement in the textual citation of Lev. 16.30 (*m. Yom.* 6.2; see also the *proskynesis* of the faithful when Simon ben Onias utters the divine name of the priestly blessing [Num. 6.24–26] in Sir. 50.20–21; cf. *m. Sot.* 7.6); (2) the custom of vocalizing the divine name in temple ceremonies but using a substitute word in the provinces (*m. Sot* 7.6); (3) the cautions expressed regarding speaking the divine name (Josephus, *Ant.* 2.275–276; Philo, *Vit. Mos.* 2.114);[20] (4) the threat of capital punishment against those who pronounce the Name (*m. Sanh* 7.5).[21] Paul no doubt encounters this textual diversity and reverence accorded the divine name in the synagogues he attends in his pre- and post-conversion life. Furthermore, the apostle would have been aware that *kyrios* in the biblical tradition often translated the divine name. When Paul quoted a *kyrios* text and applied it to Jesus, he would have been fully cognisant of the theological implications associated with the divine name. Philo provides contemporaneous evidence of an exegete who encounters YHWH in the biblical text but quotes it as *kyrios* in the fullest sense of divinity. Any appropriation of these texts to describe the person or work of Christ would carry significant christological import.

YHWH Texts in Paul's Letters

Thirteen times in Paul's undisputed letters the apostle quotes Old Testament YHWH texts. The following chart represents my own conclusions regarding how he utilizes them:

most often translated *kyrios* in Greek biblical manuscripts at the time of Paul. I now believe this previous judgement to be in error.

19. Lim, *Qumran Commentaries and Paul's Letters*, p. 156, analyses excerpts from the DSS and Paul's letters, concluding that there likely existed 'a number of biblical anthologies which circulated in Jewish and Christian circles' at the time. These excerpts would have contained important and frequently needed biblical themes.

20. Philo (*Vit. Mos.* 2.114) speaks of the name of four letters which only those with purified ears can hear and purified tongues can speak and only in the holy place.

21. D.L. Bock, *Blasphemy and Exaltation in Judaism and the Final Examination of Jesus* (WUNT, II/106; Tübingen: J.C.B. Mohr [Paul Siebeck], 1998), p. 111, writes: 'The official rabbinic position is that the use of the divine Name constitutes the only clear case of capital blasphemy (*m. Sanh* 7.5).' Though the Mishnah was not codified until around 200 CE, this rule of blasphemy may extend to the first century as well. If not, we can still understand that the faithful would exercise care in their use of the name. Bock's monograph is the clearest and most comprehensive collection of blasphemy texts.

YHWH Texts with God as Referent	YHWH Texts with Christ as Referent
Romans 4.7–8	Romans 10.13
Romans 9.27, 29	Romans 14.11
Romans 11.34	1 Corinthians 1.31
Romans 15.9, 11	1 Corinthians 2.16
1 Corinthians 3.20	1 Corinthians 10.26
2 Corinthians 6.18	2 Corinthians 10.17

Allusive uses of YHWH texts that are made to refer to Christ include 2 Cor. 3.16 and Phil. 2.10–11. Whether a passage refers to God or Christ cannot be decided based upon the presence or absence of *kyrios*; each must be worked out through contextual and exegetical analysis. The simple assumption that *kyrios* in Paul is used christologically except in Old Testament quotations and allusions does not stand up to the close scrutiny.[22]

Lucian Cerfaux addresses Paul's exegetical appropriation of YHWH texts,[23] but he does not distinguish between quotations and allusions. He classifies them as 'texts applied to God' and 'texts applied to Christ'. He concludes that when Paul quotes YHWH texts explicitly, the apostle often prefaces them with introductory formulae (e.g. Rom. 4.7–8; 9.27–28, 29) and he retains *kyrios* as a patrological title. Quotations with God as referent have greater verbal affinity to the biblical text, while christological appropriations quote more loosely. Cerfaux lists four contexts in which Old Testament YHWH texts retain a patrological focus: (1) the call of God, (2) justification, (3) the role of Gentiles and (4) the fundamental rights of God.[24]

Cerfaux acknowledges that Paul does utilize YHWH texts and refer them to Christ, but he feels the practice is rare and generally does not involve 'explicit' quotations. Rather they are loose quotations and/or expressions like 'the table of the Lord', 'the fear of the Lord', or 'the day of the Lord'. Yet Cerfaux does admit that Paul at times interprets these texts christologically and reads *kyrios* as Christ. He distinguishes three categories in which Paul applies *kyrios* texts to Christ. First, he does so in descriptions of the parousia (Rom. 10.13; Phil. 2.10–11; 1 Thess. 2.19; 4.6; 2 Thess. 1.9, 12; 2.8, 14). These, Cerfaux argues, are not explicit quotations but they do seem to refer to some type of theophanic event. Included within this category are passages dealing with judgment, eschatological deliverance and glory. Second, Paul applies *kyrios*/YHWH texts to Christ in typological readings of the Old Testament (1 Cor. 10.9, 22; 2 Cor. 3.16). Third, since he considers Christ to be the wisdom of God, the apostle applies *kyrios* to Christ in texts that speak of

---

22. For a fuller analysis of these texts and the rationale for the exegetical decisions see Capes, *Old Testament Yahweh Texts*, pp. 90–159.

23. L. Cerfaux, '<<Kyrios>> dans les citations pauliniennes de l'Ancien Testament', first published in *Ephemerides Theologicae Lovanienses* 20 (1943), pp. 5–17; also available in *Recueil Lucien Cerfaux*, 1 (Gembloux: J. Duculot, 1954).

24. *Recueil Lucien Cerfaux*, pp. 177 and 186–87; see also *idem, Christ in the Theology of Paul*, trans. G. Webb and A. Walker (French, 1954; New York: Herder & Herder, 1959), pp. 470–72.

the glory and wisdom of God (1 Cor. 1.31; 2.16: 2 Cor. 10.17). For Cerfaux, Paul's exegetical practice means the apostle to the Gentiles understands Christ as a divine functionary; yet God remains supreme. It is likely, Cerfaux thinks, that these exegetical manoeuvrings were going on prior to Paul's conversion.[25]

Unfortunately scholars have followed Cerfaux's work uncritically. There are a number of problems with his assumptions and conclusions. First, Cerfaux classifies the 'texts applied to God' and 'texts applied to Christ' based on scant contextual and exegetical analysis. A more rigorous investigation would lead to a different appraisal of Paul's practice. Related to this is, second, the assumption that, unless specified otherwise, *kyrios* in Paul's citations refers to God.[26] My own work reveals the opposite conclusion. Unless otherwise specified, *kyrios* in Paul's quotations refers to Christ. When Paul wants the reader to understand God and not the Lord Jesus, he signals that clearly in the context (e.g. Rom. 4.7–8; 11.34; 15.9, 11; 1 Cor. 3.20; 2 Cor. 6.18). Third, Cerfaux blurs the line between an explicit and a verbatim quotation. For Paul an explicit quotation appears to have had little to do with verbal affinity to a known text; it has rather to do with his exegetical purpose. 1 Cor. 1.31 provides a good example. Although the wording of this quotation (Jer. 9.22–23) differs significantly from the LXX, the introductory formula signals Paul's intent to quote the text explicitly. In fact, such decisions are rendered problematic because manuscript evidence indicates the text tradition of the Greek Old Testament is not fixed.[27] Therefore, basing a decision on how close Paul's quotation is to the wording of the LXX or the MT does not prove helpful; it may in fact skew the results.

Now let me offer another analysis of Paul's exegetical practice. First, it is noteworthy that Paul could preface both patrological and christological uses of YHWH texts with introductory formulae. This clearly marks his intent to engage in explicit citation with either God or Christ in view.[28] Second, as indicated above, the fluid nature of the manuscript tradition at the time of Paul means it is extremely difficult to determine whether a quotation is a verbatim or a loose quotation. It is therefore unwise to assume that quotations close to any known version would more likely be patrologically directed. Third, whether Paul intends God or Christ as referent must be worked out through a rigorous exegetical and contextual analysis. We find that Paul reserves YHWH texts for God primarily in theocentric passages such as Rom. 9–11. Additionally, when Paul wants the reader to understand the Father rather than the Lord Jesus, he states it clearly in the context and/or an introductory formula. When Paul is discussing justification (Rom. 4.7–8), divine wisdom (Rom. 11.34; 1 Cor. 3.20), the Fatherhood of God (2 Cor. 6.18) and the relationship of Jews and Gentiles (Rom. 9.27, 29; 15.9, 11), he customarily utilizes the YHWH text to refer to God the Father. Furthermore, whenever other descriptive titles are added to the *kyrios* predicate, such as 'Lord of hosts' or 'Lord Almighty', he retains these as patrologically directed (e.g. Rom. 9.27–29; 2 Cor. 6.18). In contrast, he seldom

---

25. Cerfaux, 'Kyrios', pp. 178 and 187.

26. W. Foerster, 'κύριος', in *TDNT*, III, pp. 1081–1098 (here p. 1087).

27. Capes, *Old Testament Yahweh Texts*, pp. 160–63.

28. For the christological use of a YHWH text with introductory formula see Rom. 14.11 and 1 Cor. 1.31.

offers a straightforward statement that he intends to refer to Christ. Perhaps this is due to the fact that Paul uses *kyrios* overwhelmingly as a christological title. The apostle applies YHWH texts to Christ in passages that are christologically focused under the following themes: (a) the universality of the gospel (Rom. 10.13; Phil. 2.10–11); (b) eschatological judgment and parousia (e.g. Rom. 10.13; 14.11; 1 Thess. 3.13; 4.6; 2 Cor. 3.16); (c) Christian ethics and belongingness to Christ (Rom. 14.11; 1 Thess. 4.6); (d) divine wisdom as 'Christ crucified' (1 Cor. 1.31; 2.16);[29] (e) the Lord's Supper (1 Cor. 10.21, 26); (f) the role of the Spirit in the lives of believers (1 Cor. 2.16; 2 Cor. 3.16); and (g) Paul's apostolic authority (2 Cor. 3.16; 10.17; cf. 2 Tim. 2.19).

We turn our attention now to two representative examples of Paul's christological use of YHWH texts. The first, Joel 2.32 (LXX 3.5), which cited in Rom. 10.13, is largely undisputed. The interpretation of the second, Isa. 45.23, quoted in Rom. 14.11, is less certain; however, a close contextual analysis demonstrates that Paul has made use of it in reference to Christ. The apostle uses the same text allusively in Phil. 2.10–11 in a remarkable appropriation of honorific language directed at the exalted Jesus. As is well known, Isa. 45 is one of the most significant monotheistic passages in the Hebrew Bible.

Calling upon the Name of the Lord – Romans 10.13

In Rom. 10.13 Paul quotes Joel 2.32 (LXX 3.5) as he elaborates on his instruction that Christ is the goal of the Law (10.4) and that faith in the resurrected Lord is what ultimately commends all Jews and Gentiles to God. He writes:

> Πᾶς γὰρ ὃς ἄν ἐπικαλέσηται τὸ ὄνομα κυρίου σωθήσεται
> ('For everyone who calls on the name of the Lord shall be saved.')

The Septuagint reads:

> καὶ ἔσται πᾶς ὃς ἄν ἐπικαλέσηται τὸ ὄνομα κυρίου σωθήσεται
> ('And it shall be that everyone who calls on the name of the Lord shall be saved.')

Kyrios translates the divine name from the Hebrew tradition. In Joel the promise of deliverance regards a remnant of Israel prior to the Day of the Lord. The phrase πᾶς ὃς ἄν ('everyone who') appears to suggest that even loyal Diaspora Jews would be included in God's promise. Paul takes it as scriptural warrant for the inclusion of believing Gentiles along with faithful Jews. The omission of καὶ ἔσται ('and it shall be') from his version of the quotation could be due to textual fluidity or, more likely, to theological concerns. The apostle is convinced that 'the Day' has already dawned and that Jesus' death and resurrection inaugurate the new age. For the Old Testament prophet this vision belongs to the future.

---

29. Divine wisdom related to God stands in contrast to divine wisdom related to Christ. The latter has to do with the specifics of Christ's death, burial and resurrection. The former (Rom. 11.34; 1 Cor. 3.20) appears connected to God's mysterious plan of the ages. Yet the two are ultimately related in the divine wisdom and mystery.

There are four reasons for concluding that Paul applies this Old Testament YHWH text to Jesus. (1) *The Christological focus.* Whereas most of Rom. 9–11 is theocentric, the multiple references to Christ and the other christological applications of scripture (Isa. 28.16 and 8.14 in Rom. 9.33 and 10.11; Deut. 30.12, 14 in Rom. 10.6–7) in this context demonstrate a christological focus. (2) *The Resurrection emphasis.* The clear statement of the belief in and confession of the resurrection (10.7, 9) associates the *kyrios* title with Jesus. As is well known, Paul frequently relates the Lordship of Jesus with the resurrection (e.g. Rom. 1.3–4; 14.8–9; Phil. 2.6–11; cf. Rom. 8.34; Eph. 1.20; Col. 3.1). (3) *The Eschatological interest.* The verb tense in 10.9, 11, and 13 indicates that Paul understands that ultimate vindication (the reversal of shame) and salvation belong to the future. For him the 'Day of the Lord' will be the 'Day of the Lord Jesus Christ'. So it is likely he employs the *kyrios* title christologically in these ultimate matters. (4) *The Christological confession.* Romans 10.9 provides decisive evidence that Paul applies this YHWH text to Jesus. Therein he characterizes his gospel and the believers' response with the confession, 'Jesus is Lord'. He then proceeds to quote Joel 2.32, a text containing the *kyrios* predicate. That Jesus is *kyrios* in both the confession and the quotation can hardly be doubted.

In the Hebrew Bible the phrase 'call upon the name of the Lord' involves cultic activity such as altar building and sacrifice, prayer and petitions, worship and praise.[30] YHWH appears to call on his own name in the theophanic experience of Moses on Mt Sinai (Exod. 33.19; 34.5). Elsewhere the phrase distinguishes God's people as those who call upon his name (Isa. 41.25; cf. Jer. 10.25; Ps. 79.6). Carl Davis describes 'calling upon the name of the Lord' as 'a religious act which characterised and even determined God's people'.[31] In his JSNTS monograph Davis traces the theological association of Joel 2.32 in pre-Christian, Jewish texts and concludes the phrase refers to cultic activity directed to Israel's one God; there is little evidence it ever applies to any other figure. The only counter evidence he can cite is Josephus who reported that Jews invoked the name of Caesar to liberate them from the tyranny of Florus (*War* 2.294). Yet he notes Josephus uses ἀνακαλέω not ἐπικαλέω to refer to this plea.[32]

Paul's use of the phrase 'call upon the name of the Lord' (from Joel 2.32 [LXX 3.5]) in Rom. 10.13 is echoed in 1 Cor. 1.2 where Paul characterizes the universal Christian community as those who 'call on the name of our Lord Jesus Christ'. The application of Joel 2.32 to Christ with its attendant cultic associations appears to imply the worship of Jesus by Paul and his churches. The christological appropriation of these texts and the veneration of Christ practised in Paul's churches relate Jesus to God in surprising ways that move beyond a mere functional identity between them.

---

30. Gen. 12.8; 13.4; 26.25; 1 Kgs 18.24–26; Isa. 12.4–6; Pss. 105.1; 116.4, 13, 17.
31. C.J. Davis, *The Name and Way of the Lord: Old Testament Themes, New Testament Christology* (JSNTSup, 19; Sheffield: Sheffield Academic Press, 1996), p. 106.
32. Davis, *The Name and Way of the Lord*, pp. 109–39.

Every Knee Shall Bow – Romans 14.11 and Philippians 2.10–11

Isaiah 45.23 provides the apostle with a remarkable image from which he fashions his convictions about the significance of Christ. The image, the bowing of every knee and the confession of every tongue, characterizes a strictly monotheistic interest and its concomitant, the disdain for idolatry and polytheism. In Rom. 14.11 Paul offers this passage as support for his belief that all must appear before the judgement seat of God (14.10). He prefaces the quotation with a standard introductory formula, γέγραπται γάρ. He writes:

> Ζῶ ἐγὼ λέγει κύριος, ὅτι ἐμοὶ κάμψει πᾶν γόνυ καὶ πᾶσα γλῶσσα ἐξομολογήσεται τῷ θεῷ.

> 'As I live, says the Lord, to me will bow every knee and every tongue will confess to God.'

In the Septuagint Isaiah 45.23 reads:

> κατ' ἐμαυτοῦ ὀμνύω...ὅτι ἐμοὶ κάμψει πᾶν γόνυ καὶ ἐξομολογήσεται πᾶσα γλῶσσα τῷ θεῷ

> 'By myself I swear...that to me will bow every knee and will confess every tongue to God.'

Immediately apparent is the difference between the two oath formulae. Does this reflect the fluidity of the biblical manuscripts available or does Paul replace κατ' ἐμαυτοῦ ὀμνύω with Ζῶ ἐγὼ λέγει κύριος? Certainty in this cannot be attained. Cranfield suggests the difference is due to Paul's faulty memory, for the latter is a more standard oath-formula (e.g. Isa. 49.18).[33] In following Matthew Black,[34] I argue that Paul intends the association of the Lord who lives (Ζῶ ἐγώ, λέγει κύριος) in 14.11 with the Lord who died and came back to life so he might be Lord over the living and the dead (εἰς τοῦτο γὰρ Χριστὸς ἀπέθανεν καὶ ἔζησεν, ἵνα νεκρῶν καὶ ζώντων). This reading accounts both for the unusual use of ἔζησεν to refer to the resurrection and the possible substitution of one oath for the other. Accordingly the text should be understood as follows: 'As I live (again by the resurrection), says the Lord (Jesus), every knee will bow to me, and every tongue will confess to God (at the judgment seat)'. The first line of the prophetic couplet would refer to Christ (the bowing of the knee); the second would refer to God (confession and giving an account at the judgment seat). Κύριος in the oath formula would therefore properly refer to Christ who died and lived again.

In the Philippian hymn (2.6–11), Paul appropriates the same language of bowing and confessing from Isa. 45.23 and applies it to Jesus who is identified as Lord in the confession. We note here only the second part of the hymn:

---

33. C.E.B. Cranfield, *A Critical and Exegetical Commentary on the Epistle to the Romans* (2 vols.; ICC; Edinburgh: T. & T. Clark, 1975–1979), II, p. 710. There are four λέγει κύριος quotations in Paul (Rom. 12.9; 14.11; 1 Cor. 14.21; 2 Cor. 6.16–18).

34. M. Black, *Romans* (NCB; Greenwood, SC: Attic Press, 1973), p. 167.

> διὸ καὶ ὁ θεὸς αὐτὸν ὑπερύψωσεν καὶ ἐχαρίσατο αὐτῷ τὸ ὄνομα τὸ ὑπερ
> πᾶν ὄνομα,
> ἵνα ἐν τῷ ὀνόματι Ἰησοῦ πᾶν γόνυ κάμψῃ ἐπουρανίων καὶ ἐπιγείων καὶ
> καταχθονίων
> καὶ πᾶσα γλῶσσα ἐξομολογήσεται ὅτι κύριος Ἰησοῦς Χριστὸς εἰς δόξαν
> θεοῦ πατρός.

> 'Therefore God exalted him highly and bestowed on him the name which is above
> every name,
> that at the name of Jesus every knee will bow of those from heaven and earth and
> under the earth
> and every tongue will confess that 'Jesus Christ is Lord' for the glory of God the
> Father.'

The christological application of Isa. 45.23, every knee bowing and every tongue confessing, is beyond doubt in his hymn. Whether Paul composes this prose or adopts a pre-formed hymn does not change his basic agreement with its Christology. Here Paul is consciously and deliberately associating this YHWH text with the crucified and now resurrected (highly exalted) Jesus. Kreitzer remarks: 'it is difficult to imagine any first-century Jew or Christian even remotely familiar with Isa. 45 hearing this final stanza of Phil. 2.9–11 without recognizing that words of theistic import have now been applied to Christ'.[35] Paul's clear use of Isa. 45.23 as a reference to Christ in the Philippians hymn makes it likely that he intends a similar use in Rom. 14.11. Moreover, one should note well the phrase 'the name which is above every name'. To what name does he refer? Some scholars interpret the phrase ἐν τῷ ὀνόματι Ἰησοῦ as 'at the name Jesus' rendering the genitive Ἰησοῦ as an epexegetical modifier of 'name'. This is grammatically possible. Given the context, however, it is best to take the genitive Ἰησοῦ as possessive, yielding the translation 'at the name which belongs to Jesus'. This would be identical with 'the name above every name' bestowed by God on the obedient Christ, and is revealed only at the climax of the hymn in the acclamation 'Jesus Christ is Lord'.

The response to God's exaltation of Christ is the universal acclamation expressed in the language of Isa. 45.23 'every knee will bow' and 'every tongue will confess'. These venerative phrases belong to one of the most significant monotheistic passages from the Old Testament and refer originally to YHWH. Although the passage alters and expands the text to accommodate Christian cosmological and eschatological interests, there can be little doubt that Jewish believers would have recognized the core phrases as scriptural language reserved for YHWH now applied to their Lord Jesus. Reginald Fuller approaches the correct conclusion when he writes:

> For this is no unreflective transference to the Exalted one of a LXX text about
> *Yhwh*, but a conscious and deliberate transference of the 'name'. It is not just a
> *functional* identity between the Exalted one and Yahweh, but an *ontic*, though not

---

35. L.J. Kreitzer, *Jesus and God in Paul's Eschatology* (JSNTSup, 19; Sheffield: JSOT Press, 1987), p. 116.

yet ontological, identity: 'Name declares dignity and nature, radiates being and makes it manifest'.[36]

Without a doubt the language here describes the universal worship of Jesus as Lord by creatures inhabiting the heavenly, earthly and subterranean realms. Such veneration, however, does not threaten God's unique position. Indeed to worship Jesus brings glory to the Father. Since God has exalted him and given him the name *kyrios*, Paul understood that the worship of Jesus was in full accord with the will and purposes of God.

A Christological and Binitarian Monotheism

Paul's christological use of YHWH texts has significant christological implications. Indeed such an appropriation of scriptural language containing the divine name appears unprecedented. It implies that he considers Jesus the Messiah to be more than a man. By applying to Jesus the divine name through scriptural exegesis, Paul includes Jesus within the Name and dignity of God. In a crucial sense then he identifies Jesus with Yahweh himself. Given Paul's view of scripture and the reverence accorded the divine name, as demonstrated in Jewish religious manuscripts and liturgical practices, this conclusion seems warranted.

The validity of any conclusion, of course, depends on how well it explains the data. To understand the risen Jesus as bearing the Name of God or as Yahweh manifest explains many aspects of early Christian faith and practice. It explains why early Christians offer prayers and worship Jesus. It provides a basis for the application of the title *theos* to Jesus (e.g. Rom. 9.5; cf. Tit. 2.13). It clarifies why early Christians give the words of Jesus authoritative status equal to Old Testament scripture. Furthermore, the conviction that Jesus occupies divine status accounts for other christological notions such as his pre-existence, his role in creation and his place as the coming eschatological Savior and Judge.

If one acknowledges this construal of Paul's Christology, it is important to note that, at the same time, the apostle never confuses Jesus with God. He continues to assert that Jesus is distinct from and even subordinate to the Father much as expressed in the Fourth Gospel (e.g. 1 Cor. 15.25–28; cf. Jn. 1 and 5). Yet this subordination does not function to undermine thoughts of his equality with God, nor, more importantly, does it preclude invoking his name in prayer or composing a hymn of praise about him for use in worship. Thus Paul remains a monotheist, as he chooses his words carefully to avoid any charge of di-theism. Nevertheless, he wants to accord Jesus the highest honor and praise. Such honor, in turn, is understood to be enhance, not detract from, the glory of God (Phil. 2.5–11; cf. Eph. 1).

Later generations of Christians will express the relationship between Jesus and God in other ways. They will face different challenges and heresies such as the denial of Jesus' full humanity (Jn 1.14; 1 Jn 4.2–3; 2 Jn 7). Ironically, the issue

---

36. R.H. Fuller, *The Foundations of New Testament Christology* (London: Lutterworth, 1965), p. 214. Fuller quotes E. Käsemann, *Exegetische Versuche und Besinnungen* (Göttingen: Vandenhoeck & Ruprecht, 1961), I, p. 83.

facing the community of the Fourth Gospel is a Christology too high, a Christology with a deficient understanding of Jesus' humanity. The present article calls into question any developmental scheme in which the earliest Christians, like Paul, held a 'low Christology', which evolves over time to a 'high Christology', represented by the Gospel of John. Paul's use of YHWH texts suggests that he is already working from a high Christology, a Christology in which Jesus bears the divine name and full religious devotion to Christ is the will of God.

The question must now be asked: how does Paul accommodate the application of YHWH texts to Jesus, according him full religious devotion, while remaining a 'monotheist'? My work on Paul's christological use of scripture reflects one among several answers to this question that has occupied the recent attention of a number of scholars. In order to place myself more precisely within the current debate, I would like recount some of the views with which I am in conversation.

Larry Hurtado, in his book *One God, One Lord*, considers the evidence carefully and concludes that early in the Christian movement Palestinian Jews worshiped Jesus. This is reflected particularly in confessions like 1 Cor. 8.6 that reflect what he calls the 'binitarian shape' of Christian devotion.[37] How did Jewish Christians accommodate the worship of Jesus and remain monotheists? Hurtado's answer appeals to a concept of divine agency that was well established in Second Temple Judaism.[38] The paradigmatically different, indeed unprecedented, religious experiences of the early Christian communities[39] could therefore be given a plausible framework, so that monotheistic belief, rather than being altogether eschewed, could be conceptually reshaped. Though in pre-Christian Jewish sources divine agents could be understood as being close to God and at times as exercising divine powers, they never posed a threat to the exclusive monotheism because they were never really worshipped.

Crispin Fletcher-Louis[40] has accepted Hurtado's criterion of cultic worship as a decisive marker for divine status. Moreover, he accepts that in relation to the status of Jesus something unprecedented did take place.[41] However, he fundamentally

37. Larry Hurtado, *One God, One Lord: Early Christian Devotion and Ancient Jewish Monotheism* (Philadelphia: Fortress Press, 1988; Edinburgh: T. & T. Clark, 2nd edn, 1998), pp. 1–15.

38. Hurtado, *One God, One Lord*, pp. 17–39. Having surveyed Jewish texts from the era, he notices that many Jewish groups believed that God has a chief agent, second to him only in rank. These carry out divine functions in creating, sustaining and administrating the world under God's hand. He classifies these agents into three main categories: (1) divine attributes, e.g., Wisdom and Logos; (2) exalted patriarchs, e.g., Enoch and Moses; and (3) principal angels, e.g., Michael, Melchizedek and Yahoel. Though close to God and at times exercising divine powers, these agents never pose a threat to the exclusive monotheism of the Jews because they are never worshipped.

39. The novelty of worshipping Jesus alongside God, for Hurtado, may be traced back to several factors: (1) Jesus' own influence on his followers; (2) the Christians' conviction that God raised Jesus from the dead and exalted him to heaven; and (3) refinements that came as Christians attempted to explain their convictions in response to theology opposition in the synagogues; see Hurtado, *One God, One Lord*, pp. 93–124.

40. Crispin H.T. Fletcher-Louis, 'The Worship of Divine Humanity as God's Image and the Worship of Jesus', in *JRCM*, pp. 112–28.

41. *JRCM*, p. 119: the worship of Jesus 'shatters the boundaries of acceptability in as much as he is worshipped as a particular *person*, Jesus of Nazareth'.

disagrees with Hurtado when he rejects the notion that the worship of Jesus was a religious-historical innovation within the framework of Jewish monotheism. Instead, he finds precedent for cultic devotion to Jesus in the worship of '*certain righteous individuals*' who are in one way or another '*God's Image, his living idols*'.[42] He cites a number of texts in which humans, especially the high priest, appear to be worshipped in a way that, at the same time, was deemed to lie entirely within Jewish monotheistic bounds.[43] The discontinuity with Jesus lay in the fact that early Christians were addressing their worship to a particular person, not just to an office.[44] Given for Fletcher-Louis the inextricable connection between 'image' and 'deity', the high priest, functioning as God's image, could regarded as 'deity' and thus be worshipped at the same time. To be precise, Israelite religion was not aniconic; rather, it was an-idolatrous; humans could function as God's image and serve as objects of cultic devotion.[45] For Christians, then, since Jesus functions as God's image, the worship of Jesus signifies the worship of God.

As an explanation for the background of Paul's application of YHWH texts to Christ, Hurtado's construal is preferable. If the question of precedent focuses on the worship of a *personal* being (rather than in relation to an office), his point that there is no analogy in pre-Christian Judaism that gave rise to religious devotion to Christ is correct. At a very early stage in Christian circles, to borrow Hurtado's term, a 'mutation' took effect with regard to Jewish monotheism. Thus Paul's exegesis, as especially observable through the appropriation of Isa. 45.23 at Rom. 14.11 and Phil. 2.6–11, may surely be said to have presupposed such a development.

A dissenting voice to this perspective belongs to James Dunn. He finds it unlikely that early Christians worshipped Jesus and therefore denies that Paul violated, or at least compromised, his monotheistic heritage. While affirming Hurtado's thesis 'in the longer term' and recognising early hymns, prayers and benedictions including Christ as 'remarkable' and 'astounding', Dunn stops short of agreeing with him that this amounts to the worship of Jesus by earliest Christians. Regarding the christological hymns, Dunn argues they are hymns about Christ not hymns directed to Christ. Prayers to Jesus, he says, were limited and did not utilize regular prayer language. Ultimately, Dunn finds nothing in Paul's language or practice that would have offended the sensibilities of the apostle's Jewish contemporaries.[46]

However, although Dunn has been quite influential in studies in Christology, his conclusions here are not compelling. First, Dunn's approach allows the formal language to distract from what the Pauline hymns have to say. Admittedly, Dunn is correct to note that, formally, the Pauline hymns (Phil. 2.6–11; Col. 1.15–20)

---

42. *JRCM*, p. 128.

43. See *JRCM* for a rehearsal of the evidence (including esp. the discussion of Sir. 50), along with a more indepth discussion of texts relating to Alexander the Great's encounter with the Jerusalem high priest (cf. esp. *Ant.* 11.331–334 and *b. Yoma* 69a), see the Fletcher-Louis' contribution to this volume.

44. *JRCM*, p. 119.

45. *JRCM*, pp. 122–25.

46. J.D.G. Dunn, *The Partings of the Ways Between Christianity and Judaism and their Significance for the Character of Christianity* (London: SCM Press; Philadelphia: Trinity Press International, 1991), pp. 204–206.

are about and not to Christ. Not unlike many of the Psalms, they are written in the third person not second. But it is not insignificant that the second half of the Philippian hymn describes an eschatological scene in which all heavenly, earthly and subterranean creatures bow the knee and confess Jesus to be Lord. The language of bowing and confessing, appropriated from the YHWH text of Isa. 45.23 and now applied to Jesus, clearly envisions a day when he will be worshipped by all creatures. If Paul regarded such worship as appropriate in the *eschaton*, would he not also have found it appropriate in the present for those who 'call upon the name of the Lord Jesus Christ' (1 Cor. 1.2)? Ironically, Dunn considers a similar scene in Rev. 5.8–12 as sufficient evidence that Jesus was being worshipped by the Christian communities who composed and read the Apocalypse. It should not be overlooked that Paul's letters contain only christological (i.e. not patrological) hymns. Second, Dunn argues that Paul's letters provide no evidence that his Jewish contemporaries were ever concerned with his violation of monotheism. This is no more than an argument from silence. The issues involved in mining Paul's letters for evidence of the thinking of outsiders are problematic. Paul's letters are pastoral responses to needs that have arisen among believers in churches he knows. They are not, for the most part, a record of Paul's debates with non-believing Jews or Greeks. The opposition faced by Paul recorded in the letters comes from believers who insist that Gentiles observe Torah. No sure evidence exists regarding what non-believing Jews may have thought about Paul's Christology beyond Paul's own statement that the preaching of a crucified Messiah was a stumbling block (1 Cor. 1.23). One cannot say for certain that the Philippian and Colossian hymns in the hands of a Jew would not have been deemed a violation of the uniqueness of God. In the end Paul's letters are silent on these matters and so Dunn's use of this criterion as a guiding principle in assessing other evidence should be rejected.

The contributions of Hurtado, Fletcher-Louis, and Dunn all raise the question of what should be regarded as 'cultic' worship that contravenes the uniqueness of God. Here, further research should attempt to introduce more clarity and precision. Moreover, they do not fully answer the question of *how* christological exegesis of the Jewish scriptures fed religious devotion to Christ or reflected already existing practices. However, what is clear, at least from my analysis above, is that exegesis and praxis went hand-in-hand. Paul's reading of the Old Testament, which can so straightforwardly substitute YHWH with Christ, cannot have hoped to convince his readers unless some degree of such an association had already taken place. However, is it right to assume that praxis and scriptural exegesis can be distinguished?

In answer to this question, my answer would be 'no'. Thus it is appropriate to refer to Richard Bauckham's recent monograph[47] in which exegesis is seen to have been a central medium that gave expression to Jesus' special status in relation to God while tenaciously holding on to Jewish monotheism. Bauckham argues that the high Christology expressed in the New Testament does not find its antecedent

---

47. R. Bauckham, *God Crucified: Monotheism and Christology in the New Testament* (Grand Rapids: Eerdmans, 1998). See also Bauckham's study in this volume on scriptural exegesis in the Christology of Hebrews 1.

in the semi-divine, intermediary figures in second temple Judaism; rather he simply proposes that 'early Christians included Jesus, precisely and unambiguously, within the unique identity of the one God of Israel'.[48] For Bauckham, to understand the interplay between Jewish monotheism and the early Christian assessments of Jesus as divine, one must understand 'the identity of God' as it is understood in Second Temple Judaism. Whereas earlier discussions of Christology suffer because of misleading and ambiguous functional and ontic categories, the notion of 'divine identity' provides a better way to grasp the evidence found in contemporary literature. As with human identity, divine identity has to do with who God is, God as a person who acts, speaks, knows and is known. As such, it distinguishes God from everything that is not God. Bauckham discusses two categories of features relevant to Second Temple Jewish thought: (1) God in his relation to Israel and (2) God in relation to all other reality. For Israel God reveals himself as a covenant partner, making himself known through his acts in history (see, e.g., Exod. 34.6). For the rest of reality God relates as the Creator and Ruler of all things. Ultimately God alone is responsible for creating and governing the world, though God uses myriads of angels to execute his purposes.

Bauckham focuses on the character of early Jewish monotheism. Against those who think that the lines of distinction between God and certain divine, mediator figures were blurred, Bauckham argues that Second Temple Judaism was strictly monotheistic. Indeed strong evidence suggests that Jews drew hard lines of distinction between God and all that is not God. In contrast the evidence for mediator figures who blur this distinction is ambiguous and limited. In particular, the notion that God has a principal angel as his 'second-in-command' is not a commonplace in the literature. Angels may serve God's purposes, but never occupy the throne of God and flatly refuse worship.[49] On the other hand, personified and hypostatized divine aspects such as the Word and Wisdom do participate in God's creation and administration over the cosmos and so should be recognized as 'intrinsic to the unique divine identity'.[50] Whether these aspects should be understood as literary devices or beings distinct from God is a question Bauckham leaves unsettled, though he seems sympathetic to the latter possibility. In the end it is important to view Second Temple Jewish monotheism as unique but not unitary. Throughout the history of Israel, the one God of Israel had manifested himself in many ways.

Bauckham assesses the evidence regarding how the New Testament writers include Jesus within the identity of the one God of Israel. They acknowledge him as Creator and sovereign Lord. They view him as bearing the divine name and without hesitation worship him. In fact, according to Bauckham, this fully divine Christology characterizes the early church before any New Testament documents appear.[51] Although this 'christological monotheism' is an innovation, it is continu-

---

48. Bauckham, *God Crucified*, p. vii.

49. For Bauckham the only exception is the Son of Man figure in *1 Enoch* (46.5; 48.5; 61.8; 62.2–9; 69.27, 29). Concerning the refusal by angels to be worshipped, see the brief discussion in Stuckenbruck's contribution to this volume, ' "Angels and "God": Exploring the Limits of Monotheism', section B.

50. Bauckham, *God Crucified*, p. 21.

51. Bauckham, *God Crucified*, p. 27.

ous with Jewish monotheism, properly understood, and does not require either a setting in a community where belief in God's oneness had eroded or the repudiation of monotheistic faith. Indeed, the very nature of Jewish belief allows for this development.

Significantly, for Bauckham the catalyst for this innovation emerges in scriptural exegesis. Generally, he thinks, Christian theology develops through creative readings of biblical texts. Early Christians mine every resource available in scripture to sculpt a theology that includes Jesus within the unique identity of Israel's one God. Specifically, Bauckham points to the New Testament's appropriation of Ps. 110.1 to portray Jesus sitting on the throne, exercising God's rule. Further, he notices how 1 Cor. 8.6 appears to be Paul's Christian version of the *Shema'*. The apostle continues to stand within his monotheistic heritage, [52] so the confession 'one God, the Father' and 'one Lord, Jesus Christ' should not be taken as ditheism. Bauckham finds divine identity to be the most satisfying category to understand how Jesus' followers included him in the identity of God.

Bauckham's category of 'divine identity' offers a refreshing way out of the functional/ontic cul-de-sac that provides few satisfying answers for understanding early Christian faith and practice. It takes seriously the undeniable evidence that Christians worshipped Jesus at a very early stage. It also challenges those who continue to insist that devotion to Christ developed in a setting where the constraints of monotheism had grown weak. Finally, it accords with the findings here, that early on Christians applied the name of God in reference to Jesus as they attempted to understand Jesus' significance by means of the scriptures they inherited.

At this stage, it is perhaps worth noting that, in substance, Bauckham's approach is not entirely novel. Earlier, in 1942, A.R. Johnson published *The One and the Many in the Israelite Conception of God*.[53] Like Bauckham, Johnson considers the Hebrew concept of the human the best analogue when thinking about God. He begins with the observation that the Israelites conceive of humans as possessing 'an indefinable "extension" of the personality'. This 'corporate personality' becomes the basis for attributing to God similar extensions of his personality, such as the Spirit, the divine Word, the Name and the Ark of the Covenant. Johnson concludes that within a monotheistic framework the Israelites envisage their one God as having multiple manifestations, and he goes on to suggest possible ramifications for Christology.[54] Bauckham's work seems to advance a similar theory under the category of divine identity.

---

52. Paul looked with contempt upon idolatry (1 Cor. 10.14–22) and confidently wrote of the oneness of God (e.g. Rom. 3.30; 1 Cor. 8.4–6; Gal. 3.20; cf. Eph. 4.4–6).

53. A.R. Johnson, *The One and the Many in the Israelite Conception of God* (Cardiff: University of Wales Press, 1942).

54. For objections to the category of 'corporate personality' see J.R. Porter, 'The Legal Aspects of the Concept of "Corporate Personality" in the Old Testament', *Vetus Testamentum* 15 (1965), pp. 361–80; J.W. Rogerson, 'The Hebrew Conception of Corporate Personality: A Re-examination' *JTS* NS 21 (1970), pp. 1–16; S.E. Porter, 'Two Myths: Corporate Personality and Language/ Mentality Determinism', *SJT* 43 (1990), pp. 289–307. For one who has a more positive assessment, see J.S. Kaminsky, *Corporate Personality in the Hebrew Bible* (JSOTSup, 196; Sheffield: Sheffield Academic Press, 1995).

Conclusion

In conclusion, Paul deliberately and unambiguously applies to Jesus Old Testament texts that contain the divine name. Along with other patterns of religious devotion, this means that Paul identifies Jesus with God or – to import Bauckham's concept – he included Jesus within the unique identity of Israel's God. Yet he continued to see Christ as distinct and subordinate to the Father. Thus 'high Christology' is apparent from the earliest extant documents of the Christian movement. At the same time Paul was a Jew, a monotheist cut from the same cloth as the prophets Joel and Isaiah. He wanted to maintain the oneness of God in a world populated with polytheists and idolaters (1 Cor. 10.14–22). While further scholarly attention to the language of worship is still needed, the present study nonetheless shows that Paul's use of Old Testament YHWH texts expressed both his own devotion to Christ and reflected his expectation that his readers would share in his interpretation of scripture.

'THE LORD IS ONE': REFLECTIONS ON THE THEME OF UNITY IN JOHN'S GOSPEL FROM A JEWISH PERSPECTIVE[*]

C.T.R. Hayward, University of Durham

1. *Introduction*

The proclamation of God's unity in the recital of *Shema'* stands at the very heart of the Jewish way of life. The Jewish world is ordered around the daily affirmation that the Lord is one, יהוה אחד, a solemn declaration not only of God's sole existence, but also of his incomparable uniqueness. It is incumbent on every Jew to witness to the Divine unity in private and public life, most especially in the keeping of the commandments set forth in the one Torah of the one God. Thus in the *Qeduššah* of the *Musaf* service for Sabbaths, the Reader chants:

> From His place may He turn in mercy and be gracious to a people who, evening and morning, twice every day, declare the unity of His Name (המחדים שמו) continually (תמיד) saying in love: Hear -

and the congregation join in saying: 'Hear, O Israel: the Lord our God, the Lord is One'.[1] This solemn prayer twice alludes to the Temple service: first, God's unity is proclaimed 'morning and evening', that is, at the time when the daily lamb sacrifices were offered on the great altar, and when the incense was burned on the golden altar in the holy place. Second, this complex of ritual acts was known as the Tamid (תמיד), the 'regular' or daily sacrificial offering to the Lord. The synagogue service, in some measure, is held to do duty for the sacrifices until the Temple is restored.[2] Yet while the Temple stood, the Rabbis inform us, the proc-

---

* Except where otherwise indicated, the Hebrew or Aramaic of the Qumran texts is cited from F. García Martínez and E.J.C. Tigchelaar, *The Dead Sea Scrolls Study Edition* (2 vols.; Grand Rapids: Eerdmans; Leiden-Boston-Köln: Brill, 1997/1998). The translations are mine.

1. For the Hebrew text, and this translation of it, see S. Singer, *The Authorised Daily Prayer Book of the United Hebrew Congregations of the the British Commonwealth of Nations* (London: Eyre and Spottiswoode, 5722/1962), p. 212. On the Musaf service in general, see I. Elbogen, *Der jüdische Gottesdienst in seiner geschichtlichen Entwicklung* (reprinted Hildesheim: Georg Olms, 1967), pp. 115–17, 125–41; and for a summary of information on the *Qeduššah*, see C.T.R. Hayward, 'Sanctus 1. Alttestamentlich und jüdisch', in *Theologische Realenzyklopädie* vol. 30/1 (Berlin: W. de Gruyter, 1998), pp. 20–25.

2. For discussion of the relationship between the Service of the Temple and the Synagogue, see now especially S.C. Reif, *Judaism and Hebrew Prayer* (Cambridge: Cambridge University Press, 1993), pp. 5, 10–13, 34–47, 57–59. Following the destruction of the Temple, the important principle was enunciated that study or reading of the laws relating to the sacrifices, and their men-

lamation of God's unity in the recital of *Shema'* was an integral part of the sacrificial service (*m.Tamid* 4.3; 5.1). The historicity of this need not be doubted, since the Temple was the place where God had made his Name to tabernacle (Deut. 12.5; 16.2; 26.2; 1 Kgs. 8.29) and was indeed the only place where the proper Name of God, the שם המיוחד as the Rabbis were later to refer to it (e.g. *b. Sanh.* 60a), might be pronounced with its proper vocalization. The unique Name of God has one Temple as a place to tabernacle: if the Name is One, it naturally follows that the dwelling-place of that Name must correspondingly be one. The Temple building, therefore, serves as a constant reminder of the unity of God. This Name is the Name of a king (see Zech. 14.9) whose earthly palace is the Temple, whose earthly ministers are the Temple priests and Levites, and whose subjects are the Jewish people, daily accepting his kingly rule as they recite *Shema'* and 'take upon themselves the yoke of the Kingdom of Heaven' (*m. Ber.* 2.5). Such, at any rate, is the ideal situation, as envisaged by Scripture and Rabbinic tradition. When the Temple was still standing, however, the realities of religious life in the land of Israel were not so straightforward.

We are accustomed, perhaps all too easily so, to perceiving the Jerusalem Temple as essentially without peer. Even when the existence of other Jewish Temples is acknowledged, the Jerusalem shrine very quickly reclaims attention and pride of place. A glance at a recent major work of scholarship in the shape of E.P. Sanders, *Judaism: Practice and Belief 63 BCE–66 CE* is instructive in this regard: the Samaritans receive two notices, the Temple of Onias at Heliopolis none at all.[3] Yet, as we shall see, these institutions undoubtedly exercised a profound influence over the 'common Judaism' of which Sanders is so eloquent an advocate. The existence of more than one Jewish Temple constituted the most profound embarrassment for the Jews of late antiquity; indeed, much more than embarrassment was involved. For it should be clear in the light of our opening remarks that nothing less than the very notion of the unity of God was called into question by the existence of these rival shrines.

These shrines were not insignificant. The Samaritan Temple on Mount Gerizim had been destroyed by John Hyrcanus I in 128 BCE; but its site was, and still is, the place of sacrificial worship.[4] In Second Temple times, the Samaritans constituted a serious political and religious threat to the Jerusalem Temple, as a close reading of Ben Sira 50.26 demonstrates.[5] The dispute between Jews and Samaritans over the

---

tion in the Synagogue Service, was equivalent to the offering of those sacrifices: see *b. Ber.* 5ab; *Sifre Deut.* 306 (on Deut. 32.2); *Tanhuma B.* אחרי 9.

3.   E. P. Sanders, *Judaism: Practice and Belief 63 BCE – 66 CE* (London: SCM Press, 1992), pp. 165 and 329–30.

4.   See E. Schürer, *The History of the Jewish People in the Age of Jesus Christ* (rev. and ed. G. Vermes, F. Millar and M. Black; 3 vols.; Edinburgh: T. & T. Clark, 1979), II, pp. 15–20; B. Hall, *Samaritan Religion from John Hyrcanus to Baba Rabbah* (Mandelbaum Studies in Judaica, 3; Sydney: Mandelbaum Publishing, 1987); R.T. Anderson, 'Samaritans', in *ABD*, pp. 940–47.

5.   Ben Sira's comments are mordant: the Samaritans are described in the Hebrew text of MsB from the Cairo Geniza (see P.C. Beentjes [ed.], *The Book of Ben Sira in Hebrew: A Text Edition of All Extant Hebrew Manuscripts and a Synopsis of All Extant Parallel Hebrew Ben Sira Texts* [Leiden: E.J. Brill, 1997], p. 90) as גוי נבל הדר בשכם, 'a lawless people which hangs out in

site of the true Temple apparently spilled over into the Diaspora: Josephus (*Ant.* 13.74–79) tells how both groups resident in Alexandria argued the respective merits of Jerusalem and Gerizim before Ptolemy VI Philometor. The Jews won their case, and the Samaritan representatives were put to death. Whatever the historical worth of this account, the intense and bitter division it describes as existing between worshippers of the unique God of Israel was undoubtedly a prominent feature of religious life in the first century CE when Josephus was writing.[6] Indeed, the historian never tires of recording Samaritan outrages against the Jews, as when he records their notorious defilement of the Jerusalem Temple by scattering human bones there at the time of Pesah when Coponius was Roman Prefect (*Ant.* 18.29–30).

The Temple of Onias at Leontopolis was of a different order from that on Gerizim. While the Jerusalem authorities could claim, probably with justification, that no Temple had stood on Mount Gerizim before the time of Alexander the Great (see the account of the building of the Temple by Josephus in *Ant.* 11.321–325), the Jewish Temple at Leontopolis in Egypt had been founded by the son of a legitimate Jerusalem high priest of impeccable Zadokite descent. This man, conventionally known as Onias IV, had effectively been ousted from his rightful inheritance of the high priesthood as a result of the turmoil engendered by the Hellenistic crisis. He went to Egypt and built a temple, claiming to fulfill Isaiah's prophecy (Isa. 19.19, 21) that there would be an altar to the Lord in Egypt, and that sacrificial worship would be offered there.[7] Josephus is again one of our principal sources of knowledge of this building: he states that Onias purposely intended to rival Jerusalem (*War* 7.431), and that Onias had built 'a small town on the model of Jerusalem and a temple resembling ours' (*War* 1.33). The Greek word here translated 'resembling' is ἀπεικασμένην, meaning 'to form from a copy, express, copy'. It conveys the sense that Onias intended to imitate Jerusalem and its Temple, and that his

Shechem'. The Hebrew is so phrased as to indicate that these people are without understanding of the Torah, that is, foolish in the sense of 'law-less': the epithet נבל also suggests their illegitimacy, and, more directly, their stupidity. This follows a glorious poem praising the high priest Simon of the house of Zadok, which also indicates the immense esteem in which ben Sira held the Jerusalem Temple. See C.T.R. Hayward, *The Jewish Temple: A Non-biblical Sourcebook* (London: Routledge, 1996), pp. 62–63. For the most recent, detailed discussion of this verse, see O. Mulder, *Simon de Hogepriester in Sirach 50* (Almelo: Wormgoor, 2000), pp. 349–54.

6.   For evidence of Samaritans in Egypt, see Schürer, *History* (see n. 4), 3.1, pp. 59–60.

7.   See M. Delcor, 'Le Temple d'Onias en Egypte', *RB* 75 (1968), pp. 188–205; S. Steckoll, 'The Qumran Sect in Relation to the Temple at Leontopolis', *Revue de Qumrân* 6 (1967–69), pp. 55–69; O. Murray, 'Aristeas and Ptolemaic Kingship', *JTS* 18 (1967), pp. 365–71; J.A. Goldstein, 'Tales of the Tobiads', in J. Neusner (ed.), *Christianity, Judaism, and Other Greco-Roman Cults: Studies for Morton Smith at Sixty* (Leiden: E.J. Brill, 1975), part III, pp. 91–121; R.T. White, 'The House of Peleg in the Dead Sea Scrolls', in P.R. Davies and R.T. White (eds.), *A Tribute to Geza Vermes* (Sheffield: Sheffield Academic Press, 1990), pp. 67–98; G. Bohak, *Joseph and Aseneth and the Jewish Temple in Heliopolis* (SBL Early Judaism and Its Literature, 10; Atlanta: Scholars Press, 1996); P. Rainbow, 'The Last Oniad and the Teacher of Righteousness', *JJS* 48 (1997), pp. 30–52; J.E. Taylor, 'A Second Temple in Egypt: A Reconsideration of the Evidence for the Zadokite Temple of Onias', *JSJ* 29 (1998), pp. 1–25; G. Bohak, 'Theopolis: A Single Temple Policy and its Singular Ramifications', *JSJ* 30 (1999), pp. 3–20.

project was undertaken for profound symbolic and theological reasons which I have attempted to sketch elsewhere.[8]

To the early second century BCE belong the buildings in Transjordan associated with the Tobiad family at the village 'Araq el Emir. Some years ago, Hugo Gressmann argued that archaeological evidence pointed to the existence of a Jewish Temple in that place for the use of the military garrison associated with it. The theory is unproven, but has not been convincingly refuted.[9] The Tobiad family was deeply implicated in the intrigues leading up to the Hellenistic crisis and in the early events of those tragic times (2 Macc. 3.11); and it was certainly powerful enough to exert its own influence in religious affairs.

The mid-second century BCE witnessed (in all probability) the formation of the Qumran group, who seem to have formed a discrete Jewish community resident on the shores of the Dead Sea.[10] Although these Jews did not construct a temple, there is abundant evidence from documents produced by the settlers at Qumran that they regarded their own establishment as constituting a temple, albeit a 'temple of men', or a 'temple of Adam'.[11] Discussion of their concerns will form the substance of this essay; but in the meantime it will be important to give an example of their thinking about the temple, as set out in the so-called *Community Rule* from Qumran Cave 1, referring to the Council of the Community. The relevant parts from column viii, lines 1–10 read as follows:

> They shall preserve the faith in the Land with steadfastness and meekness and shall atone for sin by the practice of justice… When these are in Israel, the Council of the Community shall be established in truth. It shall be an Everlasting Plantation, a House of Holiness for Israel, an Assembly of Supreme Holiness for

---

8. C.T.R. Hayward, 'The Jewish Temple at Leontopolis: A Reconsideration', *JJS* 33 (1982), pp. 429–43. On the specifically political dimensions of the Samaritan and Leontopolis temples, and of the earlier Jewish temple at Elephantine, see J. Frey, 'Temple and Rival Temple – The Cases of Elephantine, Mt. Gerizim, and Leontopolis', in B. Ego, A. Lange and P. Pilhofer (eds.), *Gemeinde ohne Tempel Community without Temple* (Tübingen: J.C.B. Mohr [Paul Siebeck], 1999), pp. 171–203.

9. See the comments of the excavator, P. W. Lapp, 'Iraq el-Emir', in M. Avi-Yonah (ed.), *Encyclopaedia of Archaeological Investigations in the Holy Land* (4 vols.; Jerusalem: Israel Exploration Society, 1976), IV, pp. 527–31, and J. Frey, 'Temple and Rival Temple', pp. 194–95; and contrast L.L. Grabbe, *Judaism from Cyrus to Hadrian* (London: SCM Press, 1992), pp. 188–89.

10. The literature on this group is vast; but those seeking convenient introductions to a range of scholarly opinions on the organization, beliefs, and practices of the group should consult G. Vermes, *An Introduction to the Complete Dead Sea Scrolls* (London: SCM Press, 1999); H. Stegemann, *The Library of Qumran: On the Essenes, Qumran, John the Baptist, and Jesus* (Leiden/New York/Köln: E.J. Brill, 1998); L.H. Schiffman, *Reclaiming the Dead Sea Scrolls* (New York: Doubleday, 1994); and F. García Martínez and J. Trebolle Barrera, *The People of the Dead Sea Scrolls: Their Writings, Beliefs and Practices* (Leiden: E.J. Brill, 1995).

11. So 4QFlorilegium (=4Q174) col. i, lines 6–7, which states that God has ordered that מקדש אדם be built for Himself. For the interpretation of this phrase as 'sanctuary of men', see G.J. Brooke, *Exegesis at Qumran* (JSOTSup, 29; Sheffield: JSOT Press, 1985), pp. 184–87. More recently, Brooke has emphasized the strongly eschatological aspects of this 'sanctuary of Adam' or 'sanctuary of men', demonstrating its links with the Eden and plantation imagery favoured by the Qumran Yahad to speak of the glorious future; see his essay 'Miqdash Adam, Eden, and the Qumran Community', in *Gemeinde ohne Tempel* (see n. 8), pp. 283–301.

Aaron. They shall be witnesses to the truth...who shall atone for the Land... It shall be a Most Holy Dwelling for Aaron, with everlasting knowledge of the Covenant of justice, and shall offer up sweet fragrance... And they shall be an agreeable offering, atoning for the Land...[12]

For the writer of this *Rule*, and for those who accepted it as authoritative, the Temple in Jerusalem has lost all claim to be recognized as the place where God's Name dwells and where alone on earth he may be worshipped. As we know from other Qumran documents, the group settled by the Dead Sea looked upon the contemporary Jerusalem Temple as hopelessly defiled and corrupt, and awaited eagerly the day when it might be rebuilt as God willed, a matter which they addressed with punctilious precision in the great Temple Scroll discovered in Cave 11, one of the longest literary compositions found at Qumran.[13] It is no exaggeration to say that they held the Jerusalem shrine in as great abhorrence as did the Samaritans.

No attempt should be made to mitigate the scandal created for thoughtful, pious Jews of the mid-first century CE by these different sanctuaries and their rival claims. This plurality of places, each maintaining that it, and not another, was the place where the Divine Name tabernacled on earth, threatened to bring disintegration and division into the very core of Judaism, the affirmation that God is One, that his Name is One and Unique, and that he has chosen one place of dwelling for that Name on earth. The plurality of temples was an urgent problem, crying out for resolution. To a student of Second Temple Judaism, therefore, St John's Gospel, with its emphasis on unity, may not unreasonably be considered as a particular Jewish attempt to address the problem set forth above, and to remove the scandal of many sanctuaries. It certainly emphasizes unity as no other Gospel, and associates this unity with the Divine Name (see 17.6, 11, 12, 21, 22, 23, 26) which Christ has manifested to believers. It is also concerned to portray Jesus as the authentic place of the Divine presence (1.32, the Spirit remains on him; 1.51, the angels go up and down upon him; 14.6, he is the truth; 4.23–24, possessing the Spirit and being the truth, he, and not Jerusalem or Mount Gerizim, is the place where the true worshippers worship the Father). Serious consideration should, I believe, be given to the question of unity in this Gospel, when it is considered alongside anxieties about unity articulated in the Judaism of the first century CE and earlier.

2. *Unity at Qumran*

There can be no doubt that the idea of unity was almost an obsession for the Jews who made up the group at Qumran. The *Community Rule*, it is generally agreed,

12. The translation is that of G. Vermes, *The Complete Dead Sea Scrolls in English* (London: Harmondsworth, 1997), p. 109. On attitudes to the temple among the Qumran Jews, see B. Gärtner, *The Temple and the Community in Qumran and the New Testament* (Cambridge: Cambridge University Press, 1965); and for a brief but masterly account drawing on the most recently published Qumran materials and secondary sources, see L.H. Schiffman, 'Community Without Temple: The Qumran Community's Withdrawal from the Jerusalem Temple', in *Gemeinde ohne Tempel* (see n. 8), pp. 267–84.

13. See Y. Yadin, *The Temple Scroll* (3 vols.; Jerusalem: Israel Exploration Society, 1983).

sets out this group's most treasured tenets and practices; from the very outset, this document places unity at the forefront of its concerns. A fragment from Cave 4 (4QpapS^a) preserves what is probably the start of the scroll and its title, namely סרך היחד, 'the rule of the *Yahad*'.[14] The first of these words is not found in Biblical Hebrew, but is common in Rabbinic parlance with the meaning of 'a clinging to; a following the example of; habit'. In the Qumran texts, it means 'order': an Aramaic fragment of Testament of Levi in the Bodleian Library, published long ago by R.H. Charles, preserves the Aramaic cognate סרך in lines 29 and 30, and is given with a corresponding Greek translation rendering the word as τάξις.[15] Like the latter, סרך may mean order in the sense of rank, rule, ordinance, order (rank) for battle, and order as opposed to disorder. Whatever the precise sense of יחד, it necessarily involves for the Qumran Jews a perception of order as understood above. This will presently become very clear.

In the above compound expression, יחד appears as a noun along with סרך. The word itself is common enough in Biblical Hebrew with the adverbial sense 'together'; but its use as a noun is very rare. All authorities agree on its substantival use at Deut. 33.5 and 1 Chron. 12.18. To these two undisputed passages, Talmon adds Ps. 2.2 and Ezek. 4.3; but they are not widely accepted.[16] What is rare in the Bible, however, becomes commonplace at Qumran: יחד as a noun is a favourite with the group, being found not only in the *Community Rule*, but also in the *Hodayot*, the *War Scroll*, the *Pesharim*, and liturgical works. We may note H.-J. Fabry's telling comment that it may have had new life given to it as a noun by the Qumran group.[17] The noun derives from root יחד, 'to be united' (in *Qal* at Gen. 49.6; Isa. 14.20; *Pi'el* in Ps. 86.11, 'to unite'). From the same root derives the adjective יחיד, 'only', 'unique', which is found as a description of Isaac at Gen. 22.2 and rendered by LXX as ἀγαπητός. All that has been said so far should make it clear that the root and words deriving from it are expressive of 'oneness'. The noun יחד, therefore, although conventionally translated 'community', is better understood as 'that which is one'. It is difficult to capture its precise sense with a single English equivalent: 'union', which might otherwise suffice, has connotations foreign to the Hebrew word. It really signifies 'the thing which

14. The fragment is also numbered 4Q255, and is transcribed and discussed by P.S. Alexander and G. Vermes, *Qumran Cave 4. XIX. Serekh ha-Yahad and Two Related Texts* (DJD, 26; Oxford: Clarendon Press, 1998), pp. 27–38. See also S. Metso, *The Textual Development of the Qumran Community Rule* (STDJ, 21; Leiden: E.J. Brill, 1997), pp. 18–21.

15. See R. H. Charles, *Apocrypha and Pseudepigrapha of the Old Testament* (2 vols.; Oxford: Clarendon Press, 1913), II, p. 365.

16. See the biblical evidence discussed by H.-J. Fabry, 'יחד yāhad', in G.J. Botterweck and H. Ringgren (eds.) *Theological Dictionary of the Old Testament* (11 vols.; Grand Rapids: Eerdmans, 1990), VI, pp. 404–48; and Sh. Talmon, 'The Sectarian יחד – A Biblical Noun', *VT* 3 (1953), pp. 133–40.

17. See Fabry, 'יחד yāhad', p. 48. As we note below, LXX renders the related adjective יחיד, 'only, unique' at Gen. 22.2 as ἀγαπητός, 'beloved'. Wendy North, in a private communication, reminds me that at Gen. 22.2, 12 the Minor Greek versions render Hebrew יחיד as μονογενής, 'only begotten', the word used at Jn 1.14 and elsewhere to describe Christ's relationship to the Father.

is one'; and its undisputed occurrences as a noun in the Bible help to clarify its meaning for the Qumran group.

The word's appearance at the beginning of the Blessing of Moses in Deut. 33 is the more important for our present purposes. After describing how God came from Sinai, shone forth from Seir, and beamed from Mount Paran, the poem tells how God carried his people and how they all shall receive of his decisions, before announcing:

> Moses commanded us a law, even the possession of the congregation of Jacob.
> And he was king in Jeshurun, when the heads of the people and the tribes of Israel were gathered together.[18]

The Hebrew text of v. 5, which begins with the words 'And he was king…', reads:

ויהי בישרון מלך בהתאסף ראשי עם יחד שבטי ישראל

A literal translation of this would read: 'And he was king over (or: in) Jeshurun when the heads of the people were gathered together, the one-ness of the tribes of Israel'. It is not clear whether it is Moses, or the Lord, who is king over Jeshurun, the last being a rare title for Israel having as its first three Hebrew consonants the letters ישר, which signify the notion of uprightness and integrity. For the people at Qumran, it was of little significance whether God or Moses should rule over them. It went without saying that God was their King; but Moses was the lawgiver to whose code they were bound in solemn covenant, as is made clear by 1QS col. v, lines 7–9. What the verse suggests is that the rulership of God or Moses over Israel is in some sense dependent on the leaders of Israel and its tribes being at one. The oldest interpretation of the verse sees this rulership as something destined to occur in the future, for LXX (cf. also Syriac) translate: 'And he shall be ruler over the beloved (ἠγαπημένῳ), when the rulers of the peoples are gathered together, together with (ἅμα) the tribes of Israel', the adverb (ἅμα) indicating a unity of time or place.[19] Three of the extant Aramaic Targums, Targum Neofiti, Fragment Targum according to Vatican Ms Ebr 440, and the Geniza fragments pursue this future reference further, and hint at a Messianic interpretation. Fragment Targum Vat Ms Ebr 440 may be quoted to exemplify their rendering: 'And a king shall arise from among those of the house of Jacob when the heads of the people are gathered together as one: all the tribes of the sons of Israel shall be in obedience to him'.[20] Both LXX and these Targums understand יחד as involved in a future polity for Israel entirely in accord with God's will.

Targum Pseudo-Jonathan, on the other hand, took the verse as follows: 'And he himself was the king over Israel when the heads of the people were gathered

---

18. Deut. 33.4–5, translated by M. Rosenbaum and A.M. Silbermann, *Pentateuch with Targum Onkelos, Haphtaroth and Rashi's Commentary* (5 vols.; New York: Hebrew Publishing Company, 1929–1934), V, pp. 170–71.

19. Our translation of LXX edited by A. Rahlfs, *Septuaginta* (2 vols.; Stuttgart: Württembergische Bibelanstalt, Stuttgart, 1935) 1.351: καὶ ἔσται ἐν τῷ ἠγαπημένῳ ἄρχων συναχθέντων ἀρχόντων λαῶν ἅμα φυλαῖς Ἰσραήλ.

20. For the Aramaic, see M.L. Klein, *The Fragment-Targums of the Pentateuch According to their Extant Sources* (2 vols.; Rome: Biblical Institute Press, 1980), I, p. 231. The translation is ours.

together as one, the tribes of Israel being in obedience to him'.[21] Here we learn that God, or Moses, was king over Israel (note this interpretation of Jeshurun) when the tribes of Israel with their leaders were gathered and obeyed him. In all this, the Targums emphasize obedience, that is, obedience to the commandments of God revealed through Moses, along with the one-ness of Israel under their appointed leaders. Such a one-ness and such obedience had, according to the Targums, been truly displayed at least once in the past, namely, when the heads of the twelve tribes gathered around the deathbed of Jacob their father. The interpretation of Gen. 49.1–2 in Targum Neofiti and its marginal glosses, and in the Fragment Targums extant in Mss Paris 110 and Vatican Ebr 440, is essentially of a piece: selected portions of MsVat Ebr 440 are quoted here as an example of the rendering.

> Now Jacob our father called his sons and said to them: Be gathered together, and I shall show to you the times which are stored up and the hidden secrets, and the gift of the reward of the righteous and the punishment of the wicked... The twelve tribes of Jacob were gathered together as one...(2) When the twelve tribes of Jacob had gathered together and surrounded the couch of gold on which our father Jacob was lying, they supposed that he was going to reveal to them the order of blessings, but it was hidden from him. Our father Jacob answered and said to them: Abraham, my grandfather – there arose from him the blemish of Ishmael and all the sons of Keturah; and Isaac my father – there arose from him the blemish of Esau my brother; and I am afraid lest there be among you a man whose heart is divided against his brothers, so as to go to worship before other 'idols'. The twelve tribes of Jacob answered, all of them as one [כולהון כחדא] and said: Hear, O Israel our father, the Lord our God is One. May His Name be blessed for ever and ever.[22]

In these Targumim of Gen. 49.1–2, the gathering together of the heads of the tribes of Israel as one, envisaged in the Targumim of Deut. 33.5, culminates in their collective assertion of the unity of God over against idolatry through proclamation of the *Shemaʿ*. Consider now the beginning of the Qumran *Rule* of the Yahad, the 'thing which is one', which is nothing less than a systematic exposition of the *Shemaʿ* with its demand that Israel love the Lord with all their heart, soul, and strength (מאד):

> [The Master shall teach the sai]nts to live(?) {according to the Book} of the order of the Yahad, that they may seek God with a whole heart and a whole soul, and do what is good and upright [וישר] before Him as He commanded by the hand of Moses... And all who freely volunteer themselves to His truth shall bring all their knowledge and their strength and their possessions into the Yahad of God to purify their knowledge in the truth of God's ordinances.[23]

21. The translation of the Aramaic given by E.G. Clarke, W.E. Aufrecht, J.C. Hurd and F. Spitzer, *Targum Pseudo-Jonathan of the Pentateuch: Text and Concordance* (New York: Ktav, 1984).

22. Aramaic text in Klein, *The Fragment-Targums*, 1.156–57; translation is mine.

23. 1QS col. i, lines 1–2//4Q255; 4Q257//1QS col. i, lines 11–12. This is a translation of the Hebrew as reconstructed from 1QS and 4QS materials by Vermes, *The Complete Dead Sea Scrolls*, pp. 98–99, with slight modifications of Vermes' rendering.

The Yahad is explicitly commanded here to do what is *yāshar*, 'upright', before God, perhaps as befits a group which is conscious of being *yeshurûn* = Jeshurun, Israel as that nation over whom the Divine Kingship is exercised when it is truly a Yahad. Note also the curses which the priests and Levites heap on the one who enters the Qumran covenant 'while walking among the idols of his heart' (1QS col. ii, lines 11–12) because 'he has turned aside from God on account of his idols and his stumbling-block of sin' (1QS col. ii, lines 16–17). This Yahad demands radical commitment to the spirit of the *Shema'*. What is good and upright before God is set out in the Law of Moses as interpreted by the Yahad: it is entirely clear, admitting no debate, each ordinance having a single, unitary meaning. So much is clear from the list of penalties for transgressions listed in 1QS col. vi, 24–vii, 25, and particularly from the statutes listed in CD cols. xv–xvi and ix–xiv. There is no room for double-mindedness here. We are forcibly reminded of a Rabbinic interpretation of the command to love God 'with all your heart' as 'with all the heart that is in you, so that your heart be not divided (חלוק) against God', a highly significant comment to which we must return.[24] The Yahad is to love the Lord with all its heart and soul: the command to love with all one's מאד or 'strength' is taken to mean with one's 'possessions', another interpretation found also among the Rabbis:[25] in the Yahad, it leads to a certain 'community' of goods, a pooling of the individual's resources into 'community' once he has passed through a period of probation and has been 'inscribed among his brethren in the order (סרך) of his rank for the Law, for justice, and for the pure meal' as reported in 1QS col. vi, lines 13–23.

Thus Yahad at Qumran refers on one level to a particular mode of organization of the group as Israel, gathered together with their 'heads' to make effective the words of the *Shema'*. In brief, it is organized like Biblical Israel (Priests, Levites, all the people, 1QS col. ii, lines 19–21; Priests, Levites, Israelites, proselytes, CD col. xiv, lines 3–4) and like the ranks of Israel's army (thousands, hundreds, fifties, tens, 1QS col. ii, lines 21–22; CD xii, 23–xiii, 1). Everyone has his allotted place in the Yahad of God in which he is inscribed (1QS col. ii, lines 22–23), and all are under the authority of the 'sons of Zadok, the priests', along with other named officers of the Yahad including the Mebaqqer (inspector or guardian) and the associated figure of the Paqid (1QS col. v, lines 1–3; CD col. ix, line 18; 1QS col. vi, line 14).[26]

But this level of organization does not exhaust the significance of Yahad. It will be instructive to return to Deut. 33.5, and to consider its interpretation recorded in *Sifre Deut.* 346:

24. *Sifre Deut.* 32, cited from the edition of H.S. Horovitz and L. Finkelstein, *Sifre on Deuteronomy* (New York: Jewish Theological Seminary of America, 5729/1969). All translations of *Sifre* are ours. On this point, see also the observations of Max Wilcox, cited by Wendy North, *The Lazarus Story within the Johannine Tradition* (JSNTSup, 212; Sheffield: Sheffield Academic Press, 2001), p. 47.

25. *Sifre Deut.* 32, in the name of R. Eliezer; see also *m.Ber.* 9.5, and Targum Pseudo-Jonathan and Targum Neofiti of Deut. 6.5.

26. On these officers, see Schiffman, *Reclaiming*, pp. 121–23.

AND HE WAS KING OVER JESHURUN. When Israel are alike in one counsel below, His great Name is praised above, as it is said: 'And He was king over Jeshurun'. When? 'When the heads of the people were gathered together'; and 'gathering' [אסיפה] refers to none other than the heads of the people, as it is said: 'And the Lord said to Moses, Take all the heads of the people' (Num. 25.4)... THE ONE-NESS OF THE TRIBES OF ISRAEL. When they make one band [אגודה], but not when they make many bands, for so it says: He builds in heaven His chambers, and He founds His band [אגודתו] upon earth (Amos 9.6). R. Simeon bar Yohai said: A Parable. It is like a man who brought two ships and bound them together with anchors and metal bars, and made them rest in the midst of the sea, and built a palace on them. All the time that the ships were bound together the palace stood. When the ships separated, the palace did not stand. So Israel, when they do the will of God, He builds His chambers in heaven...

At this point, the *Sifre* gets tied up in euphemism. It wants to say that when Israel does not do the will of God on earth, matters go badly wrong in heaven. The commentary does, however, give one example of what it means without resorting to too much circumlocution, a few lines beyond the passage quoted above:

> In like manner you interpret: 'And you are my witnesses, says the Lord, and I am God'.[27] When you are my witnesses, then I am God; and when you are not my witnesses (as if it were possible to say such a thing), in that case I am not God...

This passage from *Sifre* interprets Yahad as referring to the one-ness, not simply of the people Israel, but of the people Israel and God. More precisely, Israel is to be so bound in one-ness with God that the palace of the King, to use the words of R. Simeon's parable, stands secure. Yahad here betokens a perfect union between earth (Israel) and heaven (God and his chambers). At Qumran, too, Yahad refers to the one-ness of Israel with God and his angels. Here is 1QS col. xi, lines 7–9, which also uses the metaphor of building, speaking about the members of the 'union':

> ...and He has made them inheritors in the lot of the holy ones; and with the sons of heaven He has joined their council as a council of Yahad, and as a council of the building of holiness, as an eternal plantation for all future ages.

The imagery of the Temple, of a sort already encountered, is also to the fore in this passage: such concern with the Temple as a meeting point of earth and heaven, of the group and the angels, to which only those in a state of purity are admitted, also informs the language of the poet in 1QH col. xi, lines 19–23, when he says:

> I thank Thee, O Lord, because Thou hast redeemed my soul from the pit; and from the Sheol of Abaddon Thou hast brought me up to everlasting height. And I walk to and fro on a level place without limit; and I know that there is hope (or: an immersion pool, Hebrew מקוה) for the one whom Thou didst fashion from the dust for everlasting council. And Thou hast purified a perverse spirit from great sin, that it be stationed in a position with the host of holy ones, and that it come into a Yahad with the congregation of the sons of heaven. And Thou hast allotted for man an everlasting lot with the spirits of knowledge, to praise Thy Name in a Yahad of rejoicing, and to recount Thy marvellous deeds before all Thy works...

27. Isa. 43.12.

The poem's reference to a מקוה, a 'hope' or 'an immersion pool' for dealing with impurity is revealing: it should be observed that the 'gathering together' of the tribes of Israel around Jacob's deathbed in Targum Pseudo-Jonathan of Genesis 49.1 opens with the Patriarch's command that they 'purify themselves', just as (according to *Gen. Rab.* 98.2) R. Aha interpreted האספו ('be gathered together!') in that Scriptural verse as meaning in reality 'purify yourselves'. Since the סרך of the Yahad includes notions of ranks of soldiers in military formation, the *War Scroll*, too, insists that Yahad is not simply a matter of one-ness in human organization, but refers also to the union of the earthly and angelic hosts:

> Any man who is not pure with regard to his 'source' on the day of battle shall not join them in battle; for angels of holiness are with their hosts as a Yahad (1QM col. vii, line 6; cf. col. xii, lines 2–4).

To sum up and place this information in perspective, we may say as follows. Abominating and flatly rejecting what they perceived as the defilement and invalidity of the Jerusalem Temple and its priesthood, the Qumran group formed themselves into a 'temple of men', where the unique Name of God might tabernacle among those who were completely pure, single-mindedly devoted to the commandments of the Law, and voluntarily submitted to his Kingship. From the very outset, their foundational *Rule* makes their primary aim explicit: they are so ordered as to make effective in the world the central commands of the *Shema'*: to love the One God with a whole heart, soul, and strength, so as to manifest his Unity, his Oneness, which is nothing less than Israel's duty. To this end, they apply to themselves the Hebrew word Yahad, a noun rare in the Scriptures, but which they make very much their own. On the one hand, it expresses exactly their one-ness as a human society ordered in a very specific and hierarchical manner to achieve their goal; and on the other it articulates their participation in and one-ness with the heavenly world of God and the angels. Their understanding of Yahad as the word appears in Deut. 33.5, and the association of this verse with the *Shema'*, is to some degree shared by other Jews, as the Aramaic Targumim and *Sifre* on this verse testify. The Qumran group, however, appear to have broadened and deepened its significance to such an extent that one-ness, in the sense set out above, became their characteristic mark. Finally, they fully expected, in a near time, the appearance of one (or two) Messianic figures and the end of the present epoch. As Targum Neofiti, Fragment Targum Ms Vat440, and the Geniza fragment Targums of Deut. 33.5 indicate, this expectation also is intimately linked to a particular understanding of Yahad.

For the moment, the following modest suggestion may not be amiss. It seems entirely possible that St John's Gospel, when set alongside the concerns examined in this essay, constitutes yet another Jewish or Jewish-influenced attempt to wrestle with the scandal of many Temples, and the consequent damaging theological implications these buildings represented in respect of the divine Unity and the hopes for Israel's future. This Gospel insists that the only legitimate locus of divine presence and worship, that is, the true Temple, is henceforth to be located in Jesus himself (1.14, 51; 2.21; 4.23–24). This is hardly surprising, in that the Father has given to Jesus his very own Name (17.12), which he in turn has communicated to his followers (17.6, 26); so Jesus is able to pray for them: 'Holy Father, keep them in Thy

Name which Thou hast given me, that they may be one, even as we are one (ἵνα ὦσιν ἐν καθὼς ἡμεῖς ἐν)' (17.11). Here Jesus refers back to a fundamental statement which he had made earlier in his ministry: ἐγὼ καὶ ὁ πατὴρ ἐν ἐσμέν, 'I and the Father are one' (10.30), the neuter singular ἐν in both these verses indicating literally 'an object which is one'. We should note the same usage in 17.22 and 23, where Jesus begs the Father for his disciples 'in order that they might be one as we are one' and 'in order that they might be made complete as one' (ἵνα ὦσιν ἐν καθὼς ἡμεῖς ἐν and ἵνα τετελειωμένοι εἰς ἐν). The powerful influence of belief in the Divine Name as the ultimate expression of all unity underlies this request. But entry into the Temple where the Divine Name tabernacles is restricted to those who are in a state of ritual purity. Consequently, we find that already Jesus has pronounced his disciples pure prior to offering this prayer: in 15.3 he declares that all his disciples are καθαροί because of the word he has spoken, thus concluding what he has said about purity while washing his disciples' feet at the supper (13.10–11). It should also be noted that the subject of purity elicits comment elsewhere in this Gospel (2.6; 3.25). Finally, it should be recalled that the Jesus who says these things is spoken of explicitly as the Messiah and King of Israel (1.41, 45–49; 4.25–26; 19.19).

It is neither necessary nor desirable to deduce from what has been said so far that the Gospel is directly engaged in a covert polemic against the Qumran Yahad. Yet examination of those forces which, according to the Qumran writings and the Gospel, bring about the destruction of unity has the effect of sharpening the question whether there may not have been, directly or indirectly, some historical affinities between the people of the Sect and the writer of the Gospel. The third part of this paper will attempt to address this subject.

3. *Opposition to Unity*

Among those who stood against the Qumran sect and its founder, one group in particular is singled out by the scrolls for particular opprobrium. This is the דרשי חלקות, 'the seekers of smooth things': for mentions of it, see 1QH col. x, lines 15, 32; 4QpIsa^c frg. 23 col. ii, line 10; 4QpNah frgs. 3+4 col. i, line 7; CD col. i, line 18. The conventional translation 'seekers of smooth things' is accurate, but incomplete. It designates a group of learned Jews – such is the force of the root דרש indicating the learned searching out of the meaning of Scripture and traditional teaching – seeking the easy option, the smooth, convenient, and comfortable interpretation of the Torah. The phrase implies that the people whom it designates are more interested in their own well-being than in the commandments of the Torah and the scrupulous observance of the same, whatever the cost to the individual. The words themselves, however, imply much more than this. Hebrew has a second verbal root חלק meaning not 'to be smooth', but 'to divide'. We might, therefore, translate the expression as 'seekers of divisions', and in consequence see in it a reference to those who oppose Yahad, that one-ness which is required of those who single-mindedly affirm the demands of the *Shema'*. Here we should recall one of the Rabbinic interpretations of the command to love God with all one's heart, already noted above and appropriately repeated here: 'with all the heart that is in you, so that your heart be not divided (חלוק) against God' (*Sifre Deut.* 32).

There is widespread agreement amongst students of the Qumran scrolls that דרשי חלקות is a coded reference to the Pharisees. The arguments in favour of this identification are well known, and will not be rehearsed here.[28] It need only be said that the coded phrase is meant to indicate that the Pharisees are not only lax in their understanding and practice of the commandments: perhaps the words pun on the Pharisee concern with *halakhot*, rulings designed to apply the law in conditions not directly envisaged by the Torah of Moses, dismissed by their opponents as means of finding loopholes in the law. It also shows how their legal rulings are, in the opinion of the Qumran group, 'divisions' which undermine the most fundamental principle of Israel's vocation – the command to proclaim God's unity and to realize this in the world by loving him with a *heart which is undivided*. There can be no doubt about it: the Qumran group insist on absolute singleness of mind in matters concerned with the Torah.

So much is straightforward. Matters become more complicated, however, when it is observed that the Qumran group was concerned to make distinctions, indeed to insist on divisions, in quite another sphere. Membership of the Yahad required individuals who made up the union to separate themselves from all outside. Thus 1QS col. v, lines 1–2 orders them to be separated (להבדל) from the men of injustice, and the effects of this order are clearly set out in 1QS col. v, lines 11–20. Such division between members of the Yahad and the rest of society was fundamental: the distinction and division between one individual and another is a pre-requisite for the existence of the Yahad. Any man who wished to join the Yahad was obliged to undergo a preliminary examination by the Paqid, an inspection by other members of the Yahad, and a two-year period of 'probation' before being elected to full membership (1QS col. vi, lines 13–23). In other words, from the start the Yahad is to be made up of individuals who are separated, divided from the rest of Jewry. So much is evident already in 4QMMT, which Elisha Qimron and John Strugnell regard as belonging probably to the earliest days of the group's existence, and where the writer says, 'we have separated ourselves (פרשנו) from the multitude of the people [and from all their uncleanness]'.[29] The use here of the root פרש, from which derives the word 'Pharisee', should be noted: it will be discussed presently.

According to CD, the officer responsible for determining new members of the Yahad and enrolling them is called המבקר or 'the inspector' (see, e.g., CD col. xv, lines 8, 11, 14), who is also named at 1QS col. vi, line 12. CD provides a rule for this officer, which includes the following highly significant requirement for his duties towards members of the 'camp':

28. See, for example, Vermes, *The Complete Dead Sea Scrolls*, pp. 62–63; Schiffman, *Reclaiming*, pp. 228–30, 250; M.A. Knibb, *The Qumran Community* (Cambridge: Cambridge University Press, 1987), pp. 24, 211–16.

29. See 4Q397 frg. 7, as edited by E. Qimron and J. Strugnell, *Qumran Cave 4. V. Miqsat Ma`ase Ha-Torah* (DJD, 10; Oxford: Clarendon Press, 1994), p. 58: שֶׁ[פֹ]רשנו מרוב העֹם ומכול טמאאתם. On pp. 119–21 the editors suggest a date for the text around 159–152 BCE.

And he shall have compassion on them like a father has compassion on his children, and he shall carry them in all their distress like a shepherd carries his sheep. He shall loosen all the fetters that bind them, so that there be none that is oppressed or broken in his congregation (col. xiii, lines 9–10).

The verbal root בקר in Biblical Hebrew means 'enquire, seek'. The Hebrew of Qumran, however, already shows signs of development towards Mishnaic Hebrew, where the root in *Pi'el* (*Mebaqqer* is a *Pi'el* participle) also has the sense of 'distinguish', entirely appropriate to this officer's task. The words of CD col. xiii, lines 9–10, however, provide the underlying Scriptural warrant for the Mebaqqer's duties, in that they clearly echo the words of Ezek. 34 about the shepherds of Israel, whose failure leads God to announce in Ezek. 34.11–12:

Behold I, even I [הנני אני] am, and I shall seek [ודרשתי] my sheep and I shall search for them [ובקרתים]. As a shepherd searches [כבקרת רעה] for his flock on the day when he is in the midst of his sheep which are נפרשות, so will I search for [אבקר] my sheep and deliver them from all the places where they were scattered [נפצו] on the day of cloud and thick darkness.

So reads the MT, one word of which has been purposely left untranslated, since the unpointed Hebrew word נפרשות may have two quite divergent meanings, depending on how it is vocalized. Most modern translators and commentators read it as נִפְרָשׂוֹת, following the standard *Lexica* and deriving it from root פרשׂ, *Qal* 'to spread out', *Niph'al* 'to be scattered'.[30] Given this reading, the shepherd is described as searching for his flock when he is among his sheep who have been scattered abroad.

The Masoretes, however, vocalized the word as נִפְרָשׁוֹת, taking it from root פרשׁ, 'to separate, make plain, distinguish'. In Mishnaic Hebrew, the root means 'to separate, distinguish', as does the cognate root in Biblical Aramaic: in later Aramaic, the root in *Pa'el* means 'separate, divide, distinguish, define, express clearly'. If this vocalization be adopted, we have before us the image of a shepherd searching for his flock among sheep which have been separated, clearly defined or distinguished from other sheep. LXX and Targum accepted what is extant as MT's vocalization. Thus LXX translated נפרשות as διακεχωρισμένων, 'separated', the very verb they had used in Gen. 1.4, 14, 18 to express the separation of light from darkness and day from night, and to describe Jacob's separation of different kinds of sheep one from another (Gen. 30.32, 40). The Targum speaks of the shepherd searching for his flock on the day when he is in the midst of his sheep and separates, distinguishes, divides them, מפריש להון. St Jerome knew of both vocalizations, and gave them in his *Comm. in Hiezechielem* XI as *in medio ovium suarum dissipatarum* ('in the midst of his own sheep which are scattered'; this rendering he adopted in the Vulgate), or '...*ovium suarum*

---

30. See L. Koehler and W. Baumgartner, *The Hebrew and Aramaic Lexicon of the Old Testament* (rev. W. Baumgartner and J.J. Stamm; 5 vols.; Leiden: E.J. Brill, 1994–2000), III, pp. 975–76; BDB, p. 831.

separatarum' ('in the midst of his own sheep which have been separated, distinguished').[31]

In the Masoretic vocalization of נפרשות which concurs with LXX and Targum and which was known to St Jerome, we uncover one of the exegetical foundations for the authority of the *Mebaqqer* at Qumran. Just as God will search for (Hebrew בקר) his distinguished sheep, so the duty of the *Mebeqqer*, the 'inspector' or guardian of the Yahad, is to seek for the distinguished sheep, those who differ from and are separate from the rest of the flock. He is responsible for examining and scrutinizing all candidates who seek membership of his group (CD col. xiv, lines 10–12), for evaluating their characters and possibly even their physical appearance (here we may recall the Horoscopes found in the caves at Qumran). From these individuals, the *Mebaqqer* builds up the Yahad. Thus we encounter a remarkable state of affairs. The Yahad represents absolute single-minded one-ness with regard to God and his Torah, and rejects all division and those who seek it, especially those 'seekers of smooth things' who are commonly called פרושים, 'separated ones'. Yet this Yahad is itself composed of people who are distinguished one from another, נפרשות if you will, who have been gathered into one by the *Mebaqqer*, 'the one who distinguishes' like the shepherd of Ezekiel's prophecy. The polemic is clear: it is the Yahad who are true Pharisees, 'distinguished ones', who according to 4QMMT have separated themselves from the rest of the people, not the learned Torah scholars searching for הלקות (or, perhaps, using their own terminology, seeking for הלכות) who are commonly known as Pharisees. Inevitably, all this talk of shepherds and sheep brings us back to John's Gospel.

4. *John's Gospel: Conclusions*

The emphasis on unity in John's Gospel, which has already been briefly considered, is manifest again in the parable of the good shepherd who calls his own sheep by name, leads them out, and knows them (Jn 10.3, 4, 14). Jesus knows the sheep just as the Father knows him and he knows the Father (10.15); he has other sheep which must also be brought, so that there be *one* flock and *one* shepherd (10.16). These and other words of Jesus cause a σχῖσμα, a division or separation, among the Jews (10.19). Later in the same chapter, the mutual knowledge of Jesus and the Father is reiterated: Jesus knows his sheep, they follow him, the Father has given them to him and no-one can snatch them away; and thus he declares ἐγὼ καὶ ὁ πατὴρ ἕν ἐσμέν (10.30).

The underlying influence of Ezek. 34 on Jn 10 is often acknowledged by modern commentators on the Gospel.[32] We have seen how in particular how Ezek. 34.12 was understood at Qumran, and we may discern a similar interpretation of that verse in the Gospel in the following respects:

---

31. So Jerome's translation of Ezek. 34.12 given as preliminary to his commentary: see F. Glorie, *S. Hieronymi Presbyteri Opera, Pars I Opera Exegetica 4, Commentariorum In Hiezechielem XI* (Turnhout: Brepols, 1964), p. 481.

32. Of the many authorities who might be cited, see R.E. Brown, *The Gospel According to John* (2 vols.; AB, 29/29A; New York: Doubleday, 1966/1970), II, pp. 397–98; H. Ridderbos, *The*

(a)   Both the *Mebaqqer* and Jesus are concerned to gather 'scattered' sheep into a 'one-ness'. As regards the Gospel, see also 11.52, where Jesus' death serves to gather together εἰς ἕν the children of God who are scattered abroad.

(b)   Both the *Mebaqqer* and Jesus are gathering together people who are 'distinct, separated' from others: both bring about a public division between those whom they gather and the rest of Jewry. In a sense, both gather around them groups which could properly be called 'Pharisees' in the sense of 'separated ones'.

In other words, both the Qumran group and the Gospel perceive in Ezekiel 34.12 reference to the presence of a shepherd among נפרשׁות, 'separated' sheep who have been 'scattered' in order to bring them into one. On the other hand, significant differences appear:

(a)   The *Mebaqqer* has actively to examine people to ensure their fitness to join the Yahad. Jesus, however, already knows who are his, and they know also that they belong to him (Jn. 10.4, 14, 27), because his Father has given them to him (10.29; cf. 17.6, 9). Jesus does not require his followers to undergo a period of extended probation.

(b)   The *Mebaqqer* may, and certainly does, reject some who seek membership of the Yahad. Jesus, however, states clearly that all that the Father has given to him shall come to him, and the one who comes to him he will not at all cast out (6.37; cf. 17.12).

At the same time, the union into which both the Qumran *Mebaqqer* and Jesus bring their followers is not only an earthly organization, but a heavenly reality uniting the upper and lower worlds. Yet even here the details of this earthly and heavenly union find different modes of expression among the two groups. The Qumran Yahad as 'one-ness' made up of individuals is the legitimate (albeit temporary) Temple of God uniting its earthly members to the heavenly realms where the angels serve God. The *Mebaqqer* appears to be but one officer in this Temple polity. Jesus, however, is the true and permanent Temple in himself: it is through him as an individual that those in union with him may worship the Father.[33] Since

---

Gospel of John: A Theological Commentary (trans. J. Vriend; Grand Rapids: Eerdmans, 1997), pp. 356–65; and, for a recent analysis of the Good Shepherd parable in terms of the Gospel's particular structure and aims, see L. Schenke, *Johannes Kommentar* (Düsseldorf: Patmos Verlag, 1998), pp. 190–97.

33.   For this well known aspect of the Fourth Gospel's teaching, see Brown, *The Gospel*, I, pp. 88–91, 180–81; John Ashton, *Understanding the Fourth Gospel* (Oxford: Clarendon Press, 1991), pp. 342–45; Ridderbos, *The Gospel of John*, pp. 114–21 and 161–65, and the literature there cited. In view of the Qumran group's application to itself of Temple imagery discussed here, it is of great interest to note that Ashton, *Understanding the Fourth Gospel*, p. 237, suggests that the author of the Fourth Gospel may have been an Essene. Furthermore, on the theme of unity in John's Gospel, see the observations on the nature of Johannine Christology by Bruce Longenecker, 'The Unbroken Messiah: A Johannine Feature and its Social Functions', *NTS* 41 (1995), pp. 428–41; and the links between John's concern with unity and the recitation of *Shema'* noted by C.K. Barrett, 'The Old Testament in the Fourth Gospel', *JTS* os 48 (1947), pp. 155–69.

he has manifested God's Name (which is One) to his adherents and is himself One with the Father, he is uniquely qualified to carry out the command to love God with all the heart and bring into being on earth the 'one-ness' which is the pre-requisite for the coming of Messiah.[34] That love is the chief command of Jesus in St. John's Gospel no-one need deny; but in light of what has been said here, it should probably be carefully scrutinized in the setting of Jewish understanding of the *Shema'*.

In sum, the evidence examined here suggests that there is a *prima facie* case for an argument that Johannine statements about the Divine Unity and the role of Jesus as shepherd represent, *inter alia*, one particular stance towards matters which were particularly sensitive and controversial in first century Judaism. These controversial matters were also fundamental: they have to do with the identity of the legitimate Temple, and the proper manner of affirming God's Unity as required by the *Shema'*. The texts from Qumran provide an insight into the doctrinal views of a group which of necessity had had an urgent need to formulate a clear position on these controversial matters. The Johannine formulations appear somewhat similar to those of the Qumran group, but differ at crucial points, as we have seen. In one vital respect, however, both John and Qumran agree: both insist that the group commonly called Pharisees are utterly misguided. For the Qumran group, they are 'seekers of divisions' and all which that term of contempt implies. For the Gospel, too, they are hardly united (see 9.15–16). Some, like Nicodemus, are inclined to accept Jesus (3.1-2; 7.50; 19.39); but most of them seek to prevent others from adhering to him (see especially 12.42; cf. 7.48). We may conclude with a question. To what extent was the hostility towards the Pharisees shared by the Qumran group and the Gospel the result of the Pharisees' support for the Jerusalem Temple? It is noticeable that, unlike the other Evangelists, John associates them with the High Priests and the Temple on no fewer than seven occasions out of a total of nineteen occurrences of the designation 'Pharisee':[35] in light of the evidence set out here, we might wonder whether that association might not be worthy of further study?

---

34. On Jesus and the Name of God in this Gospel, see Brown, *The Gospel*, II, pp. 779–81; Ridderbos, *The Gospel of John*, pp. 550–52.

35. See Jn 1.24 in the light of the report in 1.19; 7.32; and the subsequent notes in 7.47–48; 11.47; 11.57; and 18.3. Given the evidence examined here, it is of some interest to note that the actions of Jesus can cause σχίσμα, 'division' or 'separation' among these 'separated ones': see Jn 9.16.

Monotheism and the Gospel of John: Jesus, Moses, and the Law

Wendy E.S. North, University of Durham

1. *Introduction*

'In the beginning was the Word, and the Word was with God, and the Word was God' (Jn 1.1). In this magnificent opening statement, the fourth evangelist declares his position to whoever would know: the Word was neither 'divine' (θεῖος), nor was it a second god; rather, the Word *was* God, θεός. Right at the beginning of his gospel, then, John states his case: whatever we are to learn in the story about to unfold, this is the witness of a monotheist,[1] by which I mean in this context that John is a self-confessed adherent to the Jewish belief in one God.[2]

Yet the witness of John the monotheist to the life of the human Jesus seems at first the very celebration of the way to undermine the principle. As John's Word then become flesh, the Jesus we meet in the gospel is omnipotent, omniscient, and seemingly oblivious to human doubt. As Son of man, he alone has descended from heaven and will return there (3.13; 6.62). As Son of God, he has been sent into the world, he does the works of God, speaks the words of God, wields God's powers to give life and to judge, and declares himself to be one with the Father (3.17; 5.19–30; 10.30; 12.49; 17.2). In fact, John not only describes Jesus in language appropriate to God, but on two occasions he explicitly calls Jesus θεός (1.18; 20.28).[3] In these respects, then, it appears that John has deliberately sought to present Jesus in the gospel story as God on earth. Indeed, one almost hesitates to use the term 'Christology' of this phenomenon; it reads much more like *Theology* in a human environment.

For all that, however, we must also be aware of the several indicators in the gospel that John also thought of Jesus as real flesh and blood in the normal sense. These range from the casual detail, such as weariness and thirst (4.6; 19.28), to the emphasis on Jesus' agitation in the face of death and on the stark reality of the Passion (11.33; 12.27; 13.21; 19.17–30). Most telling, perhaps, is his reference on two occasions to Jesus' mother and his father Joseph (1.45; 6.42).[4]

---

1. See esp. R. Bultmann, *The Gospel of John: A Commentary* (German, 1946/1947; trans. G.R. Beasley-Murray; Oxford: Basil Blackwell, 1971), pp. 33–34.

2. See also 5.44 and 17.3, where this position is echoed in the story itself. I explain my meaning here aware that the appropriateness of using 'monotheism' language in interpreting biblical texts is open to question, see the contributions of R.W.L. Moberly and N. MacDonald below.

3. Accepting the harder reading θεός, rather than υἱός, in 1.18, in agreement with B. Lindars, *The Gospel of John* (NCB; London: Marshall, Morgan & Scott, 1972), pp. 98–99.

4. John does not dispute Jesus' human parentage. The problem with 'the Jews' in 6.42 is not

On the basis of these observations, it seems clear that John was not only able to think of the person Jesus of Nazareth as the enfleshment of the Word which was God, but also to claim such a thing under the flag of Jewish monotheism. Even more to the point, perhaps, is that in some way it evidently made theological sense to him to do that, as we may rightly judge from those passages in the gospel where Jesus' exalted claims are upheld in refutation of charges of ditheism made by 'the Jews' (5.17–30; 10.30–38; cf. 19.7).

If this evaluation of John's position is reasonably accurate, it poses important questions about the character of John's monotheistic faith and the roots of his Christology. These may be expressed as follows. What is the background to this presentation? On what basis did John assume that he could ascribe deity to Jesus without compromising his devotion to the one God of Israel? Such considerations also point to a further complicating issue: if it was self-evident to John the Jewish monotheist that he could present Jesus as he did, why is it that others who shared that background did not also share his view? Why, indeed, on his own showing was he vehemently opposed by 'Jews' precisely on that score?

It is obvious that if we hope to achieve even a partial resolution of these problems, we will need to be as clear as possible not only about the context in which John wrote but also about the issues which were at the heart of the conflict in which he was a protagonist. Accordingly, beginning with a brief reminder of the immediate circumstances generally thought to have prompted the publication of the gospel, this investigation will focus on John's presentation of one particular group in that situation who appear to represent the middle ground between the hostile 'Jews' on the one hand and the Johannine Christians on the other. The preoccupations of this group will be taken to indicate those features which were of central concern to the Judaism with which John was familiar, and on that basis a description of the positions of all three groups as differing responses to those core elements will be attempted. Finally, conclusions will be offered on John's Christology as a Jewish monotheistic concept.

2. *The Gospel's Sitz im Leben*

Since the ground-breaking work of J.L. Martyn, it has become widely recognized that the fourth gospel can be interpreted on two historical levels: it not only relates the story of Jesus which is in the evangelist's past but also, in that process, conveys crucial information about contemporary circumstances which the gospel is concerned to address.[5] Three texts in particular, all referring to exclusion from the

---

that their information is inaccurate but that they are able to see nothing *more* than this in Jesus; see esp. Bultmann, *Gospel*, pp. 62 n. 4, 104 n. 1, and 229 n. 5.

5.   See J.L. Martyn, *History and Theology in the Fourth Gospel* (Nashville: Abingdon Press, 2nd edn, 1979), pp. 24–36. On the contribution of Martyn's book (1st edn, 1968) to the development of the interpretation of John's gospel, see J. Ashton, *Understanding the Fourth Gospel* (Oxford: Clarendon Press, 1991), esp. pp. 107–108. Ashton describes Martyn's book as 'probably the most important single work on the Gospel since Bultmann's commentary' (p. 107) and continues to interact with Martyn's research throughout his own lengthy study.

synagogue (9.22; 12.42; 16.2), are seen as key to the situation involving the evangelist and his readers at the time of writing. The first two reflect an inner-synagogue situation where people go in fear of authorities ('Jews', 9.22; 'Pharisees', 12.42), who have agreed to evict from that gathering any who confess belief in Jesus. The third text not only refers to exclusion from the synagogue but also envisages a time when killing believers will be seen as offering service to God (16.2).[6]

Bearing in mind the inevitable bias in these reports, it is difficult to tell with any precision what happened to cause the rift in the first place.[7] We must surely allow, however, that by the time John compiled and composed the Fourth Gospel such difficulties were in the past, and this means that whatever situation we do find reflected in the gospel is likely to tell us rather more about the *consequences* of such an upheaval than it does about a possible cause.[8] This being the case, it seems reasonable to assume that these three texts indicate the following: (a) that at the time of writing the Johannine group is already excluded from the Jewish community which is its natural home; (b) that John knows of other believers less ready to confess their faith who have not been excluded; and (c) that he fears the situation is about to enter another, deadlier, stage in which the lives of his flock may be forfeit.[9] Clearly this is a serious state of affairs and, as already indicated, one in

---

6. See Martyn, *History and Theology*, pp. 38–42.

7. On the difficulties involved in reconstructing the specific circumstances under which Johannine Christians were rejected by the synagogue, see J.M.G. Barclay, 'Who Was Considered an Apostate in the Jewish Diaspora?', in G.N. Stanton and G.G. Stroumsa (eds.), *Tolerance and Intolerance in Early Judaism and Christianity* (Cambridge: Cambridge University Press, 1998), pp. 80–98 (here pp. 90–91 and 93). J.L. Martyn's hypothesis that there was a synagogue ban operated by Judaism against Christians at the time (*History and Theology*, pp. 43–62) has not gone uncriticized; see Ashton, *Understanding*, p. 108 n. 102; also J.M. Lieu, 'Temple and Synagogue in John', *NTS* 45 (1999), pp. 51–69 (61) and 'Anti-Judaism in the Fourth Gospel: Explanation and Hermeneutics', in R. Bieringer, D. Pollefeyt and F. Vandecasteele-Vanneuville (eds.), *Anti-Judaism and the Fourth Gospel: Papers of the Leuven Colloquium, 2000* (Assen: Van Gorcum, 2001), pp. 126–43 (134). In the same volume, see also R. Bieringer, D. Pollefeyt and F. Vandecasteele-Vanneuville, 'Wrestling with Johannine Anti-Judaism: A Hermeneutical Framework for the Analysis of the Current Debate', pp. 3–44 (p. 12 with n. 28); S. Motyer, 'The Fourth Gospel and the Salvation of Israel: An Appeal for a New Start', pp. 92–110 (p. 94 with n. 10; pp. 97–98); and M.C. de Boer, 'The Depiction of "the Jews" in John's Gospel: Matters of Behavior and Identity', pp. 260–80 (267 with n. 25). See further the full discussion in A.T. Lincoln, *Truth on Trial: The Lawsuit Motif in the Fourth Gospel* (Peabody, MA: Hendrickson, 2000), pp. 269–78. For the suggestion that the disaster of 70 CE had a fateful role to play, see P. Perkins, 'If Jerusalem Stood: The Destruction of Jerusalem and Christian Anti-Judaism', *BibInt* 8 (2000), pp. 194–204 (201–204).

8. For the view that the gospel represents the Johannine group's response to rejection rather than the attitudes that may have precipitated it, see B.J. Malina and L. Rohrbaugh, *Social-Science Commentary on the Gospel of John* (Minneapolis: Fortress Press, 1998), p. 9. A.T. Lincoln judges wisely that the gospel was written at a point when sufficient time had elapsed for the Johannine group to assume an identity separate from that of the synagogue, but not enough time to heal the scars of the breach; see his *Truth on Trial*, p. 285.

9. See Martyn, *History and Theology*, pp. 66–81. J.M. Lieu observes, correctly, that John's emphasis elsewhere rests on Temple rather than synagogue ('Temple and Synagogue in John').

which the dispute between the two sides evidently has the Johannine Christology as its flashpoint: according to 'the Jews', Jesus' claims to equality with God are blasphemous and worthy of death (5.18; 10.33); according to the Johannine Jesus, they are liable to no such charge.

If, as we suppose, the gospel was forged out of conflict between groups who were once close and who laid claim to the same cultural territory, can we specify some *common* factor in that shared background which could have been appropriated by both sides in radically different – and ultimately irreconcilable – ways? If we can, then we will surely have come close, not only to the bone of contention fundamental to this dispute, but also to the key feature within Judaism from which Johannine Christology took its cue and in relation to which it developed its distinctive shape. With that in mind, I will now attempt to place us right in the centre of that dispute by focusing on a group who appear to represent the middle ground between the other two opposing extremes.

3. *John's Believing 'Jews'*

In his references to exclusion from the synagogue, John tells us that there are not two parties in the fray but three. On the one hand there are 'Jews'/Pharisees who expel from the synagogue and seek to kill and, on the other, the Johannine faithful who are estranged and threatened, but 12.42 attests the existence of a third group who also believe in Jesus but stay low-profile in the synagogue for fear of exclusion. These people are almost certainly the group John has in mind when he refers to 'Jews' who believe.[10]

For the most part, 'the Jews' in John's gospel are presented as a hostile and menacing force (cf. 5.18; 7.1, 13, 19, 25; 8.37–59; 9.22; 10.22–39; 11.8; 18.12, 40; 19.7, 12, 38; 20.19). Nevertheless, it is important to take account of the fact that not all John's references conform to this stereotype. In some cases, John's 'Jews' can be sympathetic and well-intentioned, often confused and mystified in response to Jesus rather than hostile.[11] They can also believe in Jesus although, in John's opinion, their faith is of a rather inferior miracles-centred variety by contrast with

Nevertheless, his use of the hapax ἀποσυνάγωγος, dubbed 'enigmatic' by Lieu (p. 62), must surely still remain a key indicator to the Johannine situation post-70 CE. Not only does the immediate context of 16.2 suggest a live issue, but it is important to note that 9.22 and 12.42 occur in editorial comment only, and that all three references apply exclusively to those who *believe* in Jesus, as distinct from Jesus himself (cf. 6.59).

10. The following paragraphs on 'the Jews' and on 10.40–42 summarize earlier research; see W.E.S. North, *The Lazarus Story within the Johannine Tradition* (JSNTSup, 212; Sheffield: Sheffield Academic Press, 2001), pp. 124–26 and 132–34.

11. This more positive aspect of John's presentation of 'the Jews' is not always reflected in studies on the gospel. For example, out of the twenty-four contributors to the recently published volume, *Anti-Judaism and the Fourth Gospel* (see above, n. 5), only three deal with this topic in any detail, of whom two (Dunn and Motyer) point out that it is insufficiently recognized in the debate; see M.C. de Boer, 'The Depiction of "the Jews" in John's Gospel'; J.D.G. Dunn, 'The Embarrassment of History: Reflections on the Problem of "Anti-Judaism" in the Fourth Gospel', pp. 47–67 (esp. pp. 56–57); S. Motyer, 'The Fourth Gospel and the Salvation of Israel', p. 105.

genuine faith which, he insists, is based on Jesus' word (cf. 4.41–42, 48, 50; cf. 4.53; 5.24; 6.63, 68; 8.30–31).[12] This non-hostile type seems to find its representative in Nicodemus, whom John dubs 'a ruler of the Jews' (3.1).[13] Impressed by the signs and therefore less than trustworthy (3.2 cf. 2.23), Nicodemus comes to Jesus 'by night' and never quite leaves the darkness behind (3.2; 19.39). Failing to grasp the essentials of Johannine truth, he retains a perspective focused on law, and continues to the last to act secretly and to follow the customs of 'the Jews' (3.10; 7.51; 19.38–40).[14] This particular representation of 'the Jews' resonates well with John's reference in 12.42 to certain believers – even rulers, he says – who have not confessed their faith for fear of exclusion from the synagogue. We should not fail to note the blistering comment that follows in verse 43, in which he roundly accuses them of seeking men's honour rather than God's. It may well be, however, that in scolding them, John also held out the hope of winning these closet Christians round to his point of view.

I now propose to build up a profile of these 'Jews' with reference to John's presentation of them in the Lazarus story and related material (10.40–12.19), which is where they feature most prominently. The relevant details are as follows:

(a) In 10.40–42, where John prepares the ground for the Lazarus miracle, he reintroduces the topic of signs (v. 41) and relates that to the belief of 'the many' (v. 42). Reference to the faith of 'the many' has previously been linked with the signs (2.23; 7.31) and associated with 'the Jews' (8.30–31;[15] see also Nicodemus at 3.1–2, cf. 2.23; and 'the Jews' at 7.35, cf. v. 31). This refrain will be repeated again in relation to 'the Jews' who believe because of the Lazarus sign (11.45; cf. 12.11), and will make its final appearance, again in relation to the signs, in 12.42 (cf. v. 37), John's reference to the low-profile believers in the synagogue.

(b) In the story proper, these 'Jews' are 'the many' who arrive from Jerusalem to sympathize with Martha and Mary (11.19),[16] and who follow Mary to the tomb to weep (vv. 31, 33). Never quite grasping the full implications of Jesus' love for Lazarus, and ever alert to another miraculous cure (vv. 36–

---

12. See M.-E. Boismard, *Moïse ou Jésus: Essai de Christologie Johannique* (BETL, 84; Leuven: Leuven University Press, 1988), p. 68; M. Scott, *Sophia and the Johannine Jesus* (JSNTSup, 71; Sheffield: Sheffield Academic Press, 1992), pp. 204–205.

13. See Martyn, *History and Theology*, pp. 87–88, cf. p. 116, on 'rulers', including Nicodemus, as secret believers.

14. On these and other points relating to Nicodemus' ambiguous presentation, see the bibliography in North, *Lazarus Story*, p. 125 n. 27, and add now J.-M. Sevrin, 'The Nicodemus Enigma: The Characterization and Function of an Ambiguous Actor of the Fourth Gospel', in *Anti-Judaism and the Fourth Gospel*, pp. 357–69.

15. This identification is clear whatever else we make of this difficult text. On the problem of 'the Jews' who believe in 8.30–31, but who are then charged with seeking to kill Jesus, and behave accordingly (8.37–59), see F.J. Moloney, *The Gospel of John* (Sacra Pagina, 4; Collegeville, MN: Liturgical Press, 1998), p. 277. The abrupt shift to vehement denunciation at 8.37 suggests that John has the hostile authorities in mind from this point onwards (cf. 5.18; 7.1, 19–20, 25; 11.8, 53; 12.10).

16. Note that they are quite distinct from 'the Jews' who seek to stone Jesus referred to in 11.8.

37), many believe on witnessing the sign, although some prove less than trustworthy (vv. 45–46). In ch. 12, a great crowd of these 'Jews' flocks to Bethany not only because of Jesus but also to see the spectacle of Lazarus risen from the dead (12.9). Later, their witness to the Lazarus sign is said to account for the enthusiastic reception Jesus is given on his entry into Jerusalem (vv. 17–18).

(c) Events on either side of the miracle itself deserve special attention. Before it takes place, Jesus gives voice to his thanksgiving prayer to the Father in order to appeal to the crowd standing by to believe that he was sent by God (11.41–42). In 11.45, many of the crowd, who are 'the Jews' who had come with Mary (cf. v. 31), are quick to respond.[17] Following the miracle, John makes it abundantly clear that it is precisely the signs-faith of these 'Jews' which places Jesus' life in danger. At the council meeting, the fear that all will come to believe in Jesus because of the signs drives the authorities to act decisively against him (11.47–48, cf. v. 53). By extension, the same threat to life is applied to Lazarus, on whose account, we learn, many of 'the Jews' were going away and believing in Jesus (12.10–11). Finally, following the triumphal entry, it becomes plain to the authorities that this signs-based adulation is beyond their powers to control (12.18–19). The obvious corollary is that Jesus must be stopped.

On the basis of the evidence in these chapters, we may describe this group of 'Jews' as follows. These are 'the many' who believe, who are attracted by the miraculous and who readily accept on that basis that Jesus is sent from God. As John presents them, they are shallow and lacking in insight. More than that, however, their adulation represents a danger, for it immediately prompts the authorities to seek the lives of both Jesus and Lazarus in order to prevent any further loosening of their hold over these people. In addition to this material, it is worth noting those 'Jews' passages elsewhere in the gospel in which these various characteristics are echoed.[18] 'The Jews' in chapter 6, for example, are presented as the puzzled, non-hostile type (vv. 41–42, 52) and are continuous with the crowd who earlier followed Jesus because of the signs (v. 2). The equally puzzled 'Jews' at 7.35 relate to 'the many' impressed by the signs in v. 31, who have believed in Jesus on hearing his claim that he was sent by God (v. 29), and whose faith has spurred the authorities to take action against him (v. 32). Finally, there are 'the Jews' in 8.31, who are 'the many' who believe when Jesus claims that he always pleases the Father who sent him (vv. 29–30).[19]

17. The conclusion that 11.42 targets 'the Jews', rather than the disciples, represents a change from my earlier interpretation of this verse (see North, *The Lazarus Story*, p. 158).

18. *Pace* R.E. Brown, *The Gospel According to John* (2 vols.; AB, 29–29A; Garden City, NY: Doubleday, 1966; London: Geoffrey Chapman, 1971), pp. 427–28, the treatment of 'the Jews' in ch. 11 and 12 is not inconsistent with references earlier in the gospel and therefore does not constitute evidence of the hand of a redactor.

19. Possibly also these 'Jews' reappear in 19.20 as 'the many' who read the title on the cross. Note that the Jewish authorities ('the chief priests of the Jews') act quickly to change the wording from what looks like a believable fact to a falsifiable claim (v. 21).

So much, then, for John's believing 'Jews', who occupy the uncomfortable middle ground between the other two radically opposed positions. What precisely is the nature of the faith John attributes to these fence-sitters, and in what ways does it connect with and differ from the convictions of the other two sides, namely, the hostile 'Jews' on the one hand, and the Johannine Christians on the other?

At this point, I defer gratefully to the work of a number of scholars who have convincingly argued that the signs-based faith we have found to be characteristic of these non-hostile 'Jews' represents an interest in Jesus as the prophet like Moses.[20] The basic text here is Deut. 18.18–22. This is where God promises Moses to raise up a prophet like him who will speak God's words as commanded, and whom the people must hear upon pain of divine displeasure. The text goes on to describe another prophet, the false pretender, who presumes to speak in God's name, or speaks in the name of other gods, but his word will not come true and he must be put to death. Deut. 13.1–11 (LXX: 13.1–12) elaborates on this false prophet: he is associated with signs and wonders and persuades the people to follow and serve other gods. His words must not be heeded and he must be put to death for leading the people astray. Finally, we must not ignore the epitaph on Moses at the end of Deuteronomy (34.10–12). This states that no prophet has arisen since to compare with Moses, whom God knew face to face, and none like him for all the signs and wonders God sent him to do in Egypt.[21] There are other, later, texts nearer to John's time which develop this imagery. These range from Sirach and the Jewish tragedian Ezekiel in the second century BCE to Samaritan material from the fourth century CE which incorporates older tradition. Since these texts are readily available in the secondary literature, it will be appropriate at this point simply to provide a brief summary of their main features. Basically, they assume the following: first, that when Moses ascended Mount Sinai to receive the Law (Exod. 19.20; 20.21; 24.18; 32.31), he entered into heaven and there saw God himself; second, that on Sinai, God initiated Moses into the secrets of nature and thereby endowed him with the power over the elements which is manifested in his miracles; and third, that

20. These include: J.D.G. Dunn (*The Partings of the Ways Between Christianity and Judaism and their Significance for the Character of Christianity* [London: SCM Press; Philadelphia: Trinity Press International, 1991], esp. p. 226; *idem*, 'Let John Be John: A Gospel for its Time', in P. Stuhlmacher [ed.], *The Gospel and the Gospels* [Grand Rapids: Eerdmans, 1991], pp. 293–322); J.L. Martyn (*History and Theology*); W.A. Meeks (*The Prophet-King: Moses Traditions and the Johannine Christology* [NovTSup, 14; Leiden: E.J. Brill, 1967]; *idem*, ' "Am I a Jew?"': Johannine Christianity and Judaism', in J. Neusner [ed.], *Christianity, Judaism and Other Greco-Roman Cults: Studies for Morton Smith at Sixty* [SJLA, 12/1; Leiden: E.J. Brill, 1975], pp. 163–86); M.J.J. Menken (*Old Testament Quotations in the Fourth Gospel: Studies in Textual Form* [CBET, 15; Kampen: Kok Pharos, 1996], pp. 46–65); N.R. Petersen (*The Gospel of John and the Sociology of Light: Language and Characterization in the Fourth Gospel* [Valley Forge, PA: Trinity Press International, 1993], and D.M. Smith (*The Theology of the Gospel of John* [New Testament Theology; Cambridge: Cambridge University Press, 1995], pp. 108 and 126). See further Boismard, *Moïse ou Jésus*, pp. 44–71, who also conjectures that the Cana miracle, the cure of the official's son, and the miraculous catch of fish must have originally been the first three signs in John's source, in reference to the three 'signs' performed by Moses in Exod. 4.1–9.

21. On these and other biblical texts concerning Moses, see Petersen, *Sociology of Light*, pp. 91–96.

Moses was made God's vice-regent on earth, invested with God's power and given God's name.[22]

4. *Jesus, Moses, and the Law*

This investigation into John's presentation of the non-hostile 'Jews' has led us to conclude that their faith derives from a kind of Jewish piety in which Moses the lawgiver was central and accorded the highest possible status in relation to God. For our purposes, this is a crucially important point, for there is compelling evidence that Moses traditions have played a large part in the argument of the gospel as a whole. Indeed, not only do John's *hostile* 'Jews' declare their allegiance to Moses, but it is clear enough that John's own presentation of Jesus has involved some considerable engagement with the status and significance of the lawgiver. In other words, in pinpointing the Moses-centred piety behind the faith of John's believing 'Jews', we have at once arrived at the factor which is common to all three groups as represented in the gospel, although in each case that common ground has been differently construed. By the same token, I suggest, we have also completed our search for the key feature within Judaism which, above all, saw the distinctive Johannine Christology take direction and shape. With that in mind, the last section of this study will be devoted to an analysis of the position of all *three* groups in relation to Moses and the Law. I will leave John's attitudes until last for a fuller comment.

Moses and the Law: John's hostile 'Jews'
These evidently hold fast to the Moses-centred, Torah-focused piety that we have recognized as the basis of the other two positions, but in this case, if there has been any movement at all, we must surely think in terms of entrenchment rather than progress. These are the self-styled disciples of Moses (9.28) whom they see as their advocate before God (5.45), and who engage in study of Torah as the source of eternal life (5.39). They appear to maintain this position with varying degrees of aggression. They reject outright the suggestion that Jesus is the prophet like Moses (9.29; 12.37) and are ready to threaten with exclusion those 'Jews' who are attracted to that idea (cf. 12.42). Any application of the Moses traditions to Jesus here is restricted to identifying Jesus as the *false* prophet, who presumes to speak God's words and who leads the people astray (7.47, cf. v. 12; 7.52; 11.48; 12.11, 19),[23]

---

22.   For detail, see Dunn, *Partings of the Ways*, p. 223; *idem*, 'Let John Be John', p. 307; L.W. Hurtado, *One God, One Lord: Early Christian Devotion and Ancient Jewish Monotheism* (Edinburgh: T. & T. Clark, 2nd edn, 1998), pp. 56–63; Martyn, *History and Theology*, pp. 106–111; Meeks, *Prophet-King*, pp. 110–11, 120–25, 147–49, 156–59, 205–209, and 241–44; *idem*, '"Am I a Jew?"', p. 173; 'Moses as God and King', in J. Neusner (ed.), *Religions in Antiquity: Essays in Memory of E.R. Goodenough* (SHR, 14; Leiden: E.J. Brill, 1968), pp. 354–71; Menken, *Old Testament Quotations*, pp. 56–63.

23.   In 7.12, 47, John's verb is πλανάω, as in Deut. 13.6 (LXX). See further, Menken, 'Scriptural Dispute', pp. 451 and 457; also Lincoln, *Truth on Trial*, pp. 23–24, 37, 105 and 232; Martyn, *History and Theology*, p. 115.

and so they will take action against him and see that he and his kind are put to death before more are seduced by his tricks and poached from under their noses (cf. 7.1, 32; 11.53; 12.10; 16.2).

Moses, Jesus, and the Law: John's non-hostile 'Jews'

As regards fidelity to Moses and the Torah, strictly speaking this position is no different from that of John's hostile 'Jews'. Nevertheless, it also represents a distinct advance on the former in John's terms in that Jesus is seen here to *fulfil* the requirements of the prophet like Moses in accordance with the Torah. On the basis of the signs, these 'Jews' accept that Jesus is 'the prophet' (6.14), that he is sent by God (7.29; 8.29; 11.42; cf. Nicodemus at 3.2) and, in that regard, they expect him to repeat the Exodus miracle of the manna, which they already attribute to Moses (6.29–31).[24] Nevertheless, given that they retain the Torah-centred focus of the first group (7.51),[25] they are consistently presented by John as failing to grasp Jesus' true meaning (cf. 3.4, 9–10; 6.41–42; 7.35–36; 8.22, 27; 11.36–37). He represents their signs-faith as untrustworthy (2.23–24; 4.48; cf. 11.46) and their closet-Christian position as a lily-livered compromise (12.42–43). The goal of this polemic, however, seems to be an appeal to win them over to the Johannine Christian faith (cf. 11.42; 12.44–50).[26]

Jesus: Johannine Christianity

This third trajectory is at once the most radical and the most complex in relation to Moses and the Torah. There are four main elements to be taken into account:

a. *Moses as faithful witness.* Moses and the Law are by no means rejected by the Johannine group. On the contrary, we hear that Moses wrote about Jesus (1.45; 5.46–47)[27] and foreshadowed his crucifixion (3.14). John is clear that scripture

24. See Menken, *Old Testament Quotations*, pp. 61–63.

25. On this aspect, see S. Freyne, 'Vilifying the Other and Defining the Self: Matthew's and John's Anti-Jewish Polemic in Focus', in J. Neusner and E.S. Frerichs (eds.), *'To See Ourselves as Others See Us': Christians, Jews, 'Others' in Late Antiquity* (Chico, CA: Scholars Press, 1985), pp. 117–43 (here p. 127).

26. For this view, see M. de Boer, 'Depiction', pp. 268 n. 28 and 270 n. 34; R.E. Brown, *Gospel*, pp. LXXIII–LXXV; R.A. Culpepper, *The Gospel and Letters of John* (Interpreting Biblical Texts; Nashville: Abingdon Press, 1998), p. 45; Dunn, *Partings of the Ways*, p. 229; B.W. Longenecker, 'The Unbroken Messiah: A Johannine Feature and its Social Functions', *NTS* 41 (1995), pp. 428–41; W.A. Meeks, 'The Divine Agent and his Counterfeit in Philo and the Fourth Gospel', in E. Schüssler Fiorenza (ed.), *Aspects of Religious Propaganda in Judaism and Early Christianity* (University of Notre Dame Center for the Study of Judaism and Christianity in Antiquity, 2; Notre Dame and London: University of Notre Dame Press, 1976), pp. 43–67 (here pp. 58–59); S. Pancaro, *The Law in the Fourth Gospel: The Torah and the Gospel, Moses and Jesus, Judaism and Christianity According to John* (NovTSup, 42; Leiden: E.J. Brill, 1975), p. 533; D. Rensberger, *Overcoming the World: Politics and Community in the Gospel of John* (London: SPCK, 1988), pp. 41, 114, and 145; S.J. Tanzer, 'Salvation is *for* the Jews: Secret Christian Jews in the Gospel of John', in B.A. Pearson (ed.), *The Future of Early Christianity: Essays in Honor of Helmut Koester* (Minneapolis: Fortress Press, 1991), pp. 285–300.

27. Boismard, following R.E. Brown, suggests that a precise reference to Deut. 18.18 is intended by this statement; see Boismard, *Moïse ou Jésus*, pp. 27–32; Brown, *Gospel*, p. 86.

cannot be annulled (10.35) and he takes steps to demonstrate by scriptural exegesis that in Jesus the Law of Moses is not broken but fulfilled (7.19–23; 10.34–36; cf. 15.25).[28] For John, those who *fail* to keep the Law are the hostile 'Jews'. They misinterpret the scriptures, and they will have to answer to Moses himself for that (5.39–40, 45); they do not keep the Law, but seek instead to kill Jesus (7.19; cf. 19.7); indeed, they can even behave contrary to the point of law made by Nicodemus, while ironically scorning the rabble for their ignorance of it (7.49–51).[29]

b. *Jesus and Moses.* There can be no doubt that the Deuteronomic picture of the prophet like Moses has hugely influenced John's Christology.[30] Jesus is identified as a 'prophet' by the Johannine faithful (4.19; 9.17; cf. 1.21, 25), and the gospel describes him as one 'sent' and the Father as the sender no fewer than 24 times. In true Exodus fashion, Jesus performs signs (cf. e.g. 2.23; 7.31; 9.16; 11.47; 12.37, esp. 6.14), his predictions are seen to come true (13.19; 14.29; 16.4) and he utters only the words of God as commanded (3.34; 7.16; 8.28, 40; 12.49–50; 14.10, 24).[31]

c. *Jesus, not Moses.* Nevertheless, John has no intention of allowing Moses-enthusiasts to get these similarities out of proportion. Here, any overly exalted view of Moses is flatly contradicted in favour of Jesus.[32] 'No one has ever seen God' in 1.18 must at least be partly aimed at the conviction that Moses *had* seen God (cf. also 5.37). This is true only of Jesus, John claims, in whom alone God is revealed (1.18; 6.46). Notice also the same flat denial to Nicodemus, again in a Moses context, 'No one has ascended into heaven' (3.13). John insists there is only Jesus, the Son of man, who *descended* from heaven and will return there (6.62).[33] We can add

28. See further, J.M. Lieu, 'Narrative Analysis and Scripture in John', in S. Moyise (ed.), *The Old Testament in the New Testament: Essays in Honour of J.L. North* (JSNTSup, 189; Sheffield: Sheffield Academic Press, 2000), pp. 144–63 (here pp. 158–61); Meeks, *Prophet-King*, pp. 288–89.

29. See further, Pancaro, *Law*, pp. 156 and 527–28.

30. So Boismard, *Moïse ou Jésus*, pp. 5–71; *idem*, 'Jésus, le Prophète par excellence, d'après Jean 10, 24–39', in J. Gnilka (ed.), *Neues Testament und Kirche: Festschrift für R. Schnackenburg* (Freiburg: Herder, 1974), pp. 160–71; Meeks, *Prophet-King*, esp. pp 301–308; Martyn, *History and Theology*, esp. pp. 102–30; Menken, *Old Testament Quotations*, p. 57; *idem*, 'Scriptural Dispute', p. 453. According to P.N. Anderson, this agency typology is not only fundamental to John's Christology but also underlies the whole presentation of the Father-Son relationship in the gospel; see his 'The Having-Sent-Me Father: Aspects of Agency, Encounter, and Irony in the Johannine Father-Son Relationship', *Semeia* 85 (1999), pp. 33–57. Curiously, Anderson draws his evidence from Deut. 18.15–22 only (see pp. 36–40).

31. See, for example, Boismard, *Moïse ou Jésus*, pp. 11–20 and 64–65; A. Reinhartz, 'Jesus as Prophet: Predictive Prolepses in the Fourth Gospel', *JSNT* 36 (1989), pp. 3–16. On the Mosaic background to Jesus' role as 'paraclete', see Pancaro, *Law*, pp. 256–58. It seems that the exalted Moses traditions persisted in Christianity in the east; see J. Neusner, *Aphrahat and Judaism: The Christian-Jewish Argument in Fourth-Century Iran* (SPB, 19; Leiden: E.J. Brill, 1971), pp. 68–72. Aphrahat claims that Christians may apply 'the title of divinity' to Jesus on the grounds that God did not withhold his name from righteous men like Moses, and cites Ps. 82.6 in support of his case (cf. Jn. 10.34). Neusner rightly detects here an argument akin to John's thinking (p. XII).

32. On this, see esp. Dunn, *Partings of the Ways*, pp. 225–26.

33. See R.E. Brown, *An Introduction to New Testament Christology* (London: Chapman, 1994), pp. 210–13; Dunn, 'Let John Be John', p. 310; Martyn, *History and Theology*, pp. 121–35. Petersen describes this reaction to the Moses image as an example of 'anti-language', which not only derives from the image but also transforms it through contrast (*Sociology of Light*, pp.

here as anti-Moses polemic the sharp correction that it was God, *not* Moses, who gave the bread from heaven (6.32), and that it was *not* Moses, but the fathers, who gave circumcision (7.22).

d. *Jesus, not the Law.* If John was prepared to demote Moses in favour of Jesus, he was also prepared to take a yet more radical step, a step which the believing 'Jews' had evidently not taken, and which non-believing 'Jews' could only have greeted with outrage: Jesus in John's gospel is the living embodiment of the Word of God, the Torah found in flesh and blood which surpasses and supplants the Law of Moses as the way to God.[34] For this reason, the coming of Jesus is grace in place of grace (1.16), [35] since the glory of God, to which Moses in the Law had borne witness, is now accessible in a human being. I suggest that it is this fundamental shift on John's part away from the centrality of Torah to the centrality of Jesus which accounts for the main contours of Johannine Christology as we meet it in the gospel. Here, as is often remarked, the life-giving and sustaining properties Judaism traditionally associated with the Torah as God's Word have been applied to Jesus wholesale.[36] Hence, John describes Jesus in terms of bread, light, and living water, and has Jesus insist that in him alone is the eternal life which is sought by 'the Jews' in the scriptures (6.35, 48; 8.12; 4.14 etc.; 5.39–40).[37] Hence also, it follows that the influence of Wisdom, already equated with the Torah in Judaism,[38] looms large in his presentation of Jesus, and that the intimacy of the Father-Son relationship in the gospel echoes that between God and his Word (10.30) or between God and Wisdom his darling child, his μονογενής (1.14, 18; 3.16, 18; cf. Wisd. Sol. 7.22).[39]

5–6, 89–90, and 98–99). For a recent and full treatment of John's response to the Moses traditions in terms of legitimation, see J.F. McGrath, *John's Apologetic Christology: Legitimation and Development in Johannine Christology* (SNTSMS, 111; Cambridge: Cambridge University Press, 2001), esp. pp. 149–95.

34. Note that John himself refers to the Law as the *word* of God: 10.35, cf. 5.38; 1.38; 15.25. In this he echoes a Jewish commonplace; see further, C.H. Dodd, *The Interpretation of the Fourth Gospel* (Cambridge: Cambridge University Press, 1953), pp. 269–73; R.E. Brown, *The Epistles of John* (AB, 30; London: Geoffrey Chapman, 1983), p. 252.

35. So R.B. Edwards, 'Χάριν ἀντὶ χάριτος (John 1.16): Grace and the Law in the Johannine Prologue', *JSNT* 32 (1988), pp. 3–15. See further, the discussion on Johannine Christology as supersessionist in Bieringer, Pollefeyt and Vandecasteele-Vanneuville, 'Wrestling with Johannine Anti-Judaism', pp. 32–33.

36. See, for example, Dodd, *Interpretation*, pp. 82–86 and 336–37; C.K. Barrett, *The Gospel According to St John* (London: SPCK, 2nd edn, 1978), pp. 233, 293 and 336–37; P. Borgen, *Logos was the True Light and Other Essays on the Gospel of John* (Trondheim: Tapir, 1983), pp. 104–105.

37. On Jesus as both Mosaic prophet and the meaning and purpose of the Torah as life-giving, see G.J. Brooke, 'Christ and the Law in John 7–10', in B. Lindars (ed.), *Law and Religion: Essays on the Place of the Law in Israel and Early Christianity* (Cambridge: James Clarke & Co, 1988), pp. 102–112 (here p. 112).

38. For the equation of Wisdom with the Torah, see Sir. 24.23; Baruch 1; Philo, *Migr.* 130; for Wisdom as the word of God, see Sir. 24.3; Prov. 2.6; Wisd. Sol. 9.1–2, see further J.D.G. Dunn, *Christology in the Making: An Inquiry into the Origins of the Doctrine of the Incarnation* (London: SCM Press, 1980), pp. 170–71 and 219–20; Pancaro, *Law*, p. 545.

39. See, e.g., J. Ashton, 'The Transformation of Wisdom', ch. 1 in *Studying John: Approaches to the Fourth Gospel* (Oxford: Clarendon Press, 1994), pp. 5–35 (here pp. 25 and 31).

5. *Conclusion*

The approach adopted in this study has enabled us to see John's Christology as one element in a spectrum of responses to Jesus, rooted in the Judaism John knew and which, rows and rifts notwithstanding, was no less his own cultural home. Inasmuch as the three positions identified here[40] are based on Moses and the Law, they are organically linked and come into agreement; inasmuch, however, as each has construed that basis differently in relation to Jesus, then they are seen to conflict and, in the two cases of John and the hostile 'Jews', violently so.

The fourth evangelist emerges from this context as a Christian Jew for whom faith in the one God of Israel has become centred on Jesus. Seen against his particular background, the steps he has taken seem logical enough, for he has plainly worked on the assumption that all that was venerated in Judaism as the means to God must be superlatively true of Jesus. Thus, it follows that just as in the Judaism he knew Moses and the Torah were highly esteemed in relation to God, so also John's Christology, in which those features are taken up, is correspondingly 'high'. It also follows, I suggest, that just as Judaism clearly regarded its own 'high' claims for Torah as consistent with monotheism, so John also is unlikely to have perceived his own position as in breach of that creed. In fact, the real conflict here between John and his hostile opponents seems to lie not in the principle but in its application, for if these 'Jews' were prepared to exalt the Torah as God's life-giving word, it is clear enough from the gospel that they found John's attribution of divine status to Jesus of Nazareth completely unacceptable. To do that, they insist, is blasphemy because it puts a human being on a level with God (5.18; 10.33).

John's reply is that the blasphemy charge is not justified in Jesus' case because his whole life was so open to God that he never made a move or uttered a word except at God's bidding (5.19–30; cf. 7.16–18; 8.26–29; 10.37–38; 12.44–50; 14.10, 24; 17.7–8). Eternal life thus consists in knowing the one God through Jesus, who seeks only the glory of the one who sent him (5.44; 7.18; 17.3). In such a scheme, God is not rivalled and monotheism is not breached.

This brings me to a final thought. What do you do if you are a first-century Jew and your belief in the one God is Jesus-shaped? It seems to me that there is more than one way to come to terms with that: either you safeguard monotheism by presenting Jesus in all his human vulnerability, denying that anyone is good but God, as in Mark's gospel, for example, or you do it another way, which is by showing a human life so surrendered to God's will that to encounter that person is to meet only God in word and action. We tend to think of John's Christology as posing a problem to Jewish monotheism. What if John himself saw it as a solution?

---

40. There may well be more. The range of speculation among factions in ch. 7, for example, suggests that John was familiar with pious conjecture of various kinds concerning the Messiah and access to heavenly knowledge; see further, Dunn, 'Let John Be John', pp. 311–12; *idem*, 'The Embarrassment of History: Reflections on the Problem of "Anti-Judaism" in the Fourth Gospel', in *Anti-Judaism and the Fourth Gospel*, pp. 47–67 (here pp. 56–57); Freyne, 'Vilifying', p. 140.

MONOTHEISM AND CHRISTOLOGY IN HEBREWS 1

Richard Bauckham, University of St Andrews

1. *Christological Monotheism*

This study presupposes the general argument for a christology of divine identity that I outlined briefly in my 1996 Didsbury Lectures, published as *God Crucified: Monotheism and Christology in the New Testament*,[1] and will argue in detail in a forthcoming book.[2] I shall briefly summarize the argument here insofar as it is relevant to our present purpose. I propose that we should think of the Jewish monotheistic understanding of God in the Second Temple period in terms of the identity of God rather than of divine nature. In other words, for the Jewish monotheistic belief in God what was important was who the one God is, rather than what divinity is. (This is not intended to exclude all concepts of divine nature from the Jewish theology of this period, but I do regard the identity of God as the more comprehensive and important category.) Key features of the identity of the one God which distinguish him from all other reality (and which matter most for our present purpose)[3] are:

- God is the sole creator of all things, whereas all other beings are created by him.
- God is the sovereign ruler of all, subject to none, whereas all other beings are subject to his rule.
- God will achieve his eschatological rule, i.e. his uncontested rule over all creation and the acknowledgement of his sole deity by all creatures. The difference implied here between God's providential sovereignty and his eschatological rule defines Second Temple Jewish monotheism as a kind of eschatological monotheism.

---

1. R. Bauckham, *God Crucified: Monotheism and Christology in the New Testament* (Carlisle: Paternoster Press, 1998 and Grand Rapids: Eerdmans, 1999. See also two essays closely related to this argument: 'The Worship of Jesus in Philippians 2.9–11', in R.P. Martin and B.J. Dodd (eds.), *Where Christology Began: Essays on Philippians 2* (Louisville, KY: Westminster/John Knox Press, 1998), pp. 128–39; 'The Throne of God and the Worship of Jesus', in *JRCM*, pp. 43–69.

2. Provisional title: *Jesus and the Identity of God*. I. *Jewish Monotheism and New Testament Christology*.

3. That God is the God of his covenant people Israel is also essential to his identity in the Jewish monotheistic understanding, but it does not so clearly distinguish him from all other reality, as the features listed here do, and so was not prominent in Jewish statements of God's uniqueness from this period.

- Frequently God is said to be the only eternal one, 'the first and the last' in the classic monotheistic assertions of Deutero–Isaiah (Isa. 41.1; 42.8; 48.11), the one who precedes all things as their creator and will achieve his rule over all things for ever. I include this point because God's eternity is the attribute of divine nature most often used to distinguish God from all creation: only God is inherently eternal, living from eternity to eternity. But it is noteworthy that as an attribute of divine nature it is very closely connected with creation and sovereignty, just as divine omnipotence also is.
- God has a personal name, the tetragrammaton (YHWH), which names his unique identity.
- God alone may be worshipped, and God should be worshipped, because worship in the Jewish understanding is precisely recognition of the unique divine identity.

The early Christianity, very consciously using this Jewish theological framework, created a kind of christological monotheism by understanding Jesus to be included in the unique identity of the one God of Israel. Probably the earliest expression of this to which we have access – and it was certainly in use very early in the first Christian community's history – was the understanding of Jesus' exaltation in terms of Ps. 110.1. Jesus, seated on the divine throne in heaven as the one who will achieve the eschatological lordship of God and in whom the unique sovereignty of the one God will be acknowledged by all, is included in the unique rule of God over all things, and thus placed unambiguously on the divine side of the absolute distinction that separates the only sovereign One from all creation. God's rule over all things defines who God is: it cannot be delegated as a mere function to a creature. Thus the earliest christology was already *in nuce* the highest christology. All that remained was to work through consistently what it could mean for Jesus to belong integrally to the unique identity of the one God. Early Christian interest was primarily in soteriology and eschatology, the concerns of the Gospel, and so in the New Testament it is primarily as sharing or implementing God's eschatological lordship that Jesus is understood to belong to the identity of God. But early Christian reflection could not consistently leave it at that. If Jesus was integral to the identity of God, he must have been so eternally. And so the great passages of protological christology, such as the Johannine Prologue and Hebrew 1, include Jesus also in the unique creative activity of God and in the uniquely divine eternity. This was the early Christians' Jewish way of preserving monotheism against the ditheism that any kind of adoptionist Christology was bound to involve.

Of the passages of extended christological exposition or reflection in the New Testament, Hebrew 1 is one of the most important for understanding christological monotheism, since it brings all the main components of Jewish definition of the uniqueness of the divine identity into christological service. At the same time it illustrates very well the extent to which early christology was an exegetical enterprise, skilfully deploying accepted current methods of Jewish exegesis of Scripture.

2. Hebrews 1–2 in Relation to the Whole Epistle

Although we shall be concentrating on ch. 1 rather than ch. 2 of Hebrews, we need to begin by understanding the role of both these opening chapters in the overall design and purpose of Hebrews. An introduction or exordium (1.1–4) is a compact christological statement, ending with the exaltation of Christ to the right hand of God (with allusion to Psalm 110.1) and the superiority of Christ to angels which that exaltation entails. This functions as a statement of theme for the rest of ch. 1, which is a catena of seven scriptural quotations, with a concluding comment in v. 14. Since the last of the seven quotations is of Ps. 110.1, it is clear that the aim of the catena is to demonstrate how the exaltation of Christ to God's right hand entails his transcendence over the angels, who feature prominently in the catena. Chapter 1 is followed by a section of exhortation (2.1–4), which draws a lesson for the readers from the exposition of ch. 1. This is typical of the pattern in Hebrews of passages of exhortation interspersed among passages of exposition. This exhortatory interruption should not obscure the close link between ch. 1 and 2.5–18, which is an exposition of Ps. 8.4–6, a passage frequently linked with Ps. 110.1 in early Christian exegesis.[4] Whereas ch. 1 concerns Jesus' superiority to the angels, this section of ch. 2 concerns his inferiority to the angels during the period of his human life on earth, of which Ps. 8 is understood to speak. Apart from a brief reference in 1.3, only at the end of ch. 2 does the main theme of Hebrews begin to emerge, i.e. Christ's role as the high priest after the order of Melchizedek, whose sacrifice and priesthood supersede the levitical priesthood and sacrifices.

How do these first two chapters function to introduce the rest of the book? An important clue lies in the use of Ps. 110 throughout Hebrews. The first verse of the Psalm is the Old Testament text to which the New Testament most often alludes.[5] A christological understanding of it must go back behind all the New Testament writings to the earliest period and, with some variation, its Christian interpretation was well-established and well-known. Hebrews not only alludes to and quotes it in ch. 1, but also continues to allude to this first verse of the psalm later (8.1; 10.12–13; 12.2). These later allusions, however, are distinguished by the fact that they interpret the first verse of the psalm in the light of Ps. 110.4, which Hebrews is unique among New Testament writings in quoting and interpreting (it is quoted first in 5.6, and expounded at length in ch. 7). For these later chapters of Hebrews, Jesus is exalted to God's right hand, not only as the one who is to rule all things from the throne of the divine majesty, but also as the Melchizedekian high priest

---

4. M.C. Albl, *"And Scripture Cannot Be Broken": The Form and Function of the Early Christian* Testimonia *Collections* (NovTSup, 96; Leiden: E.J. Brill, 1999), pp. 222–28.

5. Mt. 22.44; 26.64; Mk 12.36; 14.62; 16.19; Lk. 20.42–43; 22.69; Acts 2.33–35; 5.31; 7.55–56; Rom. 8.34; 1 Cor. 15.25; Eph. 1.20; 2.6; Col. 3.1; Heb. 1.3, 13; 8.1; 10.12–13; 12.2; 1 Pet. 3.22; Rev. 3.21. Cf. D.M. Hay, *Glory at the Right Hand: Psalm 110 in Early Christianity* (SBLMS, 18; Nashville: Abingdon Press, 1973); M. Hengel, 'Sit at My Right Hand!', in M. Hengel, *Studies in Early Christology* (Edinburgh: T. & T. Clark, 1995), pp. 119–225; Albl, *"And Scripture"*, pp. 216–36.

who intercedes at the throne of the divine grace. This largely novel[6] christological theme of the high priesthood of Christ is grounded in exegesis of the same psalm as forms the scriptural basis for the much more traditional christological themes of ch. 1. It looks therefore very much as though in ch. 1 Hebrews rehearses the familiar christological themes connected with the exaltation of Christ, along with their familiar exegetical foundations, in order to prepare the way for the novel christological development that follows. Hebrews also takes up the traditional association of Ps. 110 with Ps. 8 in ch. 2 in order also to rehearse a traditional understanding of the humiliation of Christ that will also feed into the new high priestly Christology that we see already at the end of ch. 2.

Martin Albl is the most recent of scholars who have argued that the catena of quotations in ch. 1 is reproduced from an early Christian *testimonia* collection.[7] This probably goes beyond the evidence, especially if one thinks, as I do, that the rather similar passage in *1 Clem.* 36.2–6 is certainly dependent on Hebrews, [8] not an independent witness to the same traditional material, as Albl thinks. Nevertheless there is enough evidence elsewhere for christological use of the same or related texts[9] to show that in ch. 1 the author of Hebrews is working very much in traditional mode, deploying his exegetical skill with already traditional materials, and postponing his freshly creative exegesis for later chapters.

3. *Why the Angels?*

The first two chapters of Hebrews are peculiarly concerned with angels. In this respect they are not preparing the way for later chapters, which make hardly any reference to angels. Angels appear at 1.4 and after 2.16, the last reference to angels in these two chapters, they reappear only at 12.22 and 13.2. In Heb. 1–2 the angels function christologically in two ways: in ch. 1 Jesus' exaltation is understood as his exaltation over the angels, while in ch. 2 Jesus' humiliation in incarnation and death is understood as the meaning of Ps. 8's statement that God made him for a little while lower than the angels. In both cases Jesus is emphatically distinguished from the angels. In his exaltation he is not one of the angels, but divine. In his incarnation he is not one of the angels, but human, as he had to be if he came to help humans, not, as 2.16 points out, angels. An explanation of the prominence of the angels in these chapters must take account of both christological relationships: the divine Son of God above the angels and the human Son of God below the angels.

The exhortatory section at the beginning of ch. 2 (vv. 1–4) draws out explicitly at least an element of the significance of the superiority of the Son to the angels.

---

6. Rom. 8.34 may indicate that this christology was not entirely without precedent, but it was substantially novel.

7. Albl, *"And Scripture"*, pp. 201–207; cf. also L.T. Stuckenbruck, *Angel Veneration and Christology* (WUNT II/70; Tübingen: J.C.B. Mohr [Paul Siebeck], 1995), pp. 128–36.

8. G.L. Cockerill, 'Heb 1.1–14, *1 Clem.* 36.1–6 and the High Priest Title', *JBL* 97 (1978), pp. 437–40; W.L. Lane, *Hebrews 1–8* (WBC, 47A; Dallas: Word Books, 1991), pp. 23–24.

9. Albl, *"And Scripture"*, p. 202.

The message from God declared by Jesus, the Son, should be taken even more seriously than that declared by angels, i.e. the Mosaic law. While this looks like a significant anticipation of the supersessionary message of the later chapters of Hebrews, surprisingly the book makes no further use of this particular comparison. Angels are never subsequently connected with the law. It is hard to believe that the whole purpose of ch. 1 is fulfilled in the exhortatory use of this comparison in 2.1–4.[10] In fact, the exhortatory passages of Hebrews do not usually exhaust the significance of the expository passages. We cannot therefore be content to follow those scholars who explain the concern with angels solely in terms of the superiority of the revelation of Christ over the law of Moses.[11]

Many scholars have suggested that the role of the angels is polemical, i.e. directed either against an angel (or angelomorphic) Christology[12] or against the veneration of angels.[13] We should be very cautious about detecting implicit polemic in passages which show no explicit concern to counter alternative views or practices.[14] The New Testament writers engage in explicit polemic frequently enough for the question to be appropriate: why should the allegedly implicit polemic not have been made explicit? Moreover, the alleged polemic in this case bears no relation to the concerns of the rest of Hebrews, and, in the case of angel Christology, there is very little evidence of its existence in the period (before *1 Clement*, at least) from which Hebrews must date.[15] If the author was concerned to counteract the attraction of an

10. Stuckenbruck, *Angel Veneration*, pp. 127–28.

11. Lane, *Hebrews 1–8*, p. 17; J.P. Meier, 'Symmetry and Theology in the Old Testament Citations of Heb 1, 5–14', *Bib* 66 (1985), p. 522; others listed in Stuckenbruck, *Angel Veneration*, pp. 25–26 n. 201.

12. For references to scholars who have taken this view, see Lane, *Hebrews 1–8*, p. 8; H.W. Attridge, *The Epistle to the Hebrews* (Hermeneia; Philadelphia: Fortress Press, 1989), p. 52 n. 33; Stuckenbruck, *Angel Veneration*, pp. 124–25 n. 98; L.K.K. Dey, *Patterns of Perfection in Philo and Hebrews* (SBLDS, 25; Missoula, MT: Scholars Press, 1975) ch. 4, sees the polemic directed against the assimilation of Christ to intermediaries such as Philo's Logos, whom Philo can call an angel. D.D. Hannah, *Michael and Christ: Michael Traditions and Angel Christology in Early Christianity* (WUNT II/109; Tübingen: J.C.B. Mohr [Paul Siebeck], 1999), pp. 137–39, acknowledges the force of arguments against the view that Hebrews 1 opposes an angel Christology, and so argues that, while angel Christology 'was not an error that appealed to his readers...it *was* in the air', and so the author is establishing his credentials with his readers by stressing his agreement with them in opposing any confusion of Christ with angels.

13. For references to scholars who have taken this view, see Lane, *Hebrews 1–8*, p. 8; Stuckenbruck, *Angel Veneration*, p. 124 n. 197.

14. Attridge, *The Epistle*, pp. 50 and 52; Stuckenbruck, *Angel Veneration*, pp. 126–27. Stuckenbruck, *Angel Veneration*, pp. 128–39, goes on to argue that the source of the catena Hebrews takes over was aimed polemically against veneration of angels and/or angel Christology.

15. Hebrews 1 has often been used as evidence for an angel or angelomorphic Christology, usually in the negative sense that such a Christology must be inferred from the opposition to it in Hebrews. But C.A. Gieschen, *Angelomorphic Christology* (AGJU, 42; Leiden: E.J. Brill, 1998), pp. 295–303 and 314, argues, on the basis of angelomorphic motifs in the catena of Hebrews 1 as well as elsewhere in Hebrews, that 'the author embraced Angelomorphic Christology as support for the superiority of Christ' (p. 314). Though he is careful to distinguish angelomorphic Christology (in which angelic features are applied to Christ) from angel Christology (for which Christ is an angel), I am not convinced that the motifs Gieschen highlights (Creator, Name, Firstborn, Glory,

angel Christology for his readers, it is remarkable that he later, without any hint of such a danger, makes innovative christological use of the figure of Melchizedek, whom we know to have been treated as a heavenly being of prime importance in some Jewish circles.[16]

However, it is hardly enough to claim that the author treats the angels simply because they occupy the same sacred space (heaven) as the exalted Jesus, [17] though it is a highly relevant fact that they do. Nor is it not enough to point out that Christ's superiority to the angels was a well-established part of the traditional exaltation schema, connected especially with Ps. 110.1, which the catena in Heb. 1 follows, [18] significant though this is (cf. Phil. 2.9–10; Col. 1.15–18; Eph. 1.21; 1 Pet. 3.22). For the author of Hebrews to elaborate this element in the traditional schema to the extent that he does, there must be a theological point to be made by it, no doubt already made in the traditional schema and appearing in the other New Testament texts that reflect this scheme, but significant enough to be treated at considerably greater length in Hebrews 1 than in other New Testament examples of this schema.

If the aim of the first two chapters of Hebrews is the positive one of restating the traditional Christian understanding of the identity of Jesus Christ, as the presupposition for any further christological reflection later in the work, then the angels, in both chapters, have a readily intelligible role as indicators of ontological status in the Jewish monotheistic world view. In Jewish literature the transcendence of God is frequently portrayed by locating God's cosmic throne in the heights of heaven, far above all other heavenly beings, the angels.[19] This imagery of height functions along with other means, which we shall mention in due course, of radically distinguishing God from all creation. The need to distinguish angels, who as radiant heavenly beings often look like God, from God, sometimes no doubt has a polemical edge, especially as Jewish monotheism was always self-consciously alternative to pagan polytheism. But the distinction also functions as a kind of negative theology, defining who God is by demarcating God from what God is not. God is not one among other heavenly beings, but radically different in kind.

That human beings rank below angels is less often stressed, being an element more or less taken for granted in the Jewish cosmological picture, though it does become apparent in those Jewish traditions in which humans who ascend through the heavens are transformed into angels and in the expectation of angelic status or nature after death. It comes to the fore in Hebrews because of the christological aim (in Jewish terms a Christian novelty) of affirming both the divinity and the humanity of Jesus. That phrase, patristic-sounding though it is, seems fully justified by the systematic way in which the first two chapters of Hebrews depict the divine identity of Jesus in distinction from the angels and his identification with humanity

---

and Enthroned Son) should be considered angelomorphic. Gieschen's argument about Heb. 1 expands on the much briefer treatment along the same lines by C. Rowland, *The Open Heaven* (London: SPCK, 1982), p. 113.

16. M.E. Isaacs, *Sacred Space: An Approach to the Theology of the Epistle to the Hebrews* (JSNTSup, 73; Sheffield: Sheffield Academic Press, 1992), p. 176; Hannah, *Michael*, p. 138.

17. Isaacs, *Sacred Space*, pp. 176–77.

18. Attridge, *The Epistle*, pp. 52–53.

19. Bauckham, 'The Throne of God', pp. 52–53.

in distinction from the angels. As the Son of God his affinity with the Father distinguishes him from the angels, placing him far above them, while his temporary humiliation below the angels is so that, as the Son, he can establish his affinity with his human brothers and sisters. The angels are neither the only-begotten divine son nor the adopted human brothers and sisters, but servants who serve the divine purpose of human salvation, as the transitional last verse of ch. 1 makes clear. Indirectly, they serve very effectively the purpose of theological and christological definition.

4. *The Exordium: Hebrews 1.1–4*

The sevenfold narrative identity of God's Son (Heb. 1.2b–4)		
ἐν υἱῷ,	by a Son,	
(1) ὃν ἔθηκεν κληρονόμον πάντων,	whom he appointed heir of all things,	(1) Eschatological rule over all things
		Ps. 2.8; 8.6
(2) δι' οὗ καὶ ἐποίησεν τοὺς αἰῶνας·	through whom he also created the worlds.	(2) Agent of creation of all things.
(3) ὃς ὢν ἀπαύγασμα τῆς δόξης καὶ χαρακτὴρ τῆς ὑποστάσεως αὐτοῦ,	Being the reflection of God's glory and the exact imprint of God's very being,	(3) Eternal divine being
		Wisd. Sol. 7.26
(4) φέρων τε τὰ πάντα τῷ·ῥήματι τῆς δυνάμεως αὐτοῦ	sustaining all things by his powerful word,	(4) Providential sovereignty over all things
(5) καθαρισμὸν τῶν ἁμαρτιῶν ποιησάμενος	having made purification for sins,	(5) High priestly atonement
(6) ἐκάθισεν ἐν δεξιᾷ τῆς μεγαλωσύνης ἐν ὑψηλοῖς	he sat down at the right hand of the Majesty on high,	(6) Exaltation to God's throne in heaven
		Ps. 110.1
(7) τοσούτῳ κρείττων γενόμενος τῶν ἀγγέλων ὅσῳ διαφορώτερον παρ' αὐτοὺς κεκληρονόμηκεν ὄνομα.	having become as much superior to angels as the name he has inherited is more excellent than theirs.	(7) Identification (name) as YHWH

The opening contrast between the prophets and the Son introduces Hebrews' overall theme of the difference between the old covenant and the newly inaugurated eschatological age, but also introduces the key term Son (of God), immediately followed by a series of seven christological descriptions, each introduced by either a relative pronoun or a participle.[20] Seven, as the number of completeness, is

20. J.P. Meier, 'Structure and Theology in Heb 1, 1–14', *Bib* 66 (1985), pp. 170–76.

also the number of scriptural texts quoted in the catena that follows (vv. 5–13), and the seven introductory descriptions do anticipate the various christological themes of the catena, but there is no correlation of sequence between the two series of sevens.[21] The seven christological descriptions (vv. 2b–4) form a statement of the narrative identity of the Son in which his inclusion in the unique divine identity is made very fully clear. Only the fifth statement ('having made purification for sins'), deliberately introduced as a first glimpse of the high priestly Christology original to Hebrews, is alone in being unparalleled elsewhere. Other statements are traditional, in a general sense if not in detail, and accumulate in this way in other extended accounts of divine identity christology, such as Phil. 2.6–11, Col. 1.15–20, Eph. 1.20–23 and the Prologue to the Fourth Gospel.

The biblical allusions, typically of Hebrews, are to the Psalms, but to psalms already prominent in christological interpretation (Pss. 2 and 8 in statement 1, Ps. 110.1 in statement 6) and psalms interpreted to refer to Christ's exaltation and rule from the divine throne. The sequence begins with exaltation in statement 1 and comes back to exaltation in statements 6 and 7, with the theme of heirship and inheritance forming a catchword *inclusio* between statements 1 and 7. But the sequence enshrines the natural movement of early Christian christological reflection back from the exaltation of Christ (statement 1) to his participation in the work of creation (statement 2) and his intrinsic and eternal relationship to God expressed in statement 3 in wisdom language, [22] with one image borrowed from Wisdom of Solomon 7.26 and the other creatively improvised. Statement 4 may also follow wisdom traditions, but the closest parallel is perhaps in a neglected Jewish apocalypse, probably of the early second century CE, the *Ladder of Jacob*, which says of God enthroned on the heavenly throne: 'bearing the whole world under your arm, yet not being borne by anyone' (2.9). It belongs to the unique identity of God that he upholds all things and is not himself upheld. Notable in statements 1, 2, and 4 is the universal language: 'the worlds' (2) and 'all things' (1 and 4). This is the standard language used in Jewish tradition to describe God's creation and rule of all things, identifying God's uniqueness by distinguishing him fundamentally from all other reality.[23] As in 1 Cor. 8.6 or Jn 1.3, the same language is used christologically to indicate that the divine Son participates in this uniquely divine relationship to all things.[24]

The last two statements of the seven emphasize the status of the exalted Christ when he is installed on the divine throne 'on high' to be given his inheritance, i.e. God's eschatological rule over all things. This is new, not in that he only now

21. Meier, 'Symmetry', pp. 504–524, finds only 'a general symmetry between the movement of thought' in the two series (p. 523; cf. p. 529).

22. Cf. Meier, 'Structure', pp. 176–89, for the 'ring structure' of movement from exaltation back to pre-existence in eternity and forward again to exaltation.

23. E.g. Isa. 44.24; Jer. 10.16; 51.19; Sir. 43.33; Wisd. Sol. 9.6; 12.13; Add. Est. 13.9; 2 Macc. 1.24; *3 Macc.* 2.3; *1 En.* 9.5; 84.3; *2 En.* 66.4; *Jub.* 12.19; *Ap. Abr.* 7.10; *Jos. Asen.* 12.1; *Sib. Or.* 3.20; 8.376; Josephus, *War* 5.218; 1QapGen col. xx, line 13; 4QD[a] frg. 11.9.

24. Also Mt. 11.27; Lk. 10.22; Jn 3.35; 13.3; 16.15; Acts 10.36; 1 Cor. 15.27–28; Eph. 1.22; Phil. 3.21; Col. 1.16–17; Heb. 1.2; cf. Eph. 1.23; 4.10.

begins to participate in the divine identity, but in that the new creative activity of God, God's eschatological achievement of his purpose for this whole creation, his kingdom, begins with Jesus' enthronement. This is why he 'inherits' the divine name: it is in his rule from God's throne that the rule of the one God is to be acknowledged by all creation. God is to be known to all by his name when all creation recognize Jesus as the one who exercises God's rule. He is identified for them by the unique divine name. Many commentators, on the other hand, suppose the name here to be 'the Son', because it is as Son that Christ is distinguished from the angels in the following verses. But the Son is *the one* who inherits from his Father, not *what* he inherits. What he inherits should be something that belongs to his Father, not something uniquely the Son's, as the title Son is. The parallel with Phil. 2.9 suggests the much more intelligible idea that the one who sits on the divine throne is given the divine name, the tetragrammaton.[25]

5. The Structure of the Catena

Catena of seven scriptural texts on Jesus' transcendence over the angels (Heb. 1.5–13)

Τίνι γὰρ εἶπέν ποτε τῶν ἀγγέλων,	For **to which of the angels did God ever say,**	A[1]	1a Son

Υἱός μου εἶ σύ,
    ἐςγὼ σήμερον γεγέννηκά σε;
	You are my Son
	    today I have begotten you"? (Ps. 2.7)		

καὶ πάλιν,	Or again,	B[1]	2a Son

Ἐγὼ ἔσομαι αὐτῷ πατέρα,
    καὶ αὐτὸς ἔσται μοι εἰς υἱόν;
	'I will be his Father,
	    and he will be my Son'? (2 Sam. 7.14)		

[6]ὅταν δε πάλιν εἰσαγάγῃ τὸν πρωτότοκον εἰς τὴν οἰκουμένην, λέγει,	And again, when he brings the firstborn into the world, he says,	C[1] Son	3a Son and angels
Καὶ προσκυνησάτωσαν αὐτῷ πάντες ἄγγελοι θεοῦ.	'Let all God's angels worship him.' (Deut. 32.43)		
[7]καὶ πρὸς μεν τοὺς ἀγγέλους λέγει,	**Of the angels he says,**	D	4 Angels
Ὁ ποιῶν τοὺς ἀγγέλους αὐτοῦ πνεύματα καὶ τοὺς λειτουργοὺς αὐτοῦ πυρὸς φλόγα,	'He makes his angels (messengers) winds, and his ministers flames of fire.' (Ps. 104.4)		4a Servants not Son 4b

25. So also Rowland, *The Open Heaven*, p. 113; Gieschen, *Angelomorphic Christology*, p. 197.

⁸πρὸς δε τὸν υἱόν,　　But of the Son he says,

Changeable not eternal

C²   **5b**

Son   Eternal

Ὁ θρόνος σου ὁ θεός εἰς τὸν
αἰῶνα τοῦ αἰῶνος,
καὶ ἡ ῥάβδος τῆς εὐθύτητος
ῥάβδος τῆς βασιλείας σου.
⁹ἠγάπησας δικαιοσύνην καὶ
ἐμίσησας ἀνομίαν·
διὰ τοῦτο ἔχρισεν σε ὁ θεὸς
ὁ θεός σου
ἔλαιον ἀγαλλιάσεως παρὰ τοὺς
μετόχους σου.

'Your throne, O God, is forever
   and ever,
and the righteous sceptre is the
   sceptre of your kingdom.
You have loved righteousness
   and hated wickedness;
therefore God, your God, has
   anointed you
with the oil of gladness beyond
   your companions.' (Ps. 45.6–7)

and
angels

---

¹⁰καὶ,　　And,

B²   **6b**

Eternal

Σὺ κατ' ἀρχάς, κύριε, τὴν γῆν
ἐθεμελίωσας,
καὶ ἔργα τῶν χιρῶν σού εἰσιν
οἱ οὐρανοι·
¹¹αὐτοὶ ἀπολοῦνται, σὺ δε
διαμένεις,
καὶ πάντες ὡς ἱμάτιον
παλαιωθήσονται,
¹²καὶ ὡσεὶ περιβόλαιν ἑλίξεις
αὐτούς,
ὡς ἱμάτιον καὶ ἀλλαγήσονται·
σὺ δε ὁ αὐτὸς εἰ
καὶ τὰ ἔτη σου οὐκ ἐκλείψουσιν.

'In the beginning, Lord, you
   founded the earth,
and the heavens are the work
   of your hands;
they will perish, but you
   remain;
they will all wear out
   like clothing;
like a cloak you will
   roll them up,
and like clothing they will be
   changed.
But you are the same, and your
   years will never end (Ps. 102.25–27)

---

¹³πρὸς τίνα δε τῶν ἀγγλων εἴρηκεν ποτε,　　But to which of the angels has he ever said,

C²   **7**

rubric   Sharing
God's
rule

Κάθου ἐκ δεξιῶν μου,
ἕως ἂν θῶ τοὺς ἐχθρούς σου
ὑποπόδιον τῶν ποδῶν σου;

'Sit at my right hand
until I make your enemies a foot-
   stool for your feet'? (Ps. 110.1)

In early Jewish and Christian literature, in which theological argument is usually inseparable from skilled and exact exegesis, a catena of texts of this kind, with only a minimal framework of interpretation, can function as the vehicle for a sophisticated theological argument, since much can be said purely by the careful selection and juxtaposition of texts. (A good example from Qumran is 4QTestimonia [4Q175];[26] a New Testament example is 1 Pet. 2.4–10.) This makes the structure of the catena an indispensable key to its correct interpretation.

---

26. H.W. Bateman, *Early Jewish Hermeneutics and Hebrews 1.5–13* (American University

That there are seven quotations is significant, not only because the number indicates the Son's complete superiority to angels, but also because the number allows the seven quotations to fall into two different, overlapping patterns.

There is a chiastic pattern (see the third column of the diagram above), in which the fourth quotation (D) forms the centre of the chiasm, while the two outer quotations (A^1 and A^2) correspond. The formulae introducing these first and seventh quotations clearly correspond, while these and the formula of the central quotation (D) is distinctive and marks out this one quotation as actually about the angels themselves. The other quotations are about the Son, but the two nearest to the centre (C^1 and C^2) *explicitly* compare the angels with the Son, whereas the others refer to the Son in terms that imply a contrast with the angels, but do not explicitly refer to the angels. In C^1 the angels are told to worship the Son (v. 6), while in C^2 they are the 'companions' of the Son above whom he is elevated (v. 9). Thus the chiastic structure serves the purpose of the catena in portraying the contrast between the Son and the angels.

However, while a series of seven can have a chiastic structure with a centre, it can also imply that the seventh item is to be set apart from the other six as the climax and consummation of the others, as the Sabbath is of the week. The last column of the diagram above shows how the chiastic structure is modified by the distinctive role of the seventh quotation as a summarizing climax to the series. The first three quotations (1a, 2a, 3a) all characterize the Son as Son. (The third quotation does not itself describe the Son as Son, but its introductory explanation does [v. 6a].) The fifth and sixth quotations (5b, 6b) both characterize the Son as eternal. These two lengthy quotations are clearly linked together in a way that shows this to be their common purpose: the first line of the fifth quotation ('Your throne, O God, is forever and ever') corresponds to the last line of the sixth quotation ('your years will never end'). This makes them a self-contained pair, whose theme is not continued by the seventh quotation. Thus, excluding the seventh quotation from the chiastic pattern, the central quotation about the angels is framed, on the one hand, by a triplet of quotations about the Son as Son and, on the other hand, by a pair of quotations about the Son as eternal. The central quotation, as we shall see, is very carefully chosen in that it has two aspects (4a, 4b), one of which (4a) contrasts the angels with the Son as Son, the theme of the preceding quotations (1a, 2a, 3a), while the other aspect (4b) contrasts the angels with the Son as eternal, the theme of the succeeding quotations (5b, 6b).

6. *The Theme of the Catena*

The two verses before the catena (1.3–4) already stated the theme of the catena as the exaltation of the Son according to Ps. 110[LXX 109].1 and the superiority to angels which both explicates this and is required by it. The catena then returns to

Studies, 7/193; New York, Bern: Peter Lang, 1997), ch. 6, compares the hermeneutical methods of Heb. 1.5–13 with those of 4QFlorilegium (4Q174), which, unlike 4QTestimonia, incorporates explicit exegetical comment on its selection of messianic texts.

Ps. 110[109].1 as its summarizing climax, and the preceding six quotations expound the theme by establishing what qualifies the Son for this status and distinguishes him from the angels. The overall point is that as Son he participates in the exercise of the divine sovereignty, whereas the angels are merely servants. Along with this eschatological christology goes the protological point that the Son is creator of all things, the angels created by him.

All the quotations in fact relate to the Son's messianic rule, though this is not immediately obvious in all cases:

1. The words of the first quotation (Ps. 2.7) are those God speaks to his anointed king to whom he promises universal rule (Ps. 2.2, 6, 8–9), as already picked up in the allusion to this psalm in Heb. 1.2.
2. The second quotation (2 Sam.[2 Kgdms] 7.14) is from the words of God to David, in which God promises to establish the throne of David's offspring's kingdom forever (2 Sam. [2 Kgdms] 7.12–13, 16).
3. The third quotation is introduced with an allusion to Ps. 89[LXX 88].27 ('I will make him my firstborn, exalted over the kings of the earth'), a psalm which also includes the promise of an eternal throne (Ps. 89[88].29, 36–37). The third quotation itself, from the Song of Moses in Deut. 32, belongs to the prophecy of God's eschatological victory over his enemies which concludes the Song.
4. The fourth quotation belongs to a psalm which describes the divine sovereignty over creation, while the actual verse concludes the psalm's opening description of the divine ruler establishing his palace in the heavens and ruling in power.
5. The fifth quotation (Ps. 45[LXX 44].6–7) opens with a reference to the Son's eternal throne as the throne of God ('Your throne, O God, is forever and ever') and continues with reference to his anointing as messianic king.
6. The sixth quotation (Ps. 102[LXX 101].25–27) concerns the divine sovereignty over the whole created world. The heavens, which the Son created, he will roll up and change (Ps. 102[101].26 = Heb. 1.12). But it is probably also relevant that the preceding section of the psalm (Ps. 102[101].13–22) concerns the eschatological action of God to redeem Zion and to establish his kingdom over all the kings of the earth.
7. Ps. 110[109].1 was the most quoted scriptural attestation that the exalted Jesus shares the cosmic throne of God in the heights of heaven and thus participates in the uniquely divine sovereignty over all things.

Even apart from the theme of superiority over the angels, which the quotations are designed to establish and illustrate, it is worth observing that the combination of all seven of these quotations makes it clear that the Son's rule is not merely the earthly rule of the Davidic Messiah established on Mt Zion, but the cosmic rule of one who shares the divine throne above all creation. Hence his rule is not merely over the nations, but even over the angels. Hence also his sovereignty, unlike the Davidic Messiah as traditionally perceived, includes participation in God's creative work of bringing all created things into being.

The general point of the catena – that the Son is included in the exercise of the unique divine sovereignty, whereas the angels are only servants of God (vv. 13–14) – is explicated in two aspects. The first three quotations, in relation to the fourth, show that it is because he is the Son of his Father that the Son participates in the unique divine sovereignty, whereas the angels are ministers to him. The fifth and sixth quotations, in relation to the fourth, show that the angels are created and therefore subject to change, whereas the Son, as sovereign Creator, is eternal and unchanging.

With regard to the first aspect, the contrast between the Son (in the first two quotations and in the introduction to the third) and the angels, described as 'ministers' (λειτουργούς) in the fourth quotation, is clear. But the contrast is further explicated in terms of worship. The difference between the Son and the angels requires that they should worship him (v. 6). The point is so important to the author that he has found a rare text (Deut. 32.43 in a Greek version)[27] in which explicitly the angels are said to worship, and he has had to apply it to the Son as Son by means of the introductory allusion to Ps. 89, since the text itself does not explicitly specify the object of the angels' worship (though the object has to be other than the speaker, whom Hebrews identifies as God).[28] In view of this it is probable that 'ministers' (λειτουργούς) in the fourth quotation should be given its cultic sense, just as 'angels' (ἀγγέλους) should be understood in its basic meaning of 'messengers, those who are sent'. Both aspects are taken up in verse 14, which resumes the sense of the fourth quotation: angels are 'all ministering (λειτουργικά) spirits sent

27. At Deut. 32.43a LXX has a fuller text than either the Qumran Hebrew text of this verse (4QDeut[q]) or the MT, which differ widely from each other. The standard LXX text has:

> Rejoice with him, you heavens,
> and worship him all you sons of God (υἱοὶ θεοῦ) (cf: אלהים in 4QDeut[q])!
> Rejoice with his people, you nations;
> and ascribe strength to him, all you angels of God (ἄγγελοι θεοῦ)!

If the author of Hebrews (or the tradition he follows) worked from this text, he has quoted the second line, but substituted ἄγγελοι θεοῦ from line 4 for υἱοὶ θεοῦ in line 2. It is easy to see why he should have done this: he is considering 'Son' the unique title of Christ, distinguished from the angels. Moreover, the parallel in Ps. 97.7 could have affected his quotation of Deut. 32.43. However, the matter is complicated by the fact that in the Odes, a Christian collection of biblical canticles that appear in Codex Alexandrinus of the LXX, as well as elsewhere, the verse equivalent to Deut. 32.43 (Odes 2.43), οἱ ἄγγελοι θεοῦ appears in line 2, and υἱοὶ θεοῦ in line 4. This form of the text was also known to Justin Martyr (*Dial.* 130). It may be a Christian text form, already in use in a *testimonia* collection used by the author of Hebrews, or influenced by Hebrews.

28. It is not the case, as Attridge, *The Epistle*, p. 57, supposes, that the text can be understood as referring to Christ because 'it has been taken out of its context'. Quite the contrary: it is because the author of Hebrews (or the tradition he uses) knew its context and understood Deut. 32.43 to be part of the divine speech that begins at v. 39 that he knew the 'him' of v. 43a had to be someone distinguishable from God but someone to whom worship is due. It is notable that a divine speech which begins with *the* (final, culminating, most solemn) declaration by God of his divine uniqueness (Deut. 32.39: 'Behold, behold, I am he, and there is no god besides me…') should be understood to include this God's command to the angels to worship someone distinguished from himself.

for service'. But if 'his ministers' in the fourth quotation should be understood in terms of the cultic service of the angels and connected with their worship of the Son in the third quotation, then the Son should be understood as the subject of the fourth quotation. The Son has created the angels to perform cultic worship in the heavenly sanctuary where he himself sits on the divine throne and receives their worship. Jewish exegesis understood Ps. 104.4 to mean that the angels of flame and fire are those who worship around God's throne (*2 Bar.* 21.6; cf. *Qu. Ezra* A27–28), and sometimes distinguished the fiery angels who worship God in the highest heaven (Ps. 104.4b) from the 'spiritual angels' (Ps. 104.4a) who carry out their orders in the lower heavens (*Ap. Abr.* 19.6).

Jewish exegesis of Ps. 104.4 also explains how the quotation of this verse relates to the fifth and sixth quotations, forming the second aspect of the contrast between the angels and the Son. In Hebrew the verse could be taken to mean either that he 'makes the winds his messengers, flames of fire his ministers' or (as in LXX, followed by Heb. 1.7)[29] that he 'makes his angels winds, and his ministers flames of fire'. In either case it was understood to mean that God created the angels (cf. *Jub.* 2.2). But 1QH col. ix, lines 10–11, which reads the first line of the verse according to the former option, also takes it literally ('powerful spirits, according to their laws, before they became holy angels').[30] Other exegetes, following the second option, took the verse to mean that God changes the angels at will into wind, when they are sent as messengers, or into fire, when they minister before him (*Pirqe de-Rabbi Eleazar* 4; cf. *Exod. Rab.* 25.2). This exegesis is found in late Second Temple literature. For example, *4 Ezra* 8.20–22 depicts God who abides forever on his immeasurably exalted throne:

> before whom the hosts of angels stand trembling
> and at whose command they are changed to wind and fire.

The contrast is deliberate between God in his eternal, unchangeable sovereignty and the angels, his creatures and servants, who are entirely subject to his sovereign command. A similar point is made in *2 Bar.* 48.8, where, in the context of reflection on God's eternal transcendence over the times of his creation, which are entirely subject to his command, the fact that even the angels change at his command is cited:

> With signs of fear and threat you command the flames
> and they change into winds

(cf. 21.6, for the evidence that these are understood as the angels; and cf. also *Ap. Abr.* 15.6–7 for the idea that the fiery angels constantly change shape as they worship God in the highest heaven).

---

29. In Greek the definite noun is more likely to be the direct object.

30. Cf. also *1 En.* 17.1, which probably interprets the second line of the verse in the same way: 'those who were there were like blazing fire, and when they wished, they took on the appearance of men'. Bateman, *Early Jewish Hermeneutics*, pp. 197–98, is mistaken in thinking this refers to the sinful angels, the Watchers of *1 En.* 6–16. The latter are not mentioned in this vision until 19.1, which refers back to 18.11–16, but not to 17.1.

The function, therefore, of the fourth quotation in the Hebrews catena, in relation to the fifth and the sixth, is to depict the angels as created beings, subject to change at the command of their Creator, by contrast with the Son, who in the fifth and sixth quotations is depicted in precisely the terms which the Jewish texts just cited use to depict God in his transcendence over his creatures and servants the angels.[31] The fifth and sixth quotations are carefully selected to refer to two complementary aspects of the eternity of the Son's participation in the divine sovereignty. The quotation from Ps. 45[LXX 44].6–7 shows that the position on the divine throne to which the Son has been exalted as God's Messiah ('anointed...with the oil of gladness') is a matter of eternal participation in the eternal divine sovereignty. The quotation from Psalm 102[LXX 101].25–27 then takes the Son's participation in the divine sovereignty back to creation. The heavens, including the angels, are the work of his, the Son's hands; they pass away and are changed and renewed at his command; he himself in his transcendence over all creation will endure unchanging forever. This correlation between the Son's *eschatological* participation in the divine sovereignty, which began with his exaltation as the messianic king to his place at the right hand on the divine throne, and the Son's participation in exercise of divine sovereignty *in creation*, had already been made in the exordium (1.1–4) which anticipates most of the theological themes of the catena: 'a Son, whom he appointed heir of all things [Ps. 8.7–8], through whom he also created the worlds' (1.2).

The fact that the sixth quotation begins with the words, 'you in the beginning, Lord' (σὺ κατ' ἀρχάς, κύριε), is not incidental to the catena's purpose; nor is the fact that the word order differs from the Septuagint Greek text (Ps. 101.26: κατ' ἀρχὰς σύ, κύριε). These words link this text with Gen. 1.1 (ἐν ἀρχῇ) and Prov. 8.22–23 (ἀρχήν; ἐν ἀρχῇ), and refer to the primordial time before the creation of the heavens and the earth (cf. Jn 1.1). The emphatically placed σύ stresses the Son's presence before creation in the divine eternity. Only as the one who eternally pre-existed all things could he be the Creator of all things. Thus the sixth quotation begins with the Son's eternity before all things and ends with his eternity beyond all things ('your years will never end'). It could hardly be better chosen to describe the transcendent eternity of the one Creator and Ruler of all things, whom the monotheistic divine self-declarations in Deutero-Isaiah call 'the First and the Last' (Isa. 44.6; 48.12). The opening and concluding affirmations of the Son's primordial eternity and his eschatological eternity frame what is said about the creation, which came into being and perishes, decays and is renewed, its existence subject to the will of the only eternal One.

---

31. J.W. Thompson, 'The Structure and Purpose of the Catena in Heb 1.5–18', *CBQ* 38 (1976), p. 358, comments: 'Whereas the mutability of angels in rabbinic tradition is no sign of inferiority, in Hebrews their changeableness and connection with the material world marks them as inferior. Such a handling of the scripture citation indicates that the author reads his text with his own metaphysical assumptions.' But this is to miss the point that the inferiority of the angels does not lie in their mutability as such, but in the fact that it shows their complete subjection to the will of the Son, as to that of God. This meaning certainly can be found in the Jewish texts cited above. The Son's superiority is in his participation in the divine creativity and sovereignty. This entails his metaphysical eternality, but not immutability. There is no Platonism here.

The third, fifth and sixth texts are all texts which, in their context, could be read as distinguishing another divine person from the one whom Hebrews takes to be God the Father.[32] The fact that in the fifth quotation this results in the application of the *word* 'God' (ὁ θεός) to the Son (v. 8)[33] should not be given too much significance, even though it is one of the mere handful of instances in which the word is applied to Jesus in the New Testament. Exegetically, this phenomenon in the fifth quotation is very similar to the application of Ps. 82.1 to Melchizedek in 11Q*Melchizedek* (col. ii, line 10). In that case exegesis required the identification of the *Elohim* of the text with a figure other than YHWH since the text was regarded as distinguishing between this *Elohim* and the *El* who must be YHWH. Similarly, in the Hebrews catena, Ps. 45(44).6–7 is understood to address someone as 'God' (ὁ θεός) who is also distinguished from 'God, your God' (ὁ θεός, ὁ θεός σου). In 11Q*Melchizedek*, the point is not to include Melchizedek in the unique divine identity, but merely that, in the exegete's views, Scripture here uses the word 'god' (אלהים) for a figure other than the one God. It is not the mere application of a scriptural use of the word 'god' to Jesus Christ which makes Heb. 1.8 more significant.[34] What makes it of special significance is that this text (Ps. 45[44].6) speaks of the eternal divine throne as 'your throne, O God'. Sitting on the divine throne was the most powerful symbol Jewish monotheism had for the inclusion of a figure in the exercise of the unique divine sovereignty over all things.[35] Standing in the divine council, as Melchizedek does, does not carry the meaning which sitting on the divine throne carries. Thus it is not the word 'god' – an ambiguous word in

32. On Ps. 102.25–27 in this respect, see T.F. Glasson, '"Plurality of Divine Persons" and the Quotations in Hebrews 1.6ff.', *NTS* 12 (1965–1966), pp. 271–72. In this sense they are 'two powers' texts like those that feature in the rabbinic discussions studied by A. Segal, *Two Powers in Heaven: Early Rabbinic Reports about Christianity and Gnosticism* (SJLA, 25; Leiden: E.J. Brill, 1977), but these specific texts do not appear in those discussions. In fact, none of the texts that do appear in the rabbinic discussions is given christological significance in the New Testament, while the absence of Ps. 110.1 from the rabbinic discussions is particularly significant for the relationship of the rabbinic discussions to the Christianity of the New Testament period.

33. H.W. Montefiore, *A Commentary on the Epistle to the Hebrews* (BNTC; London: A. & C. Black, 1964), p. 47; Attridge, *The Epistles*, pp. 59–60; Bateman, *Early Jewish Hermeneutic*, p. 228 (and others listed in M.J. Harris, *Jesus as God: The New Testament Use of Theos in Reference to Jesus* [Grand Rapids: Baker Book House, 1992], p. 218 n. 59), take ὁ θεός in v. 9 to function like ὁ θεός in v. 8, as a vocative addressed to Christ, but this seems unlikely. In v. 8 it is the most natural way to read the Greek, but not in v. 9: see Harris, *Jesus*, pp. 218–20; D.F. Leschert, *Hermeneutical Foundations of Hebrews: A Study in the Validity of the Epistle's Interpretation of Some Core Citations from the Psalms* (Lewiston, Queenston, Lampeter: Edwin Mellen, 1994), pp. 34–35.

34. Aquila's translation of Ps. 45.6 makes the address to God unambiguous by using the vocative θεέ instead of the LXX's nominative with (probable) vocative meaning. But this could be understood to mean that this verse of the psalm is addressed to YHWH, not to the king, as is certainly the case in the Targum to Psalms ('Thy throne of glory, YHWH, endures forever and ever'). See W. Horbury, *Jewish Messianism and the Cult of Christ* (London: SCM Press, 1998), pp. 148–49, for discussion of two variant targumic versions, which also read at least v. 7a as addressed to God, not the king.

35. Bauckham, 'The Throne of God'.

certain contexts, just as it is unambiguous in others – that is so important chris-tologically. The word itself says nothing that is not adequately said without it, in this catena and elsewhere in the New Testament, about the inclusion of Christ in the divine identity. Hence the rarity of its use for Christ in the New Testament is not of great christological moment.

In view of the fact that Ps. 45[44].6–7 and Ps. 110[109].1 both concern the divine throne and (in this early Christian interpretation) the Messiah's enthronement on it, there is a significant parallel between the way the former text distinguishes 'God' (addressed by the psalmist) from 'God, your God', and the way the latter (in the opening words not quoted in Heb. 1.13) distinguishes 'the Lord' (ὁ κύριος) from 'my Lord' (τῷ κυρίῳ μου). Of course, in the Greek version of Ps. 110[109].1 the first κύριος represents the tetragrammaton, while the second does not. It is proba-bly a mistake to suppose that any New Testament author was unaware of this. Even if they did not read Hebrew (as most did), they are likely to have known tetragram-maton or used a Greek equivalent (ΠΙΠΙ) or a Greek transliteration (ΙΑΩ), as well as those which substituted κύριος for the tetragrammaton.[36] They knew κύριος as the *oral* Greek substitute which they, like other Jews, always used in reading the text either to themselves (since ancient readers normally pronounced words to themselves) or to others, and which they, like many other Jews, therefore also used when they quoted Scripture in their own writings. But they also knew that κύριος *was* the oral Greek substitute for the divine name which was written in many manuscripts of the Greek Bible. However, this need not have prevented them from finding significance in the correspondence between ὁ κύριος, representing the tetragrammaton, and τῷ κυρίῳ μου in Psalm 110[109].1. They could well find very significant the parallel between this text, where 'the Lord' enthrones the one David calls 'my Lord', and Psalm 45[44].6–7, where 'God, your God' anoints as king the one who sits on the divine throne as 'God'. What the parallel suggests is that both texts speak rather clearly of the enthronement of Jesus Christ in heaven *as* his inclusion in the unique divine identity.

The way that the fifth quotation attributes to the Son participation in the divine work of creation is one of the more direct and remarkable instances of this theme in the New Testament literature. Evidently the writer connected this theme closely to that of Christ's participation in the unique divine sovereignty, just as these two aspects of the unique divine identity were linked in Jewish monotheistic assertions that the one Creator of all things is also the one Ruler of all things. The distinction from the angels in both cases also follows standard Jewish monotheistic precedent. In this exercise of the divine sovereignty, the angels are merely servants, whereas the Son exercises the sovereignty himself, sitting on the divine throne. In the work of creation, the angels play no part whatsoever, being themselves created, whereas the Son carries out this activity which was understood to be God's alone. If the eternity of the Son's rule, demonstrated by the fifth quotation, distinguishes him

36. A. Pietersma, 'Kyrios or Tetragram: A Renewed Quest for the Original Septuagint', in A. Pietersma and C. Cox (eds.), *De Septuaginta* (Mississauga, ON: Benben Publications, 1984), pp. 86–101; P.W. Skehan, 'The Divine Name at Qumran, in the Masada Scroll and in the Septua-gint', *BIOSCS* 13 (1980), pp. 28–33.

from the angels, his eternity as Creator, established by the sixth quotation, distinguishes him even more decisively. He is eternal in the full sense of the Jewish monotheistic assertion that God alone is the eternal One, preceding and therefore also transcending all creaturely existence, not subject to the transcience, change and decay of creaturely life, in which the angels, despite their superiority to earthly creatures, do participate.

Finally, we should note that what is said about angels in the catena would be uncontroversially accepted in Second Temple Judaism. That angels are created, mutable and only servants of the unique eternal sovereignty of God was not controversial. All Jews would have agreed to it. Conversely, what is said of the Son here would never have been said of an angel. Angels, even so-called principal angels, only stand in God's presence, in the attitude of servants and worshippers of God. No such angel is portrayed as seated on the divine throne, or as worshipped by other angels, still less as participating in the work of creation. All these features unambiguously and unequivocally distinguish angels, even the most exalted, from God in the literature of Second Temple Judaism. The catena places the Son above all the angels ('all' explicitly in v. 14) by placing him in the position of God in relation to the angels.

7. *The Pre-Existence of the Son*

Does Hebrews 1 then envisage the personal pre-existence of the Son? James Dunn doubts it, suggesting that the language used need only assert the continuity of God's creative and revelatory activity that reaches its climax in Jesus Christ.[37] But in my view the evidence is strongly in favour of a positive answer.[38] (1) The text clearly speaks of the same person, the Son, as both the agent of creation and the Jesus Christ who took his seat at the right hand of God. The fifth and sixth quotations in the catena are particularly instructive: they both address a person, called God in one quotation, Lord in the other, who is not God the Father. Indeed, God is in both cases understood to be the speaker. In this personal address there is no difference between the fifth quotation which addresses the enthroned Messiah and the sixth which addresses the one who created the heavens and the earth. (2) Both these quotations, the fifth and sixth, and also the third, use the same exegetical technique of finding in their texts a second divine person addressed by God. The use of this technique in the sixth quotation, just as in the third and fifth, seems a very odd way of talking merely about the continuity of the divine purpose that came to fullest expression in Jesus. It is important to note that in Hebrews 1 the pre-existence of the Son is expressed not only in the Wisdom language of vv. 2–3, but also in the quotation of Ps. 102.25–27 as addressed to the Son. The latter is certainly not to be dismissed as a kind of proof-texting that needs not be taken very seriously. The quotations in the catena are, as we have seen, chosen and arranged with great care. In the early Christian milieu this kind of exegesis is very serious theology,

37. J.D.G. Dunn, *Christology in the Making* (London: SCM Press, 1980), pp. 208–209.
38. Cf. the partially similar critique of Dunn in Meier, 'Symmetry', pp. 531–33.

perhaps even the most serious form of theology. (3) To see pre-existence here as no more than an ideal pre-existence in the mind of God is surely to miss the point of the catena, which is not merely that God acts through Jesus, even climactically. In that case the difference between Jesus and the angels, who act as God's servants in the work of salvation (1.14), would be merely one of degree. The whole catena is designed to establish a difference in kind between, on the one hand, Jesus who participates in the unique divine sovereignty and unique divine eternity, and, on the other hand, the angels who are servants and creatures. That Jesus sits on the divine throne and they do not is explicated by means of the whole array of Jewish monotheistic distinctions between the unique identity of the one God and all other reality. This would not be needed in order to say that God's activity culminates in Jesus. It says that Jesus himself is intrinsic to the divine identity.

8. *A Two-Natures Christology?*

Although we have given detailed attention in this essay to ch. 1 of Hebrews, a final comment concerns the christology of chs. 1 and 2 taken together. These chapters are perhaps the closest the New Testament texts come to the conceptuality of the Chalcedonian Christology that emerged in the fifth century from the patristic christological controversies. Jesus is identified both with God (ch. 1) and with humanity (ch. 2). In the one case he is in every respect like God ('the reflection of God's glory and the exact imprint of God's being': 1.3), in the other case he is in every respect like us ('he had to become like his brothers and sisters in every respect': 2.17). In him, as Chalcedon insisted, true divinity and true humanity are both to be recognized. One might even speak of two natures in these two chapters: the divine nature which is unchangeably eternal (1.10–12) and the flesh-and-blood mortal nature of humanity (2.14). But to call the Christology of these chapters a two-natures Christology would not be adequate. Nature is here subordinate to narrative identity. Just as the God of Israel is who he is in the story the Hebrew Bible tells, so Jesus Christ is who he is in the narrative that includes him in the unique divine identity (notably, creation and exaltation to divine rule) and in the narrative that tells of his human experience of identifying with his human brothers and sisters, learning obedience through suffering, tested but without sin, dying and being exalted to heaven. It is that divine and human narrative identity of Jesus that the rest of Hebrews goes on to retell in terms of his high priesthood, acquiring a fresh angle on who God is and who Jesus is by a scripturally based new reading of the narrative.

JESUS AND WORSHIP, GOD AND SACRIFICE[1]

J. Lionel North, University of Durham

1.

When a boy, without thought or just to be clever, repeats some oath or vulgarity which he has heard his father let drop, his mother, ever the guardian of domestic propriety, might well bark at both of them, 'Watch your language!' So must we when we deal with fundamental matters like the deity of Christ, or with the technical language which almost inevitably accompanies it, jargon such as 'monotheism', 'henotheism', 'monolatry'. One feature of these words is the relative lateness of their arrival in English academic discussion. 'Monotheism' goes back only to the 1660s, while the other two are much later, Victorian, verbal artefacts; 'henotheism' was coined in the 1860s and 'monolatry' in the 1880s (on their history see MacDonald's contribution to this volume).

Our concern about the relatively late appearance of words that have become the staple of scholarly discourse is well-placed. First, we show thereby our awareness of the danger of foisting modern constructs like the above onto ancient data, in this case notions mainly derived from our Victorian forefathers' early studies in world religions and also from reports about them emerging from travellers' tales and from representatives of the Church's overseas mission. Secondly, we show that we are aware that these notions are usually expressed in European languages foreign to the genius of that data. We recall the Italian jingle *traduttori traditori* ('translators betray'). The rabbis had a similar comment which in fact may be the origin of the Italian. It runs, 'Whoever translates literally deceives; whoever expands is a blasphemer'.[2] This sense of the passage of time and of the way that translation inevitably distorts makes us aware, thirdly, of the dangers of anachronism, of imposing *our* opinions of issues that emerge only later in church history and doctrine, upon the ancient materials.

---

1. Versions of this paper were read not only in Durham but also to a lay audience at a Theology Day School held in the University of Hull in 2001. I am grateful to my wife and our cousin Adrian Morris for initiating me into the mysteries of the computer.

2. This is the rendering of M.P. Weitzman, *The Syriac Version of the Old Testament* (Cambridge: Cambridge University Press, 1999), p. 235. As Weitzman says, there is something 'innately unsatisfactory' about translation, since both literal and paraphrastic renderings falsify the original. There is an immense hermeneutical problem here. We do the best we can, but the best will be only an approximation. In the last analysis something supplementary to linguistics is needed to bridge the gulf fixed between ancient wisdom and modern men and women.

On the BBC radio programme 'The Brains Trust' the popular post-war philosopher C.E.M. Joad would invariably preface his answer to a philosophical question from his interlocutor by countering, 'It all depends what you mean by' key term(s) in the question. We too must heed that observation as we approach the particular, even limited, way in which I propose to tackle the deity of Christ, that is, by way of the worship of Christ. 'Professor'[3] Joad's concern for precise definition comes into play; 'it all depends what you mean by' worship. As an example of the imprecision of that word and of the baggage it has been obliged to carry, we may quote the words of the Marriage Service in the *Book of Common Prayer*, 'With my body I thee worship'. In the lexicon of love a lover's profession 'I adore you' or a parent's indulgent observation 'He idolizes her' are clearly not idolatrous assertions. They imply only that the semantic spectrum of 'worship' *vel sim*. is broad. It is a loose cannon and, with weapons still in mind, ideally it is better to have the single bullet of the rifle precisely aimed than the indiscriminate scatter of duck-shot from a blunderbuss. But, sadly, most words are not so tractable. So, heeding both Joad's concern for exact definition and my own comments about the possibilities of distortion, I do not want to prejudge the meaning of the Greek words προσκύνησις and cognates; strictly they should be left untranslated, but I shall compromise with 'worship(per)'.

I concentrate on 'worship' since many Christians would urge that the deity of Christ is proven partly because the New Testament, their foundation document, says Jesus was 'worshipped'. Since monotheists insist that 'worship' is due to God alone, they conclude *ergo* Jesus is God.[4] But this conclusion is too important to be left unexamined. I shall begin with a brief study of the προσκυν- word-group in the New Testament. For necessary cultural context I shall then consider how some of the rabbis described some physical postures adopted in the act of 'worship', and, returning to language use and for more historical perspective, close with a summary of an eighth-century Christian analysis of προσκύνησις. Thereafter we proceed from 'worship' to a summary of the meaning of sacrifice and particularly its significance in defining deity.

2.

When we examine the New Testament for the προσκυν- word-group, some interesting facts emerge. Though the abstract noun προσκύνησις does not occur,[5] the

---

3. Joad remained a University *Reader* in Philosophy until his death.

4. On the other hand, as H.P. Liddon insisted, 'If Jesus is worshipped, this is simply because Jesus is God' (on other grounds, I presume); that of course is a different syllogism; cf. *The Divinity of our Lord and Saviour Jesus Christ,* lecture 7, §I.2.α (London: Rivingtons, 1867), p. 565 = (London: Longmans, 16th edn, 1892), p. 385. The whole section, pp. 538–608 (1867) = pp. 366–414 (1892), is a full (and fulsome) account of the 'worship' of Jesus in the New Testament. Liddon's logic reverses that of Phil. 2.6–11, because, while Paul does speak of every knee bowing at the name of Jesus (and this must be given its proper weight), this (προσκύνησις?) *follows* self-emptying, obedience and crucifixion (cf. διό [v. 9] and n. 33 below); it is not the corollary of deity.

5. The abstract noun is found in contemporary Jewish Greek literature hardly more often, only at Sir. 50.21; *3 Macc.* 3.7; Philo, *Leg. Gai.* 116; Josephus, *Ant.* 2.15. The example at *Test. Abr.*

cognate verb and concrete noun ('worshipper') do, sixty-one times. Their distri-
bution is uneven: Paul (once) and Mark (twice) (our earliest sources), along with
Hebrews (twice), muster only five examples between them. Matthew (thirteen),
Luke–Acts (seven) and John (twelve, but ten in 4.20–4) together have thirty-two.
Revelation has the lion's share with twenty-four instances. Of the sixty-one examples, fourteen have Jesus as the object of 'worship'. While this is our primary interest, it is instructive to list the other recipients; this will provide some illuminating
perspective. There are sixteen references to the 'worship' of God. Jesus quotes at
the devil, 'You shall worship the Lord your God and him only shall you serve', a
quotation that is part of Jesus' strategy against paganism, the shadow side of true
religion. By it Jesus justifies his refusal to 'worship' his tempter (Mt. 4.9–10//Lk.
4.7–8; see Dunn's essay in this volume). Acts also knows of pagan religion (see
n. 6) but it is Revelation that specially deals with this. Rather like the Synoptic
devil, the demons and idols, the dragon and beast with its image in Revelation (all
probably symbols of Roman ruler cult) blasphemously insist upon and usually receive 'worship' (ten examples). Aware of the abomination of blasphemy and
idolatry an angel twice declined the 'worship' offered him by John (19.10; 22.8–9),
something that Peter also had done (Acts 10.25–26).[6] But while these examples
show that legitimate 'worship' is restricted to God, there could be exceptions. At
Mt. 18.26, part of the story of the unforgiving servant or slave – when he realised
that he and his family and all he owned were on the brink of being sold off to pay
off his immense debt, προσεκύνει, which in context suggests 'grovelled'. Secondly, at Rev. 3.9, men who appear to be Jewish and perhaps oppressors of the
church at Philadelphia are promised that as punishment they will have to 'worship'
the local Christians and admit that God has preferred these *goyim* to them. Here,
like the debtor's master, human beings will be offered 'worship', legitimately; it
must mean something like 'homage'.

When we turn to the fourteen cases where Jesus is 'worshipped', analysis reveals
these results. (a) If 'worship' is often understood as an important part of the response to a prior action of Jesus, e.g. to a miracle, it is surprising to discover that
Jesus is said to be 'worshipped' after a miracle only twice: after the stilling of the
storm (Mt. 14.33) and the healing of the blind man (Jn 9.38). Astonishment is a
more common reaction. Although Resurrection and Ascension are acts of God, not
of Jesus, perhaps we should add the 'worship' that follows the former in Matthew
(28.9, 17 – the two women at the tomb and later some of the eleven disciples) and
the latter in Luke (24.52, *si v.l.*). Even if we do include them, these are all the references to the 'worship' of Jesus following a display of power, his own or God's.

(Rec. A) 20.12 may be Jewish; the one at *Greek Apocalypse of Ezra* 7.16 is clearly Christian. For
these last two cf. *The Old Testament Pseudepigrapha* (ed. J.H. Charlesworth; 2 vols.; Garden City,
NY: Doubleday, 1983–1985), I, pp. 579, 895. It does not occur in the Apostolic Fathers. Only five
examples may suggest that most Jewish writers found something unsavoury about the abstract that
did not always infect its cognates; contrast the noun at Philo, *Leg. Gai.* 116 (see n. 21), defined as
θεοπλαστῆσαι (118), with the verb at 310.

6.   Similarly Paul and Barnabas at Lystra (Acts 14.11–18), though no derivative of προσκυν-
is used; see below and Stuckenbruck's essay in this volume *passim*.

This raises the question whether they are enough to warrant the conclusion many Christians would draw about the deity of Christ, especially given the meaning 'homage' which some passages clearly require, and the legitimacy of its being offered to human beings in others. (b) The references to 'worship' before a miracle (the leper, Jairus and the Canaanite woman in Mt. 8.2; 9.18; 15.25; the Gerasene demoniac in Mk 5.6) are a different matter. The verbs are in the imperfect ('they began to...' or 'they continued to...') and are part of the humble but persistent approach of the petitioner to a possible benefactor or healer, part of the arm-twisting flattery in 'Lord, if you choose, you *can* make me clean'. I conclude that while 'worship' after a miracle is dictated by wonder and gratitude, beforehand it is dictated by need.[7] Though a miracle is not involved, this is where the respectful approach of the ambitious mother of the sons of Zebedee belongs, as she petitions Jesus in proper Oriental fashion for favours for her two sons (Mt. 20.20). (c) Outside the gospels there is only one place where the 'worship' of Jesus is mentioned. In Heb. 1.6 God invites the angels to 'worship' his Firstborn when he is presented to the world. Perhaps this example is on a par with the 'worship' offered by the Magi with their three gifts, when the Firstborn of Hebrews is born in Bethlehem (Mt. 2.2, 11). (d) Ironically, even the pretence of Herod that he too, like the Magi, wanted to 'worship' the baby, and the mock 'worship' that was part of the soldiers' taunting of Jesus on the cross (Mt. 2.8; Mk 15.19) may say something about the attitude towards Jesus that the Church felt was only his proper due.

My question in (a) above anticipated my summary of the New Testament usage; we have nothing here, not even in Hebrews, that requires us to conclude that Jesus is regarded as divine because he is worshipped. This is a case where our translation of προσκυν- as 'worship' betrays us. It does not mean 'worship' if we are thinking of the exclusive 'worship' that God demands and God alone should receive, the 'worship' that is reflected on church notice boards that advertise the times on Sunday for Divine Worship. The 'worship', better, the homage, the obeisance, the respect, is reflected in non-theological contexts not only in the words I have already quoted ('With my body I thee "worship"') but also for example in the full nomenclature of a town's first citizen, His/Her Worship the Mayor,[8] and in a review of a book of which he clearly thought very highly, where Henry Chadwick wrote, 'It is an achievement meriting *proskynesis*'.[9] That I think says it all. It means the profoundest respect and it implies no more.

3.

I now extend the investigation of the meaning of προσκυν-, first, as I have indicated, by enquiring about Jewish descriptions of the physical postures which symbolize what could be construed as προσκύνησις. This will provide the social reality necessary to contextualizing the lexical investigation, putting flesh on the

7. In the analysis of προσκύνησις offered by John of Damascus (see below), the προσκύνησις which is prompted by need is recognised as a valid subdivision.

8. This possibility is also recognised by John of Damascus.

9. *JTS* NS 23 (1972), p. 258.

bones of 'worship' and, literally, bringing it down to earth. Secondly, we turn to the Iconoclast Controversy of the eighth and ninth centuries for yet more semantic analysis. The reason for turning to these two contributions is that both explicitly ask the question that we are asking (though each looks for a different type of answer), *viz.* 'What is worship?' A rabbi asks, 'What is כריעה and what is בריכה?'; John of Damascus asks, 'τί ἐστι προσκύνησις;' In repeating their questions I am not only looking for their answers but also illustrating again the precarious nature of modern words used to say something about ancient issues, the precarious nature of arguing too enthusiastically about the 'correct' English equivalents for ancient Greek and Hebrew words, sometimes perhaps in order to express 'sound' theology.[10] We must know what 'worship' means before we are in a position to infer anything from it.

In their present form our Hebrew sources are post-biblical, but it is widely assumed that many of them could well reflect first-century practices and doctrines. I am more confident about this when we are looking at ritual since practice is more conservative than theologizing. Philo, the older contemporary of Jesus and Paul, offers some assistance. At Gen. 37.9–10 Joseph tells his father and brothers about a dream he has had: 'the sun, the moon, and eleven stars were bowing down to me' (LXX προσεκύνουν). Jacob rebukes what he sees as his young son's youthful vanity: 'Are we to come and bow to the ground before you (προσκυνῆσαι...ἐπὶ τὴν τῆν), I and your mother and your brothers?' When Philo embroiders this episode, the short question of the biblical text, 'Are we to...bow to the ground?' becomes 'Shall we all standing straight opposite ranged in order with lifted hands address our prayers to vanity? Shall we first bow and then cast ourselves to the ground in supplication and obeisance?' (πρότερον ὑφέντες [*si v.l.*], εἶτα καταβαλόντες ἑαυτούς εἰς τὸ ἔδαφος ποτνιᾶσθα καὶ προσκυνεῖν ἐπιχειρήσωμεν;) (*Somn.* 2.139–40).[11] My point is that Philo's diffuse embellishment is sufficiently close to later Jewish descriptions that I will now summarize to make me think that Philo has factored into his exegesis of Genesis details of the ritual that he witnessed and shared in every Sabbath in one of the Alexandrian synagogues. In this way we can argue that the later rabbinic evidence could well be relevant for the first century.

The Hebrew terms[12] used to describe the different postures adopted in prayer (other than standing) are not completely technical terms, in that they are to some

10. In 'Is Christianity Monotheistic? Patristic Perspectives on a Jewish/Christian Debate', *SP* 29 (1997), pp. 340–63, O. Skarsaune quotes Gregory of Nazianzus (*Or.* 29.21), 'The weakness of the argument appears to belong to the mystery itself'. Recognizing this should discourage what he calls, following Gregory, 'too much trust in arguments we construct in favour of orthodoxy, arguments which must always fall short of the reality they purport to explain' (p. 353); similarly, Augustine confesses (*Trin.* 5.9.10), 'When we are asked, "Three what?", we encounter at once a huge deficiency in human language. However, we say "Three Persons", not for the sake of saying it, but because the only alternative is silence.'

11. Cf. Josephus, *Ant.* 10.11. All quotations and translations from Philo in this paper are taken from the LCL.

12. For this section I have consulted the following editions, translations and discussions: *The Babylonian Talmud, Seder Zera'im* (London: Soncino, 1948): *Berakoth*, M. Simon (ed.); *idem,*

extent interchangeable, that is, they are not used, as we shall see, with the uniformity we may desire.[13] However, there were attempts to discriminate them. Using biblical texts as both proof and illustration, an unascribed and therefore undateable passage in *b. Berakot* 34b attempts some precise definitions of three nouns: קידה means prostration on the face; בריעה is kneeling; השתחואת is prostration with hands and feet spread out.[14] But role-play rather than words was sometimes used to illustrate differences and meanings. The rabbinic form of the question we began with above is in *j. Berakot* 1.5 (3c).[15] Perhaps repeating a student's question, an anonymous teacher asks, 'What is בריעה and what is בריכה?' From the rather strange story that follows about two rabbis, Chiyya and Levi, demonstrating the two postures in front of Rabbi, the former developing a limp after a בריכה but recovering, the latter after a בריעה not being so fortunate, I conclude that while both postures are similar and painful, a בריעה is more painful and difficult to perform than a בריכה. But we are not specifically told what the couple did; we cannot identify the postures only from the symptom of limping. But light is thrown on these demonstrations by an equally strange story told in *b. Sukkah* 53a[16]; in fact it is very probably a parallel but earlier version of the same episode. It concerns Simon, son of Gamaliel I and first-century figure known to Josephus and prominent in the Roman-Jewish war. The story first tells of Simon's successful juggling with eight flaming torches as an expression of religious joy, and then proceeds, more

Seder Mo'ed (London: Soncino, 1938): *Yoma*, L. Jung (ed.) and *Sukkah*, I.W. Slotki (ed.); *The Talmud of Babylonia, An American Translation, I: Tractate Berakhot*, J. Neusner (ed.) (Chico, CA: Scholars Press, 1984[a]); *idem, VI. Tractate Sukkah*, J. Neusner (ed.) (Chico, CA: Scholars Press, 1984[b]); *Le Talmud de Jérusalem*, M. Schwab (ed.), I, *Traité des Berakhoth* (Paris: Maisonneuve, repr. 1932); *Der Jerusalemer Talmud in deutscher Übersetzung. I. Berakhoth*, C. Horowitz (ed.) (Tübingen: J.C.B. Mohr [Paul Siebeck], 1975); *Der Tosephtatraktat Berakot, Text, Übersetzung und Erklärung*, O. Holtzmann (ed.) (Giessen: Töpelmann, 1912); *Die Tosephta, Seder Seraim, Text, Übersetzung, Erklärung*, (ed. E. Lohse and G. Schlichting; Hefte 1–2; Stuttgart: W. Kohlhammer, 1956–1957); *The Tosephta Translated from the Hebrew, Second Division, Moed*, (ed. J. Neusner; New York: Ktav, 1981); *Midrash Rabbah, Genesis* (ed. H. Freedman; London: Soncino, 1951), I, (but at p. 323, following the critical edition of J. Theodor and C. Albeck [Berlin, 1912–1927], p. 377, correct the dittography involving *keri'ah*). Most of the texts I discuss are also translated or summarized in *Kommentar zum neuen Testament aus Talmud und Midrasch* (eds. H.L. Strack and P. Billerbeck; München: Beck, 1924), II, pp. 259–62. See also S. Krauss, *Synagogale Altertümer* (Berlin-Wien: Harz, 1922), §44: *'Stellung, Verhalten, Gesten und Geberden'*, esp. pp. 400–405. F. Heiler discussed *'Gebetshaltung und Gebetsgestus'* from a *religionsgeschichtlich* point of view in *Das Gebet* (München: Reinhardt, 1921, 4th edn), pp. 98–109 and 511–13, having summarized his findings in *'Die Körperhaltung beim Gebet'*, in *Orientalistische Studien: Festschrift für F. Hommel, MVAG* 21–22 (1916–1917) (Leipzig: Hinrichs, 1917–1918), II, pp. 168–77. For a detailed study of השתחויות see M.I. Gruber, *Aspects of Nonverbal Communication in the Ancient Near East* (Studia Pohl. 12/I–II; Rome: Biblical Institute Press, 1980), I, pp. 90–123 and 187–200, though it is not clear that Gruber has established the case for a new etymology. He also deals, more briefly, with the other words mentioned in this section, pp. 123–43 and 157–62. All references in notes 13–20; 30 are to this note.

13. This is acknowledged by Strack and Billerbeck, p. 261, end of §3.

14. Soncino (Simon), p. 213; Neusner (1984[a]), p. 243.

15. Schwab, p. 21; Horowitz, p. 33.

16. Soncino (Slotki), p. 254 and nn. 4–5; Neusner (1984[b]), p. 262.

pertinently, to describe an act of prostration where the final position was achieved by Simon's lowering his body and using only his two thumbs to support his trunk. One version of this tradition uses the singular, 'his finger'.[17] No one else could do this; when someone (Levi) tried, he became permanently lame. The *b. Sukkah* calls this posture a קידה, but it is clearly what the parallel version in *j. Berakot* has called a כריעה and the version in *Genesis Rabbah* 39 a בריכה (Soncino [Freedman], I, p. 323). So we see again that the achievement of a precise nomenclature was difficult even for members of the culture in question. But whatever Simon's action was called, if the story as a whole is authentic, its early date shows that, like Philo's embellishment of Gen. 37.9–10, we could be dealing with material that is contemporaneous with the New Testament.

The passage in *j. Berakot* 1.5 (3d) reports a long prayer attributed to the third century CE rabbi, Ben Qappara. It begins, 'To thee we should genuflect, bow, prostrate ourselves, kneel, since before thee every knee must bow'. Later the prayer has the phrase 'we throw ourselves down before thee'.[18] The nouns in the first sentence are the fullest single list we possess of postures in Hebrew prayer (respectively בריכה, השתחויה, כפיפה, כריעה). The omission of קידה, an action we have already seen to be difficult and even dangerous, may be due to its rarity or because of its abuse (?) as entertainment (see n. 17).

In *Tos. Ber.* 3.5 Rabbi Akiva's disciple Judah ben Ilai reports that when praying privately in the synagogue Akiva could be found, not standing still as was usual, but moving around the synagogue because of the frequency of his והשתחוייות הכרעות.[19] Schlichting does not enlarge on why he thinks that these two postures might have induced a state of ecstasy.[20]

In summary, to judge from the range of vocabulary available to express shades of respect and so forth, Oriental manners and etiquette appear to have been more elaborate than in Greek societies, the reason being that the details were unnecessary when Greeks (i.e. Greek freeborn males) despised *all* Oriental obsequiousness.[21] Since Greek did not possess words for the fine distinctions which the

17. *Tos. Suk.* 4.4 (Neusner [1981], p. 223). In his note on another mention of the קידה (*b. Yom.* 19b), Jung interpreted it as 'pressing both big *toes* against the floor, bowing and kissing the pavement, and rising without moving the feet' (Soncino, p. 86 n. 5, my italics). Even the High Priest was encouraged to demonstrate it, almost as a party trick, to prevent his falling asleep! For a fairly close non-Jewish parallel cf. Cornutus, *Theologiae Graecae Compendium* (Leipzig: Teubner, 1881), p. 12, χωλὸς [sc. τὰς Λιτὰς] μὲν οὔσας διὰ τὸ πίπτειν τοὺς γονυπετοῦντας.

18. Schwab, pp. 21–22; Horowitz, p. 34.

19. Holtzmann, pp. 36 (line 8)–37; Lohse and Schlichting (1956), p. 36 (German); *idem* (1957), p. 18 (line 7) (Hebrew).

20. Lohse and Schlichting (1956), p. 36, n. 37. A close parallel to the description of Akiva's activities is to be found in *b. Ber.* 31a (Soncino [Simon], p. 190; Neusner [1984ᵃ], p. 220). At *Vita Numae* 14.7–9 (Teubner 3/2.73 = §§3–5 [LCL 1.356]), Plutarch describes a περιστροφή, whirling, as part of προσκύνησις, that he could not understand and had to demythologize. If Akiva's movements bear any resemblance to Numa's (and to the pathology of the religious dance, e.g. of the Sufi 'Whirling Dervish'), we may have corroboration of Schlichting's suggestion about ecstasy.

21. Cf. Philo, *Leg. Gai.* 116 where, perhaps following Aristotle, προσκύνησις is called τὸ βαρβαρικὸν ἔθος (see F.H. Colson's note *ad loc.* in LCL 10.58–59 and n. 5 above); at Herodotus, *Hist.* 1.134.1, Persian greetings are graded by the social class of the two parties: προσκύνησις

Hebrew words suggest, in LXX προσκυνεῖν sometimes had to do double duty, at Esth. 3.2 (twice); 5, for both שחה (its most common equivalent in LXX) and כרע, and at Isa. 44.15 and 17, for both שחה and סגד. So perhaps one might hazard a guess that προσκυνεῖν could be used to translate not only שחה, כרע and סגד, but כפף, קדד and even ברך as well (since its nominal cognate ברך means knee). If all this is so, we see again that from the point of view of both physical posture and also defects in the Greek language, the semantic spectrum of προσκυν- is broad. This breadth can now be put alongside the breadth we have deduced from the New Testament evidence.

4.

Five hundred years and more after these rabbis, the Iconoclast Controversy broke out to ravage the Eastern Greek church. Ever since the fourth century, and with notable exceptions, special respect had been paid by Christians of different stripes to relics, mosaics and icons bearing the likenesses of God, Christ, Mary and the saints.[22] But, apart from the inevitable political reasons, this was resisted by those whose views were shaped by the Old Testament's rejection of idolatry, by the problems posed by icons for evangelism amongst Jews and later possibly amongst Muslims, both aniconic by conviction, by their use in some Gnostic and Manichaean circles, and by their support for both Nestorian and Monophysite Christologies. However, these dangers did nothing to minimize the importance attached to icons amongst most Eastern theologians and monks and, oddly, the army, and when the emperor Leo III forbade their use in 726 and their destruction in 730, he began more than a century of controversy and violence. These ended, formally at least, in 842, with the triumph of the Iconodule or Iconophile (icon-serving or - loving) conviction which Leo had resisted.

From the beginning the Iconodules did not ignore their opponents' arguments. A new vocabulary, or at least a new precision, had to be developed to accommodate, as far as was possible, the Iconodule position to the various reasons (just listed) that the Iconoclast theologians adduced for rejecting it. For example, the Old Tes-

---

is the duty of the lowest of the low. The γονυπετ- word-group is not dissimilar (cf. Mk 1.40, γονυπετῶν [*si v.l.*]//Mt. 8.2, προσεκύνει). It is not found in LXX, Philo or Josephus. The few examples of verb and adjective in *LSJ*, augmented by new examples from Polybius and Appian, suggest that, when used of humans, Greek men thought of γονυπετ- as an Oriental, unmanly and demeaning habit, typical only of overwrought women; cf. Polybius, *Wars* 32.15.7, γονυπετῶν (a king!) καὶ γυναικιζόμενος; Appian, *Ill.* 27.1 (Teubner 1.334 = LCL 2.68), γονυπετὴς (a chieftain!) ἐδεῖτο αὐτοῦ πάνυ αἰσχρῶς. That is why it made no difference if one were also describing a goddess!; cf. *Scholia Graeca in Homeri Iliadem* (*Scholia Vetera*), (ed. H. Erbse; Berlin: W. de Gruyter, 1971), II, p. 58, where *Iliad* 5.357–358 (Aphrodite, herself wounded and frantic at the thought of losing her son, γνὺξ ἐριποῦσα...πολλὰ λισσομένη) is paraphrased by τὸ γυναικεῖον καὶ ἀσθενὲς ἐμφαίνει ἡ πολλὴ δέησις καὶ τὸ γονυπετεῖν.

22. For the fourth- and fifth-century political perspective, see I.M. Bugár, 'Zacchaeus and the Veneration of Images: Image of the Emperor – Image of a Saint', *SP* 34 (2001), pp. 11–22, with a rich bibliography and some 'pre-Damascene' lexical data.

tament's attitude towards images and idolatry could not be swept under the carpet and ignored. It had to be addressed. After all, it was in Scripture. The new analysis was elaborated by John of Damascus, in his three justly famous tracts *Against those who Slander the Holy Images,* written at the beginning of the controversy, just after Leo's first edict and, we should note, in a Muslim, aniconic, environ-ment.[23] John is after all John of Damascus in Syria and Syria was now in Muslim hands. John is claimed to have been the Muslim caliph's Chancellor of the Excheq-uer, as had his father and grandfather before him. In fact, was John a Semite, an Arab Christian, whatever that might mean in a very strongly Hellenized country? There are extant representations of him wearing a turban.[24]

John sets out his analysis and the distinctions which the Eastern church came to accept, build on and canonize at the Seventh Ecumenical Council at Nicaea in 787, when John was rehabilitated, about forty years after his death. In summary, his views are found in his three answers to his own rhetorical questions (III§15, p. 125). Asking τί ἐστι προσκύνησις; (III§27, p. 135), he gives almost a dic-tionary definition of the key word, with all the precision and discrimination of a dictionary entry. It is a sign (σημεῖον) of submission, that is, of abasement and humility (or, in John's context, self-humiliation). Next, asking, 'How many types of προσκύνησις are there?' (III§28, *ibid.*), he replies that there are five varieties which, we notice, are all only directed to the one true God. The first is what we find in worship (in the proper sense, λατρεία), and embraces all men: it is the worship that *all* offer to God, some willingly, others unwillingly; some willingly and knowingly (like the pious), others knowingly but not willingly (like the demons); others worship, neither willingly nor knowingly. For this last group no example is given, but perhaps he has Muslims in mind, whom it would not be diplomatic to specify in Damascus and Jerusalem. Secondly, προσκύνησις can also be ex-pressed in wonder at the divine glory and out of desire, presumably to know it (III§29, p. 136). The third variety is found in gratitude (III§30, p. 136), the fourth in a sense of need and hope for divine benefits (III§31, p. 136, and n. 7 above). The fifth and last kind is prompted by repentance and confession (III§32, p. 137). John's penchant for analysis and categorization is again seen in his subdividing the fifth variety into the three reasons for repentance and confession: love, fear of

23. References to these tracts are to the sections and pages of B. Kotter's edition: *Die Schriften des Johannes von Damaskos III, Contra Imaginum Calumniatores Orationes Tres* (PTS, 17; Berlin: W. de Gruyter, 1975); see pp. 1–24 for Kotter's discussion of their context and content, esp. pp. 10–11 on προσκύνησις and λατρεία.

24. *Lexikon der christlichen Ikonographie*, E. Kirschbaum and W. Braunfels (eds.) (Freiburg im Breisgau: Herder, repr. 1990), 6, col. 152 and vol. 7, col. 103. For the secular employment of John's relatives see *La Syrie de Byzance à l'Islam VIIe–VIIIe Siècles*, published by P. Canivet and J.-P. Rey-Coquais (Damas: Alef-Ba [Sidawi], 1992), pp. 90 and 140 (incidental remarks in contributions by Ignace Dick and Joseph Nasrallah respectively). The article by S.H. Griffith, *La Syrie de Byzance à l'Islam VIIe–VIIIe Siècles*, pp. 121–38, 'Images, Islam and Christian Icons. A Moment in the Christian/Muslim Encounter in Early Islamic Times', describes how things must have felt for Christians in Syria and Palestine under the new aniconic regime in the generation after John.

not receiving God's benefits, and plain fear, fear of punishment. John's third question is to enquire 'How many things do we find "worshipped" in Scripture and in how many ways do we offer προσκύνησις to creatures?' (III§33, p. 137). This is the question which perhaps we were expecting earlier, namely, who or what apart from God may legitimately receive worship? Briefly, we have the saints including Mary ('they are truly called gods, not by nature but by participation'), then holy sites and objects connected with salvation, objects dedicated to God (like copies of the holy gospels and church furniture), the images the saints see in visions, even each other, e.g. those in authority like masters and benefactors (III§§33–40, pp. 137–41, and n. 8 above). All these merit 'worship', but throughout John carefully distinguishes between the 'worship' which stems from honour and respect (τιμή) (I§8 *fin.*, p. 83; I§14, p. 87) and the 'worship' that is part of the liturgical worship of God alone (λατρεία).

To summarize: for John προσκύνησις has a very broad range and, seeking to cover himself against the Iconoclast charge of idolatry, he reserves a special word to be used only for the unique worship of God, viz. λατρεία. In earlier Greek λατρ- was a synonym of προσκυν-, used often in the LXX and even in the New Testament not only with a liturgical flavour but also to describe both Hebrew and pagan worship. But now John has clipped its wings and restricted its range, to refer solely to the worship of the only true God. But one is still bound to ask, 'For all his care, how far was the second commandment, about idolatry, observed simply by John's restricting an old word exclusively for it?' It is very difficult to say how all this worked out in practice, whether the differentiation in language could be any more than verbal and describe a fundamental difference of *attitude* in the hearts of worshippers in church as they turned from, say, BVM to God.

In spite of a considerable amount of detail, I stress that these two investigations into comparative and, as nearly as possible, contemporary materials, the one 'archaeological', the other lexical, are necessary illustrations of my general thesis that the meaning of προσκύνησις is not self-evident. It was an ancient problem, with both Jewish and Christian scholars feeling compelled to make time for their students' and readers' query, 'What precisely is it?' Rabbis answer in terms of the 'How?', i.e. in terms of physical postures – two varieties of kneeling and two of prostration. John of Damascus answers in terms of the 'Why?', of the motivation, and the 'Whom?', whom or what, apart from God, may the church legitimately 'worship'? With their answers I try to secure the loose cannon of 'worship' as tightly as possible. So, splicing together the Jewish and Christian contributions, προσκύνησις suggests a variety of physical postures adopted for any one of several reasons and directed to any number of possible recipients. It connotes homage, respect, honour, reverence. It can be offered to God or human beings or even the inanimate. The implication for the early church is that it cannot mean 'worship' in any sense that compels us to infer the deity of Christ. There is too much of the duck-shot about it; it is still unfocused; it is not exclusive enough. Something else is needed for the monotheistic parameters of the religion and cultus of Judaism to be stretched to include Jesus.

5.

Given that the phenomenon of sacrifice is universal through time and space, no one definition can ever be satisfactorily offered for it. Too many centuries have elapsed, too many societies have come and gone, leaving no trace behind them. It was and still is a part of too many networks of unrecognized presuppositions to be caught within the web of a single explanation provided by modern men and women. But we do the best we can (n. 2). A German anthropologist, Joseph Henninger, has offered this definition of sacrifice: 'A truly essential element...is that the recipient of the gift be a supernatural being (that is, one endowed with supernatural power), with whom the giver seeks to enter into or remain in communion', and, a little later, 'All the many kinds of beings to whom humans pay religious veneration, or even those they fear, can be recipients of sacrifice. Such recipients can thus be, spirits, demonic beings, and even humans, although sacrifice in the proper sense is offered to humans only when they have died and are considered to possess a super-human power.'[25]

Few in the ancient Mediterranean world seem to have attempted a definition. Perhaps rather like attending temple or synagogue, church or mosque, sacrifice (in various senses) was so common that everyone knew what it meant (or did until they were asked!). But Socrates made an attempt. In one of Plato's early dialogues he says, quite simply, 'Sacrificing is making gifts to the gods' (*Euthyphro* 14c). It was left to Augustine to attempt the precision of definition and explanation. He is writing relatively late in the day, in the first quarter of the fifth century CE, when, under the impact of Christian attack and imperial legislation, pagan sacrifice was on the wane. He is also reflecting non-Christian as much as Christian philosophical sentiment (see n. 26). 'True sacrifice', he says, 'is any act that is done in order that we may cleave in holy union to God' (*Civ. Dei* 10.6). A few lines earlier Augustine has recognized that properly sacrifice can be offered only to God. In summary, he says that while other features of the worship of God have been hijacked to the 'worship' of men, sacrifice must never be misappropriated (*Civ. Dei* 10.4); life can be surrendered only to Life. I shall exploit this point about the difference between 'worship' and sacrifice later on, but here I note the centrality of the idea that sacrifice belongs exclusively to God.

In the Old Testament sacrifice is usually understood as the offering of animal or cereal or wine or water or incense, as part of one's approach to God, perhaps particularly to show one's gratitude and the purity of one's motives. The Israelites were enjoined to offer sacrifices only to their national, territorial god Yahweh. To sacrifice to the national deities of other tribes and nations was idolatry and an insult to Yahweh. Though all this is too familiar to require proof, let me illustrate with verses that include both legitimate and illegitimate sacrifice (2 Kgs 17.35–36 NRSV): 'The LORD (=Yahweh) had made a covenant with them and commanded them, "You shall not worship other gods or bow yourselves to them or serve them or sacrifice

---

25. *The Encyclopedia of Religion*, M. Eliade (ed.) (20 vols.; New York: Macmillan, 1995), 12, pp. 544, 549.

to them, but you shall worship the LORD, who brought you out of the land of Egypt with great power and with an outstretched arm; you shall bow yourselves to him, and to him you shall sacrifice"'. All the basic elements of Israelite faith are here: the Exodus, the Sinai covenant, the jealous demand for exclusive loyalty to it and for sacrifice exclusively to Yahweh. The repetition of 'or' makes it clear that sacrifice is one thing and 'worship' another. This last point is particularly evident in the fascinating sequel to the story of the purification of Naaman (2 Kgs 5.15–19). Naaman has come to realize that 'there is no God in all the earth except in Israel'. So, after making arrangements for a portion of Israel to be transported to Syria in the form of 'two mule-loads of earth', he can promise Elisha, 'your servant will no longer offer burnt-offerings or sacrifice to any god (i.e. in Syria) except the LORD', that is, on this sacred earth. But because court protocol will oblige him to attend his elderly master the king of Syria up the steps into the temple of Rimmon to assist him in his worship of the pagan god (προσκυνεῖν, three times), Naaman asks Elisha to secure him Yahweh's understanding and pardon 'on this one count'. Elisha reassures him, 'Go in peace'. The difference between 'worship' and sacrifice could hardly be more clearly made.

With the passage of time the Jewish horror of idolatry only deepened. The discipline of the Exile had had its effect (though Horbury's essay in this volume illustrates how multifaceted the post-exilic understanding of monotheism could still be). Philo makes God say to Moses, 'The people have run after lawlessness. They have fashioned a god, the work of their hands, in the form of a bull, and to this god, who is no god, they offer worship (προσκυνοῦσι) and sacrifice, and have forgotten all the influences to piety they have seen and heard' (*Vit. Mos.* 2.165). And again, though now seasoned with the salt of sarcasm and based on personal observation in Alexandria and Egypt, 'We have known some of the image-makers offer prayers and sacrifices to their own creations though they would have done much better to worship (προσκυνεῖν) each of their two hands, or if they were disinclined for that because they shrank from appearing egotistical, to pay their homage to the hammers and anvils and pencils and pincers and the other tools by which their materials were shaped!' (*Decal.* 72; cf. 76–80).

As for the New Testament, we have Paul's appalled reaction when he hears the citizens of Lystra exclaim, 'The gods have come down to us in human form!' When he sees the plans they were making to sacrifice to them, he protests, 'Friends, why are you doing this? We are mortals just like you, and we bring you good news, that you should turn from these worthless things to the living God.' But, Luke reports, 'even with these words, they scarcely restrained the crowds from offering sacrifice to them' (Acts 14.8–18). If we prefer the Pauline Paul to the Lucan Paul, there is still the same sense of outrage: 'What pagans sacrifice, they sacrifice to demons and not to God' (1 Cor. 10.20), and earlier (in v. 7), like Jesus in the Temptation story, he had used Scripture to urge the Corinthian Christians not to behave like the idolatrous Israelites of old who 'sat down to eat and drink, and rose up to play'. (The force of 'play' is neatly caught by the verb 'party' as used in modern youth culture.)

It is no surprise that this biblical consensus that sacrifice is appropriate only to God continued into the second Christian century and beyond, though of course it is coloured by the particular circumstances of later times. The church's agreement with Judaism about sacrifice inevitably brought it into collision with other faith systems where there were other gods and human leaders functioning as gods. The Roman ruler cult and the innumerable other cults of the Mediterranean world, like the cult of Isis and, slightly later, of Mithras, come to mind. Paul himself speaks of 'many gods and many lords' (1 Cor. 8.5), and so there were. But the refusal to sacrifice was not simply a private or domestic or corporate *religious* matter. It was also a matter of state, like being a Roman Catholic in Elizabethan England or Cromwellian Ireland. Since the welfare of the Roman state, whether agricultural, commercial or military, depended on the favour of the gods (*pax deorum*), refusal to pay them that respect which sacrifice in particular embodied meant discourtesy, disloyalty and treason, and, inevitably, catastrophe. This was true of Yahweh and it was no less true of Jupiter. Again a few illustrations: perhaps the best known is to be found in a letter from Pliny, man of letters and provincial governor, to the emperor Trajan at the beginning of the second century. He informs him about the mechanism he had devised to distinguish non-Christians from Christians and to allow the former to demonstrate their continuing loyalty to their god-emperor Trajan. He had had a bust of Trajan brought in and those who denied that they were Christians offered to it wine and incense, i.e. they sacrificed (*Ep.* 10.96). 'Worship' by itself was not sufficient; it was sacrifice that was the acid test and criterion of deity. Forty years later, *ca.* 155, one charge against Polycarp, the bishop of Smyrna, was that he was 'the destroyer of our gods'; he 'teaches many neither to offer sacrifices nor to "worship"', thereby destroying the state where sacrifice was a civic duty and its omission, *lèse-majesté* (*Mart. Pol.* 12). The anonymous Christian author we call *2 Clement* claims, 'We who are living do not sacrifice to the dead gods and do not "worship" them' (3.1). Later on the historian Eusebius speaks of Christian prisoners being offered their freedom if only they sacrificed (*Hist. Eccl.* 8.6.10). (Like other totalitarian regimes, on occasion Rome could manage without martyrs.)

In summary: Jewish monotheism was not monolatry (see MacDonald's essay again). Post-exilic Judaism no longer believed in the existence of many gods of whom Yahweh was the one who had to be 'worshipped' by Jews exclusively. Whether a Jew 'worshipped' Yahweh or not, there was only one God, who not only insisted on an exclusive loyalty to himself but condemned the 'worship' of all other so-called deities. With much else, this passed into the bloodstream of the infant Christianity of the New Testament and the adolescent Christianity of the second century and beyond. In addition, the most significant part of one's approach to God was sacrifice.

6.

Thus far we have hardly had more than a statement of facts. Now for controversy. Since (a) I have just shown that there is evidence in the religious environment of the New Testament that προσκύνησις of the deity is only complete when it includes or is followed by sacrifice to the deity, and (b) I shall now endeavour to show that sacrifice in any sense is never said in the New Testament and the first centuries to be offered to Christ, I shall propose that *from yet another angle* we cannot infer that the references to the 'worship' of Christ imply that he was thought to be divine.

Some of the evidence for (b) is negative but here the argument from silence is particularly telling. Not only is it the case that there is no evidence that in the earliest centuries sacrifice was offered to Christ when understood literally; there is another understanding of sacrifice mentioned in the New Testament, and it too is never said to be offered to Christ. The early church is completely at home with the so-called 'spiritualizing' of sacrifice that is already found in some strands of the Old Testament and even more clearly in Hellenistic and rabbinic Judaism, as well as beyond.[26] With the suspension or cessation of sacrifice in the Jerusalem Temple in 70 CE, Jewish teachers were quick to substitute prayer, Torah-study and philanthropy. Even before 70 Paul can speak of the dedication of the self that is a living sacrifice (Rom. 12.1, θυσία) and reasonable cult service (λατρεία). The faith of the Christians at Philippi is a sacrifice and cult service (λειτουργία), a sacrifice over which Paul's life blood is poured as a drink offering (Phil. 2.17); the Philippians' financial assistance is an incense offering (4.18). Hebrews speaks of the sacrifice to God of praise and philanthropy (13.15–16), and 1 Peter thinks of the church as a spiritual house, a holy priesthood which offers spiritual sacrifices (2.5). So, no less than the Old Testament and post-biblical Judaism, the New Testament knows of, indeed urges, that 'bloodless' sacrifices be offered.

In four of the five passages I have just summarized, the sacrifices are said explicitly to be acceptable to *God*; none speaks of its being acceptable to Christ.[27] So I deduce that, while Paul can frequently speak of himself as a 'slave of *Christ*', the *sacrifices* he himself offers and encourages others to offer are offered to *God*. The passages from Hebrews and 1 Peter clarify the proper role of Christ in these sacrificial contexts; in the former, Christian behaviour, in the latter, unspecified spiritual, ecclesial sacrifices, are 'acceptable to God *through Jesus Christ*' (πνευματικὰς θυσίας εὐπροσδέκτους [τῷ] θεῷ διὰ 'Ιησοῦ Χριστοῦ [1 Pet. 2.5; cf. Heb. 13.15–16]).[28]

---

26. Cf. J.W. Thompson, 'Hebrews 9 and Hellenistic Concepts of Sacrifice', *JBL* 98 (1979), pp. 567–78, esp. pp. 573–78, but now see the points well made by J. Klawans, 'Interpreting the Last Supper: Sacrifice, Spiritualization, and Anti-Sacrifice', *NTS* 48 (2002), pp. 1–17, esp. pp. 12–14.

27. In general, wherever the categories of 'the acceptable' or 'being pleasing' or 'well-pleasing' are used in the New Testament – there are nearly fifty examples – there is *no* passage where Christ is clearly intended. ἀπόδεκτος: 1 Tim. 2.3; 5.4; δεκτός: Lk. 4.19, 24; Acts 10.35; 2 Cor. 6.2a; Phil. 4.18; εὐπρόσδεκτος: Rom. 15.16, 31; 2 Cor. 6.2b (*si v.l.*); 8.12; 1 Pet. 2.5; the ἀρεσκ-word-group: Mt. 14.6; Mk 6.22; Acts 6.5; Rom. 8.8; 15.1–3; 1 Cor. 7.32–34; 10.33; Gal. 1.10 (twice); Eph. 6.6; Col. 1.10; 3.22; 1 Thess. 2.4, 15; 4.1; 2 Tim. 2.4; ἀρεστός: Jn 8.29; Acts 6.2; 12.3; 1 Jn 3.22; the εὐαρεστ- word-group: Rom. 12.1–2; 14.18; 2 Cor. 5.9; Eph. 5.10; Phil. 4.18; Col. 3.20; Tit. 2.9; Heb. 11.5–6; 12.28; 13.16, 21. Where divine entities are concerned, it is usually God who accepts or who is pleased or well-pleased. In some there is no specification (Rom. 12.2; 15.16; 2 Cor. 8.12). In some it is simply κύριος (Lk. 4.19; 1 Cor. 7.32*; 2 Cor. 5.9; Eph. 5.10*; Col. 1.10*; 3.20*); in the four I have asterised, κύριος has been replaced in the course of transcription by θεός, some scribes wanting to make it clear that in their view κύριος referred to God.

28. Cf. the other uses of διά + genitive in Hebrews and 1 Peter, disproportionate even when we

But antecedent to the sacrifices of Christians is the sacrifice that is primary in every sense in the New Testament, the sacrifice of Christ. Nowhere is the relationship between the sacrificial life to which Christians are called and the primary sacrifice of Christ more clearly reflected than in the invitation of the victim to receive and so share his broken body and his spilt blood. By literally absorbing these symbols of his sacrifice into their own beings, Christians identify themselves as victims ready for sacrifice to God. But the point is that it is here once again where the true role and significance of Jesus lie: he is the one *through* whom the believer comes to God and shares God's life, not God himself. One step is always missing – the Christian's sacrifice is offered through Christ, not to Christ. The introduction into early Christology of the high priesthood of Christ emphasizes a similar point. The high priest who offered the sacrifice of himself to God (Heb. 7.27; 9.26; 10.12), both body (10.5, 10) and blood (9.12, 14; 10.19, 29; 12.24; 13.12, 20) could not be its recipient. Mediation (8.6; 9.15; 12.24) assumes *three* parties.

That sacrifice is the ultimate criterion of deity was also recognized in the wider Roman world. In addition to the snippets already quoted from Pliny the Younger and Polycarp, *2 Clement* and Eusebius, there are the pleas of Roman judges presiding at the trials of Christians in the 160s: 'Come forward and sacrifice'; 'Sacrifice both of you to the gods and do not play the fool'; 'You must sacrifice: for so the emperor has commanded'; 'So that it go no further with you, will you sacrifice?'; and finally, 'Let those who will not sacrifice to the gods and yield to the command of the emperor be scourged and led away to be beheaded in accordance with the laws'.[29] But never simply 'You must "worship"'.

We return from the wider second-century Roman and Christian world to finish with the first-century Roman and Jewish world. Here we find what appears to be a similarity between the veneration of Jesus but unaccompanied by sacrifice to him in earliest Christianity on the one hand, and the veneration of Augustus but no sacrifices to him in contemporary Judaism on the other. There are too many differences for the similarity to be called a parallel, but it concludes with an instructive refinement that neatly takes us forward to the end of the story.

The relationship between Judaism and the Roman state has nearly always been represented as uniformly hostile, the benefits of *Pax Romana* not mitigating the Chosen People's hatred of the *goy* army of occupation taxing and polluting the Holy Land. But real life is rarely black and white, and the admittedly uncomfortable relationship has interesting light thrown on it precisely at this point – 'worship', sacrifice, and deity. For whatever reason there can be no doubt that some Jews thought very highly of the first two Roman emperors, especially Augustus, and of *Pax Romana*. The reasons may well be mixed, political prudence or genuine admiration or both. Philo, the Jewish monotheist, can still devote many paragraphs to what can only be called high-flown eulogy of a quasi-divine figure and his achievements

consider their ample use in the other New Testament letters, to express the agency of Christ; e.g. τοὺς προσερχομένους δι᾽ αὐτοῦ τῷ θεῷ (Heb. 7.25).

29. Quotations from E.C.E. Owen, *Some Authentic Acts of the Early Martyrs* (London: SPCK, 1933), pp. 42–44 and 51–52.

(*Leg. Gai.* 143–54 and, put on the lips of Agrippa I, 309–18). Augustus is the one 'who in all the virtues transcended human nature' (143), 'the first to bear the name of the August or Venerable' (143), 'this great ruler, this philosopher second to none' (318). Philo piles it on: 'If it was right to decree new and exceptional honours to anyone, he was the proper person to receive them' (149), and 'the whole habitable world voted him no less than celestial honours' (149). Philo then draws his fellow Jews into his flamboyant rhetoric: 'Did they neglect any mark of the reverence that was due to Caesar? No one in his senses would say that they did' (152). In fact, according to Josephus, the Jewish priesthood was ready to accept sacrifices, two lambs and a bull, paid for by Augustus, and offer them twice a day for ever *on his behalf* and that of the Roman people (περί [*War* 2.197]; ὑπέρ [*War* 2.409–410, 416]; πρό [*Apion* 2.76–77]; see Philo, *Leg. Gai.* 157; 232; 280; 291; and 317 for his version of these sacrifices; see below for *his* prepositions). It was precisely the successful attempt by the Jewish revolutionary hotheads to stop these sacrifices being made that led to the outbreak of the Roman-Jewish war in 66 CE (Josephus, *War* 2.409–17). As a preliminary to his panegyric of Augustus and his mention of the sacrifices, offered necessarily in the Jerusalem Temple, Philo also speaks of the 'tributes to the emperors' that he knows best, those found in the synagogues of Alexandria, 'the shields and gilded crowns and the slabs [στηλαί = 'votes of thanks'] and inscriptions' (*Leg. Gai.* 133; *Flacc.* 48–49).[30] There is the deepest veneration and there is also sacrifice *on his behalf*, but never sacrifice *to* him, as god or man.

In contrast, twenty-three years after Augustus' death, his great-grandson Gaius 'Caligula' came to the throne and soon made it known that he wished to be regarded as a god and treated as such. As far as Palestine was concerned, recognition of his deity was to be the erection of a colossal gilded statue in the Jerusalem Temple, with, of course, sacrifice to be offered to it, that is, to Gaius himself. Philo, formerly so insistent that Augustus should receive all the insignia of the profoundest respect, was now no less insistent that neither deification, statue nor sacrifice to Gaius could be countenanced. Philo had served on a delegation which the Alexandrian Jews sent to Rome, to attempt to dissuade the emperor, and later he wrote up his memories. These will suffice to give us a flavour of those tense times. He recalled Gaius' very first words to the delegation: 'Are you the god-haters who do not believe me to be a god, a god acknowledged among all the other nations but not to be named by you?' The delegates insisted that the Jews had shown their loyalty by sacrificing *on his behalf* on at least three occasions, at his accession, on his recovery from a serious illness and on the eve of a military campaign in Germany.

Now Philo introduces the refinement I mentioned above, a refinement even on sacrifice *on behalf of*. He shows Gaius well aware of the difference between sac-

---

30. No doubt these dedications contributed to what some rabbis called 'the glory of Israel', perhaps the most magnificent of the Alexandrian synagogues; cf. *b. Suk.* 51b (Soncino [Slotki], pp. 244–45; Neusner [1984ᵇ], pp. 254–55); *Tos. Suk.* 4.6 (Neusner [1981], p. 224); Philo, *Leg. Gai.* 134; but cf. Krauss, pp. 163–64 and 261–63. See n. 12 above for the bibliographical details about all these Judaica.

rifice *on behalf of*, something that his great-grandfather had been ready to tolerate from the Jews and he was not, and sacrifice *to*. 'All right', Gaius agrees, 'that is true, you have sacrificed, but *to another*, even if it was *for* me; what good is it then? For you have not sacrificed *to me*' (*Leg. Gai.* 353–56; esp. 357 [ἑτέρῳ...ὑπὲρ ἐμοῦ...οὐ γὰρ ἐμοί] and 232 [ὑπέρ]; cf. Josephus' prepositions above). For the Judaism for which Philo is spokesman, and here he is probably speaking for all observant Jews, there is a 'fundamental difference' (S.R.F. Price) between sacrifice *for/on behalf of* (ὑπέρ) and sacrifice *to* (dative).[31] Only the latter points unmistakably to deity.

The material assembled in sections 5–6 and especially Philo's or Gaius' refinement impinge also on early Christianity and its Christologies. If *sacrifice to* is the most focused of the traditional criteria applied in the determination of divinity, and if divinity is claimed for Christ in early Christianity where sacrifice is *not* said to be offered *to* him, then there must be another criterion, and I have argued that it cannot be 'worship'.[32] The 'worship' of Jesus neither requires the conclusion, *ergo* divine, nor, *pace* Liddon, presumes his divinity. If divine Jesus be, we look elsewhere.[33]

31.　Cassius Dio has a very similar report. After claiming that formerly Gaius had forbidden sacrifices to be offered to his Tyche, later on, Dio continues, he gave orders that καὶ ναοὺς ἑαυτῷ καὶ θυσίας ὡς καὶ θεῷ γίγνεσθαι (*Hist.* 59.4.4). Cf. Price's treatment of this 'fundamental difference' in 'Between Man and God: Sacrifice in the Roman Imperial Cult', *JRS* 70 (1980), pp. 28–43 = *Rituals and Power: The Roman Imperial Cult in Asia Minor* (Cambridge: Cambridge University Press, 1984), pp. 207–233, esp. pp. 30–33 = pp. 209–215 ('sacrifice for') and pp. 34–36 = pp. 216–20 ('sacrifice to'). Price's book throws a great deal of light on several issues raised in this volume. There is a fairly close parallel to Dio in the criticism of Nicene Christians attributed to the Arian historian Philostorgius; describing the attention paid to Constantine's image he says that they θυσίαις τε ἱλάσκεσθαι καὶ λυχνοκαίαις καὶ θυμιάμασι τιμᾶν, καὶ εὐχὰς προσάγειν ὡς θεῷ καὶ ἀποτροπαίους ἱκετηρίας τῶν δεινῶν ἐπιτελεῖν (2.17; Bidez, p. 28).

32.　Without developing it, J.F. McGrath also sees the importance of the distinction between προσκύνησις and sacrifice; cf. *John's Apologetic Christology* (SNTSMS, 111; Cambridge: University Press, 2001), pp. 24–25 and nn. 70–71; p. 76 and n. 17. Cf. §D in Stuckenbruck's essay in this volume. I hope that my suggestion about the greater importance of *sacrifice to* offers a new approach to the current debate about the significance of the *worship* of Christ, which, in the absence of new primary data, seems to be in something of an impasse. In *One God, One Lord: Early Christian Devotion and Ancient Jewish Monotheism* (Edinburgh: T. & T. Clark, 1998) L.W. Hurtado provides an excellent introduction and contribution to the debate, but does not a full-blown 'binitarianism' stumble at the fence of *sacrifice only to God*?

33.　Was the acknowledgement of the special status of Jesus inspired by Jesus' reversal of the traditional understanding of privilege and sacrifice, perceived no more in *others sacrificing to you* but in *your sacrificing yourself to God for others*? Cf. Mk 10.35–45>Jn 15.13; Phil. 2.9 (διό [n.4]); διά (n. 28).

Part III
ASKING QUESTIONS

THE ORIGIN OF 'MONOTHEISM'*

Nathan MacDonald, University of St Andrews

> Among the questions relating to Israel's religious odyssey, that of the origin of
> monotheism is intellectually and theologically primary.[1]
>
> B. Halpern

To claim that any particular task in the study of the Hebrew Bible is 'intellectually and theologically primary' is bold, though if the flood of books and articles
on the subject is anything to go by Baruch Halpern's judgement is less audacious
than it first appears.[2] Whilst this well-trodden path is important and engaging, in
this essay I wish to venture down a quiet byway and trace the origin of the word
'monotheism'. For most this will be a journey into largely unfamiliar territory, as
it is for the writer (the footnotes indicating more experienced guides upon whom
he has relied), and it may justifiably be asked why we have abandoned 'the ancient
paths where the good way lies'. Although a complete answer will only be possible at the end of our journey, a preliminary response can be made by noting a
characteristic move in the study of Israelite monotheism. The scholar typically
defines 'monotheism' correctly, before approaching the biblical texts (arranged
chronologically) in order to ascertain the exact moment when 'monotheism' arose.[3]
My contention is that such considerations of the definition of 'monotheism' are
not thoroughgoing enough, for the conceptualization of 'monotheism' frequently
entails a particular conception of religious belief that may affect the task of historical description.

Our journey will begin with the coinage of the word 'monotheism' by the Cambridge Platonist, Henry More.[4] This first use of 'monotheism' will be placed in its

---

* This is a revised version of part of the first chapter of my forthcoming monograph, *Deuteronomy and the Meaning of 'Monotheism'* (FAT II.1; Tübingen: J.C.B. Mohr [Paul Siebeck], 2003).

1. The epigraph is from B. Halpern, ' "Brisker Pipes than Poetry": The Development of
Israelite Monotheism', in J. Neusner, B.A. Levine and E.S. Frerichs (eds.), *Judaic Perspectives on
Ancient Israel* (Philadelphia: Fortress Press, 1987), p. 77.

2. For a recent survey of this debate, see R.K. Gnuse, *No Other Gods: Emergent Monotheism
in Israel* (JSOTSup, 241; Sheffield: Sheffield Academic Press, 1997), pp. 62–128.

3. For examples see H. Rechenmacher, *"Außer mir gibt es keinen Gott!": Eine sprach- und
literaturwissenschaftliche Studie zur Ausschließlichkeitsformel* (ATSAT, 49; St Ottilien: EOS
Verlag, 1997) and J. Pakkala, *Intolerant Monolatry in the Deuteronomistic History* (SESJ, 76;
Göttingen: Vandenhoeck & Ruprecht, 1999).

4. See 'Monotheism' in *OED*. The credit for the first use of 'monotheist' is incorrectly attributed to More in 1680. In fact, it had already been used before that by More's fellow Platonist,
Ralph Cudworth in his *The True Intellectual System of the Universe* (London, 1678), p. 233.

literary context. More's work will then be examined in the wider context of the thinking of the Cambridge Platonists and their controversies. Finally, some observations will be made on recent discussions of monotheism. At this point I shall also examine the origins of the terms 'henotheism' and 'monolatry'.

1.

> To make the *World* God, is to make no God at all; and therefore this kind of *Monotheisme* of the Heathen is as rank *Atheism* as their *Polytheisme* was proved to be before.
>
> Henry More

The first use of 'monotheism' is found in Henry More's systematic presentation of the Christian gospel, *The Grand Mystery of Godliness*, published in 1660.[5] In his introduction More presents the *Grand Mystery* as a culmination of his scholarly work.[6] It had been anticipated by two of More's earlier works, *An Antidote Against Atheisme* (1653), in which he had proved the existence of God, and *The Immortality of the Soul* (1659), in which he had shown the immortality of the soul.[7] Building upon these foundations, More now sought to show in the *Grand Mystery*

> that there is no Article of the Christian Faith, nor any particular miracle happening to or done by our Saviour or to be done by him, mentioned in the Gospels or any where else in the New Testament, but I have given so solid and rational account thereof, that I am confident that no man that has the use of his Understanding shall be able ever to pretend any Reason against Christian Religion.[8]

More's work is arranged in four parts, in which he demonstrated the obscurity, the intelligibility, the truthfulness and the usefulness of the mystery of the gospel. In his section on the mystery's intelligibility, More begins by summarizing the propositions that he had already shown to be reasonable in *An Antidote Against Atheisme* and *The Immortality of the Soul*. First among these is the existence of God, whom More had shown to be an 'omnipotent, omniscient and infinitely Benign Spirit'.[9] Other matters that can be perceived by the reasonable person are the existence of good and evil spirits, that good will eventually triumph and that the time of man will come to an end, in which men will be delivered and drawn up into the 'divine life'. The 'divine life', the life regulated by faith, is not, however, the present reality. This is a consequence of the Fall. When Adam and Eve transgressed humankind fell into the world of instincts and sensuality, the 'animal life'.[10] This

---

5. H. More, *An Explanation of the Grand Mystery of Godliness* (London, 1660).

6. This most prolific of the Platonists was, in fact, to write far more despite his claim to be 'not onely free from, but incapable of the common disease of this Scripturient Age' (More, *Mystery*, p. 12).

7. More, *Mystery*, p. viii.

8. More, *Mystery*, p. ix.

9. More, *Mystery*, p. 34.

10. P. Harrison argues that the 'animal life' is a concept in the Cambridge Platonists often ignored (*'Religion' and the Religions in the English Enlightenment* [Cambridge: Cambridge University Press, 1990], p. 44).

obsession with the material characteristically expressed itself in idolatry. Prior to the coming of Christ this was the lot of humanity.

The religions of the time before Christ, and outside of the Christian world, were divided by More into five categories. First, there are those who are polytheists. Since the worship of many gods is incompatible with his definition of God as the supreme Spirit, More regarded them as equivalent to atheists. Secondly, there are those who claim to worship the sun alone. As the worship of something material it betrayed its affinities with the 'animal life'. Further Descartes had convinced More that there was more than one Sun in the universe. Thirdly, there are 'pantheists'. It is at this point that the first known use of 'monotheism' is found. More argues that

> to make the *World* God, is to make no God at all; and therefore this kind of *Monotheisme* of the Heathen is as rank *Atheism* as their *Polytheisme* was proved to be before.[11]

The attribution of deity to the world clearly collided with More's definition of God as a Spirit. Fourthly, there are those who worship an eternal, spiritual being. They worship the one God through various names and attributes, and by means of idols. In *The Divine Dialogues* More makes Cuphophron argue similarly:

> This cannot be deny'd, Euistor, but that the barbarous Nations did religious Worship to innumerable Objects of the kind, but not as to the supreme Power of all, (which was the primary or ultimate Object of all their Adoration) but rather as to Images and Symbols of that Ultimate Object.[12]

This refined form of paganism with its worship of a spiritual God is much more acceptable, in More's eyes, than polytheism, sun worship or 'pantheism'. However, whatever its qualities it was not without its failings. It characterized very few pagans, was tainted with idolatry and was probably derived from Judaism. Finally, there are the Jews, whose sensual religious festivals show that they too were obsessed with the 'animal life'. Their religion had no idolatry, however, and was given by God. It also had the types of Christ which were understood in a spiritual sense by Moses, although most of Israel did not understand their meaning.

'Monotheism' and the typology of religions

More's coinage of 'monotheism' occurs in an ambitious attempt to create a universal typology of religions. As Peter Harrison has shown in his *'Religion' and the Religions in the English Enlightenment* the first steps towards a science of religion occurred in the seventeenth century, rather than in the nineteenth century. This first attempt at a science of religion was flawed in a number of respects. First, the experience of other religions was limited. The limits of More's scholarship are clearly demonstrated by his engagement with only ancient Greek and Egyptian religion as mediated through classical writers. Despite this More is aware that there were many other religions in the world, which were in the process of being discovered by European explorers. Thus, he assures his reader that he could have selected for

---

11. More, *Mystery*, p. 62.
12. H. More, *Divine Dialogues*, II (London, 1668), p. 401.

his typology examples of religion from recently accumulated evidence about religions in 'Arabia, Persia, India, China, Tartary, Germany, Scythia, Guinea, Aethiopia …Virginia, Mexico, Peru and Brasilia'.[13] More's knowledge of these religions, however, was probably not substantial. With his readers, More, who was reluctant to leave even Cambridge, shared a lack of direct experience of these religions.

Secondly, 'while much comparison of "religions" took place in the seventeenth and eighteenth centuries, most of it was motivated not by any deep interest in the religious faith of other peoples, but by the desire to score points from theological adversaries'.[14] The use of other religions as a polemical foil is evident in More's typology. His classification of non-Christian religion can be reduced to just two categories. On the one hand, there are two deficient forms of 'monotheism', Judaism and enlightened paganism, and, on the other, there are atheists. The qualified acceptance of the deficient forms of 'monotheism' provided More with a theodicy against those who regarded the divine providence, which had restricted knowledge of the Christian faith to only a small part of the human race, as arbitrary and unjust. More's argument that both polytheism and pantheism are variant forms of atheism is both interesting and unexpected. Two reasons explain this rather curious movement. First, More had already shown the fallacy of atheism in his *Antidote Against Atheisme*. Reducing polytheism and pantheism to atheism was an effective strategy for speedy dismissal. Secondly, as More's curt disposal shows, his opponent was neither polytheism nor pantheism.

Amongst More and his contemporaries 'there was a widespread conviction that the atheists were at the gates',[15] and that this was the greatest danger facing the Church.[16] In England, More and the other Cambridge Platonists were the chief apologists for the Christian religion. What the Platonists and their contemporaries meant by 'atheism' was the doctrine of materialism,[17] whose chief exponent was Thomas Hobbes.[18] More, in contrast, believed in the existence of God, angels, demons, ghosts, other spiritual beings and the souls of human beings and animals; where the 'atheists' saw a purely material universe More saw a universe overflowing with souls.[19]

---

13. More, *Mystery*, p. 73.

14. Harrison, *'Religion'*, p. 146.

15. M.J. Buckley, *At the Origins of Modern Atheism* (New Haven: Yale University Press, 1987), p. 68.

16. C.A. Patrides, ' "The High and Aiery Hills of Platonisme": An Introduction to the Cambridge Platonists', in C.A. Patrides (ed.), *The Cambridge Platonists* (Stratford-upon-Avon Library, 5; London: Edward Arnold, 1969), p. 25.

17. Thus, More's friend and fellow Platonist, Ralph Cudworth, wrote that those, 'who derive all things from *Senseless Matter*, as the First Original, and deny that there is any *Conscious Understanding* Being *Self-existent* or *Unmade*, are those that are properly called *Atheists*' (Cudworth, *True Intellectual System*, p. 195).

18. For the criticism of Hobbes by the Platonists, see S.I. Mintz, *The Hunting of Leviathan: Seventeenth-Century Reaction to the Materialism and Moral Philosophy of Thomas Hobbes* (Cambridge: Cambridge University Press, 1962).

19. Perhaps unsurprisingly More was greatly interested in the supernatural. Demonstrating the existence of evil spirits, angels or ghosts would, in More's eyes, have provided evidence for a

In the *Grand Mystery* More clearly spelt out the dangers of materialism:

> the first and most fundamental mistake of *lapsed Mankind* [is] that they make
> *Body* or *Matter* the only true *Jehovah*, the only true Essence and first substance of
> whom all things are, and acknowledge no God but this visible or Sensible world.[20]

It is the primeval error that can be traced back to Eve and the birth of Cain. Reading Gen. 4.1 as 'I have a man, Jehovah', More argued that Eve misunderstood the promise in Gen. 3.15 and mistakenly identified her son with God.[21]

That pantheism and polytheism were mere foils for an attack on materialistic 'atheism' is clearly significant for understanding the meaning of More's 'monotheism'. Both semantically and in the immediate context of More's work it would be natural to assume that the antonym of 'monotheism' was polytheism. But, polytheism, in the sense of a belief in the existence of many gods, was not More's opponent. Nor, indeed, could it be, for neither More nor his readers would have met a polytheist, and there was not the distinct possibility that it would be considered a credible belief. The true antonym of 'monotheism' is 'atheism'. More's opponent was not the Greek religion the early Christian apologists faced, even less the beliefs and practices of Israel's neighbours that were perceived as a threat in the Old Testament.

'Monotheism', reason and innate ideas

Not all atheists were of the same ilk, in More's opinion. Some were ignorant, others morally corrupt, and the remainder had been led astray by speculative reason. It is for this latter group that More wrote, reasoning that 'not to be at least a Speculative Christian is a sign of the want of common Wit and Reason'.[22] More's approach to winning them back to the Christian faith was not by appeals to Scripture, but by reason, the cause of their apostasy. The full titles of his two earlier works, *An Antidote Against Atheisme, or, An Appeal to the Naturall Faculties of the Minde of Man, whether there be not a God* and *The Immortality of the Soul, So farre forth as it is demonstrable from the Knowledge of Nature and the Light of Reason* show that More would have fully agreed with the opinion of his one-time correspondent Descartes. 'I have always considered that the two questions respecting God and the Soul were the chief of those that ought to be demonstrated by philosophical rather than theological arguments'.[23]

---

spiritual world, and thus God. More became increasingly interested in these matters in his latter years, see R. Hall, *Henry More: Magic, Religion and Experiment* (Oxford: Basil Blackwell, 1990), pp. 128–45.

20. More, *Mystery*, p. 57.

21. In his reading of Gen. 4.1 More understands the problematic אֶת as a direct object marker, rather than as a preposition (cf. 'I have gotten a man from the Lord' [AV]). For a discussion of אֶת in Gen. 4.1, see C. Westermann, *Genesis 1–11: A Commentary* (trans. J.J. Scullion; London: SPCK, 1984), pp. 290–92.

22. More, *Mystery*, p. 43.

23. Descartes cited in Buckley, *Origins*, p. 199. Buckley's work shows the fatefulness of this apologetic move by the thinkers of the early Enlightenment.

Reason, though, could show far more than the existence of God and the immortality of the soul. More believed that reason could prove the existence of the spiritual world, that there was a battle between two kingdoms of good and evil, and the certainty of final judgement. Ralph Cudworth believed that even the Trinity was accessible to reason. The burden of his prolix *The True Intellectual System of the Universe* was 'to demonstrate that all men tend naturally to believe in one god and can, through the exercise of reason, attain even to those truths which have been argued to be the sole preserve of revealed religion'.[24]

This approach to the problem of 'atheism' was a natural consequence of the Platonist's distinctive epistomology.[25] The Platonists believed in the unity of the means of knowledge, but in this unity the role of individual reason was central. Thus More described reason as

> a Power of Facultie of the Soul, whereby either from her Innate Ideas or Common Notions, or else from the assurance of her own Sense, or upon the Relation or Tradition of another, she unravels a further clew of Knowledge, enlarging her sphere of Intellectual light, by laying open to her self the close connexion and cohesion of the Conceptions she has of things, whereby inferring one thing from another she is able to deduce multifarious Conclusions as well for the pleasure of Speculation as the necessity of Practice.[26]

This reason was not just a human quality, but a spiritual one too.[27]

This emphasis on reason distinguished the Platonists from orthodox Reformed theology, in which nature and revelation were seen as fundamentally opposed because of the noetic effects of the Fall. The Platonists insisted that faith and reason belonged together.[28] 'The legitimate seat of authority in religion is the individual conscience, governed by reason and illuminated by a revelation which could not be inconsistent with reason itself.'[29] The emphasis on reason in the thought of the Platonists naturally raises the question of the place of Scripture. Although there are affinities with the Deist thinkers of the following generation the Platonists never took the step of rejecting the need for revelation. For whilst reason was 'a light flowing from the fountain and father of lights' since man's Fall 'the inward virtue and vigour of reason is much abated'.[30] For More, Christ's revelation helped wean men from their obsession with the material and sensual.

24. Harrison, *'Religion'*, p. 32.
25. The relationship between faith and reason was one of the most fundamental theological questions of the seventeenth century. The Platonists' approach to the issue was determinative for their epistemology, see G.R. Cragg, 'Introduction', in G.R. Cragg (ed.), *The Cambridge Platonists* (Library of Protestant Thought; New York: Oxford University Press, 1968), pp. 3–31 and Patrides, 'Hills'.
26. More, *Mystery*, p. 51.
27. See Mintz, *Leviathan*, pp. 82–83.
28. Benjamin Whichcote, the most senior Platonist, wrote, 'I oppose not rational to spiritual, for spiritual is most rational' (Patrides, 'Hills', p. 10).
29. G.R. Cragg, *From Puritanism to the Age of Reason: A Study of Changes in Religious Thought within the Church of England 1660 to 1700* (Cambridge: Cambridge University Press, 1950), p. 41.
30. Smith cited in Cragg, *Puritanism*, p. 45.

The senses too were subject to reason, and thus the Platonists opposed the grow-ing influence of empiricism.[31] In particular they opposed the empiricists' idea that the mind was a *tabula rasa*. Instead, they held to a belief in 'innate ideas'. This was closely related to the Platonic Theory of Recollection.[32] Ideas were not planted in the mind by external objects; instead latent ideas were merely stimulated. The truth of a notion could be proved, therefore, by an appeal to common assent. A substan-tial part of Cudworth's *True Intellectual System* attempted to show that the belief that there existed only one God was universally attested.

'Monotheism' as the primeval religion

More, like most of his contemporaries, understood the early history of religion as a story of degeneration. The primeval religion was pure and spiritual; the Fall brought an obsession with the animal life. Polytheism and idolatry were the result of this degeneration. The belief that monotheism was the primitive religion was a view that was unchallenged for most of the seventeenth century. The dominance of this view was due to two assumptions. First, monotheism was natural and, sec-ondly, truth is older than error. The history of religion is a history of degeneration from the pure religion of the *illud tempus*.

2.

> That which enravishes me most is, that we both setting out from the same *Lists*,
> though taking several ways, the one travelling in the lower Rode of *Democritisme*,
> amidst the thick dust of Atoms and flying particles of *Matter*, the other tracing it
> over the high and aiery Hills of *Platonisme*, in that more thin and subtil Region
> of *Immateriality*, meet together notwithstanding at last (and certainly not without
> a Providence) at the same *Goale*, namely at the Entrance of the holy Bible. [33]
>
> Henry More

At the beginning of this essay I proposed taking a different approach to the question of monotheism than the 'lower Rode' of Israelite religion. It might be wondered whether our journey over the 'high and aiery Hills of *Platonisme*' has providentially landed us 'at the Entrance of the holy Bible'. Some might fear that our journey through this unfamiliar territory has been, alas, in regions too 'thin and subtil'. Our exertions may, however, not be without benefit for in returning to the issues that are usually associated with the discipline of biblical study we can ask ourselves whether we know what we mean by the term 'monotheism', which is now somewhat less familiar.

---

31. For the Platonists and empiricism, see E. Cassirer, *The Platonic Renaissance in England* (trans. J.P. Pettegrove; London: Nelson, 1953), pp. 42–65.

32. See D. Scott, 'Reason, Recollection and the Cambridge Platonists', in A. Baldwin and S. Hutton (eds.), *Platonism and the English Imagination* (Cambridge: Cambridge University Press, 1994), pp. 139–50.

33. More cited in Patrides, 'Hills', pp. 29–30.

'Monotheism' as an organizing principle and the intellectualizing of religion
More's 'monotheism' is perhaps at its most familiar when he uses it as an organizing principle in the study of religion. With the binary opposites 'monotheism'
– 'atheism' More was able to categorize the complex world of religions. With this
understanding of 'monotheism' all religions, including Christianity, can be measured. In More's *Grand Mystery* pantheism makes a false claim to be a true monotheism. Similarly in *Apocalypsis Apocalypseos* the Saracens claim to hold to
'monotheisme'. This, though is 'an ignorant pretence of *Monotheisme*, as if the
Christian Religion was inconsistent with the worship of one God, whereas the
more distinct knowledge of that one God does not make us less *Monotheists* than
they'.[34] More's trinitarian Christianity also comes under the brilliant spotlight of
this organizing principle. In *Apocalypsis Apocalypseos* polytheists charge Christian with the worship of more gods than one.[35] More allowed, however, that 'there
is a *latitude of sense* in the word *One* or *Unity* allowable in the Creed'.[36]

Powerful though this organizing principle undoubtedly was, it placed the accent
on one particular aspect of religion. This was not something unique to More, but
reflects a general trend characterizing the sixteenth and seventeenth centuries. As
Peter Harrison has shown, all religions, including Christianity, began to be defined
by their propositional expressions:

> the truth or falsity of a religion had become a function of the truth or falsity of the
> propositions which constituted it. True religion was not genuine piety, but a body
> of certain knowledge.[37]

This change is reflected in the contemporaneous explosion of '-isms',[38] of which
More's 'monotheism' is a part. Nicholas Lash draws attention to the significance of
this linguistic change. 'It is, I think, almost impossible to overestimate the importance of the massive shift in language and imagination that took place, in Europe,
in the seventeenth century; a shift for which de Certeau has two striking phrases:
the "dethroning of the verb" and the "spatialisation of knowledge".'[39]

The idea that what is truly descriptive of a religion is its propositional statements
has been aptly described by Lash as 'a simple strategy for a complex world'.[40]
Lash's point, of course, is that simple strategies carry with them a danger of distortion. That this is the case with 'polytheism' has been shown by Gregor Ahn.

---

34. H. More, *Apocalypsis Apocalypseos: Or the Revelation of St John the Divine Unveiled*
(London, 1680), pp. 83–84. R. Hülsewiesche mistakenly suggests this quotation is aimed at Judaism
in 'Monotheismus', in J. Ritter and K. Gründer (eds.) (Darmstadt: Wissenschaftliche Buchgesellschaft,
1971– present), VI, p. 124.

35. More, *Apocalypsis*, p. 89.

36. More, *Mystery*, p. 456.

37. Harrison, *'Religion'*, p. 26.

38. 'Ism' in *OED*. Perhaps the most striking example of this trend was the triumph of 'polytheism', reinvented in 1580, over 'idolatry' as the most appropriate antithesis of true religion. See
F. Schmidt, 'Naissance des Polythéismes (1624–1757)', *ASSR* 59 (1985), pp. 77–90.

39. N. Lash, 'Creation, Courtesy and Contemplation', in N. Lash, *The Beginning and the End
of 'Religion'* (Cambridge: Cambridge University Press, 1996), p. 168.

40. N. Lash, 'The Beginning and the End of "Religion"?', in Lash, *Beginning*, p. 10.

'Polytheism', he argues, reflects a classification of religions based on a monotheistic perspective. Further, the language of 'polytheism' – 'monotheism' prioritizes one particular question, that of the number of deities. This matter is rarely, if ever, a concern of polytheistic religions.[41] But it is not only polytheistic religions that are distorted. It may justifiably be claimed that the so-called 'monotheistic' religions of Judaism and Christianity are distorted in identical ways. The first use of 'monotheism' as a classification to which Christianity belongs occurs in a conflict with the philosophical doctrine of 'materialism'. The terms upon which that battle was to be fought was agreed by the Cambridge Platonists and Descartes to be philosophical, rather than theological, and the term 'monotheism' reflects that agreement. In other words, 'monotheism' reflects a classification of religions based, not on an inner-Christian perspective, but on one derived from the early Enlightenment.[42] Secondly, assent to the existence of one God does not exhaustively describe Christianity, or adequately articulate its differences from other religions. In early Christianity belief in one God is expressed in the confessional context of the creed, which included, of course, many other beliefs.

The distorting effect of an exclusively propositional focus is observable in More's work. Judaism is criticized for its sensuous religious festivals indicative of an obsession with the 'animal life'. Given the tensions in the thinking of the Cambridge Platonists upon the spiritual and the material, the 'divine life' and the 'animal life', it is not surprising that a certain ambivalence towards the outward ceremonies of Christianity developed. More, for example, asserted that 'the onely safe Entrance into Divine Knowledge is true Holiness'.[43] Like other Platonists, in the place of ceremony he emphasized ethics.[44] It is not difficult to see that, although not guilty of it themselves, the Cambridge Platonists sowed the seeds of the anti-clericalism and anti-ceremonialism that were to characterize deist thinkers of the late seventeenth and early eighteenth century.

The notion that 'monotheism' is expressed in ethics alone, and not also in religious observances, has, as is well known, been a familiar theme in biblical scholarship. The great Dutch Old Testament scholar of the nineteenth century, Abraham Kuenen, famously described the religion of the prophets as 'ethical monotheism'.[45]

41. G. Ahn, ' "Monotheismus" – "Polytheismus": Grenzen und Möglichkeiten einer Klassifikation von Gottesvorstellungen', in M. Dietrich and O. Loretz (eds.), *Mesopotamia–Ugaritica–Biblica: Festschrift für K. Bergerhof* (AOAT, 232; Neukirchen–Vluyn: Neukirchener Verlag, 1993), pp. 1–24.

42. D. Tracy notes that ' "monotheism" is an Enlightenment invention (H. More, D. Hume) that bears all the marks of Enlightenment rationalism' ('The Paradox of the Many Faces of God in Monotheism', in H. Haring and J.B. Metz [eds.], *The Many Faces of the Divine* [Concilium 1995/2; London: SCM Press, 1995], p. 30).

43. More, cited in Patrides, 'Hills', p. 14.

44. Whichcote is more astonishing with his '*the State of Religion* lyes, in short, in this; *A good Mind, and a good Life*. All else is *about* Religion' (cited in Patrides, 'Hills', p. 14). Concerning the Platonists' emphasis on ethics rather than ceremony, see Cragg, 'Introduction', pp. 19–20; A. Lichtenstein, *Henry More: The Rational Theology of a Cambridge Platonist* (Cambridge, MA: Harvard University Press, 1962), p. 23; Patrides, 'Hills', pp. 13–15.

45. See A. Kuenen, *The Prophets and Prophecy in Israel* (trans. A. Milroy; London: Longmans, Green & Co., 1877).

Despite justified criticism of a ritual – ethical dichotomy in the study of the Old Testament simple equations of monotheism with ethics are still to be found. Thus, in his recent work on the emergence of monotheism Robert Gnuse has argued that monotheism entails one divine will and one ethical imperative. This sense of address brings notions of guilt and forgiveness, rather than impurity and purification.[46] Elsewhere he argues that 'concomitant with the belief in one universal deity is a stress on human rights and dignity in some egalitarian world view'.[47]

'Monotheism' – the primeval or evolutionary climax

When he touches upon the origins of 'monotheism' More is close to the concerns expressed in the modern discussions about 'monotheism'. More's own account of the progress of monotheism differs significantly from modern accounts. Although theories of *Urmonotheism* have been articulated, the scholarly understanding of 'monotheism' since the nineteenth century has been predominantly evolutionary. This is, perhaps, seen most clearly in the coercion of the terms 'monolatry' and 'henotheism' to intermediate stages in a developmental scheme, despite their origins as attempts to describe a primeval monotheism.

The first use of 'monolatry' is probably found in Schleiermacher's *The Christian Faith*. Mankind develops from fetishism into polytheism, and finally monotheism:

> As such subordinate stages, we set down, generally speaking, Idol-worship proper (also called Fetishism) and Polytheism; of which again, the first stands far lower than the second. The idol worshipper may quite well have only one idol, but this does not give such Monolatry any resemblance to Monotheism, for it ascribes to the idol an influence over a limited field of objects of processes, beyond which its own interest and sympathy do not extend.[48]

In Schleiermacher's scheme of fetishism – polytheism – monotheism, 'monolatry' has no independent place; it is merely a variant form of fetishism. In modern discussions 'monolatry' is used of an intermediate stage between polytheism and monotheism, and is used of devotion to one god without denying the existence of others.[49]

'Henotheism' similarly had a different meaning from the one with which it has become associated. The origin of the word is attributed to Max Müller in 1860 in a review of Renan's *Histoires Générale et Système Comparé des Langues Sémitiques*. Müller understands monotheism to be the belief that there is one God alone. Hume, Schleiermacher and others had shown that as such it is a negation of the belief in many gods and must presuppose polytheism. Müller argued that polytheism must

---

46. Gnuse, *Gods*, pp. 248–52. It is unclear to me how Gnuse would make sense of P, which is usually understood as 'monotheistic'.

47. R.K. Gnuse, 'The Emergence of Monotheism in Ancient Israel: A Survey of Recent Scholarship', *Rel* 29 (1999), p. 315.

48. F.D.E. Schleiermacher, *The Christian Faith* (trans. H.R. Mackintosh and J.S. Stewart; Edinburgh: T. & T. Clark, 1928), p. 34.

49. D.L. Petersen, 'Israel and Monotheism: The Unfinished Agenda', in G.M. Tucker, D.L. Petersen and R.R. Wilson (eds.), *Canon, Theology, and Old Testament Interpretation: Essays in Honor of Brevard S. Childs* (Philadelphia: Fortress Press, 1988), p. 98.

presuppose the idea of a god. The plural presupposes the singular. For this primeval sense that there is a superior being, a 'god', Müller coined the word 'henotheism':

> If therefore, an expression had been given to that primitive intuition of the Deity which is the mainspring of all later religion, it would have been – 'There is a god', but not yet 'There is but One God'. The latter form of faith, the belief in One God, is properly called monotheism, whereas the term of henotheism would best express the faith in a single god.[50]

In Müller's judgement 'henotheism' is a natural, unreflective, but legitimate expression of monotheism. However, the term is now used of an intermediate stage between 'polytheism' and 'monotheism', often as a synonym of 'monolatry'.[51]

The coercion of 'henotheism' and 'monolatry' into evolutionary schemes for describing the development of monotheism creates a semantic field with a notable bias towards diachronic analysis. This has been particularly true of the study of monotheism in the Old Testament.[52] James Barr's recent remarks on monotheism are revealing. He suggests that

> for some sorts of enquiry, such as the Hebrew idea of humanity or of body and soul, the question of historical difference might prove to be unimportant... while for others, such as the idea of monotheism, a historical framework with dating of different sources would very likely prove necessary.[53]

What is striking is Barr's choice of monotheism as the example that makes no further argument necessary for his readers.

It seems unlikely that *Urmonotheism* will enjoy a revival in scholarly assessment, nevertheless More's understanding of monotheism features a dynamic that has been frequently lost when a brittle evolutionary schema has been combined with an intellectualized notion of monotheism. More's understanding of monotheism allows a flux in the history of monotheism on the level of the individual and the human race as a whole. Monotheism may be relinquished and regained. In

---

50. F.M. Müller, 'Semitic Monotheism', in F.M. Müller, *Selected Essays on Language, Mythology and Religion* (London: Longmans, Green & Co., 1881), p. 415. Müller's essay was originally published in 1860. Müller's argument marks an interesting return to the idea of 'primitive monotheism'. His suggestion that 'henotheism...forms the birthright of every human being' (Müller, 'Monotheism', p. 412) is somewhat reminiscent of the Platonists.

51. Petersen, 'Israel', pp. 97–98; Gnuse, *Gods*, p. 132. Attempts have been made to differentiate the terms. T.J. Meek understood monolatry as devotion to one god in which other deities were excluded, and henotheism as devotion to one god in which other deities were absorbed (*Hebrew Origins* [New York: Harper, 2nd edn, 1950], p. 206). M. Rose sees 'henotheism' as a temporary devotion to one god, 'monolatry' as the close relationship between a community and a god. He notes, however, that some regard 'monolatry' as an enduring devotion to one god (*Der Ausschließlichkeitsanspruch Jahwes: Deuteronomische Schultheologie und die Volksfrömmigkeit in der späten Königszeit* [BWANT, 106; Stuttgart: W. Kohlhammer, 1975], pp. 9–11). A definition of 'henotheism' as a temporary devotion to one god finds a basis in Müller who saw henotheism as a religious stage in which temporarily one god was adored and the plurality of gods disappeared from view (*Lectures on the Origin and Growth of Religion, as Illustrated by the Religions of India* [Hibbert Lectures, 1878; London: Longmans, Green & Co., 1878], p. 285).

52. A casual browsing of the standard volumes on Old Testament Theology will reveal this.

53. J. Barr, *The Concept of Biblical Theology* (London: SCM Press, 1999), p. 61.

many modern understandings of monotheism such an insight is absent, and this includes much of the discussion of Israelite monotheism. The supreme example of this is the desire to locate the decisive moment of the breakthrough of monotheism, a point from which Israel could not backslide.[54]

A further aspect may be recognized in both More's work and modern scholarship and that is that the task of describing the development of monotheism has frequently been affected by theological commitments to particular historical models. Stolz notes that, 'wo immer "Monotheismus" als historischer Begriff verwendet wird, ist er mit Modellen historischer Entwicklung verbunden'.[55] In each of these models of historical development monotheism has stood as the pinnacle and the organizing principle. For the Platonists monotheism was the most ancient religion since age implied naturalness and authenticity. Later interests in *Urmonotheism* resulted from Romanticism's idealization of the primitive. In the nineteenth century, when evolutionary models dominated, monotheism was viewed as the height of theological development. Schleiermacher's three levels of fetishism, polytheism and monotheism, for example, reflect not only a historical progression, but also a theological assessment.[56] As recently as 1994, Rainer Albertz complained that, 'so erfrischend diese neue Debatte ist, so sehr scheint sie mir von untergründig wirksamen dogmatischen Vorurteilen belastet zu sein'.[57]

3.

A large part of the endeavours of Old Testament scholars over the last twenty-five years has been directed towards the question that Halpern has claimed to be 'intellectually and theologically primary'. The gains of such effort are well known. I have tried to make the case for the importance of the question of the origin of 'monotheism' for 'Israel's religious odyssey'. A failure to attend to this question will have consequences for our analyses of biblical texts. In particular the dangers of an intellectualizing of religion, and the narrowing of the discussion to a simply-conceived evolutionary progression have been observed.

---

54. This point is developed at length in MacDonald, *Deuteronomy*.

55. F. Stolz, 'Der Monotheismus Israels im Kontent der altorientalischen Religionsgeschichte – Tendenzen neuerer Forschung', in W. Dietrich and M.A. Klopfenstein (eds.), *Ein Gott Allein? JHWH-Verehrung und biblischer Monotheismus im Kontext der israelitischen und altorientalischen Religionsgeschichte* (OBO, 193; Göttingen: Vandenhoeck & Ruprecht, 1994), p. 33.

56. Schleiermacher, *Christian Faith*, pp. 35–37.

57. R. Albertz, 'Der Ort des Monotheismus in der israelitischen Religionsgeschichte', in Dietrich and Klopfenstein (eds.), *Ein Gott Allein?*, p. 79.

How Appropriate is 'Monotheism' as a Category for Biblical Interpretation?

R.W.L. Moberly, University of Durham

Modern scholarly study of biblical monotheism has generally concentrated on the history of the emergence of monotheism ('doctrine that there is only one God' – *OED*) as a concept. This history has generally been formulated as a 'critical' insight in reaction to older, religiously traditional, views, which apparently took the biblical narrative 'naively' at face value and so took for granted that Israel's religious history had always been monotheistic[1] – a view which of course incorporated the recognition that some or many in Israel had regularly failed to be true to their religion and so had been on the receiving end of repeated prophetic invective. One can thus find various recurrent emphases in the modern literature.[2]

First, although the Bible presents a picture that is apparently monotheistic from the outset, monotheism (in anything like its traditional sense) only emerged relatively late in Israel's history during the biblical period, after centuries of religious and political struggle – both between Israel and its neighbours, and within Israel (though contemporary uncertainties over the dating of many primary texts allows a considerable variety of possible reconstructions). Appropriate categories for Israelite religion during most of the biblical period range from the general 'polytheism' to the more specific 'henotheism' or 'monolatry', for YHWH was conceived as one deity among others – supreme and incomparable, indeed, in Israel's literature of worship, but supreme among other deities. A succinct expression of this outlook is 'Who is like you, YHWH, among the gods?' (Exod. 15.11).

Secondly, in terms of dating, probably the most widely held view is that it was not until Deutero-Isaiah in the context of the Babylonian exile in the mid 6th century (towards the end of the Old Testament's own historical sequence) that monotheism proper (i.e. as distinct from henotheism or monolatry) was clearly

---

1. I use scare quotes for 'critical' and 'naive' because such labels hardly do justice to the subtleties of historic Jewish and Christian interpretations of the biblical portrayal of the one God in relation to other gods, even though of course these were formulated without the benefit of the conceptualizations made possible by analytical historiography and by the study of religion in the modern period.

2. A concise introduction to the debate, with representative bibliography, may be found in David L. Petersen, 'Israel and Monotheism: The Unfinished Agenda', in Gene M. Tucker, David L. Petersen and Robert R. Wilson (eds.), *Canon, Theology, and Old Testament Interpretation: Essays in Honor of Brevard S. Childs* (Philadelphia: Fortress Press, 1988), pp. 92–107. A fuller introduction is offered by Robert Karl Gnuse, *No Other Gods: Emergent Monotheism in Israel* (JSOTSup, 241; Sheffield: Sheffield Academic Press, 1997).

formulated (however much some have argued that at least the seeds of monotheism may have been present in earlier traditions associated with Elijah or even Moses). As Robert Gnuse puts it in a recent monograph on the emergence of monotheism: 'Second Isaiah, however, provides us with what is the revolutionary breakthrough to monotheism, and most scholars acknowledge that his is an absolute and universalistic monotheism developed well beyond the thought of his predecessors'.[3]

Thirdly, although the Bible apparently presents a clear-cut contrast between YHWH and deities of other nations, Israelite religion for most of the biblical period in fact existed in a symbiotic and syncretistic relationship with the religious beliefs and practices of the peoples of its nearer and wider environment. A corollary of this is that the Old Testament deity YHWH was often indistinguishable from El and Baal, the 'Canaanite'[4] deities whose characteristics are known to us from the Ras Shamra texts. John Day, for example, speaks for many when he says that 'El and Yahweh were originally separate deities who became equated'.[5] Thus the portrayal in the Old Testament as it now stands is a relatively late and in certain ways tendentious development.

Fourthly, the formulation of monotheistic belief was substantially the product of contemporary political events, particularly the confrontation between Judah and imperial Babylon and Judah's need to have something to say in the face of its defeat and Babylon's power. Gerd Theissen, for example, enunciates a social and psychological process in which cognitive dissonance is overcome: 'In the face of the destruction of Jerusalem...the only possibility was either to recognize the superiority of the victorious nations and their gods – or to hold firm to belief in YHWH by compensating for the catastrophe on earth by a victory in heaven. The other gods were said not to exist.'[6]

Fifthly, the literature of the Old Testament may be more or less unrepresentative of the actual religion practised by many/most of the people for much/most of the time within ancient Israel and Judah. As it stands the Old Testament is most likely the work of a small ideological elite – probably a 'YHWH-alone' group associated with the perspectives of Deuteronomy, which at best reinterpreted and at worst suppressed the religious perspectives and practices of those who did not share the group's ideology.[7] The attempts by scholars to retrieve some of these perspectives

---

3. *No Other Gods*, p. 207. Gnuse cites numerous representatives of mainstream scholarship in support of his contention. A recent overview essay by John Day ('The Religion of Israel', in A.D.H. Mayes [ed.], *Text in Context* [Oxford: Oxford University Press, 2000], pp. 428–53, esp. p. 438) fully supports Gnuse's position.

4.　I follow the convention whereby 'Canaanite' is applied to many an aspect of indigenous religion on the eastern seabord of the Mediterranean in the late second and early first millennia, though the rationale for such an extensive use of the epithet, well beyond the confines of geographical Canaan, seems to me open to question.

5.　*Yahweh and the Gods and Goddesses of Canaan* (JSOTSup, 265; Sheffield: Sheffield Academic Press: 2000), p. 17.

6.　*A Theory of Primitive Christian Religion* (London: SCM Press, 1999), p. 43, drawing on his earlier *Biblical Faith: An Evolutionary Approach* (London: SCM Press, 1984), pp. 45–81.

7.　Morton Smith, *Palestinian Parties and Politics That Shaped the Old Testament* (London:

and practices, so that they can be understood in their own right, can be seen not only as a concern for accurate understanding of the past but also as a charitable act towards some of history's obliterated voices.

Assuming that something like this is, as far as it goes, a recognizable and not too inaccurate (even if incomplete) account of characteristic discussions of Israelite monotheism, what is one to make of it? Much could be said. For example, the debate seems in practice (whatever the personal beliefs of some of its contributors) to have internalized a modern account of deity as a human projection in which questions about God/god/the gods are really without remainder (at least for scholarly purposes) questions about human beliefs and practices. In such a context theological and philosophical questions about metaphysics or the nature of religious language or the nature of humanity need not be addressed, while the status of historic Jewish and Christian (and, relatedly, Muslim) beliefs in Israel's God as the one true God are either unaddressed or, usually implicitly but sometimes explicitly, more or less called into question. I do not wish, therefore, to engage with the debates on their own terms, but rather to reflect on some of the assumptions which structure them, and in so doing to address certain areas which are often left unaddressed. The hope is that this will enable familiar debates to be set in a fresh light that may potentially be fruitful for growing in understanding.

1. *The Origins and Appropriateness of 'Monotheism' and Related Categories*

Our starting point will be not the biblical text itself but the interpretive categories that we bring to it. For it is neither possible nor desirable to try to interpret the Bible without making heuristic use of post-biblical categories; and it is sometimes helpful to be reminded that such basic categories as 'history' and 'theology' (not to mention 'biblical' and 'post-biblical') are post-biblical. What matters is less whether the category is biblical or post-biblical than whether it (negatively) does not force the biblical content into inappropriate moulds but (positively) enables penetrating grasp of the nature and content of the biblical text; and this, in turn, is a matter not only of the category in itself but of the way in which it is used in practice.

What, then, may we say about 'monotheism', and related terms such as 'polytheism', 'henotheism', and 'monolatry', as structuring categories? Despite their time-honoured, widespread, and generally taken-for-granted use among biblical scholars, serious questions about their appropriateness and continuing usefulness are being raised by both historians and theologians.[8]

From an ancient religious historian's perspective, consider this recent paragraph by Simon Price:

SCM Press, 1971, 1987), pp. 1–42; Bernhard Lang, *Monotheism and the Prophetic Minority: An Essay in Biblical History and Sociology* (Sheffield: Almond Press, 1983).

8.   For the argument of this section see further Nathan MacDonald's essay on 'The Origin of "Monotheism"' in this volume. I am indebted to Dr MacDonald for several references in this essay, and also for stimulus to my own thinking.

According to a Christian writer of the second century, the Greeks had 365 gods. For the proponent of one (Christian) god this alleged fact demonstrated the absurdity of Greek religion. Moderns too sometimes assume the nobility and superiority of one supreme god ('monotheism') as against the proliferation of little gods ('polytheism'). But the number of Greek gods (not as great as 365) does not mean that those gods lack significance, any more than does the multiplicity of gods in the Hindu tradition. In addition, proponents of monotheism (whether Jewish, Christian or Islamic) are often not ready to note the disruptive consequences of monotheistic intolerance or the extent to which alleged monotheisms contain plural elements. Within Christianity, what about the Trinity, the Blessed Virgin Mary, or the Saints? In fact the categories 'monotheism' and 'polytheism' do not promote historical understanding. In both ethnography/anthropology and ancient history scholars have sometimes sought to 'rescue' polytheism by arguing for an element of monolatry or henotheism, in which the power of one god in the pantheon is proclaimed as supreme. But the manoeuvre is conditioned by a Judaeo-Christian evaluation of monotheism. The terms 'polytheism' and 'monotheism' are best abandoned to the theologians.[9]

There appear to be two main factors in Price's argument (apart from a certain sense that this is not really an important question needing careful and discriminating reflection in its own right). On the one hand are issues of what one might perhaps call phenomenology: historic monotheisms are in important senses less 'mono-' than their adherents sometimes claim, and this reduces the value of using a distinction between one and many as a key to classifying understandings of deity.[10] On the other hand are issues of evaluation; although within a Christian culture the superiority of 'monotheism' was long taken for granted, why should this be so in a post-Christian culture?[11] Monotheisms can be intolerant and divisive, while belief in a plurality of deities may be religiously rich and significant. These considerations have obvious force.[12] How then should one proceed? Price is happy simply to abandon 'monotheism' to the theologians. But do, or should, all theologians really want it?

Some recent work of Nicholas Lash should at least make us think twice.[13] 'Monotheism' as a term was coined by the Cambridge Platonist, Henry More, in

9. *Religions of the Ancient Greeks* (Cambridge: Cambridge University Press, 1999), p. 11.

10. Apart from the issues involved in Greek religion, my colleague Stuart Weeks has pointed out in discussion that the terminology and concepts of polytheism and monotheism are seriously inadequate for the depiction of ancient Egyptian religion; see esp. Erik Hornung, *Conceptions of God in Ancient Egypt: The One and the Many* (trans. J. Baines [German, 1971]; London: Routledge, 1983).

11. Inversion of the value traditionally attached to 'monotheism' as opposed to 'polytheism' can be found in a significant number of influential thinkers prior to recent times – Machiavelli, Rousseau, Hume, Nietzsche (conveniently summarized in Moshe Halbertal and Avishai Margalit, *Idolatry* [Cambridge, MA: Harvard University Press, 1992], pp. 247–50).

12. The atrocity of 9/11 has given renewed force to contemporary critiques of 'monotheistically' motivated inhumanity.

13. Nicholas Lash, *The Beginning and the End of 'Religion'* (Cambridge: Cambridge University Press, 1996), ch. 1; cf. also ch. 4.

1660, at around the time when the terms 'deism' and 'theism' were first introduced into scholarly and popular parlance. Early modern England was the context when, according to Lash (who draws on major studies of the thought of the period), [14] the very concept of 'religion' and 'religions', in the senses in which the modern West has used these terms, was invented. Lash argues that this was a period when fundamental understandings of God and theology were transformed so that they became other than that which classically they had been.

At least three features of Lash's enormously suggestive argument are important for our concerns. First, in terms of the general intellectual milieu of the period, Lash sees one characteristic as:

> a new ideal for the working of the mind, namely [quoting Amos Funkenstein]: 'a science that has an unequivocal language with which it speaks and uniform objects of which it speaks'… [Thus] all knowledge is of objects, and objects are to be measured and described, as objectively and simply and straightforwardly as possible… [Consequently,] within this scheme of things, the relation of human beings to the Holy One, once understood as creaturely dependence relearned as friendship, is now reduced to knowledge of an object known as 'God'. All objects of enquiry are shaped by the methods used for their investigation. The invention of 'religion' carried with it the reduction of faith's attentive wonder to the entertaining of particular beliefs.[15]

Secondly, the idea that there are a number of different religions, which relate to each other as species of a common genus, is an invention of this intellectual milieu:

> the construction of the 'genus and species' model of relationships between 'the religions' was but one component in the project of 'enlightenment'. This project, suspecting all 'local' reasoning, all particular custom and convention, as arbitrary, divisive, insecure, sought, in its stead, 'to place reason upon a secure and universal foundation'. To say that the modern world is ending is to acknowledge that this universalising project can now, in turn, be seen to be little more than the expression of one particular set of 'local' circumstances: the circumstances of seventeenth-century Europe.[16]

Thirdly, and more specifically, religious diversity was seen in this period as a result of human degeneration and sin. The increasingly used terms 'theism' and 'deism' (initially interchangeable), terms which affirmed a Supreme Being while dispensing with revelation and Christian faith, were part of a religious world view in which:

---

14. His primary modern accounts are Peter Harrison, *'Religion' and the Religions in the English Enlightenment* (Cambridge: Cambridge University Press, 1990); Amos Funkenstein, *Theology and the Scientific Imagination from the Middle Ages to the Seventeenth Century* (Princeton, NJ: Princeton University Press, 1986); Michael J. Buckley, *At the Origins of Modern Atheism* (New Haven: Yale University Press, 1987); and he commends also William T. Cavanaugh, '"A Fire Strong Enough to Consume the House": The Wars of Religion and the Rise of the State', *Modern Theology* 11 (October 1995), pp. 397–420.

15. *Beginning*, pp. 12–13.

16. *Beginning*, p. 11. The quotation in the middle is from John Milbank.

pluralism was unnatural, and combined with intolerance, gave rise to untold human misery. The cure was to be a return to the unsullied religion of the *illud tempus* which would result in a universal worship of the one God, and bring an end to religious strife.[17]

Thus 'monotheism' arose in the context of a fundamental conceptual distinction between 'natural' and 'revealed' religion (which in the eighteenth century became the distinction between 'natural' and 'positive' religion), in which all 'revealed' religions were appraised by their extent of corruption and degeneracy in relation to the true and pure 'natural' original; and one positive criterion was when a religion displayed 'monotheism', for the more this was present, the closer that religion was to the truth of the one God of 'natural' religion. Thus the concept of 'monotheism' was not a heuristic category to grasp the particular contours of biblical (or other) faith but rather a self-standing and self-evident yardstick, an *a priori* by which all religions, including the biblical and those rooted in it, could be appraised.

Lash shows how subsequent religious discussions of the nineteenth century instinctively used these seventeenth century categories as somehow self-evident, with no recognition as to what they were actually doing. Moreover, Lash reminds us that the kind of religious understanding that was self-evident in the seventeenth and eighteenth centuries became problematic and set on course for extinction in the nineteenth and twentieth centuries:

> in due time, of course, natural religion, in turn, was understood to be a kind of fiction: the projection onto some divinity of human fears and aspirations. Thus ends the story of 'religion' and 'the religions', as conceived from the standpoint of 'enlightenment'; a story which had its beginnings in the seventeenth century.[18]

Lash's contention is that what has thus ended is a concept of 'religion' which was part and parcel of the modernity which is also now ending. As we move on from that modernity, theologians should not unlearn the many positive (and often painful) lessons of modernity; but nor should they seek to cling to or reclaim modernity's construal of 'religion'. Rather the task is to delve more deeply into the classic sources of Christian faith in scripture, the Fathers, and the medieval theologians so as to rediscover a concept of God and life which is more faithful to the tradition and which has the capacity to challenge the idolatries of secularization in the name of truth.

If Lash is at all on the right lines, the implications are considerable. In line with his thesis that the very category of 'religion'/'religions' represents a potentially distorting narrowing of that phenomenon which it seeks to depict, he implies that the adoption of 'monotheism' as a category has involved a subtle but profound skewing of Christian (and, by extension, biblical and Jewish) thought. 'Monotheism' in the 17th century entailed a certain intellectualizing whereby believing in one God becomes assent to the proposition that the class of deity has only one member, a proposition of self-evident philosophical significance, rather than a kind

---

17. *Beginning*, p. 14. Lash here is quoting Peter Harrison.
18. *Beginning*, p. 16.

of transformative and demanding awareness of reality that is rooted in, and inseparable from, a range of moral disciplines and symbolic practices. It of course
remains necessary to study how the category of 'monotheism' has in fact been used
over the last three centuries, not least by biblical interpreters, but it would be
surprising if its use was not in certain ways indebted to its original significance.
This would mean that, in a contemporary context where some of the assumptions
of modernity are increasingly questioned, there is a need for scholars to do some
lengthy and rather difficult rethinking of assumptions and frames of reference
which have come to seem as natural as the air one breathes.[19] What all this might
mean for a renewed understanding of the biblical portrayal of God is a task which
is still in its early stages.

2. *Truth Claims and their Presuppositions*

There are difficult questions about the nature of religious truth and epistemology
which are less addressed in biblical study than they might be. On the one hand,
how could one ever know whether or not there is only one deity or whether there
are many? What could count as knowing, and what might appropriate grounds of
knowing be, in regard to the realm of the divine? On the other hand, why is the
question of whether there is one deity or many a question worth bothering with in
the first place? Our familiarity with the biblical tradition's insistence that this (in
some form) is a significant issue, and the maintaining of that insistence in the
related contexts of Judaism, Christianity and Islam, may enable us to forget that in
many other contexts it may be a non-issue.

The first, epistemological, issue may be introduced via an essay by Menachem
Haran, 'The Religion of the Patriarchs'.[20] Haran writes:

> The Bible assumes that the Patriarchal God was identical with the God of Israel in
> the post-Mosaic era, although He made himself mostly known to the Patriarchs
> under names other than Yahweh. This view has become deeply rooted in Judaism...
> [and] was passed on to Christianity... This view evolved into an incontestable prin-
> ciple in medieval thought, sometimes influencing, albeit indirectly, even modern
> research. Yet, it cannot serve as a starting-point today, all the more so as it has
> become obvious that the biblical tradition itself contains decisive evidence against
> such a view.[21]

Haran's assertion that a traditional view 'cannot serve as a starting point today'
because 'the biblical tradition itself contains decisive evidence against it' surely
displays serious confusion. Perhaps one should ask: 'a starting-point' for what? To
be sure, a modern historical reconstruction of the developing human formulations

19. For a (wonderfully lucid) more general account of the pressing contemporary need to
rethink frames of reference inherited from the 17th century, see Mary Midgley, *Science and Poetry*
(London and New York: Routledge, 2001).

20. 'The Religion of the Patriarchs', *ASTI* 4 (1965), pp. 30–55. I discuss Haran's essay also in
my *The Old Testament of the Old Testament: Patriarchal Narratives and Mosaic Yahwism* (OBT;
Minneapolis: Fortress Press, 1992), pp. 111–13.

21. 'Religion', p. 30.

of ancient religion (such as Haran undertakes) is a different kind of task from that in which most premoderns were engaged, and a traditional view need be of little special significance for such a task. But what is so odd is Haran's assumption that the complex religious developments surmised by the religio-historical scholar somehow disprove the traditional understanding that the God of Israel made himself known to the patriarchs in ways other than those by which he made himself known to Mosaic Israel. Does Haran not realize how difficult it is rightly to articulate the relationship between his agenda and that of the traditional view? What is the 'decisive evidence' contained within the biblical tradition? Is it for the most part other than material with which proponents of the traditional view were fully familiar[22] but which they simply analyzed in categories other than those of Haran? That is, premodern scholars thought in terms of the one God revealing himself in differing ways, rather than, say, in terms of a syncretistic merging of diverse deities. Or, to put it differently, how does Haran know that the God of Israel was not the patriarchal God (except in so far as they are differing human constructs)? How, for that matter, does anyone know how diverse religious practices and understandings relate to the reality (if such it be) of the divine? The fact that Haran can make confident assertions about the apparently destructive implications of modern religio-historical reconstructions upon more ancient beliefs about divine identity and action, without feeling any need even to mention, let alone discuss, the epistemological problems involved, is surely eloquent of a kind of insufficiently self-critical positivism which he is not alone among biblical scholars in displaying.

In short, Haran seems to work with a model of God as a human projection, in which questions about the ontological reality of God and/or warrants for true beliefs about God are not on the agenda, and does not clearly see how this differs from an agenda where God's ontological reality and/or the validity of human response is a prime concern. In theological terms, what is at stake is the concept of revelation. Whether or not the concept of revelation is meaningful, and how revelation, if meaningful, might relate to religio-historical enquiry, are questions needing more recognition than Haran gives them.[23]

What of the related question, why the issue of whether there is one deity or many is worth pursuing anyway (not least in the light of the formidable epistemological difficulties just mentioned)? Why, for example, in the paradigmatic Old Testament narrative of 1 Kgs 18 does Elijah insist that there is a fundamental difference between YHWH and Baal, and that there is a life-and-death choice to be made between them, when the matter could easily be seen otherwise? Gary Anderson, in a representative contemporary account of Israelite religion, [24] puts it nicely:

22. To be sure, extra-biblical material has been discovered, which has played a significant role in modern accounts, perhaps most famously in Albrecht Alt, 'The God of the Fathers', in his *Essays on Old Testament History and Religion* (trans. R.A. Wilson [German, 1929]; Oxford: Basil Blackwell, 1966), pp. 1–77. Haran's point, however, relates specifically to the biblical tradition itself.

23. I begin to develop these issues a little more fully in my 'How May We Speak of God? A Reconsideration of the Nature of Biblical Theology', *TynBul* 53.2 (2002), pp. 177–202.

24. Gary A. Anderson, 'Introduction to Israelite Religion', in Leander E. Keck *et al.* (eds.), *The New Interpreter's Bible* (Nashville: Abingdon Press, 1994), I, 272–83, quote cols. 275–76.

> Because this confusing of YHWH and Baal was so widespread in ancient Israel, it
> is important to understand why such an identification would have suggested itself
> in the first place. The most obvious explanation is the similar natures of YHWH
> and Baal, as we have just seen [i.e. preceding review of familiar material about Baal
> as a storm and fertility deity, and the ascription of similar attributes to YHWH].
> These similarities would have led many Israelites to presume that YHWH (the
> more 'recent' figure in the history of ancient Canaan) was not a unique god but
> rather just an alternative local title for an older pan-Canaanite deity. From the
> perspective of the common Israelite, it was not so much a matter of rejecting
> YHWH in preference for Baal, but of seeing the two as equitable or interchange-
> able in certain fundamental ways. For the prophets, however, this merging of
> deities was nothing other than a rejection of the absolute uniqueness of the biblical
> God and the requirement to revere God alone. Not only does this comparison of
> the biblical story to Canaanite religion allow us to understand the Israelites' ten-
> dency toward syncretism, but it also puts in far greater relief the innovative and
> radical theological program of the prophets. How easy it would have been for
> these religious leaders to acquiesce to the convention of the times and correlate
> the activity of Israel's God to that of its neighbours.

Quite so. But if one asks *why* one should privilege the prophetic perspective – other
than the fact that the canonical text, and the faiths rooted in it, do so – how should
one respond? If someone suggests (compare Simon Price, above) that the prophetic
perspective is not only divisive, but needlessly and harmfully divisive – what real
mischief is there in syncretistic thought and practice (especially when the theologians of the Old Testament are themselves supposed to have indulged extensively in
it)? – what kind of answer, and on what basis, could be appropriate?

The question is the more pressing because the biblical text clearly does not envisage the issue in the kinds of categories which seem to have characterized certain
formulations of the concept of a single deity in ancient Greek thought. There the
issue is a philosophical one to do with an original primary cause. One thinks, for
example, of Aristotle's famous (albeit in context untraditional) affirmation: 'We
hold then that god is a living being, eternal, most good; and therefore life and a
continuous eternal existence belong to god; for that is what god is'.[25] Such a view
may or may not commend itself as a satisfactory metaphysical option. Clearly, however, it does not have the kind of life and death significance or practical implications that the Old Testament prophetic conception has. Might one suggest that the
less charged philosophical context of Greek discussion should commend itself as a
more appropriate way of dealing with the issue, if it must be dealt with at all (as it
commended itself to thinkers of the seventeenth and eighteenth centuries)? Alternatively, would not an application of the label 'monotheistic' to both Elijah (as
portrayed) and Aristotle, as though they held fundamental common ground over
against other 'polytheistic' conceptions, risk obscuring far more than it illuminates?
All of which brings us back to the appropriateness of 'monotheism' as a category
in the first place.

---

25. *Metaphysics* 12.7.9, 1072b.

3. *History of Israelite Religion, or the Theological Meaning of Israel's Scripture?*

Recent biblical criticism has seen an enormous increase in the diversity of methods and perspectives whereby the biblical text may be studied. (It is ironic that this has arisen in reaction to the apparently limiting constraints imposed by the dominance for several generations of an 'historical-critical' approach to the text, [26] when the 'historical-critical' approach was itself initially felt to be a liberation from a multiplicity of seemingly undisciplined approaches to the text.) In any case, it has become clear that the question of *how* one interprets the biblical text is to some extent inseparable from the question of *why* one is interpreting it; *context* may be as significant for the interpreter as for the text that is interpreted; difference of purpose may validly entail some difference of method.

These general reflections lead to a more specific observation about Old Testament study. The name of Julius Wellhausen remains the convenient shorthand for the insight, shared by all mainstream biblical scholars (however much they continue to dispute details), that the history of Israel and its religious development as perceived through the lens of modern critical historiography looks very different from the picture presented by the Old Testament itself. Thus, for example, the Old Testament's picture of the one God known already to Abraham gives way to a picture of religious pluralism and syncretism in which monotheism is a late, exilic development. This differing picture is widely held to be not just more complex, but also more original, closer to the actual course of Israelite history, and so in some sense more valuable, or indeed truer, than the canonical presentation.

On the other hand, advocates of so-called 'canonical'[27] approaches, for which perhaps the name of Brevard Childs may serve as convenient shorthand, have argued for reconceptualizing the way the scriptural text is handled. Here there is a concern to find positive significance in Israel's own picture of its history without feeling any need to justify it as 'really more or less historical after all' (the standard 'conservative' approach). Rather one may take for granted (while still reserving the right to argue any particular issue or detail) the kinds of developmental, traditio-historical, and compositional understandings that are commonly hypothesized; but one then sees the text in their light as representing Israel's mature insight into the meaning and significance of its history. So, for example, even if it is granted (for the sake of argument) that belief in the one God is a relatively late and perhaps unrepresentative development in the biblical period, and that the texts portraying the one God in relation to Abraham and Moses are to a greater or lesser extent

---

26. I use scare quotes because 'historical-critical' is a simplifying epithet which risks obscuring the diversity of methods and assumptions which have characterized modern biblical scholarship.

27. I use scare quotes because 'canonical' is also a simplifying epithet which risks obscuring the diversity of concerns and arguments which characterize such approaches. In particular I am aware of not doing justice to James A. Sanders who has argued for a monotheizing process within Israel's literature (*Canon and Community: A Guide to Canonical Criticism* [Philadelphia: Fortress Press, 1984]).

indebted to these later developments, the fact that portrayal of the one God has been used to structure the formative moments in Israel's faith should be taken with total imaginative and interpretative seriousness. Whatever the historical development of Israel's religion, belief in the one God has become the normative pattern within which Israel's story and Israel's faith should be understood and appropriated by those who subsequently seek to stand in continuity with it – for it is to such that the Old Testament as a canonical collection is addressed.

One difficult question is to know what is the value of characteristic 'historical-critical' rearrangements of the text into their putative original historical sequence for the interpretation of the 'received canonical' text and its possible appropriation by (would-be) believers. For if the sequential development is not granted intrinsic superiority *tout court* (as in most biblical scholarship of the 19th and 20th centuries), but may represent that which the editors and compilers of the canonical texts deliberately wished to relegate to the background or margins, then in what ways may the developmental account potentially skew (as well as at times enable) a reading of the canonical text? If part of the point of the canonical text is in fact to present an understanding of God in categories other than those of its historical origins and development, what is actually gained (for what purposes, and appropriate to which contexts?) by critically reconstruing it in those developmental categories?

These questions cannot properly be addressed here. The point of these remarks is not to deny the validity of those developmental accounts of 'monotheism' that fill the pages of modern Old Testament study, which must be argued in their own terms, but rather to problematize and so reconsider their interpretative significance. It may be that such accounts of the possible human origins and development of that understanding of God which is categorized as 'monotheism' may be less self-evidently illuminating than often supposed for believers, or open-to-be believers, today to grasp either the intrinsic meaning or the enduring significance of the biblical portrayal of the creator God (*'elohim*) who is known to Israel by the proper name *YHWH* and confessed by Israel to be 'one' (*'ehad*).[28]

For example (to return to the patriarchs), I have argued elsewhere that the patriarchal traditions of Gen. 12–50 contain a clearly recognizable and consistent portrayal of one God, which is strikingly different from that associated with the normative Mosaic Yahwism of Exodus to Deuteronomy.[29]

> Although the patriarchs worship only one God, no particular significance attaches to this; there is no implied opposition to the worship of other gods. Although the patriarchs have extensive dealings, and sometimes conflicts, with the native inhabitants of both Canaan and Egypt, the question of religious allegiance is never at

---

28. In a not dissimilar vein Childs comments, 'Although the historian of religion has every right to employ the term monotheism to the religion of Israel in contrast to polytheistic religions, the term itself is theologically inert and fails largely to register the basic features of God's self-revelation to Israel. For one thing, God's existential demand for absolute loyalty relativizes the theoretical question of the existence of other deities, assigning it to a peripheral role' (*Biblical Theology of the Old and New Testaments* [London: SCM Press, 1992], p. 355).

29. *The Old Testament of the Old Testament*, quotes from pp. 87 and 104.

stake... Worship of one God is a matter of straightforward religious fact rather than, as in Mosaic Yahwism, a matter of urgent religious choice...

The difference between patriarchal and Mosaic religion is perhaps most conveniently epitomized by the notion of holiness... [which] from Exod. 3.5 onward focuses the exclusive, demanding, regulated, mediated, and sanctuary-centred relationship between YHWH and Israel, while the absence of holiness in patriarchal religion equally epitomizes its open, unstructured, nonlocated, and unaggressive nature, its 'ecumenical bonhomie'.

Although the textual evidence is well known, the possible theological implications of the canonical presentation have been consistently transposed into religio-historical accounts of the development of 'orthodox' (deuteronomic) and 'unorthodox' (non-deuteronomic) Yahwism. What is remarkable is that the Old Testament itself, in its received form, envisages knowledge and worship of the one God – for the text is clear that the deity who calls the patriarchs is not other than the deity who calls Moses – taking place in two quite different, and in important senses incompatible, ways (i.e. two kinds of 'monotheism'). Theologically, it poses the questions of continuity and difference within the self-revelation of the one God, and of the legitimacy of different modes of knowledge of God in different contexts. Since these questions are also at the heart of problems posed by the New Testament's confession of Jesus as now definitive for the identity and nature of Israel's God (as discussed elsewhere in this collection), the Old Testament in its received form may have unrecognized resources and conceptuality for basic issues of both theology and christology.

4. *Exegesis and Interpretation of Selected Old Testament Texts*

It is time to consider a text – perhaps the most obvious one to consider in this context, the prime (indeed sole, apart from its likely citation in Zech. 14.9) text in the Old Testament which depicts the deity as 'one': the *Shema'* in Deut. 6.4–9.[30] One key question is, of course, how 'one' should be understood. In Jewish contexts, where the text has been most used and discussed, there has developed an extensive theological and philosophical tradition of discussion of the divine 'oneness' and its possible implications. Much modern study, by contrast, suspecting that the traditional Jewish debate bears too little relation to the likely meaning of the text in its deuteronomic context, has transposed the debate into different, religio-historical categories: 'one' is part of a slogan of religious reform around the time of Josiah – in Gottwald's depiction, '*one* God for *one people* in *one land* observing *one cult*',[31] a depiction which indeed echoes some ancient Jewish formulations.[32]

---

30. I have offered a detailed exegesis and interpretation of the text in my 'Toward an Interpretation of the Shema', in Christopher Seitz and Kathryn Greene-McCreight (eds.), *Theological Exegesis: Essays in Honor of Brevard S. Childs* (Grand Rapids: Eerdmans, 1999), pp. 124–44. My comments here are based upon this essay.

31. Norman K. Gottwald, *The Hebrew Bible: A Socio-Literary Introduction* (Philadelphia: Fortress Press, 1985), p. 390.

32. Josephus summarizes Mosaic laws for the Jewish constitution: 'Let there be one holy city

This may, however, be potentially as misleading for understanding the text as anything in medieval Jewish tradition (the difference is that many contemporary biblical scholars are happier with religio-historical speculations than with religio-philosophical speculations). This is so not least because the Hebrew word for 'one' (*'ehad*) is nowhere in Deuteronomy or the deuteronomistic history repeated in the kind of sloganistic way which this hypothesis requires; and also because it tends to misconstrue the nature of the linkage between the affirmation that YHWH is one and the immediately following, correlative, injunction that Israel is to love YHWH wholly and unreservedly (*w^e 'ahabta* in v. 5 should be rendered 'so you shall love', expressing what it entailed by the affirmation that YHWH is 'one').

I suggest that the best guide to the usage of 'one' in the *Shema'* is Song of Songs 6.8–9, where the man twice uses the term in praise of his beloved. Here 'one' has the sense of 'one and only', 'unique', not in the sense that there are not in fact other women [the biblical text envisages 'sixty queens, and eighty concubines, and young women beyond counting', who might be rivals for the man's favours but who in fact join him acclaiming the uniqueness of his beloved], but in the sense that this woman matters in a way that other women do not and evokes a uniquely positive response.[33] When such a sense of 'one' (*'ehad*) is applied to Deut. 6.4, it becomes clear that the text does not envisage it as possible to depict YHWH as 'one' without speaking at the same time of Israel's response to YHWH. 'To say that YHWH is 'one' is not to say something about God that is separable from its human counterpart of 'love', but rather designates YHWH as the appropriate recipient of unreserved human "love".'[34]

The appropriateness of understanding the *Shema'* as depicting something about YHWH that is inseparable from Israel's need to respond to YHWH is strengthened by wider contextual considerations. Within Deuteronomy itself, two passages will suffice to illustrate this. First, every Old Testament scholar knows that Deut. 7.7–8 is a *locus classicus* about election. What is too rarely mentioned is the context of this *locus classicus*, in the chapter directly following the *Shema'*. Here (7.6 in relation to 7.1–5) Israel's election, which serves to provide the rationale for the practice of *herem* (already, most likely, a metaphor for undivided allegiance),[35] is a prime corollary of the logic of the *Shema'*. The affirmation that YHWH is one, and the affirmation that Israel is a chosen people who must love and serve YHWH unreservedly and exclusively, are different facets of one and the same precious stone.

Secondly, consider the logic of Deut. 10.14ff. On the one hand, to YHWH belongs the totality of creation (v. 14). Yet this is specified so as to sharpen the

---

in that place...and let there be one temple therein, and one altar of stones... In no other city let there be either altar or temple; for God is one and the Hebrew race is one' (*Ant.* 4.200–201).

33. 'Shema', p. 132.

34. 'Shema', p. 133.

35. For a preliminary exposition of the thesis that *herem* in Deut. 7 is a metaphor which does not envisage actual warfare and the taking of life but rather prescribes undiluted allegiance in terms of shunning intermarriage (7.3–4) and destroying those objects that symbolize and enable allegiances other than to YHWH (7.5), see my 'Shema', pp. 134–37.

wonder and mystery of YHWH's commitment to the patriarchs and his choice of their descendants (v. 15). The consequence of this is that Israel must respond appropriately to YHWH and overcome their recalcitrance (v. 16). On the other hand, YHWH is the sovereign and incomparable God, whose character is displayed in integrity and justice, especially towards those who are marginal (vv. 17–18), and so Israel, who know at first hand the lot of the marginal, must live likewise (v. 19). They must look unswervingly to YHWH (v. 20), as they recognize that their life and destiny is inseparable from what YHWH has done for them (vv. 21–22). The first affirmation about YHWH leads into an affirmation of election and a call for proper responsiveness to YHWH. The second affirmation about YHWH leads into a requirement for moral response towards those who are dependent upon Israel. It is not just that we have here a kind of combination of love of God and love of neighbour, but that speech about YHWH as supreme is inseparable from the call of Israel to be a particular kind of people.

Put simply, the book that contains the *Shema'* also contains a prime exposition of YHWH's election of Israel, and the two are, or at least should be, conceptually inseparable (in rabbinic thought the inseparability of the uniqueness of YHWH from the uniqueness of Israel was commonly expressed by linking YHWH as *'ehad* in Deut. 6.4 with Israel as *'ehad* in 2 Sam. 7.23).[36] The linkage between YHWH as one and election is, in significant ways, that between a theological affirmation and its corequisite within history. In other words, the confession and recognition of YHWH as 'one' is not a view from anywhere or nowhere in particular, but rather a view from the particular context of that people who know themselves to be called and chosen by that God; theological confession entails human vocation and responsiveness. In terms of the epistemological issues raised in the previous section, God cannot be known without humans knowing themselves also in specific ways.[37] (Such an account of the inseparability of theological affirmation from human responsive engagement with that which is affirmed is not to be confused with a reductive transposition of theological affirmation into solely human categories).

Finally, I would like to suggest that the way in which the *Shema'* affirms that YHWH is 'one' is the clearest affirmation of what is the consistent understanding of the Old Testament as a whole, and that it is never displaced by any other kind of (more explicit, more developed, more 'monotheistic') affirmation about YHWH. Usually appealed to in this regard are certain texts which depict recognition of YHWH as God with the added specification 'there is no other' (*'en 'od*). These are

36. *Num. R.* 14.4, *Song of Songs R.* II.16.1, *Pesikta Rabbati*, Piska 21.12, *Targum Pseudo-Jonathan* to Deut. 26.17–18. Most modern translations of 2 Sam. 7.23 obscure this linkage by preferring the LXX, whose *allo* ('other') seems to presuppose a Hebrew *Vorlage* of *'aher* rather than *'ehad*.

37. The relatedness of theological affirmation with human vocation and responsibility has not featured prominently in modern discussion beyond the depiction of Israel's monotheism as ethical monotheism. An interesting recent exception is Walter Brueggemann, 'Exodus in the Plural (Amos 9.7)', in his *Texts That Linger, Words That Explode* (Minneapolis: Fortress Press, 2000), pp. 89–103, esp. pp. 89–92, though Brueggemann does not consider the epistemological issues but rather the potential narrowing of vision of God that can be entailed by election.

most common in Isa. 40–55 (45.5, 6, 14, 21, 22; 46.9), where there is regularly a further strengthening expression, though there are also comparable examples of *'en 'od* in Deuteronomy (4.35, 39) and elsewhere (1 Kgs 8.60; Joel 2.27). If such expressions are read against a background of a question such as 'Do any deities other than YHWH in any way exist?' then it is of course natural to read such texts as expressing Israel's conviction that deities other than YHWH are non-existent. But are we right in supposing that the way that the conceptuality was commonly articulated in certain post-biblical contexts is also present in these texts? For at least three reasons, I suggest not.

First, the Hebrew for 'there is no other (sc. deity)', in the sense of non-existence, might naturally utilize the Hebrew term for 'other' (*'aher*), and so be *'en 'aher* – an expression which is never used in these contexts. An alternative formulation of the non-existence of other deities could be *'en 'elohim 'aherim*; but since the Old Testament writers (especially those standing within the tradition of Deuteronomy) regularly warn of the ever-present temptations to go after *'elohim 'aherim*, and the Old Testament expresses Israel's normative relation to other deities in the first commandment of the decalogue where their significance and importance for Israel is denied (*lo' yihyeh leka 'elohim 'aherim*), it is hardly surprising that the non-existence of such is nowhere expressed.[38] The expression *'en 'od* in its contexts surely suggests something along the lines of 'there is nothing further', 'there is no alternative', 'there is nowhere else to go'; not in the sense that alternatives are as such non-existent, but rather in the existential sense that to look elsewhere than to YHWH is misguided and futile. One should reflect on the rhetorical function of similar language in comparable contexts. The political leader who tells his/her followers that 'there is no alternative', 'we have no choice' always means that of the many courses that might be taken only one actually should be taken.

Secondly, in Isa. 46.9 the phrase in parallelism to *'en 'od* is *we'epes kamoni*, 'and there is none like me', an expression of the incomparability of YHWH in relation to all other deities; that is, the common and characteristic Old Testament expression of the relation of YHWH to other deities as in Exod. 15.11. Moreover this same claim of incomparability is set also on the lips of Babylon (Isa. 47.8, 10), presumably to indicate Babylon's pretensions to a power that rivals that of YHWH; but Babylon's claim would not mean that other great cities did not in fact exist but rather that other cities were insignificant in comparison with Babylon.

Thirdly, the consistent context of all these passages is the recognition of YHWH as alone the one who creates and saves; the concern always is the powerlessness or irrelevance of other deities in relation to YHWH, which is why there is no reason for those who recognize YHWH to look anywhere else. Alternatives, indeed apparently attractive alternatives, do exist, but for all their seeming attractiveness they ultimately represent byways leading to disaster or death rather than the road to life that can be found in loyalty to YHWH.

---

38. For an eye-opening treatment of the possible construals of 'other gods' and idolatry, see Moshe Halbertal and Avishai Margalit, *Idolatry* (Cambridge, MA: Harvard University Press, 1992).

Thus the consensus that Isa. 40–55 (and related texts) expresses an understanding other than that of the *Shema'* or the rest of the Old Testament is, I suggest, a misreading of the texts.

5. Conclusions

Where does all this leave us, and what difference might this argument make to the overall concern of this collection of essays, that is 'christological monotheism' in relation to the New Testament? I offer three observations and three suggestions.

The first observation is that, even if the seventeenth century saw a certain narrowing and intellectualizing of its concept of God through its adoption of 'monotheism' as a prime category, the problem is perennial. For one needs only to turn to the pages of the New Testament, and the letter of James (2.19-26), to be reminded of the withering critique which could be directed against a diminished understanding of God, an intellectual recognition (*pistis*) which is diminished precisely because it is a recognition divorced from responsive obedience (*erga*): 'You believe that God is one? Fine. The demons also believe – and they tremble…'. Yet even if the thinkers of the seventeenth century did not create the problem, one might wonder whether they did not institutionalise it in a new way.

The second observation is that much in my argument is hardly novel. Exegetically, for example, it has not infrequently been recognized that the Isaianic texts may not bear the significance customarily ascribed to them.[39] A striking recent example is Christopher Seitz's relating of the exegesis and interpretation of Second Isaiah to the wider issue of 'monotheism':

> To put this in modern terms, nowhere in Second Isaiah would 'monotheism' amount to a practical elimination of all gods but one, such that it could be said, 'we all worship the same God'. Precisely the opposite is true in these chapters: representatives of other nations 'shall make supplication to you, saying, "God is with you only and there is no other, no god besides him"' (45.14). That is, they will make the same sort of claim Israel was commanded to make in the Ten Commandments, that against the rival claims of other gods, YHWH demanded sole allegiance. Now that claim is emboldened with the assertion that other gods are in fact only illusions. This is not a sublime monotheism capable of differentiation from a more concrete henotheism – rather, it is henotheism of a particularly potent stripe.[40]

Other eminent Old Testament scholars have also pointed out the inadequacy of 'monotheism' and related categories. Gerhard von Rad, for example, said in 1961:

---

39. P. de Boer, *Second Isaiah's Message* (Oudtestamentische Studien, 11; Leiden: E.J. Brill, 1956), p. 47; James Barr, 'The Problem of Israelite Monotheism', *Transactions of Glasgow University Oriental Society* 17 (1957–58), pp. 52–62, esp. p. 54; Ulrich Mauser, 'One God Alone: A Pillar of Biblical Theology', *Princeton Seminary Bulletin* 12 (1991), pp. 255–65, esp. p. 259 n. 5.

40. 'The Divine Name in Scripture', in his *Word Without End: The Old Testament as Abiding Theological Witness* (Grand Rapids: Eerdmans, 1998), pp. 251–62, quote p. 255.

It could be, indeed, that to pose the alternative monotheism-polytheism postulates a system of thought into which the phenomenon of Mosaic faith cannot be incorporated at all... Monotheism is a thesis the truth of which a philosopher could possibly unfold. But the prophet [sc. Second Isaiah] believes that the singleness of God as the Lord of world history and as the only helper can be made believable only by those who bear witness to him; and he leaves no doubt that those who bear witness to him will have to assert themselves against an oppressive majority.[41]

Or, more recently, Walter Brueggemann has commented:

Monotheism, as presented in classical Western Christian theology, is an intellectual claim that only one God presides over all existence. Such an intellectual claim is, as conventionally articulated, of little interest for the Bible and has caused endless mischief in understanding the Bible.[42]

Indeed, central aspects of my thesis were well articulated ten years ago by Ulrich Mauser in an inaugural lecture at Princeton Theological Seminary:

It is my thesis that *the Biblical insistence on the oneness of God is so different from the monotheistic consciousness of our time that the almost universal procedure of reading the Bible through the spectacles of a modern monotheist must result in a serious misreading of its message.*[43]

The third observation is that such voices have not been heard. The steady flow of books now appearing on Israelite religion and monotheism do not characteristically display any serious reflection on the adequacy of the categories and frames of reference within which the debate is conducted.[44] Though C.J. Labuschagne expressed

41. 'The Origin of Mosaic Monotheism', in his *God at Work in Israel* (trans. John H. Marks [German, 1974]; Nashville: Abingdon Press, 1980), pp. 128–38 (here, pp. 129 and 138).

42. 'Monotheism', in his *Reverberations of Faith: A Theological Handbook of Old Testament Studies* (Louisville, KY: Westminster/John Knox Press, 2002), pp. 137–40 (here, p. 137).

43. 'One God Alone' [see n. 39], p. 257 (his italics). In a range of other contexts also, unease with the term 'monotheism' has been expressed. From a religio-historical perspective, Peter Hayman has argued 'that it is hardly ever appropriate to use the term monotheism to describe the Jewish idea of God', because for much of Jewish history 'God is the sole object of worship, but he is not the only divine being' ('Monotheism – A Misused Word in Jewish Studies?', *JJS* 42 [1991], pp. 1–15 [pp. 2 and 15]); while from a systematics perspective Jürgen Moltmann has argued that 'the Christian Church was...right to see monotheism as the severest inner danger', a danger which took its 'purest form' in Arianism (*The Trinity and the Kingdom of God* [London: SCM Press, 1981], pp. 131 and 133). Moltmann idiosyncratically uses 'monotheism' as an opposite of 'trinitarianism', and his concern is with a certain kind of claim to power implicit in monarchical kinds of 'monotheism'.

44. For example, M.S. Smith, *The Origins of Biblical Monotheism: Israel's Polytheistic Background and the Ugaritic Texts* (Oxford: Oxford University Press, 2001), interestingly discusses context-setting assumptions in the Introduction (pp. 3–24) but at best skirts around the kind of concern central to this paper; he mainly argues for the importance of dispassionate and not intrinsically reductive historical work that attends as much as possible to the concrete contexts of ancient religious language and life. See also the 2nd edition of his *The Early History of God: Yahweh and the Other Deities in Ancient Israel* (Grand Rapids: Eerdmans, 2002), pp. xii–xxxviii for a survey of recent literature and debate.

an awareness of some problem a generation ago, he nonetheless blocked the best way ahead through a move typical of many. His recognition that 'Nobody has yet given a definition of 'monotheism' which will satisfy everyone!' is followed by the contention that 'It is therefore imperative to approach the factual data without any preconceived system or '-ism', to examine them in their historical context...'[45] One may entirely agree with the need to avoid inappropriate imposition upon the text, and yet wish that this did not lead to a kind of positivism in which all one has to do is 'approach the factual data' without rigorously considering the adequacy of one's conceptual categories of interpretation.

My first suggestion, therefore, is that we need a kind of Socratic *aporia*, a recognition of not knowing as the context for fresh knowledge. Instead of our knowing what 'monotheism' is in the context of ancient Israel and early Judaism, and it then being a problem to know how the literary deposit of Israel's religion can be correlated with it or how Jesus can be fitted into it, we should rather acknowledge that we may not have rightly understood Israel's canonical religion because the preferred category of 'monotheism' may in important respects impede our grasping the nature of the Old Testament's understanding of God in the first place.[46]

Secondly, there is an important strategic question that arises if the above argument is at all on the right lines. Should 'monotheism' as a category be retained or abandoned? Probably the most obviously appealing strategy is to retain it (it is time-honoured, and what hope would some neologism have of widespread acceptance?), but to concentrate on careful definition of what is, and is not, meant by the term in its various contexts. A model discussion along these lines for the nature and meaning of Jewish monotheism at the time of Christian beginnings is that by Tom Wright in his *The New Testament and the People of God*.[47] Nonetheless 'monotheism' remains related to a range of other terms ('polytheism', 'monolatry', etc.) which are all part of a modern attempt to conceptualize 'religion' in a particular kind of way. If the logic of our argument is consistently followed it might be preferable to prescind from these terms and their frames of reference – not in favour of instant alternative terms (which would only arise in due course), but in favour of a renewed attempt to articulate through thick description, with nuanced and revisable interpretative categories, how the Bible, and the faiths rooted in it, do, and do not, conceive the relationship between the God who is 'one' and human life.

Finally, if the existentially engaging nature of Israel's belief in YHWH as 'one' is kept in focus, together with the epistemological issue that to say anything meaningful (i.e. not mere projection) about the divine at all requires as its corollary a particular kind of human self-knowing and way of living, then Christians should perhaps look most of all at those New Testament passages where these issues

45. C.J. Labuschagne, *The Incomparability of Yahweh in the Old Testament* (Leiden: E.J. Brill, 1966), p. 143.

46. Compare N.T. Wright: 'The christological question, as to whether the statement "Jesus is God" is true, and if so in what sense, is often asked as though "God" were the known and "Jesus" the unknown; this, I suggest, is manifestly mistaken. If anything, the matter stands the other way around' (N.T. Wright, *The New Testament and the People of God* [London: SPCK, 1992], p. xv).

47. Wright, *The New Testament*, pp. 244–59.

come together in relation to Jesus. The letters of Paul, unsurprisingly, are prime candidates. Paul reformulates the *Shema'* in such a way as to include Jesus as Lord (*kyrios*, a prime LXX designation for God), in a context in which he readily acknowledges many rival claimants for human allegiance (*theoi*) and yet insists that 'for us' there can only be one (1 Cor. 8.4–6).[48] Alternatively, confession of Jesus who gave up all and has now received all (Phil. 2.5–11) entails the transformation of his own life according to the pattern of Jesus (Phil. 3.2–16). The exclusive, demanding, and transformative nature of the Old Testament's confession of YHWH as 'one' is clearly present, *mutatis mutandis*, in Paul's confession of Jesus as Lord, a confession which is not an end in itself but which is to the glory of God, a God now known as father (Phil. 2.11). Here we may well be as close as we are likely to get (within the literature of the period) to seeing what is going on in the New Testament's incorporation of Jesus Christ into Israel's confession of the one God. But we need appropriate categories for understanding and articulating what the text is saying.

---

48. For I Cor. 8.6 as a reformulation of the *Shema'*, see e.g. N.T. Wright, 'Monotheism, Christology and Ethics: I Corinthians 8', in his *Climax of the Covenant: Christ and the Law in Pauline Theology* (Edinburgh: T. & T. Clark, 1991), pp. 120–36.

EARLY JEWISH AND CHRISTIAN MONOTHEISM:
A SELECT BIBLIOGRAPHY

Compiled by James F. McGrath, Butler University, Indianapolis,
and Jerry Truex, Tabor College, Kansas

The present bibliography originally had as its ambitious aim to provide a 'compre-hensive' bibliography of works dealing with early Jewish and Christian monothe-ism. It soon became apparent, however, that if one were to include *every* article, book, dissertation or monograph that touches on these subjects, then one would have to include a dauntingly large proportion of all that has ever been written on the subjects of God, Trinity, Christology, and numerous other topics. Thus, our aim for the present bibliography is a more modest one. We have sought to include all of the relatively recent works that focus on early Jewish and Christian monotheism as their primary subject. This meant that we omitted most works that focused on the origins of ancient Israelite monotheism and books concerned with dogmatics and contemporary issues.

Beyond those works specifically addressing early Jewish and Christian monothe-ism, we have also included publications that devote at least a small but significant discussion to these topics. Among these are Barclay's *Jews in the Mediterranean Diaspora*, Dunn's *Partings of the Ways*, Rowland's *Christian Origins*, and Schäfer's *Judeophobia*. Each of these books has a section or chapter that focuses, in its own way, on the issue of early Jewish monotheism. In addition, monographs on *mediator figures* and *worship* have significant implications for understanding early Jewish and Christian monotheism. Hence, we have included seminal works by scholars such as Bauckham, Dunn, and Hurtado, who have stimulated a great deal of dis-cussion. The present bibliography also includes recent works by Ashton, Carrell, Gieschen, and Stuckenbruck, who focus on the importance of *angels*. Furthermore, we have occasionally included works that focus on monotheism in relation to the wider Greco-Roman world, Rabbinic writings, and/or the early church. Such works are useful for tracing trajectories of development and for identifying sources for comparative study.

At present, perhaps the most crucial issues are those of *methodology* and *defini-tion*. Particularly since the appearance studies by Barker and Hayman, the question has been raised whether early Judaism should be referred to as 'monotheistic'. Among works that attempt to tackle these issues are those by Bauckham, Davila, Gieschen, Hurtado, Mach, and Stuckenbruck. Not only is there room for further work on the question of what is meant by 'early Jewish or Christian monotheism' or by a 'mediator figure', but also clarifying and understanding the relationship between different forms of belief in and devotion to one God found in early Jewish and Christian writings. It is our hope that the present bibliography will serve those who devote themselves to researching and clarifying the issues and options in this important area of ongoing research.

Aschim, A., 'Melchizedek and Jesus: 11QMelchizedek and the Epistle to the Hebrews', in *JRCM*, pp. 129–47.

Ashton, J., 'Bridging Ambiguities', in *idem, Studying John: Approaches to the Fourth Gospel* (Oxford: Clarendon Press, 1994), pp. 70–89.

Ball, D.M., '*I Am*' in *John's Gospel: Literary Function: Background and Theological Implications* (JSNTSup, 124; Sheffield: Sheffield Academic Press, 1996).

Barclay, J.M.G., *Jews in the Mediterranean Diaspora: From Alexander to Trajan (323 BCE– 117 CE)* (Edinburgh: T. & T. Clark, 1996), pp. 429–34.

Barker, M., *The Great Angel: A Study of Israel's Second God* (London: SPCK, 1992).

—'The High Priest and the Worship of Jesus', in *JRCM*, pp. 94–111.

Barrett, C.K., '"The Father is Greater than I" (John 14:28)'. Subordinationist Christology in the New Testament', in *idem, Essays on John* (London: SPCK, 1982), pp. 19–36.

—'Christocentric or Theocentric? Observations on the Theological Method of the Fourth Gospel', in C.K. Barrett, *Essays on John* (London: SPCK, 1982), pp. 1–18.

Bauckham, R.J., *God Crucified: Monotheism and Christology in the New Testament* (Didsbury Lectures, 1996; Carlisle: Paternoster Press, 1998).

—'Jesus, Worship of', in *ABD*. III, pp. 812–19.

—'The Throne of God and the Worship of Jesus', in *JRCM*, pp.43–69.

—'The Worship of Jesus', in *idem, The Climax of Prophecy* (Edinburgh: T. & T. Clark, 1993), pp. 118–49. Reprinted, with minor revisions, from 'The Worship of Jesus in Early Christianity', *NTS* 27 (1980–81), pp. 322–41.

—'The Worship of Jesus in Philippians 2.9–11', in Ralph P. Martin and Brian J. Dodd (eds.), *Where Christology Began: Essays on Philippians 2* (Louisville, KY: Westminster/John Knox Press, 1998), pp. 128–39.

Borgen, P., '"Yes", "No", "How Far?"': The Participation of Jews and Christians in Pagan Cults', in *idem, Early Christianity and Hellenistic Judaism* (Edinburgh: T. & T. Clark, 1996), pp. 15–43.

Callan, T., 'The Exegetical Background of Gal. 3.19b', *JBL* 99 (1980), pp. 549–67.

Capes, D.B., '*Imitatio Christi* and the Early Worship of Jesus', in *JRCM*, pp.293–307.

—*Old Testament Yahweh Texts in Paul's Christology* (WUNT, II/47; Tübingen: J.C.B. Mohr [Paul Siebeck], 1992).

Carrell, P.R., *Jesus and the Angels: Angelology and the Christology of the Apocalypse of John* (SNTSMS, 95; Cambridge: Cambridge University Press, 1997).

Casey, P.M., *From Jewish Prophet to Gentile God: The Origins and Development of New Testament Christology* (The Edward Cadbury Lectures at the University of Birmingham, 1985–86; Louisville, KY: Westminster/John Knox Press, 1991).

—'Monotheism, Worship and Christological Development in the Pauline Churches', in *JRCM*, pp. 214–33.

Chester, A., 'Jewish Messianic Expectations and Mediatorial Figures and Pauline Christology', in Martin Hengel and Ulrich Heckel (eds.), *Paulus und das antike Judentum* (WUNT, II/58; Tübingen: J.C.B. Mohr [Paul Siebeck], 1991), pp. 17–89.

Cohon, S.S., 'The Unity of God: A Study in Hellenistic and Rabbinic Theology', *HUCA* 26 (1955), pp. 425–79.

Collins, A. Yarbro, 'The Worship of Jesus and the Imperial Cult', in *JRCM*, pp. 234–57.

Collins, J.J., 'Jewish Monotheism and Christian Theology', in H. Shanks and J. Meinhardt (eds.), *Aspects of Monotheism: How God Is One* (Symposium at the Smithsonian Institution, October 19, 1996; Washington, DC: Biblical Archaeology Society, 1997), pp. 81–105.

—'A Throne in the Heavens', in *idem, The Scepter and the Star: The Messiahs of the Dead Sea Scrolls and Other Ancient Literature* (New York: Doubleday, 1995).

Crump, D., *Jesus the Intercessor: Prayer and Christology in Luke–Acts* (Grand Rapids: Baker Book House, 1999).

Culianu, I.P., 'The Angels of the Nations and the Origins of Gnostic Dualism', in R. van den Broek and M.J. Vermaseren (eds.), *Studies in Gnosticism and Hellenistic Religions: Festschrift for G. Quispel* (Études préliminaires aux religions orientales dans l'Empire Romain, 91; Leiden: E.J. Brill, 1981), pp. 78–91.

Dahl, N.A., 'The One God of Jews and Gentiles (Romans 3.29–30)', in *idem, Studies in Paul: Theology for the Early Christian Mission* (Minneapolis: Fortress Press, 1977), pp. 178–91.

Daly-Denton, M., 'Singing Hymns to Christ as to a God (cf. Pliny *Ep.* X, 96)', in *JRCM*), pp. 277–92.

Daniélou, J., *The Theology of Jewish Christianity*. I. *A History of Early Christian Doctrine before the Council of Nicaea* (London: Darton, Longman & Todd, 1964).

Davila, J.R., 'Of Methodology, Monotheism and Metatron: Introductory Reflections on Divine Mediators and the Origins of the Worship of Jesus', in *JRCM*, pp. 3–18.

Davis, C.J., *The Name and Way of the Lord: Old Testament Themes, New Testament Christology* (JSNTSup, 129; Sheffield: Sheffield Academic Press, 1996).

Davis, P.G., 'Divine Agents, Mediators, and New Testament Christology', *JTS* 45 (1994), pp. 478–503.

de Conick, April D., 'Heavenly Temple Traditions and Valentinian Worship: A Case for First-Century Christology in the Second Century', in *JRCM*, pp. 308–41.

de Jonge, M., 'Monotheism and Christology', in John Barclay and John Sweet (eds.), *Early Christian Thought in its Jewish Context* (Cambridge: Cambridge University Press, 1996), pp. 225–36.

de Lacey, D.R., ' "One Lord" in Pauline Christology', in H.H. Rowdon (ed.), *Christ the Lord: Studies Presented to Donald Guthrie* (Leicester: Inter-Varsity Press, 1982), pp. 162–82.

Di Segni, L., 'Εἷς Θεός in Palestinian Inscriptions', *SCI* 13 (1994), pp. 94–115.

Donahue, J.R., 'A Neglected Factory in the Theology of Mark', *JBL* 101 (1982), pp. 563–94.

Dunn, J.D.G., 'Christology as an Aspect of Theology', in *CSC*, pp. 377–87. Originally published in A.J. Malherbe and W.A. Meeks (eds.), *The Future of Christology: Essays in Honor of L.E. Keck* (Minneapolis: Augsburg Fortress, 1993), pp. 202–212.

—*Christology in the Making: An Inquiry into the Origins of the Doctrine of the Incarnation* (London: SCM Press, 2nd edn, 1989).

—'How Controversial Was Paul's Christology?' In *CSC*, pp. 212–28. Originally published in M.C. de Boer (ed.), *From Jesus to John: New Testament Christologies in Current Perspective* (JSNTSup, 84. Sheffield: JSOT Press, 1993), pp. 148–67.

—'Incarnation', in *CSC*, pp. 30–47. Originally published in *ABD*, III, pp. 397–404.

—'Let John Be John: A Gospel for its Time', in *CSC*, pp. 345–75. Originally published in P. Stuhlmacher (ed.), *Das Evangelium und die Evangelien: Vorträge vom Tübinger Symposium 1982* (WUNT, II/28; Tübingen: J.C.B. Mohr [Paul Siebeck], 1983), pp. 309–39.

—*The Partings of the Ways. Between Christianity and Judaism and their Significance for the Character of Christianity* (London: SCM Press, 1991).

—'The Making of Christology: Evolution or Unfolding?' In *CSC*, pp.388–404. Originally published in J.B. Green and M. Turner (eds.), *Jesus of Nazareth, Lord and Christ: Essays on the Historical Jesus and New Testament Christology* (Grand Rapids: Eerdmans, 1994), pp. 437–52.

—'Was Christianity a Monotheistic Faith from the Beginning?' , in *CSC*, pp. 315–44. Originally published in *SJT* 35 (1982), pp. 303–336.

—'Why "Incarnation"? A Review of Recent New Testament Scholarship', in *CSC*, pp. 405–423. Originally published in S.E. Porter *et al.* (eds.), *Crossing the Boundaries: Essays in Biblical Interpretation in Honour of M.D. Goulder* (Leiden: E.J. Brill, 1994), pp. 235–56.

Ellis, E.E., 'Deity-Christology in Mark 14.58', in J.B. Green and M. Turner (eds.), *Jesus of Nazareth: Lord and Christ. Essays on the Historical Jesus and New Testament Christology* (Grand Rapids: Eerdmans, 1994), pp. 192–203.

Evans, C.A., 'Jesus' Self-Designation: The Son of Man and the Recognition of His Divinity', in S.T. Davis, D. Kendall and G. O'Collins (eds.), *The Trinity: An Interdisciplinary Symposium on the Trinity* (Oxford: Oxford University Press, 1999), pp. 29–47.

Fee, G.D., 'Paul and the Trinity: The Experience of Christ and the Spirit for Paul's Understanding of God', in S.T. Davis, D. Kendall and G. O'Collins (eds.), *The Trinity: An Interdisciplinary Symposium on the Trinity* (Oxford: Oxford University Press, 1999), pp. 49–72.

Fennema, D.A., 'Jesus and God According to John: An Analysis of the Fourth Gospel's Father/Son Christology' (PhD Dissertation, Duke University, 1979).

Fletcher-Louis, C.H.T., *Luke–Acts: Angels, Christology and Soteriology*. WUNT, II/94; Tübingen: J.C.B. Mohr (Paul Siebeck), 1997.

—'The Worship of Divine Humanity as God's Image and the Worship of Jesus', in *JRCM*, pp. 112–28.

Fossum, J.E., 'Colossians 1.15–18a in the Light of Jewish Mysticism and Gnosticism', *NTS* 35 (1989), pp. 183–201.

—*The Image of the Invisible God: Essays on the Influence of Jewish Mysticism on Early Christology* (NTOA, 30; Freiburg, Schweiz: Universitätsverlag and Göttingen: Vandenhoeck & Ruprecht, 1995).

—*The Name of God and the Angel of the Lord* (WUNT, 36; Tübingen: J.C.B. Mohr [Paul Siebeck], 1985).

—'The *New Religionsgeschichtliche Schule*: The Quest for Jewish Christology', in Eugene H. Lovering (ed.), *SBL 1991 Seminar Papers* (Atlanta, GA: Scholars Press, 1991), pp. 638–46.

Fowden, G., *Empire to Commonwealth: Consequences of Monotheism in Late Antiquity*. (Princeton, NJ: Princeton University Press, 1993).

Fowler, W.W., *Roman Ideas of Deity in the Last Century before the Christian Era; Lectures Delivered in Oxford for the Common University Fund* (Freeport, NY: Books for Libraries Press, 1969).

Francis, R.T. 'Worship of Jesus: A Neglected Factor in Christological Debate?', in H.H. Rowdon (ed.), *Christ the Lord. Studies Presented to Donald Guthrie* (Leicester: Inter-Varsity Press, 1982), pp. 17–36.

Gerhardson, B., 'Monoteism och högkristologi I Matteusevangeliet', *SEÅ* 37–38 (1972–73), pp. 125–44.

Giblin, C.H., 'Three Monotheistic Texts in Paul'. *CBQ* 37 (1975), pp. 527–47.

Gieschen, C.A., *Angelomorphic Christology: Antecedents and Early Evidence* (AGJU, 42; Leiden: E.J. Brill, 1998).

Grant, R.M., *Gods and the One God: Christian Theology in the Graeco-Roman World* (London: SPCK, 1986).

Grässer, E., ' "God is One" (Rom. 3.30)', in *"Ich will euer Gott werden" Beispiele biblischen-Redens von Gott* (Stuttgarter Bibelstudien, 100; Stuttgart: Katholisches Bibelwerk, 1981), pp. 179–205.

Hagner, D.A., 'Paul's Christology and Jewish Monotheism', in M. Shuster and R. Muller (eds.), *Perspectives on Christology: Essays in Honor of Paul K. Jewett* (Grand Rapids: Zondervan, 1991), pp. 19–38.

Hahn, F., 'The Confession of the One God in the New Testament', *HTR* 2 (1980), pp. 69–84.

Hall, R.G., 'Astonishment in the Firmament: The Worship of Jesus and Soteriology in Ignatius and the *Ascension of Isaiah*', in *JRCM*, pp. 148–55.

Harner, P.B., *The 'I Am' of the Fourth Gospel* (Facet Books; Philadelphia: Fortress Press, 1970).

Harris, M.J., *Jesus as God* (Grand Rapids: Baker Book House, 1992).

Hartill, P., *The Unity of God: A Study in Christian Monotheism* (London: A.R. Mowbray; New York: Morehouse-Gorham, 1952).

Hartman, L., 'Johannine Jesus-Belief and Monotheism', in L. Hartman and B. Olsson (eds.), *Aspects of the Johannine Literature* (Coniectanea Biblica New Testament Series, 18; Uppsala: Almqvist & Wiksell International, 1987), pp. 85–99.

Harvey, A.E., 'The Constraint of Monotheism', in *idem, Jesus and the Constraints of History* (Philadelphia: Westminster, 1982), pp. 154–73.

Hayman, P., 'Monotheism—A Misused Word in Jewish Studies?', *JJS* 42 (1991), pp. 1–15.

Hellwig, M.K., 'From Christ to God: The Christian Perspective', in A.E. Zannoni (ed.), *Jews and Christians Speak of Jesus* (Minneapolis: Fortress Press, 1994), pp. 137–49.

Hengel, M., ' "Sit at My Right Hand!" ', in *idem, Studies in Early Christology* (Edinburgh: T. & T. Clark, 1995), pp. 119–25.

—'The Song about Christ in Earliest Worship', in *idem, Studies in Early Christology* (Edinburgh: T. & T. Clark, 1995), pp. 227–91.

Holtz, T., 'Gott in der Apokalypse', in J. Lambrecht (ed.), *L'Apocalypse johannique et l'Apocalyptique dans le Nouveau Testament* (BETL, 53; Leuven University Press, 1980), pp. 247–65.

—'Theologie und Christologie bei Paulus', in E. Grässer and O. Merk (eds.), *Glaube und Eschatologie: Festschrift für Werner Georg Kümmel zum 80. Geburtstag* (Tübingen: J.C.B. Mohr [Paul Siebeck], 1985), pp. 105–121.

Howard, G., 'Phil 2.6–11 and the Human Christ', *CBQ* 40 (1978), pp. 368–87.

Hurst, L.D., 'The Christology of Hebrews 1 and 2', in L.D. Hurst and N.T. Wright (eds.), *The Glory of Christ in the New Testament: Studies in Christology in Memory of G.B. Caird* (Oxford: Clarendon, Press, 1987), pp. 151–64.

Hurtado, L.W., *At the Origins of Christian Worship* (Carlisle: Paternoster Press, 1999).

—'The Binitarian Shape of Early Christian Worship', in *JRCM*, pp. 188–213.

—'Christ-Devotion in the First Two Centuries: Reflections and a Proposal', *TJT* 12 (1996), pp. 17–33.

—*One God, One Lord: Early Jewish Devotion and Ancient Jewish Monotheism* (Philadelphia: Fortress Press, 1988; Edinburgh: T. & T. Clark, 2nd edn, 1998).

—'First-Century Jewish Monotheism', *JSNT* 71 (1998), pp. 3–26. This is a major re-writing of an earlier paper, 'What Do We Mean by "First-Century Jewish Monotheism"?', in E.H. Lovering (ed.), *SBL 1993 Seminar Papers* (Atlanta, GA: Scholars Press, 1993), pp. 348–68.

Klutz, T.E., 'The Grammar of Exorcism in the Ancient Mediterranean World: Some Cosmological, Semantic, and Pragmatic Reflections on How Exorcistic Prowess Contributed to
the Worship of Jesus', in *JRCM*, pp. 156–65.

Kreitzer, L.J., *Jesus and God in Paul's Eschatology* (JSNTSup, 19. Sheffield: Sheffield Academic Press, 1987).

Laato, A., *Monotheism, the Trinity, and Mysticism: A Semiotic Approach to Jewish-Christian
Encounter* (New York: Peter Lang, 1999).

Lang, B., 'Der monarchische Monotheismus und die Konstellatin zweier Götter im Frühjuden-
tum: Ein neuer Versuch über Menschensohn, Sophia und Christologie', in W. Dietrich
and M. Klopfenstein (eds.), *Ein Gott allein?* (Freiburg, Schweiz: Universitätsverlag; Göttingen: Vandenhoeck & Ruprecht, 1994), pp. 559–64.

Mach, M., 'Concepts of Jewish Monotheism in the Hellenistic Period', in *JRCM*, pp. 21–42.

—*Entwicklungsstadien des jüdischen Engelglaubens in vorrabbinischer Zeit* (Texte und
Studien zum Antiken Judentum, 34; Tübingen: J.C.B. Mohr [Paul Siebeck], 1992).

Marshall, I.H., 'The Development of Christology in the Early Church'. *TB* 18 (1967), pp. 77–93.

—*The Origins of New Testament Christology* (Leicester: Apollos/IVP, rev. 1990).

Mastin, B.A., 'A Neglected Feature of the Christology of the Fourth Gospel'. *NTS* 22 (1975–
76), pp. 32–51.

Matsunaga, K., 'The "Theos" Christology as the Ultimate Confession of the Fourth Gospel',
in M. Sekine and A. Satake (eds.), *Annual of the Japanese Biblical Institute* (Tokyo:
Yamamoto Shoten, 1981), VII, pp. 124–45.

Mauser, U.W., 'Εἰς Θεός und Εἰς Κύριος in Biblischer Theologie', *Jahrbuch für biblische
Theologie* 1 (1986) 71–87.

—'One God Alone: A Pillar of Biblical Theology', *PSB* 12 (1991), pp. 255–65.

May, G., *Creatio ex Nihilo: The Doctrine of 'Creation out of Nothing' in Early Christian
Thought* (Edinburgh: T. & T. Clark, 1994).

McGrath, J.F., *John's Apologetic Christology: Legitimation and Development in Johannine
Christology* (SNTSMS, 111; Cambridge: Cambridge University Press, 2001).

Meeks, W., 'Equal to God', in R.T. Fortna and B.T. Gaventa (eds.), *The Conversation Continues: Studies in Paul and John in Honor of J. Louis Martyn* (Nashville: Abingdon
Press, 1990), pp. 309–322.

—'Moses as God and King', in J. Neusner (ed.), *Religions in Antiquity: Essays in Memory of
Erwin Ramsdell Goodenough* (Leiden: E.J. Brill, 1986), pp. 354–71.

Metzger, B.M., 'The Punctuation of Rom. 9.5', in *Christ and Spirit in the New Testament*,
B. Lindars and S.S. Smalley (eds.). Cambridge: Cambridge University Press, 1973), pp.
95–112.

Meyer, P.W., '"The Father": The Presentation of God in the Fourth Gospel', in R.A.
Culpepper and C.C. Black (eds.), *Exploring the Gospel of John in Honor of D. Moody
Smith* (Louisville, KY: Westminster/John Knox, 1996), pp. 255–73.

Moule, C.F.D., *The Origin of Christology* (Cambridge: Cambridge University Press, 1977).

Neyrey, J., *An Ideology of Revolt: John's Christology in Social-Science Perspective* (Philadelphia: Fortress Press, 1988).

—'"My Lord and My God": The Divinity of Jesus in John's Gospel', in E.H. Lovering (ed.),
SBL Seminar Paper Series 25 (SBLSP, 25; Atlanta, GA: Scholars Press, 1986), pp. 152–
71.

Nilsson, M.P., 'The High God and the Mediator', *HTR* 56 (1963), pp. 101–120.

O'Neill, J., *Who Did Jesus Think He Was?* (Leiden: E.J. Brill, 1996).

Osborn, E., *The Emergence of Christian Theology* (Cambridge: Cambridge University Press,
1993).

Perkins, P., 'Identification with the Savior in Coptic Texts from Nag Hammadi', in *JRCM*, pp. 166–84.

Peterson, E., ΕΙΣ ΘΕΟΣ. *Epigraphische, formgeschichtliche und religionsgeschichtliche Untersuchungen* (FRLANT, NS 24; Göttingen: Vandenhoeck & Ruprecht, 1926).

Rainbow, P.A., 'Jewish Monotheism as the Matrix for New Testament Christology: A Review Article', *Novum Testamentum* 33 (1991), pp. 78–91.

—'Monotheism and Christology in 1 Corinthians 8.4–6' (Unpublished DPhil Dissertation, Oxford, 1988).

Reim, G., 'Jesus as God in the Fourth Gospel: The Old Testament Background', *NTS* 30 (1984), pp. 158–60.

Richardson, N., *Paul's Language About God* (JSNTSup, 99; Sheffield: Sheffield Academic Press, 1994).

Rowland, C., *Christian Origins: An Account of the Setting and Character of the Most Important Messianic Sect of Judaism* (London: SPCK, 1985).

—*The Open Heaven: A Study of Apocalyptic in Judaism and Early Christianity* (London: SPCK, 1982).

Schäfer, P., 'The Jewish God', in P. Schäfer, *Judeophobia: Attitudes Toward the Jews in the Ancient World* (Cambridge, MA: Harvard University Press, 1997), pp. 34–65.

Segal, A.F., 'Outlining the Question: From Christ to God,' in A.E. Zannoni (ed.), *Jews and Christians Speak of Jesus* (Minneapolis: Fortress Press, 1994), pp. 125–35.

—'Paul's *"Soma Pneumatikon"* and the Worship of Jesus', in *JRCM*, pp. 258–76.

—' "Two Powers in Heaven" and Early Christian Trinitarian Thinking', in S.T. Davis, D. Kendall and G. O'Collins (eds.), *The Trinity: An Interdisciplinary Symposium on the Trinity* (Oxford University Press, 1999), pp. 73–95.

—*Two Powers in Heaven: Early Rabbinic Reports About Christianity and Gnosticism* (Studies in Judaism in Late Antiquity, 25; Leiden: E.J. Brill, 1977).

Shutt, R.J.H., 'The Concept of God in the Works of Flavius Josephus', *JJS* 31 (1980), pp. 171–87.

Smith, M., 'Two Ascended to Heaven—Jesus and the Author of 4Q491', in James H. Charlesworth (ed.), *Jesus and the Dead Sea Scrolls* (New York: Doubleday, 1992), pp. 290–301.

Steenburg, D., 'The Worship of Adam and Christ as the Image of God', *JSNT* 39 (1990), pp. 95–109.

Stolz, F., *Einführung in den biblischen Monotheismus* (Darmstadt: Wissenschaftliche Buchgesellschaft, 1996).

Stuckenbruck, L.T., 'An Angelic Refusal of Worship: The Tradition and its Function in the Apocalypse of John', in E. Lovelace (ed.), *SBL 1994 Seminar Papers* (Atlanta, GA: Scholars Press, 1994), pp. 679–96.

—*Angel Veneration and Christology: A Study in Early Judaism and in the Apocalypse of John* (WUNT, II/70; Tübingen: J.C.B. Mohr [Paul Siebeck], 1995), pp. 45–204.

—' "One like a Son of Man as the Ancient of Days" in the Old Greek Recension of Daniel 7,13: Scribal Error or Theological Translation?', *ZNW* 86 (1995), pp. 268–76.

— 'Worship and Monotheism in the *Ascension of Isaiah*', in *JRCM*, pp. 70–89.

Sundberg, A.C., '*Isos To Theo* Christology in John 5.17–30', *BR* 15 (1970), pp. 19–31.

Theobald, M., 'Gott, Logos und Pneuma', in H.J. Klauck (ed.), *Monotheismus und Christology: Zur Gottesfrage im hellenistischen Judentum und im Urchristentum* (Quaestiones Disputatae, 138; Freiburg: Herder, 1992), pp. 41–87.

Thoma, C., and M. Wyschogrod (eds.), *Das Reden vom einen Gott bei Juden und Christen.* (Bern: Peter Lang, 1984).

Thompson, M.M., *The God of the Gospel of John* (Grand Rapids: Eerdmans, 2001).

Turner, M.M.B., 'The Spirit of Christ and Christology', in H.H. Rowdon (ed.), *Christ the Lord: Studies in Christology presented to Donald Guthrie* (Leicester: Inter-Varsity Press, 1982), pp. 168–90.

—'The Spirit of Christ and "Divine" Christology', in J.B. Green and M. Turner (eds.), *Jesus of Nazareth: Lord and Christ. Essays on the Historical Jesus and New Testament Christology* (Carlisle: Paternoster Press; Grand Rapids: Eerdmans, 1994), pp. 413–36.

Urbach, E.E., 'The Belief in One God', in *idem*, *The Sages: The World and Wisdom of the Rabbis of the Talmud* (Cambridge, MA: Harvard University Press, 1987). Reprinted from (Jerusalem: Magnes Press, The Hebrew University, 1975, 1979).

van der Horst, P.W., 'Moses' Throne Vision in Ezekiel the Dramatist', *JJS* 34 (1983), pp. 21–29.

Vogel, M.H., 'Monotheism', *Encyclopaedia Judaica* (Jerusalem: Keter, 1971), XII, cols. 260–63.

Wiles, M., 'Person or Personification? A Patristic Debate about Logos', in L.D. Hurst and N.T. Wright (eds.), *The Glory of Christ in the New Testament* (Oxford: Clarendon Press, 1987), pp. 281–89.

Williams, C.H., *I am He: The Interpretation of "Anî Hû" in Jewish and Early Christian Literature* (WUNT, II/113; Tübingen: J.C.B. Mohr [Paul Siebeck], 2000).

Wright, N.T., 'First-Century Jewish Monotheism', in *idem*, *The New Testament and the People of God* (Minneapolis: Fortress Press, 1992), pp. 248–59.

—'Monotheism, Christology and Ethics: 1 Corinthians 8', in *idem*, *The Climax of the Covenant: Christ and the Law in Pauline Theology*. (Edinburgh: T. & T. Clark, 1991), pp. 120–36.

Young, F., 'Christology and Creation: Towards an Hermeneutic of Patristic Christology', in T. Merrigan and J. Haers (eds.), *The Myriad Christ: plurality and the quest for unity in contemporary Christology* (BETL, 152; Leuven: Peeters, 2000).

INDEX

INDEX OF REFERENCES

OLD TESTAMENT

NEW TESTAMENT

EARLY JEWISH WRITINGS
(excluding Dead Sea Scrolls and Rabbinica)

DEAD SEA SCROLLS

m.Niddah (*m.Nid.*)
5.6   107

m.Sanhedrin (*m.Sanh.*)
4.5   22, 27
7.5   124

m.Sotah (*m.Sot.*)
7.6   123–124

m.Tamid (*m.Tam.*)
4.3   139
5.1   105, 139

m.Yoma (*m.Yom.*)
6.2   124

Numbers Rabba
(*Num.Rabb.*)
14.4   229

Pesikta DeRav
Kahana (*Pes.Rab.*)
14.15   74
21.12   229
24   67

Pirqe de-Rabbi Eleazar
180

Sifra Leviticus (*Sif.Lev.*)
19.18   108

Sifre Deuteronomy
(*Sif.Deut.*)
32   146, 150
61   35
148   37
306   139
346   146–147

Song of Songs Rabba
2.16.1   229

Tanhuma B. (*Tanh. B.*)
9   139

Tanhuma Vayesh
9   75

Targum Neofiti
            145–146,
            148

Targum Psalms
            182

Targum Pseudo-Jonathan
            48, 75,
            146, 148,
            229

Fragment Targum
Paris 110
            145

Fragment Targum
Vatican Ebr. 440
            144–145,
            148

tos.Aboda Zara
(*tos.Ab.Zar.*)
5.4   36

tos.Baba Mezia
(*tos.Bab.Mez.*)
4.8   36

tos.Berakhot (*tos.Ber.*)
3.5   192

tos.Hagiga (*tos.Hag.*)
2.1   118
2.3–4   118

tos.Hullin (*tos.Hull.*)
2.18   48

tos.Kellim (*tos.Kel.*)
            36

tos.Sukkot (*tos.Sukk.*)
4.4   192
4.6   201

EARLY CHRISTIAN WRITINGS

Acts of John
77   27

Apocryphal Gospel
of Matthew
3.3   48

Aristides, Apology
(Syriac)
            48
12   28

Ascension of Isaiah
7.18–23   48
7.21–22   68

8.1–10   48
8.2–3   50
8.4–5   68
8.15   48

Athenagoras, *Legatio*
            (*Legat.*)
5–7   28
22.9   28

Augustine
De civitate Dei (*Civ.Dei*)
10.4   196
10.6   196

De trinitate (*Trin.*)
5.9.10   190

Barnabas
19.5   109

1 Clement
            171
36.2–6   170
64.1   21

2 Clement
3.1   198

INDEX OF AUTHORS